Brutal Intimacy

TIM PALMER

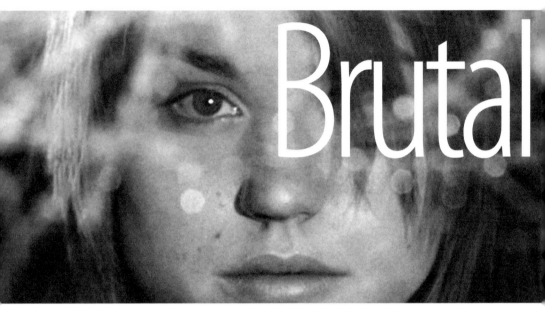

Brutal

WESLEYAN UNIVERSITY PRESS · MIDDLETOWN, CONNECTICUT

Intimacy

**ANALYZING CONTEMPORARY
FRENCH CINEMA**

WESLEYAN

UNIVERSITY PRESS

Middletown CT 06459

www.wesleyan.edu/wespress

© 2011 Tim Palmer

Manufactured in the

United States of America

Wesleyan University Press is a member of the Green Press
Initiative. The paper used in this book meets their minimum
requirement for recycled paper.

Library of Congress Cataloging-in-Publication Data appear
on the last printed page of this book.

5 4 3 2 1

For Liza

CONTENTS

Acknowledgments ix

INTRODUCTION

The Contemporary French Film Ecosystem 1

CHAPTER ONE

5 X 1

Young Cinema and First-Timers 15

CHAPTER TWO

The *Cinéma du Corps* 57

CHAPTER THREE

Popular Cinema, Pop-Art Cinema 95

CHAPTER FOUR

Feminine Cinema 151

CONCLUSION

Instructive Cinephilia

Film Literacy and la Fémis 195

APPENDIX

"The 156 Films That You Must Have Seen"

The List 217

Notes 223

Select Filmography 245

Select Bibliography 259

Index 265

ACKNOWLEDGMENTS

As I was writing this book, many people cleared my path and helped me find my way. Thank you first of all to the people who agreed to be interviewed, for giving up their time so generously. I am especially grateful to Marina de Van, Lola Doillon, and Julie Lopes-Curval. Thanks to Matthieu-David Cournot for our conversations in person and via email, and especially for the insider's tour of la Fémis in 2008. Thanks to the staff of the BiFi in Paris, to Delphine Selles and the French Embassy, and to the organizers of the vcu French Film Festival, for giving me access to so many worthy materials.

To my colleagues in the Film Studies department at the University of North Carolina Wilmington—Todd Berliner, Nandana Bose, Chip Hackler, Mariana Johnson, Carlos Kase, Jim Kreul, Terry Linehan, Melinda Miles, Dave Monahan, Glenn Pack, Sue Richardson, André and Shannon Silva—I owe thanks, especially to those who did battle with my more troublesome sections. I must single out the impact of Lou Buttino, my chair during the years in which this book was written, for being such a staunch mentor, energetic advocate, and friend. Also in King Hall, thanks to Megan Helsley and the irreplaceable Pat Torok for all their help in making my professional life so much easier. Thanks to Sophie Williams for her interlibrary loan endeavors, as well as all the Randall librarians and staff who aided my research process. My home institution, the uncw, also supported me many times in America and France, with Charles L. Cahill research grants, summer research funds, and a research reassignment leave in the fall of 2009. Thanks also to the Office of International Programs for a series of travel grants.

Elsewhere, a big thank you to Kelley Conway, for her generous and unfailing long-term encouragement on this and many other projects. Thanks also to Mike Benedetti, Whitney Byrd, Sam King, and the American vanguard of Intellect Press, and Charlie Michael, who got his much-deserved Ph.D. while this book was completed. From my years in Madison, thanks to Four Star Video Heaven for the two-year grant; and my officemates Tom Yoshikami, Madhavi Mallapragada, Mobina Hashmi, Chris Sieving, and Jen Cook. I must also acknowledge the intellectual debt I owe to David Bordwell, from my time in Vilas and beyond it.

For direct or indirect professional help, thanks to Pascale Borenstein,

Susan Hayward and Phil Powrie, Richard Neupert, Alan Williams, and Jonathan Buchsbaum. Thanks to Leigh Gibson for starting the ball rolling, Eric Levy and Parker Smathers for keeping it going, to Margaret Way, and all at Wesleyan University Press. I'd also like to thank the many students who've joined me in the classroom with such enthusiasm, especially those who've worked with me on French cinema.

Acknowledgment is also due here to the diverse and talented community of people who make French cinema happen, whose work is discussed in the pages that follow. Pessimism and faint praise are all too often directed at French cinema, a gloom I've never shared. To those men and women responsible for the extraordinary films which have inspired so many of my activities as teacher, programmer, and writer, I hope I do your work justice.

On a more personal note, thank you to my Mum and Dad, for keeping an eye on me from across the Pond. Thanks to my brother, John, for, among other things, visiting me in America so many times laden down with European DVDs. To David Shippey and the indefatigable Betty Shippey, thank you so much for your unflagging back-up, support far above and beyond the call of duty, before, during and after the writing of this book. I hope you all know how grateful I am.

My son, Riley Tate Palmer, was born while this book was starting to take shape; I hope one day he comes across these words. Riley, you have given me so many new perspectives about so many things, filling my life with wonderful mayhem. Seeing the world through your eyes, with your boundless curiosity, reminds me each day to try and keep a sense of discovery. I hope this book captures at least part of your zest for life.

To Liza, my wife, coviewer and coconspirator, collaborator in all things, I owe the biggest thanks of all. From my earliest days gathering my thoughts, to the final stretches of writing and revisions, you have kept me going with your tireless faith and support, and endless insights. You inspire me every day. A lot of this book is about courageous and talented women, making it especially fitting that it's dedicated to you. The best thank you I can offer is to tell you that I've always wanted to write a book, since my earliest memories of growing up in England. Here it is, and it's for you, with all my love.

Brutal Intimacy

The Contemporary French Film Ecosystem

The December 2007 European edition of *Time* magazine, prompted by Marcel Marceau's death that September, used for its cover a sorrowful mime staring tearfully at the ground. The accompanying headline proclaimed: "The Death of French Culture." Unsurprisingly, in the light of recent Franco-American relations, this incident quickly roused passions. One official response, widely reproduced, came from Culturesfrance, an agency supervised by France's Ministries of Foreign Affairs and Culture & Communications. Its director, Olivier Poivre d'Arvor, published a bilingual "Letter to Our American Friends," at once conciliatory and caustic. D'Arvor began: "On the announcement of the extinction of French culture, we wanted to react rather than simply revel in the silence of the tomb into which you had hurled us."[1] The letter next cited American luminaries, from Paul Auster to Woody Allen, as advocates for France's position as an epicenter of global culture. Defensive yet expansive, d'Arvor's conclusion then offered an A to Z of contemporary French artistic luminaries, an "address book [which] has brought in a notable haul of fish . . . men and women of culture originating in France and whose impact is making itself felt all over the world."[2]

Delivered with spirit in a high-profile forum, this manifesto broaches key points about French culture — and, more specifically, French film culture. The first point is how vital cinema still is to France's artistic and national identity. Nearly half of d'Arvor's A to Z are either filmmakers or film stars, from an arthouse icon, Isabelle Adjani, to the more commercial figure of Lambert Wilson. Besides asserting the strength and breadth of French cinema, the Culturesfrance essay also revives longstanding debates about cultural protectionism, France's response to American hegemony. On this front, d'Arvor pointedly refers to the 2005 Paris trade agreements, when the United Nations Educational, Scientific, and Cultural Organization (UNESCO) voted overwhelmingly (the United States was the only negative vote among 191 member countries)[3] in favor of preserving cultural diversity. With film on his mind, d'Arvor recalls the Cultural Exception ideology, France's oft-cited belief that the commercial circulation of its culture must be complemented, whenever necessary, by institutional safeguards against the pressures of the global marketplace, especially versus North American incursions. In sum, d'Arvor's essay distills certain paradoxes of contemporary French cinema: that this is a vigorous industry but also a subsidized artform; a field with intellectual ambitions that also courts widespread popularity; a craft extending from idiosyncratic experiments to commercial operations; a medium identified with a local audience yet one that also allows France to export itself on-screen around the globe, even to America.

While we open here with an image of French culture's alleged demise, this book argues from the outset for the vivacity of French film, its embattled but enduring health. In fact, the central premise is that twenty-first-century French cinema is one of the most expansively interesting in the world. A brief but representative selection of films confirms the extraordinary range of different approaches on offer, from the popular to the antagonistic, the opulent to the austere, the generic to the unclassifiable. There is, for instance, *Brice de Nice* (2005), a scurrilous comedy and star vehicle for Jean Dujardin in which a bleach-haired surfing wannabe craves the perfect wave, while worshipping his icon, Patrick Swayze, who eventually appears to him in a sun-baked vision. There is also Patrice Chéreau's *Gabrielle* (2005), which adapts a Joseph Conrad short story in a devastating period drama of marital collapse, punctuated by intertitles of anguished dialogue that resemble a neo-Brechtian exercise or a presound short. And there is *La France* (2007), set in World War I, about a young bride searching for her soldier husband; while she combs the battlefront we witness soldiers inexplicably performing song numbers after their weapons are replaced by musical instruments. Alternatively, we might consider *In My Skin* (*Dans ma peau*, 2003), one of France's continuing tide of debut features, female-centered like many recent French films, one of the most lyrical yet challenging works in recent world cinema, an intimate and open-ended depiction of a young woman's descent into graphic self-mutilation.

Responding to productions like these, a key hypothesis here is that to understand contemporary French cinema we should explore its diversity, from the broadest of mainstream products to the most esoteric arthouse practices. To pursue this, we must depart from traditional critical methods, which usually tend towards selectivity and abstraction—privileging either certain auteurs or else isolated genres or movements (Impressionism, the French New Wave, the *cinéma du look*, etc.). Instead, this book treats contemporary French cinema as an interconnected continuum, a series of concentric circles, a range of craft techniques from all walks of filmmaking life. What then emerges is a fascinating kind of cinematic ecosystem, a population of French filmmakers that is highly cineliterate, a group very much engaged by and in conversation with the work of their peers. Beyond the production process, we will also observe that the resulting films are themselves subject to a reception of intense cinephilia, based upon the energetic interventions of critics, sponsors, financial and governmental agencies, academics, and even, of course, from mass paying audiences. (A subtext to this book is that France's film culture, centered in Paris, is still far and away the world's most advanced; in some ways France gets the cinema it expects, or demands.)

At issue, then, is our need to conceptualize the extent of French cinema, on-screen, but also to analyze broadly the habits of its practitioners (newcomers and veterans alike), off-screen, together with their critical respondents and industrial advocates. In this frame we will consider French filmmakers to be active and rational agents, cultural entrepreneurs as well as the creators of film texts. Within France's bustling film culture, indeed, we see how its filmmakers behave as professional craftspeople — attuned to cinematic developments around them; attentive to their own self-promotion and self-presentation; alert to institutional opportunities like grants and festivals; creatively informed by pedagogical experiences; engaged by the discourses of the French trade and popular press. Hence the act of filmmaking involves an *array* of roles: work as writers, interviewees, self-promoters, students, teachers, cultural activists, applied cinephiles, and so on. While French cinema has drastically evolved in recent years — today it has something for everyone — its materials are continually reinvented by cineliterate professionals, creating models in flux, films produced according to innovative formulae, connected to the past yet versatile, adapting to the changing appetites of the twenty-first century. On these terms, we can begin to grasp contemporary France as a major center of world film.

Brutal Intimacy also emphasizes empirical inquiry and revisionist analysis. The chapters that follow respond to recent French cinema by devising, where appropriate, a new set of critical approaches, resisting the temptation to pour new wine into old bottles. To characterize contemporary French cinema (defined here as films produced since 2000, including detours to earlier moments when needed) we will study it on its own terms, without recourse to reviving preexisting templates for their own sake — updating the résumés of famous auteurs, say, or plugging new films into breakdowns of historical genres or putative movements. As we see repeatedly, contemporary French cinema relies upon continual overhaul and renewal, an industry famously committed since the 1950s to advancing the filmmaking careers of untested newcomers. (This *jeune cinéma* phenomenon is analyzed in detail in Chapter 1.) In this context, new and relatively obscure filmmakers emerge as part of the group conversation that sustains the recent work of well-known veterans. We will find icons like Claire Denis and Olivier Assayas working alongside, and related to, budding professionals like Diane Bertrand and Serge Bozon.

As a result, my intention throughout is to offer any critical methods as defined by the actual range of films encountered, not, as is regrettably customary, coercing a smaller set of cherry-picked texts into preexisting ideological or critical categories, inherited trains of thought. Although not as scientific as the "unbiased sample" used by David Bordwell, Janet Staiger, and Kristin Thompson to characterize classical Hollywood cinema, their hundred random titles drawn from 1916 to 1960,[4] *Brutal Intimacy* nonetheless shares a proximate approach, a systematic editorial response to an unfiltered and wholesale engagement with the continuum of French cinematic practice, as many films as possible, supplemented by the testimonies of filmmakers and professionals. Over the last decade, my reading, viewing, interviews, campus and festival programming, and teaching have come from hundreds of contemporary French films taken from as wide a range of sources as possible: at American film festivals in places like Boston, New York City, and Richmond, Virginia; through specialist region-1 DVD companies; during the theatrical releases of French films in the United States; a consideration of those films highlighted, for good or bad, in trade papers like *Le Film français* and more popular magazines like *Studio* and *Première*; in mainstream movie theaters during regular visits to Paris; in specialist repositories like the Bibliothèque du Film and the Cinémathèque Française; and, most free-ranging of all, through the constant flow, the torrent of films released (in recent years far more comprehensively than ever before) on French DVD. (The Select Filmography includes the availability of these with English subtitles.) Our major objective is to broaden the canon of contemporary French cinema, especially the texts that are discussed here for the first time in the English language.

Returning to *Brutal Intimacy*'s rationale, my survey reflects another pivotal tendency: that French cinema evolves at speed, from an industry and culture machine built around continuity but also rapid flux, the new and old poised in creative friction. Regarding the films and their shaping contexts, certain critical gospels are simply no longer apt; some have become ossified and out of touch. An example of this, explored in Chapter 3, is the traditional belief in a rigid antagonism between France's arthouse auteurs and their more commercially oriented colleagues, the notion that French cinematic practices high and low do not mingle. This, like some other conventional theories of French film, we can abandon, but hopefully in a productive spirit, as something from the past that no longer rings quite true, becoming less an overarching truism than just one point of departure among many. Exploring newer developments like France's contemporary pop-art cinema, my aim is not only to revise our critical repertoire, but also to open up new avenues within which to situate the shifting techniques — conceptual, stylistic, thematic, promotional, and so on — of French filmmakers at large. While each section that follows details a particular model of French cinema, these models are often interrelated and are not mutually exclusive. As a result, the case studies are worthy ambassadors of French cinema in their own right, but also represent larger tendencies, markers to chart the changing contours of French cinema, as well as, where pressing and salient, its wider connections to French society.

On the issue of French cinema's versatility, its reputed strength in depth, we can briefly survey France's recent production landscape. This introduces the French cultural-commercial complex, subsidized film art underpinned by capitalism. France's cinema industry, indeed, often resembles a financial minefield, a heavily regulated business coupling mandated top-down government initiatives to the economic resources of, variously, production bodies, national television networks, regional and international grant agencies, artists and artistic enterprises, and cautious investment companies. A hypothetical production scenario demonstrates the system — sometimes flexible, sometimes precarious — in action.[5] In 2008, the average French film cost 6.4 million euros. Say you are the enterprising producer in charge, negotiating the French film industry, how might you raise these funds?

Besides assembling your creative and technical personnel, you would first seek institutional support. Your first port of call becomes the state-sponsored Centre National de la Cinématographie (CNC), at the heart of the French film industry. The CNC primarily offers a *compte de soutien* aid program, which disburses taxation revenues — principally from film tickets and DVD sales — to would-be producers (a more lucrative prospect if you are experienced and your previous film made money). In addition, the CNC annually awards *avances sur recettes* (advances on takings) grants: first and primarily for debutants, second for everyone else (less commercial ventures are prioritized), and third, more rarely, for at-risk productions after principal photography is complete. Around 10 percent of applicants receive the *avances sur recettes*, however, which in 2008 averaged around 400,000 euros each (this financial kernel is, though, typically decisive: over 90 percent of *avances sur recettes* recipients complete their productions and make it to the big screen).

After the CNC, your real financial deals begin. First, you would almost certainly approach Canal+, the pay-per-view and subscription media empire described impishly by Michel Palmiéri as "the good fairy of French cinema."[6] In exchange for screening rights and continued state accreditation, Canal+ is obliged to invest at least 20 percent of its revenues into film production, of which just under half must be French in origin. (In 1988, Canal+ founded Studio Canal, a separate and extremely active film and DVD production company.) With or without Canal+, your next step is to consider France's terrestrial or indigenous television channels, all of which are similarly directed to fund filmmaking (3.2 percent of their total investments into prepurchasing and/or coproducing; 2.5 percent into French cinema specifically). At this stage, your ability to pitch your film as a prime-time candidate, suitable for broad audiences, and, most marketable of all, as a property with a star attached, is certainly useful. Beyond your potential television benefactors, you would soon need to attract distributors, domestic and international. Their input, typically, will take the form of a *minimum garanti* (MG), up-front capital, which is subsequently reimbursed from the takings of theatrical and/or DVD release.

What other funding sources are available to you as producer? One financial fixture, created in 1985 by France's renowned Minister of Culture Jack Lang, is the Société pour le Financement du Cinéma et de l'Audiovisuel (SOFICA), which generates tax shelters to encourage investment in filmmaking. In 2008, a SOFICA could net you as much as 500,000 euros or more. Similarly vital to the ambitious producer are regional agencies—dominated in France by that of the greater metropolitan Paris/Île-de-France—which allocate cash grants in exchange for commitments to base location shoots, with all the local incomes they stimulate, within their particular domain. Elsewhere, there is a further fiscal option: since 2004, you can apply directly to the state for further tax credits under the *crédit d'impôt*, provided that your production satisfies criteria about the French nationality of its financiers, creative pool and staff; and that it has suitable CNC credentials.

At this point, as a typical French producer you are probably not yet out of the woods. Counting your total investments, you would discover that you still lack about 20–30 percent of your total production budget. Balancing your books might, in turn, require additional coproducer partnerships, or simply oblige you as producer to stump up the extra money yourself, either from your production company or from your own pocket. Many contemporary French producers hence describe their work as a mixture of practical fiscal negotiations and dedication to films they creatively and financially believe in. As Olivier Delbosc of Fidélité Films, the adventurous producer of *5x2* (2004) and *Actresses* (*Actrices*, 2007), who currently makes about five films annually, remarks ruefully: "Among the 200 films produced in France each year, many are almost self-produced by enthusiasts ready to risk their homes or their futures to get a film shot."[7]

From the vicissitudes of our hypothetical film project, we can turn to a broader assessment of the French production situation. Statistically at least, the key data, collated meticulously by the CNC, do point to a measure of stability, especially as the dwindling revenues of the turbulent 1990s (the nadir being the years following the 1993 General Agreement on Tariffs and Trade [GATT] treaty) gave way to the more vigorous business of the early-to-mid 2000s. Most industrial analysts express ambivalence but also a measure of confidence about France's cultural-commercial production conundrum, despite the perennial perception that crises loom. Two recent studies, by Jonathan Buchsbaum and Laurent Creton, conclude on the same note of cautious optimism—that French cinema will weather storms by devising contingent top-down solutions to financial exigencies. As Buchsbaum puts it, "The French support system is built on elaborate national definitions in order to identify, track, and capture currency flows . . . [with] the CNC direct[ing] the proliferating mix of aids distributed in all directions. . . . As France values cinema as an essential cultural achievement . . . it is unlikely that France will fail to design a new system to preserve cinema's vitality."[8] More succinct, Creton reflects that "in the throes of crisis we find mixed the two poles *difficulty-danger* and *chance-opportunity*."[9]

Turning to the figures, certainly as far as the last fifteen years go, a trajectory of fiscal and production gains is clear. Tracking the data, we can discern several defining trends. One is a pattern of obvious production growth, from just 89 French features released in 1994 to a solid pattern of more than double this figure by 2009, the two hundred annual film threshold routinely bandied about as a new norm in the French trade press. Investment in French cinema, concomitantly, has soared, more than tripling during the same period, a phenomenon linked to the rapid development of France's blockbuster mega-production sector, popularized by Luc Besson. (Only in 2009's slight shrinkage of productions and budgets is evidence of the 2008 global economic downturn evident.) Analysts of these CNC statistics offer us broad perspectives about contemporary French film production. *Le Film français*, an important mouthpiece for the French film industry, much as *Variety* is for Hollywood, is arguably the most systematic respondent. One of its consistent refrains is to note the influx of production capital: as early as 2000 Sarah Drouhard noted presciently that, as far as French film was concerned, "there's always more money"[10]—the discrepancy being, however, that these funds were concentrated on fewer, hyper-commercial ventures. In general, annual reports in *Le Film français* on the industry describe increasing prosperity and continuity throughout the early twenty-first century. Among its assessments are motifs: that the CNC's and regional fiscal support mechanisms were stable and beneficial (2000, 2001, 2002, 2004, 2005, 2007, 2008); that first-time directors were augmenting the industry, especially those able to

Table 1 *Films Produced in France, 1993–2009*

	Total French Film Production	100% French-financed Productions	Coproductions
1993	101	67	34
1994	89	61	28
1995	97	63	34
1996	104	74	30
1997	125	86	39
1998	148	102	46
1999	150	115	35
2000	145	111	34
2001	172	126	46
2002	163	106	57
2003	183	105	78
2004	167	130	37
2005	187	126	61
2006	164	127	37
2007	185	133	52
2008	196	145	51
2009	182	137	45

Source: CNC.

continue their careers (2001, 2002, 2005, 2007); a degree of uncertainty about the fluctuating yet vital role of SOFICA, Canal+, and television networks (2001, 2002, 2004, 2005); and, almost every year, confirmation that budgets were on the rise. By 2004, *Le Film français* declared that French cinema (boosted by its new *crédit d'impôt*) had left its period of crisis; by 2006 it announced that it had stabilized at unprecedented high production standards; by 2008 it went so far as to suggest a "beautiful permanence"[11] about the industry as a whole, a rather ironic statement given the global financial turbulence to come.

To other parties, the state of affairs in twenty-first-century French film production appears more controversial. Especially contentious was a *Le Film français* finding about the 2007 industry—that a "bipolarization" process was evident, in which low budget (less than 4 million euros) and high budget superproductions (more than 10 million euros) were starting to dominate the field, leaving little or no room for middle budget features in between.[12] At the 2007 César awards, France's annual celebration of its cinematic achievements, Pascale Ferran, director of five-prize-winner *Lady Chatterley* (2006), took the

Table 2 *Finances in French Productions, 1993–2009*

	Total Investment in French Film Production (French + foreign, millions of euros)	Average Budgets of French Productions (millions of euros)	Number of French Productions Costing More Than 10 Million euros
1993	475.0 (341.1 + 133.9)	3.4	3
1994	438.9 (340.4 + 98.5)	4.0	8
1995	548.2 (406.2 + 142.0)	4.3	7
1996	501.0 (386.2 + 114.8)	3.7	6
1997	705.3 (567.8 + 137.5)	4.8	9
1998	753.3 (607.6 + 145.7)	4.4	9
1999	691.9 (568.7 + 123.2)	3.9	10
2000	803.3 (665.3 + 138.0)	4.7	14
2001	905.2 (728.7 + 176.5)	4.4	20
2002	860.7 (678.2 + 182.5)	4.4	14
2003	1,153.3 (789.3 + 364.0)	4.6	18
2004	1,048.8 (819.8 + 229.0)	5.3	24
2005	1,286.1 (917.0 + 369.2)	5.0	22
2006	1,148.5 (834.3 + 314.2)	5.3	24
2007	1,201.1 (951.8 + 249.3)	5.4	28
2008	1,490.5 (1,223.8 + 266.7)	6.4	35
2009	1,098.7 (927.5 + 171.2)	5.1	25

Source: CNC.

opportunity to attack what she saw as "the system of financing films which leads on the one hand to films that are increasingly rich, and on the other to films that are extremely poor."[13] In effect, Ferran argued, the French industry was losing its capacity to support *films du milieu*, midrange productions that were historically the domain of commercial artists like Jacques Becker, Jean Renoir, Alain Resnais, and François Truffaut. Following this broadside, between March and December 2007, Ferran convened a hand-picked Club des 13, excluding studio insiders and film critics and instead representing the profession with three directors (Ferran herself, Jacques Audiard, and Claude Miller), a scriptwriter (Cécile Vargaftig), four producers (including Patrick Sobelman), a distributor, three exhibitors, and an export agent. After extensive investigations, in 2008 the Club des 13 published its findings, widely debated ever since, as *Le Milieu n'est plus un pont mais un faille—The Middle Is No Longer a Bridge But a Faultline*.

The Club des 13's 321-page report, in some ways mimicking the format of the CNC's own exhaustive yearly surveys, seizes upon a number of allegedly fatal flaws in the French industrial system. The main problem, the Club des 13 claims, is the undue pressure the contemporary French film industry places upon its so-called *films du milieu*, a category shifting amorphously between productions with midrange budgets to those defined by more independent and/or artistic (yet presumably quite costly) aspirations. At times, *Le Milieu n'est plus un pont mais une faille* is quite specific and industrially acute, noting that the proliferation of French film production is squeezing the fixed grant resources available through the CNC to ambitious producers; that funding sources have not grown proportionately to inflation and escalating production costs; and that conservative and/or commercially oriented exhibition practices (apparent in multiplexes and in Canal+'s programming alike) are hindering the quality of French cinema. Elsewhere, the Club des 13 yearns romantically for the past: when the mainstream ideology of French television channels did not dictate film investment, when scriptwriters were able to work closely with directors and producers, and when, in a shamelessly idealized fantasy, times were vastly different from "today, when the cinema of auteurs is attacked on all sides."[14] As Isabelle Vanderschelden points out, while the Club des 13's analysis highlights productive areas for financial reform, it can be and indeed has been criticized for its "stereotypically French auteurist bias . . . an ideal of directorial control . . . [that drops] market and reception issues rapidly from the discussion."[15] A point in common, however, between writers as diverse as the largely optimistic *Le Film français* and the more pessimistic Club des 13 is their shared sense that the twenty-first century has changed the production equation in France, that the perennial interests of commerce and art are producing an unprecedented diversity of French filmmaking.

How does this book engage with this continuum of contemporary French cinema? Chapter 1 analyzes one of the main aspects of French filmmaking for several generations, especially pressing in the early twenty-first century. This is the matter of France's debutant cinema, an industry predicated on the institutional and artistic support awarded to first-time filmmakers, from sources like the CNC and the French Film Academy. The first chapter explores the particular contexts that give rise to France's contemporary young cinema, the relationship between newcomers present and newcomers past, the fiscal resources and official bodies that shape the careers of emergent French filmmakers, often propelling them into the international spotlight as part of France's mission to safeguard its indigenous film culture and showcase it abroad. This chapter also analyzes this first-time cinema on-screen: its painfully frank yet often dispassionate coming-of-age narratives, as well as its representation of burgeoning sexuality, adolescence, and teenage identity politics. As we will see, a paradox that emerges is the notion of a "rebellious" young cinema, texts about alienated youths and juvenile delinquency, which derive from institutional mandates. To examine the major conventions of France's first-time cinema, both on- and off-screen, this chapter's representative sample is the five debut features nominated, hence officially sanctioned as French success stories, for the 2008 Best First Film César awards: Lola Doillon's *Et toi, t'es sur qui?*, Céline Sciamma's *Water Lilies* (*La Naissance des pieuvres*), Mia Hansen-Løve's *All Is Forgiven* (*Tout est pardonné*), Anne le Ny's *Those Who Remain* (*Ceux qui restent*), and Vincent Paronnaud's and Marjane Satrapi's *Persepolis* (*Persépolis*).

In the second chapter, *Brutal Intimacy* responds to the contemporary phenomenon of the *cinéma du corps*, a defining strand of France's most experimental and textually fraught art cinema. This, arguably the most notorious tendency in recent French filmmaking, is a cinema profoundly centered on the body, dwelling on the visceral processes of corporeal acts, from body crimes to self-mutilations, often savage behaviors derived from unchecked sexual and carnal desires. This chapter explores the emergence of the *cinéma du corps*, its leading practitioners and their critical reception, its resonance beyond France, and its contemporary culmination in the work of figures as diverse as Claire Denis, Bruno Dumont, Gaspar Noé, Marina de Van, and Diane Bertrand. In the hands of filmmakers like these, we consider how the *cinéma du corps* has been controversial yet misunderstood, its stylistic conception and execution overlooked, as have the bravura means by which diegetic defamiliarization occurs, the construction of social spaces that are apprehended in the context of such stark, atavistic, threateningly amoral case studies. This brutal intimacy template most profoundly extends to the actual viewer, a role that becomes highly unconventional, challenged overtly by the artful proximity of such formally and physically confrontational events.

Chapter 3 broaches another fascinating paradox or cultural incongruity within contemporary French filmmaking: its emergent pop-art cinema. This I define as a confluence of what have traditionally been seen, certainly since the New Wave, as distinct discourses in France — the materials of high art and mass cinema. Instead, this chapter argues that many representative pop-art filmmakers are increasingly motivated to interweave the ingredients of France's mainstream sector with its more esoteric, intellectual *art et essai* works. On the one hand, this chapter begins by studying case studies of French cinema at its most ingeniously commercial: the Mesrine and OSS 117 franchises, which are designed around stars like Vincent Cassel and Jean Dujardin, oriented to popular genres like the comedy and the crime thriller or policier, and attuned to audiences both local and international. From here, I explore how France has recently entered a hyper-commercial, global phase of its mainstream production sphere, focusing especially on how such popular French cinema targets American markets. But the neglected facet of this equation, defined in this chapter, uses the examples of leading and lesser known French filmmakers — from Valeria Bruni Tedeschi to Olivier Assayas to Serge Bozon to Robin Campillo and others — to define France's pop-art cinema as a collision, an intermingling, a productive textual intersection between the forms and subjects of two such ostensibly opposed approaches to film.

Feminine cinema is the focus of Chapter 4, which charts the historical emergence of women in France, and the corresponding growth of French women filmmakers since the 1980s. The chapter considers how women increasingly permeate the French industry, from the popular mainstream to the more radical domain of the arthouse. Considering the materials of figures such as Lucile Hadzihalilovic and Siegrid Alnoy, the chapter outlines the salient critical models connected to women filmmakers in France, the theoretical notions and critical terminologies applied to what is a comparative success story within French production: the advance of females in a highly competitive, and traditionally chauvinistic, trade. On-screen, by result, in many representative feminine films we see evidence for a more textually progressive cinema, departing from the closed formal system of traditionally male-centered cinema in favor of more lyrical, polyvalent, rhetorically open forms. Once again, such cinema is highly empowering for the alert viewer, as witness the energetic reception of films that offer complex but compelling screen portraits of female characters, within diegetic worlds that represent the domains of women as at once liberating yet contingent, idyllic yet under threat.

Brutal Intimacy's final section draws together the preceding case studies, resituating the continuum of French cinema in the context of its applied cinephilia. The model presented here as a shaping context to French production is not merely passive, cinephilia as a pattern of intensely appreciative reception and critical scrutiny, but also as an *active* principle, something that consciously defines the production habits of its filmmakers. Relating back to a sample of representative works, this final segment explores a vital catalyst for modern French cinema, the elite national state-funded film school, la Fémis. Using pedagogical analyses, interviews with professionals, and outlines of the school's methods and impact, we discover the cinephilic ideology as a configuring force among a growing and catalytic population of France's film craftspeople. Drawing all these points together, the book's climactic case study is the work of Jean Paul Civeyrac, instructor and critic, cinephile filmmaker, whose work emblematizes many currents of French cinema today. Contemporary French cinema, then, offers us a paradigm of dialogue between the craft of filmmaking and France's system of critical reception and promotion. It presents us with the impact of a range of activities that are actively taken on by contemporary professionals, from being a student to becoming a teacher, working as an industrial advocate as much as an artist, engaging with critics and scholars through cineliterate self-promotion, behaving as a highly motivated citizen within a film culture that is one of the world's most invigorating, often surprising, and wonderfully dynamic.

CHAPTER ONE

5x1

YOUNG CINEMA AND FIRST-TIMERS

CAHIERS DU CINÉMA

STREET VENDOR:
Excuse me, Mister —
do you have something
against Youth?
MICHEL: Yeah, I prefer
old people.

Breathless
(A Bout de souffle, 1960),
Jean-Luc Godard's
debut feature

Among critics and filmmakers, the expression *le jeune cinéma français* is often used to refer to any striking or especially creative surge in contemporary French filmmaking. It translates literally as young French cinema, a useful way of considering what Réné Prédal calls the film industry's "incessant renewal,"[1] its velocity and forward momentum. Young cinema: the term suggests enthusiasm and vigor, youthful films made by ambitious newcomers, something to reinvigorate a stale tradition. Such traits can be qualified, though, by more negative aspects of textual youthfulness — films that are culturally ephemeral, perhaps, or faddish and immature. Weighing up both sides, as one recent French first-time director observed: "There is surely more clumsiness or errors in a first film, but they're often effaced by the feeling of sincerity, of energy and passion for the work."[2] Either way, this notion of young cinema — a generative force that supplants old cinema, shaping a field in constant flux — is vital for understanding contemporary French film. So prompted, this chapter will explore the phenomenon of young, first-time cinema in France today, a surprisingly neglected issue. As we will see, modern French film culture relies heavily on a vanguard of emergent professionals, debutants, whose unpracticed but often startlingly accomplished talents are foregrounded forcefully within a highly competitive industrial marketplace. This systematic emphasis upon young cinema makes France unique.

Pursuing the French young cinema model, often described as an elastic or rather slippery term,[3] does confirm the importance of debutant filmmakers, both historically and in the contemporary moment. This is an industry built strategically around getting untried first-timers, often with little or no professional experience, into the trade quickly, then soliciting disproportionate attention to their work. This system is a legacy, of course, of France and arguably world cinema's most beloved moment, the French New Wave, which based much of its (self-) promotion, artistic profile, and commercial viability on the fact that its Young Turks were amateur-professionals, unschooled movie brats both on- and off-screen. As a group, the *Cahiers* cohort and its acolytes traded off the rupture with the past they embodied, as uncorrupted outsiders breaking—rapidly—into an outmoded profession, reinventing the medium from more unorthodox, personal, and, above all, youthful perspectives. So attractive was this New Wave paradigm—young cinema as rebellious as freethinking as modern— that it became French cinema's definitive global export. Today, still, the work of contemporary debutants pays homage to the legacy of landmark debuts from this period, like Jean-Pierre Melville's *The Silence of the Sea* (*Le Silence de la mer*, 1949), Agnès Varda's *La Pointe-Courte* (1954), and their more famous descendents *Breathless* and *The 400 Blows* (*Les 400 coups*, 1959).

Since the 1950s the figure of the first-time filmmaker, usually young, has become an institutional fixture of French cinema, integral to its national and international identity. A sizeable portion of French production now hinges upon CNC sponsorship of emergent filmmaking, part of the French state's mission to safeguard French cinema domestically and boost its profile abroad. Although the CNC had intervened in the film industry since its 1946 inception, its efforts became more aggressive throughout the 1950s, eventually consolidating around the *avances sur recettes* grants. These *avances sur recettes* were tested in different forms between 1955 and 1959 (the year after André Malraux moved the CNC from the Ministry of Industry and Commerce to the Ministry of Culture), and then implemented as formal policy in 1960.[4] *Avances sur recettes* responded to two of French cinema's most chronic problems. The first point, a bottom-up concern, was that the 1950s film industry seemed unable to integrate its younger professionals with any alacrity. In an era when obligatory traineeships lasted up to ten years, and conservative producers resisted hiring newcomers in advanced roles like director anyway,[5] it was widely felt that the trade was ossified. The second matter was a top-down perception, that despite the commercial rejuvenation of postwar French cinema, to many, its artistic imperatives were being overlooked. Hence, pressure mounted on the CNC to support more creatively ambitious projects, worthy flag-bearers for French film culture. Responding to both issues, the CNC designed the *avances sur recettes* in its own words "to promote the creative renewal and to encourage the direction of first films, and to support an independent cinema, audacious in relation to marketplace norms, which could not maintain its financial equilibrium without public aid."[6]

Following this logic, *avances sur recettes* applicants (typically French directors, although scriptwriters, producers, and even filmmakers of other European nationalities were eligible) submitted production proposals based on their demonstrated artistic ambition and French-language orientation, with strong preference given to debutants. Soon, a young cinema began en masse, while the *avances sur recettes* became arguably the world's most famous and influential film grants, credited widely, as Charlie Michael suggests, with encouraging "a slew of young directors and low-budget productions, soon to be embraced as the aesthetic of the New Wave."[7] More than 120 first-time directors, in fact, made commercially released features between 1958 and 1964 alone. (Between the late 1940s and mid-1950s, by contrast, first-timers were responsible for fewer than thirteen features a year.)[8] And while the New Wave always snatches the headlines, today it is worth noting that 15 percent of all films produced in France each year still result from successful *avances sur recettes* pitches, many of them by new directors.

Following this production dynamic, the cult of young cinema has become central to the way that French cinema showcases its wares, at home and abroad. The model underpins government-sponsored agencies like Uni-France, which exists to "play a role at every stage in the life of a French film abroad: from its selection at a recognized film festival or its screening at an international market to its commercial release in one or more international territories. . . . In this way, UniFrance works to increase the visibility of all recent French films."[9] A number of organizations affiliated with UniFrance explicitly cite the *jeune cinéma* mantra, such as the Saint-Ouen-based *Collectif Jeune Cinéma*. This independent cooperative, founded in 1971, supports upcoming filmmakers through events like its Paris *Festival des Cinémas Différents*, and a foreign sales division which gives export opportunities for new short filmmakers, as was recently the case with figures like Frédéric Tachou, Emmanuelle Sarrouy, and Augustin Gimel.[10] More generally, a crucial part of the French mission to valorize its newest cinema is highlighting the latest breakthrough directors. UniFrance's regular collaborations with the New York City-based *New Directors New Films* festival is just one effort to position recent French cinema as internationally distinctive, pioneering. In the same vein, also in America, is the French Ministry of Culture's *Nouvelles fictions* series, a package of ten to twelve debutant films which are pitched annually as a heavily subsidized touring screening package to schools and higher education institutions in North America. In such instances, young cinema travels internationally as the distillation, or epitome, of what French cinema has to offer.

Reinforcing this mentality, many French institutions, some iconic, champion the nation's young cinema. Most prestigious of these is the debutant filmmaking prize at France's annual national film awards, the Césars.[11] After the French Film Academy (*L'Académie des Arts et Techniques du Cinéma*) was formed under the direction of Georges Cravenne in 1974, the Césars began the following year, with a debutant category inaugurated in 1982 as the award for Best First Work (*César de la meilleure première œuvre*). The prize not only recognized, belatedly, the importance of a debutant generation to French cinema, but also neatly differentiated the Césars from their American counterparts, the Academy Awards. Additionally, the Best First Work was a nice antidote to cinema awards programs dominated by veterans being compensated for long professional service. In 1982 — retrospectively a symbolic moment — the first ever Best First Work César went to Jean-Jacques Beineix's controversial *cinéma du look* harbinger *Diva*: to many eyes a vulgar, apolitical, and excessively youth-oriented commercial piece; to its supporters a lively and welcome break with a dour recent cinematic past.[12] In keeping with its youthful ideology, moreover, the first-timer César is constantly repackaged and reinvented by the French Film Academy. In 2000 it became the César for Best First Work of Fiction (*César de la meilleure première œuvre de fiction*), and then in 2006 it received its current, more streamlined title, simply the Best First Film (*César du meilleur premier film*).

Whatever its name, the debutant César award is just part of a constellation of French cinematic events that favor, and honor, the newcomer. These include, notably, the *Prix Jean Vigo*, a highly prestigious award for artistic originality and excellence, which since 1951 has been heavily weighted towards first-timers. Its recipients include Claude Chabrol, for *Le Beau Serge* (1959), Godard, for *Breathless*, and, more recently, Bruno Dumont, for *La Vie de Jésus* (1997). In 2000, the venerable *Prix Louis-Delluc* committee followed suit by adding a Best First Film prize, given that first year to Laurent Cantet's *Human Resources* (*Ressources humaines*). Even more systematically, the principle of youthful cinema and emergent filmmakers shapes France's highest profile site of global film culture, the Cannes Film Festival. At Cannes, the pro-new doctrine informs the *Un Certain Regard* panel (which awards one to three annual grants to enable distribution for newer directors in France); the annual *Caméra d'or* prize for Best First Film (awarded, for instance, to a French film in 2002, Julie Lopes-Curval's *Seaside* [*Bord de mer*]); and the International Critics Week series, which screens both features and shorts that are limited to first- or second-time films.

Table 3 *Debut Films Produced in France, 1997–2009*

	Number of Debut Films Produced in France	Total French Film Production	Percentage of French Productions Made by First-timers	First Films That Received the *Avances sur Recettes* Grant
1997	46	125	36.8	18
1998	58	148	39.2	23
1999	62	150	41.3	24
2000	53	145	36.6	19
2001	53	172	30.8	19
2002	67	163	41.1	27
2003	68	183	37.2	28
2004	54	167	32.3	24
2005	69	187	36.9	23
2006	56	164	34.1	21
2007	72	185	38.9	15
2008	74	196	37.8	18
2009	77	182	42.3	17

Source: CNC.

Turning to a contemporary frame, the vitality of debutant cinema is clear across the French production landscape. Consider, as evidence, the figures compiled by the cnc about first-time productions in France. Statistically, the data confirm that first-timers now reliably contribute around 40 percent of all films made or coproduced in France, a process augmented by the *avances sur recettes*.

From our evidence so far, the phenomenon of young French cinema, and specifically the contingent of films directed and released by first-timers, seems undeniably important to an assessment of contemporary French cinema. Obstacles to such an approach, however, soon become clear, as does a corollary critical reluctance to address, or an outright bias against, debutant filmmaking, not only in relation to French cinema but also in film studies itself. (Here and elsewhere, analyzing recent French cinema yields productive conclusions about the state of an entire critical discipline.) There is, most pressingly, the ubiquitous auteur complex, a methodology predicated on an established *oeuvre* and coherent body of texts bearing a signature style and themes. Respondents to recent French cinema, it must be said, return time and time again to familiar auteur candidates (especially Luc Besson, Jean-Pierre Jeunet, and Mathieu Kassovitz) whose impact, while obviously important, becomes disproportionately inflated. In an industry predicated on newness and high cultural turnover, this lure of the familiar—critics nuancing the known rather than broaching the unknown—narrows the canon and neglects the discourses, and texts, that continually propel French cinema forwards.

Focusing instead on French debutant cinema creates invigorating challenges. How do we appraise a filmmaker or group of filmmakers with only one feature, and possibly a handful of student works or shorts, to their name? Must critical intervention wait until the newcomer becomes an established auteur, or at least survives the passage of time? (The cnc's data confirm that approximately half of France's debutant filmmakers do manage to complete at least one follow-up feature.) The hazards—but also rewards—facing the analyst of young French cinema are incisively explored by Michel Ciment in a 2003 *Positif* editorial, *"Premières œuvres."* Ciment's agenda, drawn up for an issue dealing with a slew of debut features, claims that many prejudices circulate around debutant cinema—accounts of which, he reports, are surprisingly rare in any case. Most reductive, Ciment suggests, is the fatally patronizing tone which permeates analyses of first works, as if the qualities of a debut text emerge merely as precursors to subsequent achievements; the first work can only ever be a work-in-progress. Almost never, moreover, does the critic rest content with an overarching analysis of a filmmaker or an emergent work based *on that emergent work alone*. Although the litany of never-repeated debut masterworks is clear—the editorial cites as obvious targets *Citizen Kane* (1941), *L'Atalante* (1934), and *Hiroshima mon amour* (1959), plus lesser known contenders like Luchino Visconti's *Ossessione* (1943) and Joseph Losey's *The Boy With Green Hair* (1948)—Ciment argues that few explore the common principles guiding the first work *sui generis*. This is to our loss, Ciment concludes, for the debut work, considered on its own terms, offers the engaged critic "an audacious madness, a praiseworthy lack of concern for the rules of the trade, its setbacks, the economic contingencies that can bring [the filmmaker] down."[13] Among many artists, indeed, from Welles to Truffaut, a case could be made that the first feature is often their richest and most lasting contribution of all.

Already, we have seen that a sustained analysis of first-time cinema is crucial to understanding contemporary French film. We should follow Ciment, however, in approaching this debutant cinema as a distinctive tendency, as neither a set of "precursor" works by nascent auteurs-to-be, nor "pure" works abstracted from France's cultural-industrial complex. Instead, we can analyze contemporary French debutant cinema on its own terms: its transtextual features, the attributes that so engage—and are consciously configured by—the mechanisms of France's pro-young cinema industry. None of this is to deny, of course, the extraordinary accomplishments and artistic flair often shown by individual filmmakers among French first-time productions. But a guiding rationale here is that seeking out new or breakthrough films, some of them obscure outside France, is a vital tool to assess the true breadth of French cinema, the source of its perpetual regeneration. In this way, we enrich the twenty-first-century French canon, while also understanding the subsidized newness that is designed to elevate French film above its peers.

To pursue this agenda we will now address chiefly, as a representative sample, the five features that were nominated for the Best First Film César on January 24, 2008, films that were all released in 2007. The films are: Lola Doillon's *Et toi, t'es sur qui?*, Vincent Paronnaud's and Marjane Satrapi's *Persepolis (Persépolis)*, Mia Hansen-Løve's *All Is Forgiven (Tout est pardonné)*, Céline Sciamma's *Water Lilies (La Naissance des pieuvres)*, and Anne le Ny's *Those Who Remain (Ceux qui restent)*. In their design, execution and reception, this group provides an array of materials, a benchmark with which to analyze French debutant cinema. (Hansen-Løve, Paronnaud, Satrapi, and Sciamma all received *avances sur recettes* grants for their work.) While all the 2008 nominees were hailed in the trade press as a keenly competitive batch, representative of a vigorous industry, the First Film category was especially singled out for praise — François-Pier Pelinard-Lambert, for instance, referred to it in *Le Film français* as "a beautiful palette of talents."[14] Another fact universally noted was that all five films were either directed or codirected by women, a prompt about the impact of feminine cinema that will be taken up systematically in Chapter 4. For our purposes, this first-time quintet poses interrelated questions. Why were these particular films seen as pinnacles, best case scenarios, of the craft of first-time French cinema? What circumstances created such debutant productions, and how were they marketed? What textual features unite them, as first-time works, and in what ways do they address their status as novice projects with auteurist ambitions? How did these debutants intervene in their own cultural reception in France, ingratiating themselves with critics? A final issue to consider is the matter of this quintet's engagement with the currents of cineliteracy that so decisively shape contemporary French cinema.

Maliciously Tender: Lola Doillon's *Et toi, t'es sur qui?*

Among our debutant quintet, the name Lola Doillon is perhaps the most auspicious, the most connected to the film industry at large. She is the daughter of director Jacques Doillon and editor Noëlle Boisson, both mainstays of the trade. Lola's father, now an instructor at la Fémis, has been an active filmmaker since the late 1960s, less well known outside France, but acclaimed for his intimate family dramas, often focusing on women, children and youthful relationships. More recent, widely distributed examples of Doillon Senior's work include *Ponette* (1996), his powerfully unsentimental study of a four-year-old girl's life after her mother dies in a car accident; and *Petits frères* (1999), about the descent into criminality of a group of latchkey kids living in Pantin, a working-class Parisian suburb. For a filmmaker seeking access to a profession that historically privileges auteurs, having a seasoned brand for a surname is an undeniable advantage, the basis for a viable and well-established passage into French cinema. This is the case, taking just several among legions of examples, with directors Jean Becker (son of Jacques), François Desagnat (son of Jean-Pierre), and Julie Gavras (daughter of Costa), as well as actors Mathieu Demy (son of Agnès Varda and Jacques Demy), and Julie and Guillaume Depardieu (daughter and son of Gérard).

Doillon's name and its professional connotations raise an important point about how filmmakers promote themselves, a part of the job that often gets neglected. The issue is very relevant to the first-timer, of course, and especially so in France. In the contemporary French press, much more so than in North America or England, scores of magazines, newspapers, and specialist journals devote column space to interviews with filmmakers by critics, a forum surprisingly accommodating to newcomers. (Even in essays without firsthand interviews, French film critics routinely cite filmmaker testimony, usually with respect.) Like many of her peers, Lola Doillon took this opportunity to advance her artistic credentials and cineliteracy. On the one hand, much of Doillon's reception did, in fact, situate her nascent career by way of her father's screen legacy, like an auteur by proxy. Barbara Théate, for instance, writing in *Le Journal de Dimanche*, opened her review of *Et toi, t'es sur qui?* with the remark: "In the Doillon family, here comes the elder sister Lola . . . who seems to have inherited her talent from her father, Jacques."[15] Quite skillfully, though, Doillon turned such predictable journalistic gambits into more considered self-promotion by depicting herself—accurately, if truth be told—not as the lucky beneficiary of nepotism, but rather as a committed cinéaste-professional, tested beyond her years (she was thirty-two when her debut feature was released). In many of her interviews Doillon first paid wry lip service to the filial connection—"Yes, my father evoked childhood, the world of adults, love stories . . . so if I wanted to avoid what he did, all that was left was for me to direct Westerns, or pornos?"[16]—before reinforcing her own independently rigorous capacities: "My family name gave me options, but it also forced me to work hard . . . I had to wait a long time before making a name for myself as a feature director."[17]

Certainly, prior to her debut feature Doillon had spent half of her life immersed in cinema. As Elodie Lepage notes, Doillon's was "a childhood spent between her dad's film sets and her mother's editing suites."[18] And while cinephilia prevails among many contemporary French filmmakers, Doillon's route to direction rivals Jean-Pierre Melville's for its dogged cineliteracy. Starting as a young adult, Doillon trained over a gamut of professional roles, a course that ironically recalls the painfully protracted, decade-long apprenticeships common to French cinema during the newly professionalized, pre-New Wave late 1940s and early 1950s, prior to the *avances sur recettes* initiative.[19] Doillon worked as an on-set still photographer, casting director (notably for both *Ponette* and *Petits frères*), actress, editor, assistant director (on Cédric Klapisch's *Ni pour, ni contre (bien au contraire)* [2002] and *L'Auberge Espagnole* [2002]), then the writer-director of three short films: *Majorettes* (2005), *Deux filles* (2006), and *Déjà fait* (2006).

How does Doillon's work represent contemporary France's debutant cinema? Two major strands emerge from her short films alone. *Majorettes* is a fifteen-minute film which intersects three remarkably deadpan mininarratives about a disaffected group of young teenagers—boys who play soccer and girls who cheerlead the matches—showing each gender faction lying and calmly manipulating friends and family to attract would-be boyfriends or girlfriends. Confirmed by Doillon on Studio Canal's DVD release via an on-screen statement, it was *Majorettes* that first evoked in her the desire to "make a full-length feature with, and on adolescents." Coupled to this pro-youth declaration—as important to young French cinema as it is to Doillon—is the premise of *Déjà fait*. This micro-short, a single long take of eighty-six seconds, shows a young man (Zinedine Soualem) sitting outdoors at a table, surrounded by books, trinkets, plants, and CDs. A pen and blank stack of paper lie before him. As the camera slowly tracks in, the man gets increasingly animated, then frustrated, as he ponders what to write. Jolts of fast motion further agitate his self-diagnoses: "I'll write about politics—no, it's already been done. I'll write about women—no, that's already been done. . . . Religion's been done. Botany's been done. Football, been done. Sixteenth-century painting, been done." His consternation grows, as does the list of rejected topics—poetry, menopause, cigarettes, psychoanalysis, the effects of cell phones on the brain, the Cold War, architecture; they've all been done. All of which leads to an inevitable conclusion as the film cuts to black: "Everything's already been done, so I'll write about myself—*me*, nobody's ever done *me* before!"

Majorettes and *Déjà fait* wittily depict issues that are pivotal to debutant cinema, in our quintet of films and beyond. There is first the pervasive sensibility of sheer belatedness. Doillon's early shorts proclaim how all that has passed, the preceding body of (cinematic) experiences, has basically mined everything out, run the river dry, leaving a medium made banal through end-less repetition. The only viable course left is to turn to the next generation, the nihilistic milieu of the contemporary adolescent, those hedonistic and antisocial young adults in conflict with the older generation, their peers, themselves. This subject and approach are then rendered all the more pro-vocative, of course, through textual cues that identify such filmmaking as honest, unflinching autobiography: *me*, nobody's ever done *me* before. The young cinema text proclaims its newness, in style and content, through a delinquency aesthetic—an authentic treatment of disenfranchised youth, real people pent up with reckless appetites.

All of which returns us inevitably to the legacy of French (and possibly world) cinema's most celebrated and influential debutant text, *The 400 Blows*. This, it seems, perennially relevant film depicts the young life of Truffaut and the New Wave's adolescent alter ago, Antoine Doinel (Jean-Pierre Léaud)—his brutalizing collisions with a repressive school, dysfunctional parents, and relentlessly overbearing authority figures. Such events are punctuated by Antoine's romanticized escapes: bouts of film-going, a day of fairground truancy, his rapturous flights through the streets of Paris, and then, climac-tically, in one of the most infamous freeze frames ever composed, the boy left stranded on a beach, alone and uncertain but at liberty at last. The ide-als which *The 400 Blows* offered a new generation in 1959—its delinquent frankness—come, Richard Neupert suggests, just as "the backbone of *The 400 Blows* springs from the real-life experiences of François Truffaut filtered through the universe of Antoine Doinel . . . [which is nonetheless] a universal and mature tale of childhood rather than just a veiled autobiography."[20] In its playfully radical style as well as this pro-youth address, Truffaut's debut fea-ture created a practical model to which contemporary generations of French filmmakers still attend. The point was confirmed in understated style during another of Doillon's interviews, when she dryly referenced Truffaut within her baggage of motivations. Asked about the relationship between her own life and *Et toi, t'es sur qui?*'s adolescent genre (*genre d'ados*) Doillon replied that, "I raised my own hell [*Je faisais mes quatre cents coups*] discreetly. I was forc-ibly inspired by what I'd lived through myself, mixed with the universe and the vocabulary of the youth [*des ados*] of today."[21] On the subject of Truffaut's actual film, Doillon was more emphatic: "*The 400 Blows* is a moment of grace which affected everyone, especially me; it's something that accompanied me on my own projects."[22]

Replete with New Wave sympathies, *Et toi, t'es sur qui?* focuses on the sex-ual urges, peer pressures, and wavering social ties within a group of fourteen-

Lola Doillon on set with the cast of *Et toi, t'es sur qui?*

and fifteen-year-olds. The film follows best friends Elodie (Lucie Desclozeaux) and Julie (Christa Theret), who decide on the brink of high school summer holidays that they will lose their virginity by the start of autumn classes. Julie, a skeptical outsider nicknamed Batman for her gothic dress sense, ends up having hasty sex with Vincent (Gaël Tavares), Elodie's close male friend, during a work placement at a meat processing plant. This creates jealousy between the two girls, which intensifies as they jostle for the attention of Nico (Nicolas Schweri). Nico bets Vincent that he can bed Julie before switching his interest to Elodie, who permits him a one-evening-stand but fantasizes about the disinterested Kevin (Vincent Romoeuf). The unsparing cynicism of these intertwined encounters (the film's poster featured arrows linking the characters by way of their dalliances) is offset, though, by more poignant moments: Vincent's genuinely persistent affection for Elodie, her stubborn loyalty to Julie, and the trio's underlying friendship, confirmed hesitantly in the film's final sequence as Elodie leaves by train to head south on vacation. As Cécile Mury suggests, the tone of *Et toi, t'es sur qui?*'s plot comes from Doillon's "malicious tenderness, [observing] the comings and goings of her young heroes, as they take unsteady flight and burst into energetic life."[23]

Amplifying its tangled narrative web of teenaged yearnings, the film's youthful braggadocio is also the product of its pugnacious style, a common motif of the first-time French feature. Turning limited production means to her advantage (*Et toi, t'es sur qui?* cost 1.26 million euros, the cheapest of our quintet whose average budget was just 2.98 million euros)[24] Doillon shot on digital video (DV),which made the logistically complex long take a viable option, as was her frequent recourse to carrying out more than thirty takes per scene.[25] (Isild le Besco took the same approach, a kind of home movie aesthetic, for her debut as director, the quasi-documentary *Half Price* [*Demi-tarif*, 2003], focused on an unconventional family, characterized from the point of view of children.) By consequence, like the work of many of her peers, Doillon's design strategically erupts, with flourishes that not only highlight textual motifs but also exist to flaunt her technical ingenuity. Debutant directors are apt to swagger cinematically, showcasing their mastery of the craft. Consider Doillon's opening, a beguiling two-minutes-fifteen-seconds sequence shot that distils the premises of the entire film.[26] After a title sequence—the camera scans high school lockers that reveal the credits—we cut to an extreme long shot of Julie standing in a street before a row of tenement houses. She droops, staring down the road, then walks to a window and knocks. Elodie emerges from the front door and they kiss each other's cheeks in cheerful greeting. The girls trot briskly towards the camera, a steadicam, which smoothly retreats, holding them in long shot as passersby crisscross the frame. Elodie gossips about a party at which two of their friends had drunken sex ("She gave him a blow job—that's horrible!") and the camera loops around, tracking the duo up a long staircase that leads to a park. Julie smiles, thinking out loud—"By next year most of us will have done it, and I don't want to be last"—to which Elodie responds: "Me neither—not a spinster, but not a slut; it's got be with someone you love." Two flights of stairs up, the girls disparage all the boys they know as bumbling idiots, finishing each other's sentences, before hitting on the idea of a timeline for losing their virginity ("We get laid by September, ok!") which neatly presents the deadline of the plot.

The long take, Doillon's thesis shot, continues. On the third flight of steps, both girls' expressions abruptly change (Elodie glances up nervously and gnaws at her lip; Julie sighs heavily, frowning) as from off-screen right Kevin struts confidently into view. Kevin embodies Julie's distaste (he greets her with, "Bonjour, Batman!" and she tells him to "fuck off") but is the object of Elodie's nervous desire. As Kevin arrives mid-frame, moreover, the choreography of Doillon's mobile frame, its deft use of on- and off-screen space, offers new points. Before and after Kevin acknowledges Elodie offhandedly, he furtively eyes passing girls who stroll right-to-left (foreground) then left-to-right (background). Elodie labors to sustain their conversation while Kevin gazes up at the sky, aloof, rocking on his heels, distractedly flipping his fringe behind an ear. Elodie tries and fails to catch Julie's eye for support, so the girls set off forwards again, while Kevin saunters blithely down the stairs behind them. Julie blurts a protest about her friend's would-be boyfriend, and finally we cut, but not before the shot has instantiated *Et toi, t'es sur qui?*'s agenda. Juggling intimacy and vulgarity, this is, first of all, a wonderfully organic study of body language, probing the brittle nature of teenage social life, the behavioral shifts of young girls when alone, together, and in the company of the opposite sex. Doillon also maps out the attraction-repulsion dynamic between different genders during the teenage years; the intersections between burgeoning sexuality and social-peer pressure; and, most forcefully, the inconstancy of friendships, especially between girls, as boys intervene and then inevitably recede. A deceptively simple yet painstakingly orchestrated piece of dramatic happenstance, Doillon's shot is cinematically virtuoso.[27]

Also emblematized by this preface is another key part of young French cinema — its (quasi-sociological) treatment of the adolescent milieu, youthful pursuits and youthful pleasures. For Antoine Doinel in *The 400 Blows* these were highly active pastimes — raucous misbehavior with classmates, visceral glee at the fairground and in the movie theater, physical flight from teachers in the streets of Paris or by the sea — whereas Julie and Elodie, twenty-first-century young adults, inhabit a static, highly technologized *mise-en-scène*. As Serge Kaganski suggests, part of *Et toi, t'es sur qui?*'s project is "to integrate naturally new modes of communication among adolescents (Orange and MSN rule)."[28] Certainly, there is an implicit point about globalization made when these French teenagers' interests in music, television, fashion, and technology are almost exclusively the products of American brands, from *Buffy the Vampire Slayer* TV episodes to Eminem, the Red Hot Chili Peppers, and Adidas sportswear.

The theme of commodified or virtual communication infuses Doillon's design. One delicately staged motif — a ritual that shows the understated norms of teenaged relationships — shows pairs of characters, posed in medium or medium long shot, sitting and listening to music together, one white earphone apiece, plugged into the same iPod. The iPod itself is Elodie's: we first see her sharing it in this fashion with Vince, very casually; later, again comfortably, with Julie; then finally, by contrast, as the uneasy prelude to a supremely terse seduction scene between her and Nico, to whom she loses her virginity. In the same vein, Doillon builds sequences around cellphone calls and online chat site sessions between her protagonists, during which, of course, they talk far more candidly. Throughout these exchanges, moreover, Doillon pointedly retains classical conversation devices like shot-reverse shot, reaction shots, and even eyeline matches, cutting back and forth as lines are tapped onto keyboards, emoticons created, or exclamations muttered into handsets. The formal system underlines a sense of physical proximity lost, contemporary teenaged dialogues shown as absent presence, a virtual world apart, the distanced communities of what Cécile Mury calls "the adolescent empire of chatrooms."[29]

Doillon's fixation on teen technologies reflects a growing French social unease about twenty-first-century adolescents' affinity for virtual devices, especially cell phones and the internet. In *Et toi, t'es sur qui?* these habits are rife: we see adolescents texting each other during classes, merrily emailing hard-core pornography clips, hanging out online in public chatrooms at the expense of family conversations, and almost constantly talking on handheld phones. At times, Doillon showcases teen multimedia like a subcultural epidemic, tapping insidiously into widespread fears about parents losing control over their children. France's concerns over the secret virtual lives of its adolescents were addressed in a major 2009 survey by Taylor Nelson Sofres, one of the world's largest market research groups. Its findings were arresting: 96 percent of France's twelve-to-seventeen-year-olds now have personal (potentially unsupervised) access to the web, and 76 percent of fourteen-to-fifteen-year-olds (Doillon's demographic) own and use cell phones regularly, a figure that rises to 83 percent among children of divorced parents.[30] In 2007, the year *Et toi, t'es sur qui?* was released, political campaigning began in earnest for stricter laws against teen cell phone use, particularly in schools, on educational grounds as well as those of health risks (the issue of potential brain damage that Doillon's protagonist rejected as a topic in *Déjà fait*) and adolescents' vulnerability to web advertising and online predators.

In tandem with these technological interactions, *Et toi, t'es sur qui?* characterizes adolescence through spoken discourse. Linguistic behaviors, Doillon suggests, develop the social mores that separate—and abstract— each generation from its predecessor. The idea starts with the very title of Doillon's film—an obscure piece of current adolescent slang, which most (middle-aged) French film critics struggled to define; some were not amused. (Julie says the phrase to Nico, asking whom he's literally getting it on, or in real terms, "coupled" to.) Clearly, a young cinema about young people gains authenticity from such spontaneous-sounding, unconventional, lines and performances. Patois dialogue and nonprofessional acting are crucial features here, key to Doillon's methods. As Stéphane Batut, Doillon's casting director, reports, during preproduction they abandoned the idea of using experienced actors in scripted roles, preferring unorthodox auditions in which they studied the mannerisms of unknowns they had mostly chosen at random from adolescent hang-outs like bars, cafés, and schoolyards. During these improvisations, Doillon went so far as to rewrite her final script based on what the guest teenagers did and said, even retaining input from those not eventually cast. Subsequent rehearsals were minimized to allow the cast just to spend time together, developing off-camera relationships that flavored the filmed sequences. As Batut argues, the creative process was not about foisting dramatic situations upon a troupe of trained actors, but "more about unearthing the personalities"[31] they discovered in the adolescent community.

The culmination of this process, a trait widely admired by critics, is Doillon's ear for the formulations and cadences of teenage slang. The film's dialogue, profane and often bewildering, ranges from the banal to the almost poetic, distinctively French as well as nontraditionally multicultural, all the while laced with American-English neologisms, adding zest to the quotidian conversations. (The effect is heightened for viewers following the English subtitles, which attempt about 70 percent of what is said on-screen; the French closed captions similarly struggle to transcribe the more colorful streams of consciousness.) The dramatic-comic-unsettling effect is most striking during more heated moments, such as when Nico reacts with a mixture of delight and disgust to Vincent's admission that he just had sex with Julie: *"Putain, j'en r'viens pas, t'as niqué Batman!"* ("Fuck, get outta here, you screwed Batman!"). Indeed, after naturalizing her script with lines overheard during pre-production, Doillon, a writer in her fourth decade, fashions a true polyglot vernacular — an adult's manipulated transcription of free-form adolescent speech — that at times she admitted to understanding only partially. As Doillon reflected, "There was [one expression] I particularly liked, it's *'Oeuch'bien ou quoi?'* which comes from Arabic. . . . I don't know its precise significance but in the mouths of my actors it came to mean, 'So, how's it going?' [*'Alors, ça va?'*]."[32]

So memorably dense — and forcefully delivered — is Doillon's dialogue that at times it veers close to the stylized part-Russian, part-Cockney rhyming slang, part gibberish Nadsat devised by Anthony Burgess and used in Stanley Kubrick's tale of radically alienated youth, *A Clockwork Orange* (1971). Catchphrases, banter, quips, and offhand epithets are codes for teenage identities slowly slipping away from the linguistic and social mainstream. Doillon's approach recalls two other culturally proximate examples of young French cinema whose scripts derive from *banlieue* milieux: Abdellatif Kechiche's *L'Esquive* (2003) and Audrey Estrougo's debut feature, *Regarde-moi* (2007). (Estrougo's tagline was the snappy syncopated threat: *"Rien qu'avec mon boubou, je t'habille pour l'hiver, connasse!"* or, loosely, "Don't mess with my baby, I'll shake you down, bitch!") Further back, of course, the ghetto slang/lost younger generation model was propelled into the cultural spotlight by the huge success of Kassovitz's *Hate* (*La Haine*, 1995) and, to a lesser extent, Jean-François Richet's *Ma 6-T va crack-er* (1997). As Alison Murray Levine suggests generally, and particularly in regards to Malik Chibane's first feature, the *beur* narrative *Hexagone* (1994), such films blend "standard French, *argot* (French slang in wide use), region-specific slang, *verlan* (back-slang), and some Arabic words," to underline how their characters "are versed enough in French culture to pass for insiders, and yet in the eyes of the mainstream . . . they are outsiders."[33] While this point has been commonly made in relation to ethnic and racial divisions (and Vincent in *Et toi, t'es sur qui?* is black, a point about which nothing at all is made), it applies just as much to the generation gap, youth versus adults, created on-screen in French young cinema culture. Doillon, who cited Kechiche's film as an influence, simply stated that: "I didn't want to cheat when it came to the language of young people."[34] Mury makes the broader case that the film's "constant recourse to dialogue, very contemporary, engaging yet often strange . . . is the key to the dramatic flow. It works, blow by blow, as a means of self-definition, of finding a place in a group and testing your links with others . . . [it shows] all the painful contradictions of this transitory age."[35]

An obvious objection to the film's youthful sympathies is to dismiss its protagonists as stereotypically disaffected, rebels too apathetic for a cause. Anticipating this more cynical reading (perhaps from an older viewer), Doillon inserts strategic cues for reflection, social contexts to France's disenfranchised younger generation. One scene is pointedly didactic. Before her work placement begins, Elodie drifts into conversation with a classmate, who attacks the training scheme with dispassionate gusto: "Frankly it's completely idiotic—even if a guy does a three-month internship, he won't find a job because he's got no experience. . . . Wasting all that National Education money is scandalous, demeaning." The dialogue ends there, abruptly, but to a French audience Doillon's point already hits home. Nearly a quarter of all France's eighteen-to-twenty-five-year-olds are currently unemployed (23 percent in the year *Et toi, t'es sur qui?* was shot), a festering statistic that causes perennial unrest; a fate that awaits Doillon's characters. Implicit to the film, in this light, is the rioting that erupted in early 2006, during Doillon's preproduction. After

Dominique de Villepin, Jacques Chirac's recent appointee as Prime Minister, outlined legislation for a *contrat première embauche* (CPE), allowing employers to fire new workers more readily, hence, following neoliberal theory, also encouraging them to hire more readily, Paris descended into chaos. Echoing the October 2005 banlieue riots but in the heart of France's capital city, student protestors occupied the Sorbonne, a third of all universities shut down, images of police brutality were posted on YouTube, and by March 2006 over 1.5 million people, most of them younger adults, took to the streets to demonstrate.[36] Villepin backed down the next month, but the uncertain future of France's youth, a backdrop invoked within Doillon's story, remained.

The final ingredient of the film's youthful palette is its candid treatment of teenaged sex. A common feature of the debutant films in our quintet and beyond, a painfully apt analogy, is that quintessential first-time act, the loss of virginity. From the widespread influence of Catherine Breillat and Bruno Dumont (whose *cinéma du corps* we will explore in Chapter 2), inaugural sex is staged in the starkest, least romantic terms possible. This so-called loss of physical innocence, the most intimate rite of passage, is treated instead like an awkward obligation, pleasurable to neither gender, a peer-pressured, mechanical deed that leaves little positive emotional trace. (Three of the lead characters in *Et toi, t'es sur qui?*, not coincidentally, have first-time sex on a bet.) Julie and Vincent's sexual interaction is a sharp case in point. Meeting in a locker room while on a break at the meat processing factory (love in a sterilized abattoir), Doillon first supplies a point-of-view shot of him appraising her torso and naked midriff, eyes lingering on her exposed navel. Two more medium shots follow: she smiles back; he stares on, dumbly. A brief rightward long shot track then shows them copulating on the floor, almost fully clothed, in absolute silence. Next — in an extraordinarily brutal cut, worthy of Dumont if not Sergei Eisenstein at his most agitational — we jolt to a close-up of a dead mackerel being sliced in half, complete with a slurping foley effect on the soundtrack. Here, the film makes first-time sex like filleting meat, flesh violently rendered, an unappetizing preparation process.

Similarly dispassionate is Elodie's first sexual encounter. Her virginity is also lost in clinical fashion, a transaction with Nico that Vincent hypocritically protests as loveless. It begins with another wordless shot, the couple perched uneasily on a bed in a tiny borrowed apartment. They share a Coke and belatedly some uncomfortable small-talk: "Do you listen to Eminem?" "No, I like the Chili Peppers." Finally, he kisses her roughly, retreats to get a condom, and she undresses under the sheets. They complete their arrangement as before, in long shot, in silence, with no sign of gratification on either side. And like the cut to fish shredding for Julie and Vincent's postcoitus, Doillon takes pains to show us the cynical, pathetic aftershocks of virginity lost. For Nico, it entails bragging about his — frankly, robotic — prowess to the friends he has listening outside their room. Elodie's dissatisfaction is more lyrically pessimistic: she walks home, weary and impassive, and in another mobile long take we see behind her, out of focus, a series of adult couples meeting in a café, laughing, physically at ease. How does one get from her life to theirs? Doillon's agenda here, like many of her contemporaries, seems to contradict utterly the conflation of sexual desire with romantic idealism that Tanya Krzywinska argues is still ubiquitous in "mature" mainstream cinema: the standard treatment of "the pleasures of romantic dalliance as a sensual 'holiday' from the tedium of everyday routine, but also from emotional and sexual confusion, dissatisfaction or complexity."[37] The sexual encounter here, by contrast, unfolds like an arbitrary and even abstract experience, drained of emotion, lifeless and mechanical. First-time sex, the most consummately intimate act in French young cinema, is maliciously tender indeed.

Synchro Girls: Céline Sciamma's *Water Lilies*

Many of the facets of young cinema raised by *Et toi, t'es sur qui?* relate closely to Céline Sciamma's debut feature, *Water Lilies*. The two are sister texts, equally compelling parts of an ongoing conversation within twenty-first-century French film. While the subject materials interconnect, however, the two filmmakers' routes to completing a debut feature were different: Doillon worked her way up through the profession step by step, whereas Sciamma graduated from the scriptwriting division of la Fémis. In fact, *Water Lilies*[38] originated as Sciamma's 2005 *travail de fin d'études* (final student project), a script she was persuaded eventually to direct by her graduating jury committee, chaired by noted filmmaker Xavier Beauvois. Sciamma was twenty-seven when she made her first film, five years younger than Doillon. Both films were released in Paris in the summer of 2007; *Water Lilies* followed *Et toi, t'es sur qui?* by two months. The pro-youth agenda of Sciamma's film was defined, from the outset, by a skilful marketing campaign, which targeted teenagers in the press (through organizations like *Libération*, *Flavor*, and *Muze*), on the radio (*Radio Nova* and its website novaplanet.com), on the French satellite music video TV channel MCM, online through a MySpace site, and even with posters and ads distributed at rock concerts like Vieilles Charrues and La Route du Rock.[39]

Water Lilies centers on three young teenaged girls, Marie (Pauline Acquart), Floriane (Adèle Haenel), and Anne (Louise Blachère), all of whom are involved with a synchronized swimming team in Cergy, a New Town built in the 1960s to the northwest of Paris. The personalities of these so-called "synchro girls" are defined by their body types. The introverted Marie is skinny and petite, whereas Anne, her cast-off best friend, is a much larger girl in build and height, boisterous in her behavior yet painfully lacking self-esteem. The film starts with Marie fixated on the swim team captain, Floriane, a more conventionally attractive and physically mature girl, popular with boys yet the subject of vicious gossip among her female peer group, who accuse her (falsely) of sexual promiscuity. Floriane, initially put off by Marie's attentions, soon becomes more responsive and, when it suits her, openly flirtatious: she allows Marie to join the swim team training sessions, solicits her romantic advice, then uses her as an alibi when she sees her on-off boyfriend François (Warren Jacquin). The bond between the girls intensifies, its lesbianism implicit, yet Marie remains Floriane's supplicant, passively in thrall. Their relationship culminates when Marie provides Floriane's first sexual experience — a one-way corporeal act for the (basically heterosexual) older girl, a far more emotionally loaded moment for her sexually uncertain admirer. Two final ironies complete the narrative during a final set-piece at a party in the Cergy youth center. First, François turns abruptly to Anne to relieve his sexual frustrations when he is again rebuffed by Floriane; then, climactically, Marie returns to, and seemingly takes solace from, her more conventional yet by now compromised relationship with Anne.

Considered in tandem, Doillon's and Sciamma's films represent the adolescent state as fraught, alienating. These first-time films immerse us in an unfulfilling and cryptic subculture, a numbing dead time with jolts of painful self-exposure. Both filmmakers use non-professional actors for lead roles that are frequently opaque, volatile yet uncommunicative, at best unevenly sympathetic. Both films counterpoint burgeoning female sexual impulses with the deterioration of sincere and long-term friendships, a dynamic that prefigures virgin sex acts which neither gratify nor satisfy. (Marie-Noëlle Tranchant describes Marie and Floriane's sex scene in *Water Lilies* as a medical procedure: "more an operation than an erotic outburst.")[40] Both films also characterize emergent social and physical teenage identities through rash, selfish, and ultimately self-destructive behavior. Above all, though, *Et toi, t'es sur qui?* and *Water Lilies* treat the coming-of-age process as highly ritualized, a social integration process taken to an extreme in the grueling, martially choreographed team discipline of synchronized swimming routines. This, the contemporary French *cinéma d'ado*, was linked by many critics to the first-time French film text itself, extending from the past to the present moment. Jean-Marc Lalanne, for instance, suggests insightfully that "there's an organic link, quite typically French (under the auspices of Vigo/Truffaut), between the two first-time types: the direction of a first feature and the passage from childhood into the world of the adult."[41]

What distinguishes Sciamma's work, upping the ante, is its highly stylized conception and execution, emphasizing abstraction. Since so much young French cinema is shaped by the inchoate passions of the fledgling adult, *Water Lilies* renders such encounters correspondingly obscure, understated yet strangely lyrical. This is a film about assertive yet uncommunicative teenagers that is itself abrasively, painstakingly indirect. On this point, Sciamma gives what amounts to a highly ambitious debutant manifesto, a formal pledge to subvert conventional models and dismantle cinematic cliché. As we saw with Doillon, the task of the first-time director is to project cinematic maturity. Sciamma stated: "I wanted to play with the codes of adolescent cinema—these archetypal characters, the actresses who inhabit these roles, their over-determined physicalities, the problem of emerging desires—by taking counter-steps through radical stylistic choices."[42] Again, the debutant's issue is textual belatedness. These rites-of-passage materials are so self-evidently well-worn that they need reinvention on-screen, a conscious process of defamiliarization. Concomitant to this, through textual citation and off-screen self-promotion, is the opportunity for the first-time director to advance her cinephilia and nascent auteurist credentials. In Sciamma's case, the motif was minimalism, a wholesale dramatic and stylistic deflation. The figure of Robert Bresson, an uncompromising advocate of formal reduction and a perennially cited influence among la Fémis students, loomed especially large; Sciamma also repeatedly referenced Gus Van Sant's pared-down work on films like *Gerry* (2002), *Elephant* (2003), *Last Days* (2005) and *Paranoid Park* (2007).

The principal deletion in *Water Lilies* is dialogue, and any larger domestic and social contexts to Marie's, Floriane's, and Anne's lives. (One problem with teen slang like Doillon's is how quickly such chatter dates; an advantage of muted textual abstraction is its timelessness.) In the transition from script to screen Sciamma removed all mention of parents and families: the girls are left with no on-screen home lives, they don't share meals with mothers or fathers, they never attend school, and they inhabit deserted houses. The generation gap here widens precipitously, young and old divorced to an absurdist degree. Even beyond the confines of family, *Water Lilies* has only five adult speaking roles: none of these characters is named, and among them they muster barely a dozen lines, most of which are banalities, like a swimming pool attendant reciting membership rules to Marie. An unidentified and largely out-of-frame woman, who asks Marie to "sit down, please" during a swimming competition in the film's opening sequence (her line doesn't even

Marie (Pauline Acquart) and Floriane (Adèle Haenel) in *Water Lilies*

warrant translation for the English subtitles), is clearly a representative figure. For Sciamma's adolescents, the adult is absolutely marginal, a trace element that barely registers on-screen.

More provocatively, Sciamma uses the same principle of reduction with men. *Water Lilies* lacks any individuated adult male roles; it has just two masculine speaking parts, a solitary boy with a name (François), and only eleven lines, less than forty words, allocated to boys on-screen. No boy ever speaks to another boy: intra-male vocalizations are limited to rowdy roars of approval among the boys' swim team, an animalistic growl first heard when Anne presents a necklace to François in front of his friends, then reprised during the film's climactic party scene. From this approach comes a clear gender imbalance but also a disorienting sense of the world of girls, girls alone. Outspoken always about her aggressive cinematic choices, Sciamma stated in the press that her aim "was to take away [the boys'] point of view, to apprehend everything from the girls' side. At that age boys understand nothing, don't talk among themselves, are brute forces. . . . [*Water Lilies*] offers a feminine perspective on what it means to become a girl. . . . For this precise moment of the birth of desire, of the problem of falling in love, it's also the birth of the problem of femininity. I wanted to talk more about girls than adolescence itself."[43] Besides the political subtext here—a feminine film in which men are just vestigial traces, a point we will pursue in Chapter 4 with Lucile Hadzihalilovic's *Innocence* (2003)—*Water Lilies* conveys powerfully its hermetic, estranging world. The process is accentuated by the film's peculiarly modernist setting, Cergy itself, Sciamma's home town. (Again, from *The*

400 Blows to *The Silence of the Sea* to our contemporary quintet, the debutant text highlights strategic autobiographical markers.) In *Water Lilies*, Sciamma configures Cergy on-screen as a landscape of jutting, monumentalist architecture and sprawling plazas. It is a paradoxical city of claustrophobic vistas with no passersby, an oddly dehumanized new town designed by Spaniard Ricardo Bofill and known cinematically as the *mise-en-scène* backdrop of Eric Rohmer's *Boyfriends and Girlfriends* (*L'Ami de mon ami*, 1987).

Permeating its intrusively stylized diegetic world, *Water Lilies* is highly elliptical at the level of narration and stylistic design. Neither overarching plot causality nor time-space continuity connect individual scenes, which accumulate rather than cohere. As Sciamma declared in another public interview, using an aphorism that consciously recalls Bresson's famous *pensées* in *Notes sur le cinématographe*:[44] "No parents, no temporality, not much dialogue."[45] Instead, the film's segments coalesce around extended, narratively distinct sequence shots, or else brief clusters of sensory impressions, fleeting teenaged encounters. In one sequence, a counterpart to Doillon's opening flourish in *Et toi, t'es sur qui?*, there is a pivotal exchange between Marie and Floriane, sealing their unusual pact while removing any sense of closeness or intimacy, the yearnings of the young girls juxtaposed with the brutalist Cergy landscape. Sciamma stages the interaction in four shots, prefaced with a deliberate mismatch from the preceding scene: there's a straight cut, but long shadows have shortened, light levels risen, early dusk has become late daytime. (After the quartet of shots ends, Sciamma conversely cuts to pitch black night.) The first shot, a high angle, is a starkly symmetrical extreme long shot of the two girls walking away from the camera, for seventeen seconds, towards a row of huge concrete pillars at the end of a massive concrete square high above the surrounding countryside. We discern the Paris skyline under grey cloud cover, dwarfed by the shot scale, distantly visible in the rearground. The rumbling of an airplane reverberates overhead; the rhythm of the girls' footfalls corresponds exactly with its passage. Next, we cut across the axis to a low angle medium shot taken from below the girls, who perch, in shadows, on the steps underneath the pillared causeway. The sky behind them has now turned azure blue.

After a brief cutaway to the rolling landscape below, the pay-off shot, eighty-four seconds long, begins. Under the towering concrete columns, Floriane offers a series of dispassionate confessions: about her swimming trainer's advances ("He never lets up, cornering me in dressing rooms, saying he loves me"), her contempt for her female teammates, and the relentless scrutiny she feels subjected to by men (one swimmer has even exposed himself to her in the pool). Sciamma, meanwhile, tracks very slowly right to left, favoring Marie in the frame, shifting (it seems arbitrarily) the balance from speaker to listener. The film's distinctive electronic score, two or three interwoven treble tones, underlines the camera's sideways movement; drifting white cloud masses have now abruptly appeared again. Finally, Floriane asks Marie to recount her own similar experiences—yet none are forthcoming: Marie wordlessly shrugs, and Floriane suggests that this actually makes her "lucky, really lucky." Essentially, the girls' quasi-friendship builds from this one-sided (implied) understanding about mutual sexual dissatisfaction and social disconnect. And Marie and Floriane's mercurial engagement is entirely offset by the mathematical, brittle intensity of Sciamma's young cinematic designs: a highly stylized, laborious rendition of such emotionally erratic teenaged relationships. As Lalanne observes perceptively about Sciamma's approach—a microcosm of *Water Lilies* overall—there is self-consciously a "mastery of framing, of rhythm, of direction of its actors . . . a discipline that feels a little like an anxious debutant worried about maintaining absolute control."[46]

Sciamma's formal abstraction, this defamiliarization of teenaged behavior, particularly extends to the soundtrack. Here again, *Water Lilies* follows minimalist dogma, and Bresson's famous admonition for aural precision above aesthetic stimulation: "Sound cinema invented silence"; "What is for the eye must not duplicate what is for the ear."[47] Sciamma typically removes dialogue and limits her actors (especially Pauline Acquart as Marie, who isn't even named until twenty-two minutes into the film) to remote, doleful stares. Strikingly, *Water Lilies* is a film that unfolds—often up to ten minutes at a stretch—with no verbal exchanges and minimal eye contact. The technique is pressed, at times perversely, during flashpoints of dramatic tension which avoid conversation or restrict it to disproportionately laconic asides; the film and its adolescents are articulately inarticulate. Often, Sciamma allows her actors just one performative gesture, a dismissive or contemptuous tic, to track the inevitable teenaged course of disaffected sexual desire. In one scene, for instance, Anne spits into the mouth of François instead of kissing his proffered mouth: the boy makes no response at all, freezing, and Sciamma cuts away from any potential aftermath. Similarly, to imply Marie's resistance to her same-sex desire for Floriane, a major thematic issue, Sciamma favors contained introspections, like a brief shot in which the younger girl spits on and rubs at her hand on which her quasi-friend had written her address. Later, in another anticlimax, Floriane rejects Marie after their only kiss, which leads to a four-minute sequence without talking that—very assertively—concludes the film. In this vein, more disconcertingly, almost nothing at all is said after Floriane loses her virginity to Marie. The word *lesbian* is never spoken, no

Marie and Anne (Louise Blachère) in the final shot of *Water Lilies*

ramifications of the act unfold: the girls instead wordlessly make the bed; Marie murmurs, "Wait"; Floriane replies, "I have to go," and leaves. In all these cases, as Tranchant remarks, Sciamma's silences are "as orchestrated as music."[48]

So what takes the place of dialogue, for dramatic exposition? *Water Lilies* returns repeatedly to highly abstracted patterns of bodies in motion: teenaged activities represented as densely lyrical, expressively charged routines, often derived from extended passages of swimming and dancing. Many of these segments quite systematically recall Maya Deren's influential avant-garde studies of protracted, wordless bodily movements in shorts like *Ritual in Transfigured Time* (1946) and, more famously, *Meshes of the Afternoon* (1943). One recurrent aesthetic feature is the way that Sciamma shoots her synchronized swimming set-pieces (rehearsals and competitions mix interchangeably) with extremely long lenses, removing all depth cues, condensing the girls' body parts into whirls of splashing limbs, flesh and water, a close-up suite of kinetic fragments. The same process affects Floriane's and Marie's interactions, many of which (their strolls through Cergy after dark, a visit to a nightclub, their subsequent walk home alongside a motorway) are staged in very low lighting, designed like a particularly strong Kuleshovian tableau:[49] stark key light on black background, darkness highlighting bright skin and faces, the bodies of the performers thrown into exaggerated aesthetic relief.

While *Water Lilies* dwells on the pure physicality of swimming, its ritualistic energy, it follows the same logic of stylistic abstraction with the act of dance. Both swimming pools and dancefloors, moreover, offer Sciamma a rich *mise-en-scène* of visceral corporeality: individuals grouped actively with others yet not really in their company; bodies together, alone. (Not coincidentally, on dancefloors we repeatedly see Floriane abandoning Marie, who is similarly isolated as an observer of the girls' swim team, at one point swimming underwater by herself at the fringes of a practice session.) Added to this, Sciamma's final stylistic catalyst is the meticulously synthesized score, created by her fellow la Fémis graduate (from the direction track), Jean-Baptiste de Laubier, who records and produces under the name ParaOne. The *Water Lilies* soundtrack, often nondiegetic and heavily syncopated, blends shrill, tinny electronic strings, distended minor-key treble slides often distorted by pitch bends, with intermittently off-beat rhythms, to create a weirdly disjunctive accompaniment to the wordless image-track. At times, ParaOne's ambient soundscapes resemble John Carpenter's unsettlingly minimalist keyboard refrains for science-fiction thrillers like *The Thing* (1982) and *They Live* (1988). The timbre and textures of ParaOne's acoustically manipulated score also relate in France to the jarring experimental noise-soundtracks created by a number of more assertive sound designers. These include, notably, the work of electronic artist (and co-founder of Daft Punk) Thomas Bangalter for *Irreversible* (2002), and Raphael Elig and Eric Wenger (a programmer known for his software Metasynth, which translates images into aural patterns) for *Dante 01* (2008). Applied to the teenaged context of *Water Lilies*, Philippe Azoury suggests evocatively that "The sound, supplied by [Sciamma's techno producer] accomplice ParaOne . . . conveys the aural qualities of the world of the deaf, an adolescence heard yet bottled-up and enclosed . . . a whole universe immersed like in a pool."[50]

Returning to the first-timer's agenda, the debutant film as calling card, *Water Lilies* showcases another device to self-promote a would-be cinéaste. This is the artful directorial cameo, the filmmaker as product placement, a signature feature adopted by the New Wave generation. Like Jean-Luc Godard's brief role as a newspaper-reading passerby in *Breathless*—who slyly points out Michel (Jean-Paul Belmondo) to a patrolling *gendarme*, in effect informing on his own protagonist—a tactic for aspirant auteurs is to materialize textually, announcing their presence, signing off their work with a self-reflexive flourish. Before the *Cahiers* cognoscenti, of course, this motif of overt directorial fingerprints had long been popularized in Franco-American circles by a series of attention-getting devices. The first iconic examples are in the Lumière brothers' works, like Auguste and family arranged in tableaux for shorts like *Baby's Dinner* (*Repas de Bébé*, 1895); Méliès's showmanship simply made the process more grandiose. Other major directors followed suit: from D. W. Griffith observing his heroine in danger at the climax of *Birth of a Nation* (1915),[51] to Chaplin's brief appearance as a porter in *A Woman of Paris* (1923). With sound came more options for personal directorial touches: Sacha Guitry contributing a droll, continuous voice-over for his *The Story of a Cheat* (*Le Roman d'un tricheur*, 1936); a tactic echoed by Orson Welles with his omniscient opening monologue in *The Magnificent Ambersons* (1942); revived by the ever self-conscious Melville in his various roles, as extra or narrator, in *Les Enfants terribles* (1950) and *Bob the Gambler* (*Bob le flambeur*, 1955). In 1952, by which time Hitchcock had made the directorial walk-on notorious, even the self-effacing classicist Howard Hawks was following suit, indulging himself in a series of voice-over cautions ("Not yet, Cary!") addressed during the titles to the befuddled lead of his comedy *Monkey Business*. For *Cahiers* critics keen to champion such storied directors as auteurs, the filmmaker's cameo was a sign of self-conscious pedigree, a feature they quickly built into their own early works. Debutant filmmakers thereby mimicked the hallmarks of long-established celebrity directors, stating their own prodigious textual ambitions.

Less ostentatious but still wittily self-presentational, Sciamma's cameo comes as Marie and Anne visit that most sacred of teenaged shrines, the shopping mall McDonald's. Beforehand, Anne has been shoplifting in a jewelry store; the sequence begins with her plucking a stolen necklace (which she later gives to François, who subsequently passes it on to Floriane) from its hiding place in her mouth. As she does so, in another wry intertextual touch, Anne declares: "Just like in *Peau d'âne*!" (The cinephilic reference is to Jacques Demy's fairy-tale fantasy *Donkey Skin* [1970], about a magical beast of burden which egests jewels.) The girls proceed to the McDo's counter, where they order children's Happy Meals. There, they meet Sciamma, a surly, gum-chewing server, one of the handful of adults in *Water Lilies* who talks. Visibly irritated, Sciamma asks the girls their age, and on hearing the answer (fifteen) responds brusquely, one eyebrow raised, that they are too old for Happy Meals. At this, Anne is incensed about her rights both as an adult ("What, I need an ID card to get a cheaper burger?") and a child: "I want the toy, it's cool, mini-binoculars!" We then cut to their ensuing lunch, moments later, as Anne triumphantly plays with her new gadget. Ultimately, if *Water Lilies* is a film about burgeoning desire and rites of passage, the awkwardly defining passages of adolescent cravings, then Sciamma reserves final judgment on the process, herself, on-screen. Coming-of-age, articulated as a joke with a highly self-reflexive undercurrent, is about how much you have to pay in the fast food outlet, commercialized teenaged identity as fighting for the right to be simultaneously a child *and* a grown-up. And it is Sciamma, the debutant director, given the task, or right, of deciding who belongs and who doesn't.

Domestic Dissolutions: Mia Hansen-Løve's *All Is Forgiven* and Anne le Ny's *Those Who Remain*

Two films which productively intersect, the feature debuts of Mia Hansen-Løve and Anne le Ny, further elaborate our young cinema paradigm, while also connecting it to larger issues within contemporary French cinema. In the first place, these inaugural filmmakers share a common professional trajectory in France, that of performers-turned-directors, actors moving behind the camera.[52] Hansen-Løve, the youngest of the 2008 César nominees, just twenty-six when *All is Forgiven* was released, began acting as a sixteen-year-old for Olivier Assayas, in *Late August, Early September* (*Fin août, début septembre*, 1998) and *Les Destinées* (*Les Destinées sentimentales*, 2000). Hansen-Løve then entered the Paris Theater Conservatory in 2001, before writing for *Cahiers du cinéma* between 2003 and 2005 while also shooting short films. Here, like Doillon and many of her contemporaries, Hansen-Løve consciously modeled herself after the New Wave generation, preferring practical cinephilia and the job of writing film criticism above formal instruction at an institution like la Fémis.

Once again, a salient discourse to the French debutant is her means of self-representation: as a cineliterate, critically empowered, historically engaged artist-in-training. Hence, in an interview for *Le Monde* (a newspaper that appears prominently on-screen in *All Is Forgiven*), Hansen-Løve declared: "When I arrived at *Cahiers*, I knew that I wanted to make films . . . most of the cinéastes that I admired were also writers and I needed to learn like them, even if it was difficult . . . for me, the rapport between the writer and cinema is inseparable."[53] In the pages of *Cahiers* itself—which published a very sympathetic interview with its ex-employee that was reproduced in *All Is Forgiven*'s DVD booklet—Hansen-Løve was more expansive still. She reflected: "What I wanted [as a *Cahiers* critic] was to build little-by-little a cinematic train of thought. . . . When one wants to practice an art, it seems essential to me to engage with what others have done, so as not to be isolated by yourself, immersed only in your own work."[54]

For le Ny, an acting career was more long-term and formative in her route to professional direction. Before *Those Who Remain* was released in August 2007, she had acted in no fewer than forty-four feature projects, interspersing regular TV appearances with supporting film roles, some of which gained international exposure, like Sophie Fillières's *Aïe* (2000), Zabou Breitman's *Happy Memories* (*Se souvenir de belles choses*, 2001), Claude Miller's *La petite Lili* (2003), and, albeit offering her just a comedic cameo, Patrice Leconte's hit *My Best Friend* (*Mon meilleur ami*, 2006). But in her self-presentation in the trade press after *Those Who Remain* opened, le Ny unsurprisingly stressed her cinephilia rather than the professional dues that led her to consider directing for the first time. One interview in *Le Nouvel Observateur*, called "The Woman with Two Faces," included an entire section, "Réferences," in which le Ny was asked to describe—or, alternatively, put on the spot to prove—her appreciation of film history. Dutifully yet elegantly, le Ny supplied not just a list of favorite auteurs, but also the story of a favorite cinema, her regular haunt, the l'Action Christine, a two-screen *art et essai* theater housed in an old seventeenth-century apartment complex in the Saint-Germain-des-Prés. In this context, le Ny cited "nourishing" inspirations including Howard Hawks, Ernst Lubitsch and Billy Wilder, as well as neatly positioning *Those Who Remain* as a contemporary version of David Lean's *Brief Encounter* (1945).[55] While Donald Richie describes the ideology of professional rivalries among filmmakers in the classical Japanese film industry as, effectively, "My work is more elegant than your work,"[56] in contemporary France, the formulation comes across more as, "My work is more cineliterate than your work."

In broader terms, Hansen-Løve and le Ny's eventual role of actor-filmmaker provides yet another marketable category to export French cinema officially as an industry of vigorous debutants. Again, the institutional support of UniFrance is significant; it has, in one prominent promotional campaign, organized an Actors-Turned-Directors series at the Cannes Film Festival, celebrating variously the debuts of figures like Yolande Moreau (*When the Sea Rises* [*Quand la mer monte*, 2003], winner of the Best First Film César in 2004), Laure Duthillel (*À ce soir*, 2004), and Eric Caravaca (*Le Passager*, 2005). Just as prestigious are the regular actor-turned-director events at the Rendez-Vous with French Cinema series. This gala festival, an annual collaboration between UniFrance and the Film Society of Lincoln Center in New York City, presents screenings, panel discussions, and practical seminars with French filmmakers, and has become one of the leading venues for French cinema in North America, a more prestigious neighbor of the yearly French Film Festival at the Museum of Fine Arts in Boston. The French debutant filmmaker is once more a valuable asset—especially if already known for acting—in an industry bent on global circulation and prestige.

All Is Forgiven and *Those Who Remain* both deal with the fragmentation of families and marriages, a theme of domestic dissolution that resonates widely in recent French cinema. This bourgeois melancholia is reworked in innumerable films from *La Séparation* (1994), to *My Sex Life . . . or How I Got into an Argument* (*Comment je me suis disputé . . . [ma vie sexuelle]*, 1996), to *Sitcom* (1998), *Lemming* (2005), *Summer Hours* (*L'Heure d'été*, 2008), *Leaving* (*Partir*, 2009), and so on. Today, this model perhaps finds its most prominent voice with Philippe Lioret, whose *Je vais bien, ne t'en fais pas* (2006), about a teenaged girl returning home to find her family disconsolate after her brother has apparently vanished, received five César nominations in 2007. Such on-screen materials relate in part to social upheavals off-screen: the fairly typical data that almost half (49.1 percent) of all French marriages now end in divorce, as well as, more alarmingly, the fact that marriage itself is a French institution in steady decline: from 334,400 annual unions in 1970, to 287,100 in 1990, to just 266,500 in 2007.[57] Related to all this is the debutant's work, needing to pitch effectively, establishing a track record, connecting a proposed feature to a bankable cinematic tendency built on a social faultline. On this subject, both Hansen-Løve and le Ny confirmed candidly in interview the work of would-be directors as self-promoters: how they secured relationships with producers, and eventually financing, by presenting their scripts as following this vaunted French screen tradition of precarious domestic relationships.[58] These are films that Stephen Holden, writing in the *New York Times* from an American perspective, describes glossily as "those sexy, bittersweet marital comedies that [are] a hallmark of sophisticated French cinema."[59]

Certainly, both films depict families that are unraveling, in terminal disarray. *All Is Forgiven* begins in Vienna in 1995, where Victor (Paul Blain), a failing aspirant writer, is married, uneasily, to Annette (Marie-Christine Friedrich), with whom he has a daughter, Pamela (Victoire Rousseau as a child; Constance Rousseau as a teenager). The marriage strains and breaks, in part because a demoralized Victor lapses into his former habits as a heroin addict. After a jump of eleven years, to Paris, the film then shifts to the perspective of an older Pamela, who rediscovers her lost father and begins a relationship with him, in part conducted through letters and shared poetry, which starts to deepen touchingly, only to end with his abrupt and premature death. Equally mournful in tone, *Those Who Remain* concerns Lorraine (Emmanuelle Devos) and Bertrand (Vincent Lindon),[60] who meet on the ward of a Parisian hospital. Bertrand's wife is finally succumbing to breast cancer after five years of illness, while Lorraine's boyfriend is undergoing a series of permanently debilitating treatments for cancer of the colon. Although they have drastically different personalities—he is a laconic, routine-bound German teacher; she a flighty graphic designer—the two connect personally, and briefly romantically, over their shared guilt as flawed caregivers to deteriorating life partners, neither of whom ever actually appears on-screen.

Belying their backgrounds as performers, as first-time directors both Hansen-Løve and le Ny (who has a customary supporting role in *Those Who Remain*, playing Bertrand's overbearing sister) pursue, in conception and design, an actorly aesthetic. This is a common and pragmatic course among debutant French directors. As Marina de Van, another performer-filmmaker,

Lorraine (Emmanuelle Devos) and Bertrand (Vincent Lindon) in *Those Who Remain*

analyzed her own choices about inaugural direction on her first feature *In My Skin* (2002): "A lack of money and time makes you focus on the actors."[61] Systematically, Hansen-Løve and le Ny design their scenes as seamlessly and efficiently as possible around the work of their performers. Unlike *Water Lilies*, these are dialogue-intensive films with a highly classical repertoire: typically medium shot conversations with shot-reverse shot emphases, set off with occasional close-ups or long takes to preserve any particularly sequential nuances of a given scene. At the same time, both women reserve directorial flourishes for highlighting the key details of their actors' performances — an interesting reversal of the more conceptually assertive styles of Doillon and Sciamma, a more tic-driven or swaggering approach.

In this light, rejecting the self-reflexivity endemic to young cinema, Hansen-Løve described her motivations: "I didn't want to make a film which came across as modern, or radical. We're surrounded by a false radicality, a false subversion. . . . I didn't dwell on my relationship with what's expected of a first film."[62] Le Ny echoed the sentiment, arguing that her actor-centered direction derived from the legacy of quintessential classicist Howard Hawks: "I tried to apply Hawks's rules, edicts which much affected me."[63] While ostensibly self-effacing, however, Hansen-Løve and le Ny are as much engaged with auteurist ambitions and the debutant belatedness issue as any of their more formally precocious contemporaries. Rather than preferring stylistic mannerisms that are blatant or showy, this duo's principle is graceful restraint, an organic, performer-focused execution. Either way, none of these first-time filmmakers could be accused of lacking self-consciousness or being conformist. Understated realism is just as studied an approach as flamboyant artificiality; rather than mavericks, Hansen-Løve and le Ny take pains to present themselves defiantly as stylistic throwbacks.

The actorly aesthetic is particularly clear in sequences about ingrained intimacies — parents attending to children, spouses interacting in unthinking routines — which precipitate ruptures in the relationships. This is the structure of *All Is Forgiven*, established from its opening, which hints clearly at the tensions eroding this family unit. It is Pamela's sixth birthday, and we meet her and Victor naming her new dolls ("You can't call them both 'Doll' — they'll get confused!") while sitting on a mat surrounded by toys. Leaving the apartment to play tennis, father and daughter hit their ball off walls, the ground, and each other, and the two actors simply play, in impromptu reaction to where the ball bounces, who retrieves it and serves, who leads the way. Hansen-Løve's camera tracks the pair in a static long shot as they exit their building, a rightward pan as they move through an adjacent courtyard, then a series of wobbling handheld close-ups when the game degenerates — happily — as Victor grabs Pamela ("Meanie!"), and she sees him off with a swipe of her racket. Hansen-Løve's cinematography underscores the unforced tenderness of the characters, the actors' physical improvisations accentuated gently by the increasingly close, bustling camerawork. The payoff comes, though, when Annette arrives in a static insert that interrupts both the stylistic flow and the tennis. The effect is compounded when she calls out ("I've been looking for you everywhere!") in loud German, rather than Pamela and Victor's conversational French. When Victor now hastily abandons Pamela to her mother's care, the dramatic seed is sown. Victor, we infer, is the source of anarchic fun in this household whereas Annette is the reluctant disciplinarian; one parent, not two, is present in this family tableau. Albeit in different style to Doillon's opening long take in *Et toi, t'es sur qui?*, Hansen-Løve provides exactly the same kind of beautifully rendered thesis sequence, the hallmark of a debutant filmmaker establishing a dramatic rhythm.

A potential strength of this actorly aesthetic is its lack of strident or sentimental emphases, a fraught point when dealing with highly charged materials like divorce and terminal illness. As in the tennis scene above, Hansen-Løve and le Ny favor performance cues over intrusive stylistic means, skillfully marshalling their limited textual resources. Two pivotal moments in *All Is Forgiven* and *Those Who Remain*, short scenes in which marriages quietly end, illustrate the technique. In *Those Who Remain*, marital closure comes after Bertrand's wife has finally died, off-screen, and le Ny focuses for more than five minutes on Lindon's trance-like face and numbed body language during scenes of banal domestic conclusion: Bertrand removing the pictures that pathetically personalized his wife's hospital room, standing alone in the garage after his stepdaughter has left to live with her biological father, tidying and boxing the clutter of the house, then finally sitting, as if

The final family meal: Breakfast with Victor (Paul Blain), Pamela (Victoire Rousseau), and Annette (Marie-Christine Friedrich) in *All Is Forgiven*

ground to a halt, on the downstairs sofa, unsure of his next move, vacantly smoking a crumpled cigarette, one of his wife's, turned up from the back of a drawer.

The same moment of understated domestic demise, realized largely through performance, comes a third of the way through *All Is Forgiven*. Victor stumbles home drunk, late at night, and for the first time hits his wife. Instead of aftermath, we immediately cut to breakfast the next day, a medium long shot held for nearly a minute, in which Pamela obliviously munches on her cereal, in motion constantly, while her two parents, sitting on either side of the frame, hold their bodies in awkward symmetrical poses, their faces rigid masks. Victor tries and fails to make eye contact, then blurts, "I'm really sorry, Annette." Silence follows, broken only by the sound of Pamela eating. Finally we cut to a closer view of Annette, who states calmly that she'll return to Vienna with Pamela for Christmas, without him. (An irony of *mise-en-scène* is that over her shoulder, slightly out of focus, hangs Pamela's crayon drawing of the three of them happily together.) Cut to Victor, hunching over in defeat; then finally to Pamela, blithe, unaware that her life is forever changed by what has just taken place.

Cued by this moment, a final element that unites Hansen-Løve and le Ny's films is the catalytic on-screen role of children, an element reiterated constantly in French debutant cinema. Besides the adolescents in films like *Et toi, t'es sur qui?* and *Water Lilies*, younger children are central, for example, to

Isild le Besco's directorial debut, *Half-Price*, mentioned earlier, as well as Julie Gavras's highly successful first feature, *Blame it on Fidel!* (*La Faute à Fidel*, 2006), in which the growing politicization of two young parents is framed, offset, and at times critiqued, by the stubborn bourgeois viewpoint of their nine-year-old daughter, Anna (Nina Kervel). Similar in method is Carine Tardieu's poignant debut feature, *La Tête de maman* (2007), in which a deadpan fifteen-year old, Lulu (Chloé Coulloud) speculates and fantasizes about the cause of her single mother's (Karin Viard) depression. Even a more generic comedy debut, Anne Fassio's *Je déteste les enfants des autres* (2007), reserves for its punch-line a child-framed segment: before the end credits roll, Fassio inserts DV shots of her juvenile cast cavorting in the sun, their antics a sharp contrast to the careworn adult lives the preceding film has exposed. In a similar context, studying *Etre et avoir* (2002) and *Les Diables* (2002), Phil Powrie suggests how child-derived French films create a dichotomy: "The subtext in the first type is 'I wish I could find that state of innocence again' (nostalgia tinged with self-pity); the subtext in the latter is 'thank God my childhood was not like that' (nostalgia tinged with pity)."[64] Based on our examples, more recent French debutant films often intermingle such representational strands, with pointed ambivalence.

Those Who Remain and *All Is Forgiven* equally rely on children for their resonance and closure. In the former, Bertrand simply absents himself from Lorraine's life, severing their relationship; the main sense of narrative resolution comes from the fragile peace he finally makes with his withdrawn, embittered sixteen-year-old stepdaughter. Even more so, in *All Is Forgiven*, a film about two adults increasingly focuses on the young Pamela, ultimately the real victim of the split family, and her lost time with her dead father. This is brought home in Hansen-Løve's artful final shot, after Victor's funeral, in which Pamela removes herself from the family gathering, subdued, wandering alone towards a nearby forest; her watching mother's tiny wince is our sole hint that she regrets the effect of divorce on her daughter's childhood. From both these conclusions, it seems, for the debutant director the figure of the child onlooker offers an invigorating view of the mystifying adult world, its vicissitudes refracted through the perceptual ambitions of these emerging filmmakers.

Hansen-Løve's short film *Un Pur esprit* (2004), an experimental calling card[65] made while she was still a *Cahiers* critic, emblematizes this child-centered rationale, its importance for the beginning French filmmaker. A composite of images framed by Isabelle, a young girl, Hansen-Løve's black-and-white short contains no dialogue, just fleeting glimpses of autumnal parklands, blurred fronds of foliage, gathering dusk along a deserted roadway,

Isabelle Marchandier in *Un Pur esprit*

whip pans across a soccer game in progress, then shots of the young girl herself, alone in repose yet strangely pensive. Harking back to the famed debuts
of Vigo and Truffaut, more recently cited in the work of Doillon and Sciamma,
the first-time French director returns compulsively to this motif of measured
but fraught youthful observation — coming-of-age used in part as an analogy
for a filmmaker's feature debut. This is the world perceived through immature
eyes, creating a vulnerable yet keenly aware consciousness, a fresh and highly
cinematic perspective on cynical adult deeds.

Iran in Black and White: Marjane Satrapi's and
Vincent Paronnaud's *Persepolis*

Among our quintet of César-nominated debuts, the texts held up by the French
Film Academy as leading first-time breakthroughs, it is *Persepolis* that achieved
the highest profile. First, *Persepolis* actually won the Best First Film César, as
was widely predicted by journalists. *Persepolis* became, in fact, the epitome
of a debutant success story in France: a charismatically international project,
almost universally acclaimed, possibly the most voluminously discussed film
in the twenty-first-century French trade press, politically committed yet play-

ful and popular, a profoundly personal story about a young woman's coming-of-age in war-torn Iran. In its film version, *Persepolis* claimed the Jury Prize at the 2007 Cannes Film Festival, where its premiere ended with a twenty-five-minute standing ovation. During its four-month theatrical release in France between July and October 2007, playing initially on more than 200 screens, the film had over 1.1 million paid admissions, passing the million threshold by which *Le Film français* and most industrial analysts gauge blockbuster status in France. Better still, *Persepolis* was picked up for distribution around the world, including territories as far afield as South Africa, Bulgaria, Indonesia and Japan. The film's international circulation even climaxed with a run in North America for Sony Classics, in both subtitled and dubbed forms,[66] during which it grossed over $4.4 million, one of the most successful French exports of recent decades, leading to an Oscar nomination for Best Animated Film. *Persepolis*, indeed, has become a true international phenomenon. One representatively swaggering write-up, in *Le Film français*, hailed the film as the event of 2007, distinctively French despite its international connections, whose artistic momentum has culminated in nothing less than a "conquest of the United States."[67]

While the film's route to success was dramatic it was also protracted, a gestation shaped by multicultural contexts. In this frame, like many respondents, Patrick Caradec notes how the genesis of *Persepolis* offers an "exemplary career" for any first-time filmmaker seeking widespread dissemination, local and global, for an uncompromisingly personal and idiosyncratic project.[68] One of *Persepolis*'s defining elements is its translation of recent Iranian history into French *bande dessinée* (comic book or literally "drawn strip") culture.[69] The text originated as a series of four graphic novels written by Iranian-born Marjane Satrapi, a droll quartet of memoirs chronicling her life between the age of eight and twenty-five, growing up in the house of politically active parents during the Islamic Revolution in Iran of 1979, then the disastrous Iran-Iraq war during the 1980s. These turbulent events lead the young girl into exile twice: first, on the suggestion of her family, as a fourteen-year-old, studying abroad in Austria in 1983; then, permanently, as a French resident and graphic artist based in Strasbourg and Paris after 1994. Alternating self-deprecating farce with poignant (sociopolitical) self-discovery, *Persepolis* charts the physical, intellectual and artistic growth of Marji, the feisty incarnation of Satrapi herself.

Persepolis relates closely to France's recently revitalized *bande dessinée* format. It was first published between 2000 and 2003 by l'Association, a prestigious and independent publishing house launched in 1990, dedicated to comics and graphic novels, and home to notable artists such as Joann Sfar.

For l'Association, Satrapi's series was a major hit, with over 400,000 copies sold on its initial run alone. Satrapi's drawing style, vivid yet pared-down and monochromal, widely characterized as pseudo-childish or faux naïve, was heavily influenced by David Beauchard (known as David B. and a founding member of l'Association). A particular intertextual model for *Persepolis* was Beauchard's *Epileptic* (*L'Ascension du haut mal*, meaning the rise of high evil, an archaic medical term), a critically acclaimed autobiographical re-imagining of its author's brother's illness, which initially appeared in six l'Association volumes between 1996 and 2003. Like *Epileptic*, Satrapi's graphic novels present ironic disjunctions between mock-innocent childhood experiences and fantasies (the young Marji discussing Iran's failures with God, mimicking her parents by chanting "Down with the Shah!" while parading through their living room, performing Western rock songs from cassettes bought on the Tehran black market, discovering Simone de Beauvoir and Karl Marx as a teenager, disavowing her Iranian identity while at parties in Europe) interwoven with more skeptical asides informed by an obviously self-conscious, emancipated woman editorializing these events decades later, from the geographical and political distance of France. As with Doillon and Sciamma, the coming-of-age condition is laced with autobiography, its youthful spontaneity mediated by retrospective intelligence, a disillusioned *postfacto* reconstruction of the not-yet-adult's world.

As Ann Miller argues in her theoretical history of the *bande dessinée*, *Persepolis* also belongs to a recent series of autobiographical treatments of gender construction and/or national identity, like the Québécoise Julie Doucet's *Ciboire de Criss!* (1996) and Jean-Christophe Menu's *Livret de phamille* (1995). As such, Satrapi's work is both universal and highly particularized: a rather banal rites-of-passage narrative (childhood games, going to school, first love, marrying and divorcing, finding one's [artistic] self while abroad) defined by the repressive contexts of such events during the rise of Islamic extremism in Iran. While Marji's precocious subjectivity configures every event depicted, her fledgling identity is compromised by an Iranian regime that delimits her behavior at every turn. Embodied by Marji, therefore, *Persepolis* paradoxically celebrates feminist individuality in circumstances that make such individuality impossible. This trajectory finds its clearest form with the motif of the constricting *chador* headscarf. Marji is indoctrinated into adopting it as a school uniform, turns it into a dress-up prop during schoolyard recess, draws the ire of hardliner old women for not wearing it tightly enough in public, then eventually denounces it during a university lecture about differing, hence hypocritical, dress codes for male and female students. Back and forth: *Persepolis* oscillates constantly between this feminist exuberance and fundamentalist (self-) repression. At issue, Miller suggests, is how "the oppression that she faces and resists afflicts [Satrapi] as a woman and an Iranian. . . . But the careful rationality that she deploys in representing herself is a way of snatching back her own experience, and that of her family and friends, from definitions of 'woman' or 'Iranian' that would deny her subjectivity."[70]

Marji's *chador*, the Islamic female dress code and its violation, also broaches sociopolitical issues that simmer beneath the surface of the stringently secularist French republic. (As our debutants prove in different ways, bringing up socially controversial materials on-screen is seldom unwise professionally.) The public use of Islamic clothing, especially women clad in the full length *burqa*, is a highly contentious question in France today, a lightning rod for anti-Islamic, anti-immigration, pro-feminist and pro-Muslim factions alike. A growing list of recent cases highlights the role of religiously ordained clothes for modern French women, a touchstone case among which took place in September 1989, when three students in Creil were expelled from school for wearing *chadors*, taken as an affront to the institution's secularity. Dozens of similarly divisive incidents have followed, as Françoise Gaspard and Farhad Khosrokhavar discuss, inspiring heated debate about whether Islamic garbs are tokens of oppression or statements of individuality made by liberated women — and, in either case, whether such garments are acceptable within the increasingly strained homogeneity of the French nation state.[71] This is an argument raging with no end in sight. It extends from Nicolas Sarkozy's infamous June 2009 address at Versailles, made in the wake of the contested Iranian elections, in which he condemned the *burqa* as "not welcome on French soil", to more neutral and searching accounts of Franco-Islamic identities like Joan Wallach Scott's 2007 *The Politics of the Veil*, which suggests that such political denunciations date back as far as French colonial subjugations in Algeria in the 1830s.[72]

What about *Persepolis* as a film? In the first place, the text's passage from *bande dessinée* to screen involves a part of contemporary French cinema that is often overlooked: animation. As Caradec summarizes, "Beyond the *Persepolis* phenomenon, the film validates the dynamism of French-produced animation which has found a new way of exposing a wider audience to the auteurs of a very personal universe."[73] Echoing the sentiment, Bernard Génin surveys recent French animation in an essay circulated by the Ministry of Foreign and European Affairs, ranking France's animation production "first in Europe and third in the world."[74] In France, the animation profession comprises over 50 companies housing more than 2,000 jobs, including a Disney subsidiary in Montreuil, near Paris, and three French studio majors of sorts: la Fabrique, outside Montpellier; Folimage, in Valence; and le Pôle Image in Angoulême.

Derived from these contexts, many critics linked *Persepolis* to other contemporary artistic and commercially galvanizing French animated films: Michel Ocelot's *Kirokou and the Sorceress* (*Kirokou et la sorcière*, 1998) and *Princes and Princesses* (*Les Princes et les princesses*, 2000), Jacques-Rémy Girerd's *Raining Cats and Frogs* (*La Prophétie des grenouilles*, 2003), and Sylvain Chomet's *The Triplets of Belleville* (*Les Triplettes de Belleville*, 2003). More recent additions to this list, successful international French-language animation features, are Christian Volckman's science-fiction *Renaissance* (2006), and the horror anthology *Fear(s) of the Dark* (*Peur[s] du noir*, 2007).

In its aesthetic conception, *Persepolis* favors the same mix of stylistic old and new that we have seen elsewhere as characteristics of the first-time text. Like *Et toi, t'es sur qui?* and *Water Lilies*, the film self-consciously adopts the mannerisms of canonical greats, flaunting its cineliterate heritage, while also showcasing new, more flamboyant technical innovations. On the one hand, Satrapi and her collaborator Vincent Paronnaud revived traditional, in some cases archaic animation methods, citing the figure designs in Disney classics like *101 Dalmations* (1961) and *The Jungle Book* (1967). For the principal characters, Satrapi and Paronnaud rejected all modern computer-sculpting software, on the grounds that it failed to render precisely facial traits and bodily gestures. Instead, over two years and with ninety creative staff on hand (all of whom were French), the duo mimed out sequences from the books that were then hand drawn, cel by cel, in pen and ink, by twenty animators tracing out twelve sketches per second of eventual film. As the film's producer, Marc-Antoine Robert, pronounced proudly, "This is a [forty-year-old] process that's almost completely died out, which we rehabilitated for this project."[75] After all the resulting drawings were scanned, however, the *Persepolis* team anachronistically coupled their traditionalist methods to advanced CGI cinematography, morphing each frame into kinetic sequences of multi-plane motion and parallax scrolling. Stéphane Roche, the editor, described how "thanks to special effects, we simulated movements: zooms, pans. . . . We juxtaposed drawings, figures and décor, and made them move. In fact, we directed a film without a camera."[76] The final touch, described by Olivier Seguret as Satrapi's trademark on the page and now on-screen,[77] was that except for bookending sequences of Marji at the Mehrabad airport in Tehran, the entire film takes place in stark, sensuous, chiaroscuro black-and-white.

Textual product differentiation and overt auteurist idiosyncrasy—the debutant's stylistic palette is especially pronounced in *Persepolis*'s execution. The film is indeed charmingly retrograde, staged in emphatically flat tableaux with horizontal more often than diagonal axes, a two-dimensional *mise-en-scène* that highlights, rather than effaces, the film's roots in old-fashioned

Expressionist riots in *Persepolis*

cartoons and *bande dessinée*. Backgrounds are restricted to swathes of air-brushed grey or black, with incidental details of furniture, doors and window frames. This aesthetic of obsolescence creates knowing self-parodies. Early on, when Marji's Dad gives her a history lesson about the rise of the Shah ("Here's what really happened!"), the scene opens under a theatrical prosce-nium arch and curtains, with the shady political maneuverings performed by bouncing cardboard cut-outs with paper-clip limb attachments. During such set-pieces, *Persepolis*'s satire is at its most acute: here, Iran's modern history is enacted as a matinée entertainment for children, the players in its government a literal puppet regime. More generally, though, Satrapi's and Paronnaud's aesthetic follows Ocelot's work in *Kirokou and the Sorceress*, with stylized and characteristically artisanal French techniques that diverge from more technically cutting-edge Hollywood animations. (Many of *Persepolis*'s reviewers judged it superior to Dreamworks' slick yet vacuous *Shrek the Third* [2007], which was released simultaneously in Paris.) As Richard Neupert observes in this vein, a film like *Kirokou* "offers a radical alternative to the three-dimensional illusions of contemporary computer animation. Unlike the hyperrealistic three-dimensional norms for Pixar's toys, monsters, and cars, the characters in Ocelot's cinematic worlds display almost no cues for texture or volume . . . they often slide laterally across the screen rather than moving to or from the 'camera' in perspective, further reinforcing the artifice of their bodies and Ocelot's representational codes."[78] Conversely, perhaps perversely, is the fact that intermingled with these deliberately outdated de-signs are the CGI accents so prized by Roche and his postproduction team.

While *Persepolis*'s tableaux favor 2D theatricality, they are punctuated with computer renderings that distort or manipulate the human form, but more often mimic virtuoso camera movements, graceful reframings, iris shots, and sudden perspectival shifts like zoom-ins and -outs. The pattern is most emphatic in the opening credit sequence, a fanciful magic carpet ride which propels us through all planes of motion (left-right, up-down, forward-backward) over mountaintops, cloudscapes, snowstorms, and forestlands filled with swirling flowers and denizens of Persian folklore. The landscapes resemble fragments of traditional Japanese *ukiyo-e* woodblock prints, delicately drawn yet forcefully composed, while the CGI graphic jolts — a series of staccato pauses and swoops — blur them together via twenty-first-century compositing effects. Sequences like these are both highly kinetic but also graphically refined, evocative and strangely timeless. Again, the debutant filmmaker lays down the gauntlet with bravura techniques, stressing her stylistic repertoire and control, especially in these ambitious opening scenes.

In another studied paradox, Satrapi's and Paronnaud's use of CGI, the digital future, underscores their links to the past — particularly their cinephile credentials and engagement with an auteurist heritage. Reiterating the first-timer's seemingly obligatory declaration of principles, in one of their many interviews the filmmakers stated: "It was crucial for us to follow the course of [film] history, but also, above all, to reinvent it all."[79] Most obviously, a talking point Satrapi and Paronnaud brought up repeatedly, are their film's homages to Italian neorealism and German expressionism, along with iconically baroque classics like *Night of the Hunter* (1955) and *Touch of Evil* (1958). CGI, surprisingly effectively, became the means to resurrect and textually embed such canonical elements within their debut creation. Pervasively, the graphically angular and claustrophobic designs of German expressionism feature as graphic motifs. The trope is foregrounded during an anti-Shah street protest, a scene prefaced by Marji falling asleep in bed, as if what follows comes directly from the realm of nightmare. Set to ominous music without dialogue, lines of running black silhouettes laterally cross a shadowed Tehrani cityscape, while viscous tear gas blurs dusk into night. Rocks are thrown at faceless advancing troops, whose gasmasks hiss in pent-up fury. Tanks rumble through the streets, panicking citizens. One soldier fires off a rifle shot, and a protestor falls to the ground, his dense black blood seeping over the image, as a web of disembodied hands reaches out to lift up their fallen comrade. So stylized as to appear rotoscoped, such images transplant the sinister chiaroscuro aesthetic of films like *Nosferatu* (1922) to the urban present.

In fact, German expressionism's treatment of internal and external horrors, visceral yet graphically abstract, informs many of the film's most violent,

Marji is menaced in *Persepolis*

disturbing moments. These include scenes of undifferentiated outlines of brainwashed young Iranian troops marching needlessly off to war with Iraq, or atrocities carried out on political prisoners, like Marji's beloved communist Uncle Anouche, shown as emaciated shadows dying in jail cells drawn to resemble pitch-dark medieval torture chambers. The same techniques configure a surprise nocturnal bombing raid by Iraqi planes over Marji's neighborhood, which sends her family scurrying downstairs through their gloomy apartment complex in long shot, racing for cover like terrified rats. But *Persepolis* even imbues the quotidian with Germanic menace. After Marji solicits illegal street vendors for Western pop music tapes (they call out furtively: "Julio Iglesias!" "Pink Floyd!" "Jichael Mackson!") she is set upon by two disapproving matrons. The pair glides into view in full-length Islamic *burqas*, aghast at Marji's decadent tastes in culture and clothing (especially her "Punk is Not Dead" jacket and *Thriller* buttonhole badge). The women loom over Marji, bodies without arms or legs, sinuously bearing down on her like writhing leeches or blood-sucking tentacles; in close-up their black forms swallow Marji's pale white child's face in insidious darkness. Merging neorealist social polemics with expressionist aesthetic tensions, the film's Iranian *mise-en-scène* is at times eerily similar to the Weimar Germany of *The Cabinet of Dr. Caligari* (1920) and *Faust* (1926). Satrapi's Iran is a lunatic asylum with an open door policy, a country that has sold its soul, a grotesque metropolis where no one is safe, a society teetering on the brink of violent meltdown. As Satrapi concludes about her film's design and impact: "Think of Murnau."[80]

The issue of belatedness, perennially close to the contemporary first-timer, is another vital ingredient of *Persepolis*, especially in its international address.

In this category, the film marks a culmination of Franco-Iranian cultural relations, but also a decisive textual rupture. Returning to Cannes, where *Persepolis* began its triumphant campaign, the film revived the long-standing and volatile exchanges between the two countries, a dialogue in which cinema has played a major role. The pivotal moment was probably Abbas Kiarostami's winning of the 1997 Cannes Grand Prize for *A Taste of Cherry*, a sober film that dealt openly with the subject of suicide, forbidden in Iran. Since the 1990s, in fact, France and especially Cannes have provided a safe haven for Iranian filmmakers censored by their country's dominant Farabi Cinema Foundation: Kiarostami, Majid Majidi, Mohsen Makhmalbaf, Samira Makmalbaf, Jafar Panahi, and others. As a result, these embattled auteurs' films—*Blackboards* (2000), *Kandahar* (2001), *Ten* (2002), *Crimson Gold* (2003), *At Five in the Afternoon* (2003)—have had a bipolar reception: beloved in France, fêted by international critics panels, successful on DVD abroad, but denounced by Iran's theocratic authorities via the French Embassy in Tehran. Related to *Persepolis* are the conventional materials of this type of Iranian cinema. These are films—Hamid Reza Sadr calls them docudramas[81]—characterized by arthouse solemnity and understated styles, notably nonprofessional and subdued performances (often given by children), minimalist cinematography and natural lighting, little or no nondiegetic music, unobtrusive editing, and authentic and cost-efficient location shooting.

In the context of this muted tradition, Satrapi's and Paronnaud's film is a bracing breach of protocol. As we have seen already, *Persepolis* insists on a wildly anarchic fantasy aesthetic, a gleefully subversive, deliberately uneven, frenetic and often literally cartoonish vision of life in Iran. Compounding this is the film's final, perhaps most decisive, element of all—its pitch black, nihilistic, absurdist sense of humor. This textual sensibility juxtaposes, or in real terms intermingles, Marji's erratic and often self-indulgent rebellious streak with the ghastly, remorseless, extremist advance of Iranian history. The gravely serious political coexists on-screen with the comically irreverent personal; matters of life and death are made trivial, and vice versa. This is, after all, a film which edits from Marji moshing her head in her bedroom, sneering, performing a heavy metal anthem, "Master of the Monsters," on a tennis racket air guitar, to images of hapless troops being slaughtered in the Iran-Iraq war, while a stern male voice-over recounts the official discourse of martyrs' blood being spilled for the glorious homeland. Brash to the point of incoherence, self-deprecating yet supremely self-confident, stylistically self-aware, staunchly autobiographical, and above all engaging unpredictable, *Persepolis* absolutely warrants its César crown as the best, most quintessential first-time film made in France.

CHAPTER TWO

The *Cinéma du Corps*

*I expect an artist to show
me the edge. And to show
me that edge, they must go
over a bit to the other side.*

BRUNO DUMONT,
quoted in *Twentynine
Palms . . . off* (2003)

As an art form and a professional practice, cinema thrives on its ability to induce vivid sensations—a tendency that some readily take to extremes. Yet while the majority of world film engages its viewers to convey satisfaction or gratification, an opposite tendency occasionally emerges, abrasive forms of cinema that seek more confrontational experiences. In this context we can start to gauge the impact of a group of high profile French-language filmmakers responsible for a new wave of controversy. In particular, a spate of recent French films that deal frankly and graphically with the body, and corporeal transgressions, has provoked an international scrutiny at times nearing hysteria. Leading examples, many of which are notorious, include: *The Ring Finger* (*L'Annulaire*, 2005), *Baise-moi* (2000), *Dancing* (2003), *Demonlover* (2002), *L'Histoire de Richard O.* (2007), *In My Skin* (*Dans ma peau*, 2002), *Intimacy* (*Intimité*, 2001), *Irreversible* (*Irréversible*, 2002), *Ma mère* (2004), *Novo* (2002), *Romance* (1999), *See the Sea* (*Regarde la mer*, 1997), *Sombre* (1998), *Trouble Every Day* (2001), and *Twentynine Palms* (2003). These extraordinary films form the core of what we will define here as the *cinéma du corps*, whose basic agenda is an on-screen interrogation of physicality in brutally intimate terms.[1]

This *cinéma du corps* consists of arthouse dramas and thrillers with deliberately discomfiting features: dispassionate physical encounters involving filmed sex that is sometimes unsimulated; physical desire embodied by the performances of actors or nonprofessionals as harshly insular; intimacy itself depicted as fundamentally aggressive, devoid of romance, lacking a nurturing instinct or empathy of any kind; and social re-lationships that disintegrate in the face of such violent compulsions. In com-parison to the New Wave movement, the *cinéma du corps* is connected more loosely, through commonalities of content and technique. The recent work of Denis, Dumont, and Noé, in particular, a trio best thought of as filmmak-ing catalysts, offers incisive social critiques, portraying contemporary society as isolating, unpredictably horrific and threatening, a nightmarish series of encounters in which personal relationships—families, couples, friendships, partnerships—disintegrate and fail. But at the center of this cycle, a focal point most famously emblematized by *Trouble Every Day*, is an emphasis on human sexuality rendered in stark and graphic terms. The agenda here is an increasingly explicit dissection of the body through its sexual capacities: unmotivated or predatory sex, sexual conflicts, male and female rape, dis-affected and emotionless sex, ambiguously consensual sexual encounters, arbitrary sex stripped of conventional or even nominal gestures of solidarity.

Within global film culture, those filmmakers—or figureheads—associated with the *cinéma du corps* have either drastically advanced their reputations as distinguished iconoclasts (Olivier Assayas, Catherine Breillat, Claire Denis), or else become agit-prop auteurs seemingly overnight (Marina de Van, Bruno Dumont, Gaspar Noé, Damien Odoul, Philippe Grandrieux). To some, this group and the related projects of its contemporaries embody filmmaking at the cutting edge: artistically incisive, unflinching, without compromise. Philippe Azoury, highly sympathetic, calls it the work "of cinephile purists . . . cinema and contemporary modern art bound together."[2] In contrast, its detractors label such cinema as indefensible and grotesque, pushing screen depictions of physicality to unwelcome limits. Either way, few respond to the *cinéma du corps* with anything less than energetic commitment. The impassioned skepticism of Frédéric Strauss is quite representative. These are films, Strauss argues, which "bring together the body and the cerebral, animal drives and intelligence . . . [creating] a film-nightmare dreaming things we'd be better off not sharing . . . a 'cordoned-off' cinema [with] artistic ambition yet a vulgar appetite for carnival monsters."[3] Whatever the reaction it arouses, though, the *cinéma du corps* puts one segment of contemporary French film culture squarely into the global critical spotlight.

There is more to this cycle, however, than the sheer depiction of corporeal, sexual, and social dysfunction. Although much critical attention has focused on evaluating this new French cinema, few have recognized its collective ambitions for the medium itself, as the means to generate profound, often challenging, sensory experiences. In the age of the jaded spectator, the cynical cinephile, this brutal intimacy model is a test case for film's continued poten-

Coré (Béatrice Dalle) during a nocturnal prowl in *Trouble Every Day*

tial to inspire bewilderment—raw, unmediated reaction. For these narratives of the flesh, the projects of Denis, Dumont, Noé, and their peers, are rendered via a radical, innovative use of film style, an ingeniously crafted barrage of visual and aural techniques. Denis herself describes a creation process that is defiantly formalist: "Cinema is, first of all, images and sounds."[4] Besides the undeniably inflammatory subject area, it is this startlingly experimental stylistic treatment that makes these films so affecting in conception and execution. The texts that result, insidious yet arresting to the point of shock in their design, engage forcefully at both an intellectual and visceral level. In fact, this stylized representation of filmed bodies within agitational visual art recalls a discernible avant-garde trajectory. Important precursors in this light are taboo-breaking *films maudits* such as Salvador Dali's and Luis Buñuel's *Un Chien andalou* (1928), Stan Brakhage's *Window Water Baby Moving* (1959), Barbara Rubin's *Christmas on Earth* (1963), Jack Smith's *Flaming Creatures* (1963), and Carolee Schneeman's *Fuses* (1967).[5]

Responses to this strain of cinema have indeed been predictably combative. First hand, there has been volatile audience feedback—evident notably in the mass walk-outs that greeted *Trouble Every Day* and *Irreversible* at their Cannes premieres in 2001 and 2002, although similar fates met many of the cycle during festival screenings elsewhere.[6] Typically excitable press coverage also focused on the huge crowds, and boisterously polarized reception, that *Irreversible* enjoyed after its Parisian premiere—before, during, and after the screening—at the UGC Normandie theater on the Champs-Elysées.[7] Open hostility also defines both popular and scholarly reviews of these films.

Even when select critics offer sympathy, or defenses, their comments, in publications as internationally diverse as *Positif, Télérama, Sight and Sound*, and *The Boston Globe*, have frequently appeared in print alongside dismissive, hence mitigating, counter-reviews. Immediate rejection, indeed, remains the dominant reaction to films which, as Richard Falcon points out, manifest "an aggressive desire to confront their audiences, to render the spectator's experience problematic."[8] It is simple, consequently, to dismiss this *cinéma du corps* for its disturbing use of graphic physicality, but far harder to recognize its exacting stylistic ambitions, to gauge its status as a vigorous, conceptually dynamic new model of filmmaking. For, as Olivier Joyard argues astutely in *Cahiers du cinéma*, at issue here is a group of filmmakers whose work "build[s] from the image itself as raw material, noting the importance of colors and sound, using fragmentary storytelling . . . believing in cinema as a violent experience of the extreme."[9]

Echoing Joyard's sentiments, to characterize this *cinéma du corps* more rigorously we must approach it objectively, on its own terms, identifying the experimental minutiae of design that configure its formally assertive address to the spectator. On first viewing—or at a glance—these motifs of physical and/or sexual debasement are undeniably challenging. They are categorically not, however, the sole basis, or only interest, of this mode of cinema. Our entry point must be the analysis of the *cinéma du corps* as a type of avant-garde phenomenon. We need to explore how such filmmaking attenuates or strategically abandons narrative; how it conceives of acting and physical performance on-screen as the site of exposure and trauma; how it brilliantly radicalizes conventions of film style; and how, crucially, it overhauls the role of the film viewer, rejecting the traditionally passive, entertained onlooker to demand instead a viscerally engaged experiential participant. In essence, filmmakers like Denis, Noé, Dumont, and their contemporaries, have engineered a profoundly empirical cinema. Retaining dramatic and character arcs only in vestigial traces, they prefer effects derived from an innovative composite of perceptual encounters—a raw and occasionally confrontational array of cinematic sensations.[10]

This chapter discusses the art and contexts of this contemporary French cinema of the body, outlining the grounds for its reappraisal, and importance, as an unconventional new development in world film. We start with an account of the recent emergence of this filmmaking tendency, exploring its major figures, projects, and professional motifs. Next, we will survey the contours of its critical reception, resituating the films within the often heated scholarly, trade, and popular debates they have instigated. Climactically our focus will turn to closer analyses of representative *cinéma du corps* texts, beginning with *Trouble Every Day*, *Twentynine Palms*, and *Irreversible*. This foundational trio, its medium-specific manipulations, reveals a mode of cinema invoking a sensory experience at times threateningly, violently attuned to corporeal processes, the visceral interactions of bodies on-screen. From these pioneering examples, we will address two counterpoint cases: the work of Marina de Van, which offers a poignant rendition of corporeal disaffection, especially through the motif of self-mutilation; and Diane Bertrand's *The Ring Finger*, drawing on the work of Yoko Ogawa to pursue a more poetic, less confrontational cinematic evocation of the body as a physical repository of memory.

Professional Provocations: The *Cinéma du Corps* Emerges

In today's film marketplace, a transgressive cinema carries obvious commercial risks, yet also the prospect of a raised artistic profile, as well as, more pragmatically, an increased visibility in the crowded schedules of arthouse cinemas and international film festivals. Corporeal cinema offers the prospect of widespread attention, and intensive public engagement. In fact, such filmmaking and its concomitant creation of scandal at the Cannes film festival has recently proved beneficial, even foundational, to the fledgling careers of both Dumont and Noé: the former derived from the interest and backlash inspired by *Humanity* (*L'Humanité*) in 1999, and the latter provoked by *Irreversible*, in 2002.[11] Perhaps unsurprisingly, this has motivated a spate of projects from a diverse range of filmmakers, male and female, and, of late, both French and international. Alongside Denis, Dumont, and Noé, this group includes dynamically reinvented veterans, as well as less well-known, younger iconoclasts, whose careers have been lent shape and purpose. Despite the ongoing financial uncertainty in the contemporary French filmmaking industry — which in its structure, funding, and organization is constantly faced, in the words of Laurent Creton and Anne Jäckel, with "the danger of collapsing the aesthetic into the economic and commercial"[12] —the progress of France's more radical contemporary cinema has in part been buoyed by an ongoing dialogue among a minority of provocative filmmakers whose work has attracted a (disproportionate) degree of scrutiny and success, both in France and abroad.

A contemporary survey reveals a corpus of films and filmmakers, cultural-industrial catalysts for this new French cinema of the body. A seminal presence is Catherine Breillat, known since the 1970s for her caustic and groundbreaking treatments of female sexual desires. Breillat enjoyed a sudden renaissance in 1999 with her picaresque parable of a young woman's harsh sexual awakening, and the fundamental incompatibility between the sexes, in the bitterly titled *Romance*. In the wake of this breakthrough, among the most widely discussed French films of the 1990s, a feminist landmark, Breillat has pursued variations on the same theme. Reworking her customarily severe filmmaking palette—muted color schemes, exacting long takes, minimal editing and limited set-ups, little or no non-diegetic music, static dramatic tableau with few camera movements—Breillat continued her analysis of graphic yet arch sexual liaisons in *Romance*'s counterparts: *Brief Crossing* (*Brève traversée*, 2001), *Fat Girl* (*A ma soeur!*, 2001), *Sex Is Comedy* (2002), and *Anatomy of Hell* (2004). In a surprising continuity of material but breach of *mise-en-scène*, Breillat then transferred to the heritage genre: the nineteenth century in *The Last Mistress* (*Une Vielle maîtresse*, 2007), and (intermittently) the seventeenth century in *Bluebeard* (*Barbe bleue*, 2009).[13] At heart, these films use sex to emblematize the power struggles that arise within patriarchal societies, gender duels which Breillat intensifies through deliberate casting mismatches. Typically, beautiful but implacable and wooden male leads (often nonprofessionals) spar with far more charismatic female performers. The relationships between Fu'Ad Aïd Aattou and Asia Argento in *The Last Mistress*, for example, or Gilles Guillan and Sarah Pratt in *Brief Crossing*, are pointedly one-sided on a personal level; the irony being, of course, that on a social level, these women enjoy merely fleeting victories.

Besides Breillat, similar brutal intimacy motifs have underlined the rise to global celebrity of François Ozon, whose work is typically—uncomfortably—poised between farce and horror, brutal intimacy again, incorporating graphic representations of hetero- and homosexual desire. After shorts made as a nonprofessional, Ozon paid homage to *Persona* (1966) with the mini-feature *See the Sea*, in which a young female drifter's fixation upon a sexually repressed mother, vacationing in a remote seaside cottage, climaxes in bursts of psychological and physical violence. Following this, Ozon was invited to the 1998 Cannes film festival as part of its official selection—again a site of recognition for this vein of filmmaking—with his blackly comic satire of pent-up bourgeois (sexual) energies, and an unraveling idealized patriarchal family, in *Sitcom* (1998). Ozon progressed to a savagely explicit lovers-on-the-run thriller, *Criminal Lovers* (*Les Amants criminels*, 1999), before scrutinizing, in another after-echo of *Persona*, the psychological-sexual warfare between a mismatched female duo in the international hit *Swimming Pool* (2002); then a terminal heterosexual marriage, depicted backwards, in *5x2* (2004). In an extended interview for *Positif*, Ozon gave what amounts to a partial *cinéma du corps* manifesto. Asked about his frequent recourse to wordless, unromantic, and often antagonistic sexual encounters instead of more concrete exposition, Ozon argued that "for me, these are the moments when characters no longer project their discourse, but reveal themselves through their bodies.

Like at the start of *5x2* when Stéphane Freiss interrupts his banal exchanges with Valeria Bruni Tedeschi and rapes her. Right away his personality reveals itself, and there, he tells the truth. . . . Whether these bodies are moving to make love or to dance, these are always truthful moments."[14] In the context of remarks like these, Ozon's sympathetic reception by international audiences and critics has done much to raise the profile of French cinema itself, and more specifically its contemporary emphasis on dissections of sexual and bodily functions.

Concomitant to the *cinéma du corps*, it should be noted, is a closely related tendency in contemporary French-language literature. From a male perspective, literary counterparts exist among novelists whose works have solicited a similarly polarized reception. Leading practitioners here are Michel Houellebecq and Frédéric Beigbeder, whose writing traces the amoral sexual desires of their male protagonists to the contexts of late-phase capitalism, its imperative to translate everything, all personal and professional impulses, into marketable, commercial gains. In this train of thought, sexual exploitation and commodification are the inevitable, logical outcomes of masculine corporate indoctrination. This profoundly disillusioned model broke into the cultural mainstream with Houellebecq's *Whatever* (*Extension du domaine de la lutte*, 1994), *The Elementary Particles* (*Les Particules élémentaires*, 1998; film version directed by Oskar Roehler in 2006), and, perhaps most provocatively, *Platform* (*Plateforme*, 2001), a fictionalized suicide note about a man's attempts to found a sexual tourism business in Thailand. (Subsequent to these, Houellebecq adapted and directed his own screen version of his novel, *The Possibility of an Island* [*La Possibilité d'un île*, 2005; film produced in 2008].) In the same way, Beigbeder represents (and arguably critiques) contemporary hypercommercial sexual hedonism from the autobiographical perspective of a young, male advertising executive, in *99 Francs* (2000; translated as *9.99* in 2002; the highly ambivalent film version was directed by Jan Kounen in 2007). From a female framework, conversely, a proximate literature has also been produced, in which, as Shirley Jordan contends, "its authors eschew eroticism and scrutinize coolly the gestures, routines, and words of coupling. The inventiveness of such writing lies in its notational determination, its insistence on exhaustive recording, and its positioning of the author as a back-to-basics participant observer intent on picking away at the foundational symbolic order by re-focalizing sexual bodies and sexual relations."[15] Leading examples here include, from Jordan's primary sample, Catherine Millet's infamous confessional piece *La Vie sexuelle de Catherine M.* (2001), Breillat's *Pornocratie* (2001; the basis for her *Anatomy of Hell*), Anna Rozen's *Plaisir d'offrir, joie de recevoir* (1999) and Marie-Laure Dagoit's *Et les lèvres et la bouche* (2002), to which can be added the work of Marie Darrieussecq and Céline Curiol, among a number of others. (The work of this latter duo we will investigate in Chapter 4.)

Returning to visual media, we can discern how the *cinéma du corps* derives from an array of aesthetic practices, technological developments in the medium, and especially the rise of digital video and low-budget cinema. Minimizing production costs by relying on DV has, in fact, proved one way of realizing extremely confrontational, risky projects by newer directors who were untried prospects as far as financiers were concerned. The actor-turned-director Jean-Marc Barr, for example, shot his Franco-American "Free Trilogy" — a group of sexually frank romantic parables, *Lovers* (1998), *Too Much Flesh* (2000) and *Being Light* (2000) — for just 18 million French francs, which was at the time the cost of a single average French feature production. Elsewhere, the opportunities of DV as a cheap and accessible filmmaking method led to unprecedented recognition for Coralie Trinh Thi and Virginie Despentes, whose *Baise-moi* revived the 1970s rape-revenge format from a female point-of-view. Their film, on its release threatened with censure[16] and defended by many, including Breillat, used the DV format to derive new shock value and claustrophobia from its sexually explicit imagery, and casting of actors from the porn industry, while replicating the grimy, free-form, black-and-white cinematography of a low-budget, impromptu documentary. In *Dancing*, Patrick-Mario Bernard and Xavier Brillat similarly adopted the unflattering and pixilated DV aesthetic for a same-sex treatment of *cinéma du corps* issues, in this case a sexually fraught and psychologically disjunctive gay relationship set in a baroque, crumbling ballroom, using for its backdrop, like *See the Sea*, the wild coastlines of Northern France. Noé, equally, is a filmmaker alive to the possibilities of digital imagery, an efficient method logistically and artistically. Thus he shot *Irreversible* on Super 16, then transferred it to high definition video for digital postproduction manipulation, before finally converting it to 35mm in a 2.35:1 widescreen ratio for its theatrical release.

Above all, however, this new French cinema of the body has facilitated bold stylistic experimentation, a fundamental lack of compromise in its engagement with the viewer. Many filmmakers have deployed visual designs and imagery to create decisively original, unsettling aesthetic encounters. Philippe Grandrieux, a documentarian and multimedia artist whose work is still not widely known or distributed outside France, is a clear example of the fusing of mainstream plot elements with genuinely avant-garde cinematic motifs. Grandrieux's serial killer road movie, *Sombre* (1998), his even more graphically obscure tale of carnal obsession, *A New Life* (*La Vie nouvelle*, 2002), and the domestic-rural saga *A Lake* (*Un Lac*, 2008) at times approach a level of visual abstraction most famously associated with Brakhage, conveying piecemeal narratives of implicit murder and brutality through lyrical flashes of unfocused colors, dense visual textures, handheld camerawork, and barely perceptible figure movements. Equally formalist but at another aesthetic extreme is Jacques Nolot's *Porn Theatre* (*La Chatte à deux têtes*, 2002), a much less confrontational drama which is set entirely in and around the eponymous venue of its title. Nolot's project is in part to juxtapose ironically the sordid, emphatically sexual setting with a beatific, even meditative visual logic. Thus, *Porn Theatre* depicts the pornographic habits of his characters via a suite of meticulous and elegant long takes, showing the impersonal sexual interactions of the theater's community within serene extended tracking shots that highlight multi-layered compositions in depth. In Grandrieux and Nolot's filmmaking, abstract formal beauty coexists uneasily with visceral brutality.

More broadly, as film festivals and indigenous film cultures have become increasingly globalized, a trend towards internationalization has also informed the careers of key practitioners of the new French cinema of the body. Another recent phenomenon is that of well-established French filmmakers using equally explicit imagery—occasionally including that most enduring of artistic-cultural taboos, unsimulated sex—and oblique narrative design in international coproductions shot partially or entirely in the English language. Important in this regard is Patrice Chéreau's *Intimacy*, which was cofinanced by companies from England, France, Germany, and Spain. Shot with English actors and set amidst dingy London suburbs, *Intimacy* offers a naturalistic depiction of an adulterous sexual relationship, motivated by neither love nor friendship, between a bitter divorcé and an alienated wife. Olivier Assayas followed suit in 2002 with a transcultural conspiracy thriller about internet pornography, corporate espionage, and sexual consumption in his elliptically structured narrative, *Demonlover*, an English-French-Japanese coproduction with a multinational cast. In 2003, Dumont for the first time moved his predominantly French crew to America to make *Twentynine Palms*, a meandering Californian narrative of a couple's sexual and physical demise, which marked an abrupt departure from his typical production protocols of shooting with nonprofessional actors in the rural Bailleul region of northern France.

The methodologies of this new French cinema have also informed a number of projects made by filmmakers of different nationalities. In this framework have appeared explicit sexual dramas such as Bernardo Bertolucci's *The Dreamers* (2003), David Mackenzie's *Young Adam* (2003), Lars von Trier's *The Idiots* (1998) and *Antichrist* (2009), John Cameron Mitchell's *Shortbus* (2006), and two contemporary sensations at Cannes: Vincent Gallo's *The Brown Bunny* (2003) and Michael Winterbottom's *9 Songs* (2004). All of these films foreground scenes of graphic copulation within otherwise conventional, sometimes even calm (excepting Mitchell's and von Trier's) fictional nar-ratives. Overall, this form of contemporary French cinema has proved an influential model within both indigenous and international filmmaking—a successful formula for notoriety. But it is also a cultural development that has been hotly challenged on a global scale.

The *Cinéma du Corps* and the Critics

What are we to make of such a deliberately contentious type of cinema? The tentative efforts made by critics and scholars to characterize this new French cinema of the body have revived a cluster of discourses central to film study and cultural debate: whether it is appropriate for widely circulated films (and later DVDs) to incorporate such extreme forms of aesthetic, sexual, and social provocation; or, conversely, whether even high film art should be limited to more sanctioned forms of physical desire and social interaction. While dealing with these films, critics and scholars have built entrenched positions around the notion that a basic function of cinema is, alternately, to infuriate or to placate. One of the earliest attempts to engage with the *cinéma du corps* came in the November 25, 1999 issue of *Libération*, which published an anonymous essay that berated the grim nature of much recent French film. The article, reprinted in *Le Monde diplomatique* the following February and attributed belatedly to "journalist-cinéaste" Carlos Pardo, took to task both rising and established French auteurs by critiquing their artistic goals. Very much in the vein of François Truffaut's infamous 1954 polemic, "A Certain Tendency of the French Cinema," Pardo undertook a national filmmaking diagnostic, root-ing out a deep-seated cultural malaise while scathingly rebuking his contem-poraries. Pulling no punches, Pardo accused Breillat, Dumont, Grandrieux, Mathieu Kassovitz, Noé, Ozon, and Erick Zonca (a veritable who's who of 1990s French cinema) of embodying in their work "despair and defeatism . . . [a] fascination with the abject and the sordid."[17] Attacking the content of contemporary French cinema, Pardo nonetheless conceded its directors' stylistic ambition, poised "between naturalism at its most bleak, its most hopeless, and the mannerisms of the most affected formalism." But for his overarching conclusion Pardo objected categorically to France's ubiquitous on-screen sexual misanthropy. To him it represented nothing less than a taste for "crime, pornography, and contempt of people."[18]

In retrospect, Pardo's main insight was to observe fruitfully the emergence of a new and previously overlooked trend within French filmmaking on the brink of the twenty-first century. His broadly dismissive final analysis, very conservative, to most eyes did the films scant justice, and a number of stimulated writers have since offered rejoinders. Given the controversy attached to the films, the commentaries produced tend towards extremes, with critics and scholars alike fiercely divided about films labeled by some debased and (in pejorative terms) pornographic, and, by others, pioneering and genuinely bravura. The films have also produced political debate on the subject of freedom of speech and artistic expression. Even France's *Première* magazine commissioned in 2007 an extended treatment of the phenomenon, coinciding with the release of the sexually explicit portmanteau film *Destricted* (2007), which featured contributions from Matthew Barney, Larry Clark, and Noé, among other interested parties. The respectful tone of its interviews — with figures like Dumont and Noé — was clear from questions like, "Is representing sex the fantasy of all artists?" and "Is cinema lagging behind the other arts?"[19]

Fascinated curiosity informs most accounts — curiosity laced with either suspicion or solidarity. In the former group is James Quandt, who outlines a "new French Extremity," but then goes on rather perversely to cite the films of Dumont, Grandrieux, Ozon, and others merely to castigate their graphic content, dismiss their artistic agenda as disingenuous, and deride their alleged pretentiousness.[20] Similar in tone is Will Higbee, whose main, sometimes sole, criterion for assessing recent French cinema is the presence or absence of (leftist) political engagements. In this frame, Higbee first separates his readings by directorial gender (*Romance* and *Baise-moi* are thus marginally progressive; *Irreversible* and *Seul contre tous* inherently regressive) then attacks Noé (as if he is the only filmmaker connected to the *cinéma du corps*) for depicting sexual violence and social *insecurité* in France without overtly condemning them.[21]

An equally combative but alternative voice comes from René Prédal. At one point in *Le Jeune cinéma français*, his first survey of contemporary French filmmaking, Prédal makes acerbic reference to a vocal critical minority, namely Pardo, for dismissing directors whose texts are nihilistic, hence whose politics disconnect from their own (Pardo from a right-wing position, and, by extension, Higbee from the left). Prédal goes so far as to call such commentaries a slippery slope towards censorship: interpreting a distasteful social diagnosis from brief textual analyses, closing off any counterpoints, then calling the works in question ideologically bankrupt. This intolerance for extreme forms of cinema, exploring sexual or violent materials without trite social judgments, to Prédal reflects nothing less than a "systematic hatred for culture, intelligence and all freedom of artistic expression."[22]

Among recent film scholars, the notion of a confrontational brand of new French cinema has been more sympathetically debated. A number of writers, upholding the premise that certain French filmmakers display an affinity for baser human instincts, nuances Pardo's model by assessing more particularly the focus on starker depictions of sexuality. One libertarian take is simply to champion this freer cinematic depiction of sex, as something that broadens the possible catalog of human behaviors represented on-screen, positive or negative, finally removing sex from the domain of the culturally taboo. In what is already a seminal essay, "Cinema and the Sex Act," Linda Williams argues convincingly, mainly through Breillat's *Romance* and *Fat Girl*, along with *Intimacy* and *Baise-moi*, that such cinema acts to "defy the soft-focus erotic prettiness, the contained lyrical musical interlude, that has marked the 'sex scene' of mainstream Hollywood."[23] Neither gratuitous in the pornographic tradition, nor watered down in the prudish Hollywood mode, this unhindered portrayal of sex, Williams suggests, grants "an unprecedented emotional and physical honesty" from which derives a cinema concerned with sexual identity, personal control, and youthful character psychology.[24]

In *Screening Sex*, Williams develops her argument, putting our *cinéma du corps* model more broadly in the context of contemporary European art cinema, defining it against what she calls the artificially extended adolescence of American cinema (thanks to censors like the Motion Picture Association of America), and Hollywood's arrested on-screen development. In contrast, pragmatic yet decisive, Williams calls sexually explicit European films the "bold inheritors of Oshima's *In the Realm of the Senses* [1976] even if they no longer share the politics of revolutionary transgression marking that singular benchmark film."[25] Recalling Ozon's points about *5x2* — that explicit corporeal interactions enhance a director's ability to reveal psychology and characterization — Williams observes that films like *Intimacy* are "neither tastefully erotic nor insistently hard-core . . . [making] us realize how impoverished are the gestures and emotions of most cinematic sex acts."[26] Through a thoughtful series of carefully elaborated analyses, Williams concludes that uncensored sexual materials no longer need to make strident political statements, nor cynically work to attract controversy for their makers. Instead, such filmmaking merely, finally, allows us access to "the emotional nature and physical specificity of the sex acts that so importantly punctuate our public and private lives."[27]

Beyond these debates about the political and aesthetic legitimacy of films such as *Romance*, *Baise-moi*, and *Intimacy*, the critical unrest simmers still. Particularly after the international arrival of *Trouble Every Day*, *Irreversible*, and *Twentynine Palms*, the furor surrounding French cinema and its engagement with filmed sex has become, if possible, even more pronounced. As a group, these films continue but rework the trajectory of the preceding work of Breillat, Chéreau, and the group above, by depicting sex not just graphically but also more emphatically in the framework of horror and criminal depravity. In *Trouble Every Day*, carnal appetites now literally consume others; in all three films, sexual consummation is depicted as wanton and animalistic, inherently destructive. But the renewed intensity of the *cinéma du corps* agenda—stylized but unromantic sex acts, encounters now often devoid of any emotional contexts except berserk aggression and rage—has nonetheless still served to advance the careers of these figures, its leading practitioners, developing their reputation as auteurs, and differentiating their films from the more pallid and puerile American cinema.

The violence in these particular films has certainly been reflected in their reception in the popular and trade press. *Trouble Every Day* and *Irreversible* received their world premieres, in successive years, at the Cannes Film Festivals of 2001 and 2002, where they were greeted with at best bemusement and at worst strident disbelief. There, and at film festivals around the world, screenings of both those films and *Twentynine Palms* led to mass walk-outs and lurid dismissals among attendant journalists. The example of *Irreversible* is representative of the fate of all three. At Cannes, newspaper reports claimed that over 10 percent of its 2,400 opening night audience stormed out, and many of those who remained did so only to yell catcalls at the screen.[28] The crossfire continued at other film festivals, including outcries in London, Toronto, and New York. Once in limited release, all three films continued to receive emphatically polarized reviews. Isolated voices offered support for the embattled trio of filmmakers, but frequently in the case of *Irreversible*— certainly the least liked of the group—such defenses were, in a series of unusual editorial decisions, often published alongside, or cancelled out by, a more accusatory account. Thus in journals as diverse as *Sight and Sound*, in England, and *Positif*, in France, critics such as Mark Kermode, Nick James, Philippe Rouyer, and Grégory Valens literally sparred in print, damning or acclaiming Noé's feature.[29] One faction demanded censure for an amoral treatment of sexual violence; the opposing group called for artistic freedom for an uncompromising portrait of social and sexual dysfunction.

A final critical point about this trio of filmmakers, suddenly embattled, is that like our debutant directors in Chapter 1, self-promotion again emerges as a crucial means of professional mediation. Whether a debutant director courting (auteurist) notoriety, or a more established figure trying to offset or reconstitute it, a filmmaker's ability to engage with France's film culture through interviews remains a pivotal part of the job. The main tool for configuring such critical reception, moreover, is again cineliteracy, the capacity to situate one's project in the context of film history, divulging its debts to past masterworks. Reacting to an unusually inflamed film press, Denis repeatedly maneuvered to cite *Trouble Every Day* as an extension of sensuous fantasies or horror films, tinged with surrealism, from Jean Cocteau's *Beauty and the Beast* (*La Belle et la bête*, 1946) to Jacques Tourneur's *Cat People* (1946). For Noé, the stated source of artistic impulse was Pasolini's *Salo* (1975), avant-garde flicker films, and selected works by Kubrick. Dumont's inheritance was the so-called primitivism or sophisticated barbarity of American B-movie iconoclast Samuel Fuller. Yet again, cineliterate self-awareness distinguishes the French filmmaker, even when the context is sustained hostility. As Monica Bellucci, one of Noé's most ardent supporters, argued the case: "*Irreversible* made me think . . . of films which show humanity's capacity for cruelty. . . . Gaspar is a pure cinéaste, through and through, who accepts no compromises: for that I had to have respect and admiration for him."[30]

Ballads of the Body: Claire Denis's *Trouble Every Day*, Gaspar Noé's *Irreversible*, and Bruno Dumont's *Twentynine Palms*

If we jettison the pejorative approaches to the *cinéma du corps*, this need to dismiss that which does not beguile or immediately cohere, critical possibilities arise. A fundamental question remains unanswered: what is it about these works as *films* that renders the experience of them so memorable, so vivid? While there is clearly a textual relationship, a discernable conversation in progress amongst Denis, Dumont, Noé, and their peers, these films have been scrutinized for their subject material but essentially ignored for the specifically cinematic means through which brutal intimacy is actually conveyed. This is a drastic oversight, as there is evident both collectively and individually a remarkable, powerful exploitation of the medium within this trio — echoes of which reverberate through the rejuvenated art cinema of contemporary France, and beyond. In this context, Jean-Pierre Dufreigne believes the real force behind these films to be their "terrifying elegance."[31]

To analyze these films closely is to discover an array of devices designed to engross, bewilder, repel, but not entertain in any conventional sense. Important to note in this context is that, contrary to the unstated assumptions of most contemporary film criticism, even that which deals with film festivals, not all filmmakers seek to charm and engage the audience in regulated, upbeat terms. Cinema need neither please nor amuse. The structures endemic nowadays to the majority of international mainstream *and* art cinema — sympathetic characters that progress and develop, talking us through their problems in order to solve them; carefully plotted scenarios with inevitably positive resolutions; underlying social issues that can be tidily surveyed and usually surmounted — can be undermined or else abandoned entirely. Further to this, the stimuli of film style routinely used to gratify—attractive settings and appealing *mise-en-scène*; a lively yet reassuring soundtrack; smooth, logical editing and elegantly omniscient cinematography—can also be rejected. But what then? As *Trouble Every Day*, *Irreversible*, and *Twentynine Palms* demonstrate, the systematic pursuit of an opposite objective, the craft of agitation, sensation, and provocation, gives rise to an artful cinema. Indeed, the subversive practices that European art cinema of the 1950s and 1960s once enacted against classical film norms are, in certain sectors of twenty-first-century French filmmaking, being meticulously revived.

The tactics for such studied disorientation are often bravura, especially in regards to narrative design. The first point is that *Irreversible* was shot not from a completed script but from a three-page treatment, which divided the shoot into its constituent sequences and summarized the gist of their content. The scenes were expanded through improvisation and intensive on-set rehearsal, then filmed up to twenty times in a gradual process of dramatic and stylistic evolution. (Noé's approach in some ways echoes Lola Doillon's for its calculated spontaneity, drawing substantially from the cast's input.) *Twentynine Palms*, similarly, was written by Dumont (who never adheres to the conventional screenwriting format) as a 40-page outline, and expanded on location as principal photography went on. Only *Trouble Every Day* began life as a completed script, by Denis and long-term writing partner Jean-Pol Burgeau. But even here, as Denis admits wryly, her motivation as a filmmaker is often in "playing her script and her aesthetic against each other,"[32] using a densely novelistic point of departure (vampire literature for *Trouble Every Day*; Herman Melville's short stories and poems for *Beau Travail* [1999] and so on) and laconic dialogue, which she then cinematically supplants during her shoots. In effect, Denis intuitively substitutes sounds and images for words. Indeed, as brilliantly represented by Denis, Dumont, and Noé, the *cinéma du corps* unnerves on one level through its systemic dismantling of screenwriting norms that are absolutely—we might say tyrannically—ubiquitous. There is little room here for dialogue-driven character formulation or clear character arcs. The great fallacy endorsed by most forms of cinema, that adult human beings are psychologically transparent and learn from their mistakes, is abandoned in favor of on-screen figures that are brutish, unyielding forces of nature. Gone also are over-ordered dramatic pay-offs, codified structures of screenplay design that reduce human interactions to regulated patterns of events. Indeed, the *cinéma du corps* heeds Jane Campion's protest against what she sees as world cinema's "three-act fundamentalism."[33]

Befitting this distaste for conventional screenplay logics, like much of the *cinéma du corps*, our trio of films uses plots that oscillate between the

Marcus (Vincent Cassel) and Alex (Monica Bellucci) in blissful repose in *Irreversible*

demented and the commonplace. *Trouble Every Day* uses parallel editing to depict the sexual and psychological decay of Coré (Béatrice Dalle, cast to invoke her iconically carnal role in *Betty Blue* [37°2 *le matin*, 1986]), and Shane (Vincent Gallo), who suffer, we surmise, from a horrific medical disorder that induces cannibalistic urges in them during sexual arousal. Shane, ostensibly on his honeymoon, travels to Paris in search of a cure, but his enquiries fail. Instead, in an unsettling open ending he is left apparently embracing his condition, having carried out a series of murders. *Irreversible* is even more emphatically disorienting in its narrative structure, consisting of twelve segments which defy the film's own title by unfolding in reverse chronological order. On-screen events begin with a gory killing in a gay nightclub, carried out by Pierre (Albert Dupontel) in frenzied but misdirected retribution for the rape and apparent murder of Alex (Monica Bellucci). Later (earlier), by contrast, are beatific scenes: Alex sleeping with her lover, Marcus (Vincent Cassel), the father of her unborn and presumably lost child; and then for the film's hugely incongruous climax, a scene of her alone, content, in a sunny park surrounded by joyful families. *Twentynine Palms*, which in its deliberate pace and compositions outdoes Michelangelo Antonioni's art cinema of the 1960s—a cited influence on Dumont—recounts the picaresque journey of Katia (Katia Golubeva) and David (David Wissak), who it is implied is married to someone else (there is a tattooed band on his wedding finger). In extended sequences bracketed by fades, this couple drives his increasingly battered red Hummer through Californian scrublands. They wander, intermittently having sex, arguing heatedly, and then falling victim, in the film's final segment, to a series of sudden attacks: David is savagely beaten and raped, and in inarticulate rage kills both Katia and himself. The final shot, a distantly framed long take, shows his body lying face down in the desert next to the abandoned

Hummer, while a frustrated cop calls for backup. No compromise, or satisfying closure, is offered by these conclusions.

A defining feature of these films is their systematic distortion of the diegetic space, the confused worlds on-screen. While the actual acts of violence and sex are represented as intrusive and alarming, more nondescript events and settings also represent a brooding, nonspecific malaise. As Denis reports, her aim is to "create a feeling of danger everywhere . . . [so] every situation contains a sense of threat, anxiety." [34] In part this builds from measured narrative pacing, an insidious form of storytelling, with plots fragmented to the point of simplicity, attenuated to relentlessness. The most shocking and unflinching sexual interactions are situated, in effect, within narratives that oscillate between experiential extremes: drawn-out sequences of passive meditation, inscrutable character interactions, at times an abiding sense of boredom, and contrasted bursts of sudden, overwhelmingly abrupt movement and action. (A clear forerunner to this model is Chantal Akerman's *Jeanne Dielman, 23 Quai du Commerce, 1080 Bruxelles* [1976].) Graphic and/or violent sexual encounters are repeatedly prefaced, connected, and even sometimes intercut with banalities: Shane in a café sipping gently from a coffee mug (*Trouble Every Day*), a long take of a deserted main street (*Twentynine Palms*), Alex's lengthy attempts to find a cab (*Irreversible*). Dumont underlines the strategy: that in films like these, "nothing happens, and this nothingness creates suspense." [35]

Elements of style, furthermore, grate on our comprehension of these desolate events in progress. A daring aspect of what becomes an assault on our senses is these filmmakers' oppressive use of sound. If soundtracks can be used to situate and to accompany, they can also be used to disturb. Most strikingly, *Irreversible* uses for sixty minutes of its running time a barely perceptible but aggravating bass rumble that was recorded for Noé's purposes at twenty-seven hertz, the frequency used by riot police to quell mobs by inducing unease and, after prolonged exposure, physical nausea. Noé also hired Thomas Bangalter, a member of the electronic band Daft Punk, to dub in sound designs — beats, drones, riffs, and pitch slides — many of which were performed live on DJ decks as the shoot went on. Throughout the film there is often slippage in acoustic fidelity, a wavering connection between image and sound. Alongside, under, and over scenes — as the density, mix, and volume of the soundtrack abruptly shift — a subterranean barrage of off-screen and nondiegetic sound peaks and ebbs in waves, an arresting but dislocated clamor that interrogates the events we see. The total effect, as Robin Wood argues, is an ingeniously crafted soundscape of pure noise, registered by the audience as "ominous, ugly, threatening," [36] a queasy range of pulsing textures that intensifies our malaise at events on the imagetrack. Especially in the opening scenes set in and around a tenement building and outside the Rectum nightclub where the opening murder takes place, we approach sensory overload, sheer aural chaos.

In different but related ways, Denis and Dumont also use the soundtrack as the means for challenging viewers, making them acutely conscious that they are also listeners. In both *Trouble Every Day* and *Twentynine Palms* dialogue is removed for long stretches of time, including some segments of up to twenty minutes in duration. Silence often prevails, which in and of itself makes audiences restless, particularly when the convention is for exposition and backstory—especially during the opening sections of a narrative. Coré herself, played by Dalle, whose acting style usually depends upon volubility, is given just two lines to say, or rather, whisper: "I don't want to wait any more . . . I want to die." The minimal spoken exchanges between Katia and David in *Twentynine Palms*, barely comprehensible in her halting English and his broken French—Dumont's casting harnesses the absurdity of a couple that cannot communicate—become even more muted through the actors' uncertain, mumbled delivery. French cinema, historically noted for its tradition of dense, witty scripted dialogue, here takes a disconcertingly different turn.

All three filmmakers, in fact, use an inverted sound hierarchy to dissipate the impact of speech. As orchestrated by Denis, Dumont, Noé, and their postproduction technicians, beautifully designed sound mixes deaden or excise human voices and disproportionately privilege denser ambient forms. The soundtracks build from auditory claustrophobia rather than structured vocal interactions. Alone, silent, and (we infer only much later) on the hunt for victims, Coré's nocturnal prowls in *Trouble Every Day* are set to sweeping gusts of wind and nonspecific rumbles, as are the repeated establishing shots of industrial and city skylines. Throughout *Twentynine Palms*, Dumont heightens the clamor of distant towns, passing police sirens, clattering traffic moving at speed, scraps of noise from passersby, and ubiquitous blasts of wind. For most of *Irreversible*—in and outside two nightclubs, on Paris streets—fragments of voices collide and compete with a cacophony of sound fragments both diegetic and nondiegetic: shouts, footsteps, cries, urban and abstract noise. The audience is obliged to relate what is heard to what is seen, reconciling the two only intermittently into a meaningful, coherent whole.

Visual style also intervenes to amplify the disorienting experience offered, or rather insisted upon, by these films. As with the soundtrack, any comfortable grasp of events in progress is blocked; raw or symbolic sensation is routinely preferred to narrative synthesis. For *Trouble Every Day*, Denis and her long-term director of photography, Agnès Godard, chose to shoot pivotal se-

Bodies and rocks: Katia (Katia Golubeva) and David (David Wissak) in *Twentynine Palms*

quences either at dusk, at night, with virtually no illumination, or, conversely, in garish blood red and orange pools of light. Characters come and go, move and interact in gloom or complete obscurity. The motif is highlighted in the film's extended opening scene of a couple kissing in darkness, images which are nearly illegible even when freeze-framed on DVD. Throughout their collaboration, as Godard describes, *Trouble Every Day* was configured by "colors, volumes, luminous ambiences, which took the place of concrete settings."[37] In their cinematography, moreover, both Denis and Dumont (who began his directorial career as an industrial documentarian) often favor shots of transitory spaces, details, props, or abstract symmetrical patterns rather than the actors themselves. On-screen space — a vestigial sense of Paris in *Trouble Every Day* or tangible landscapes in either film — is profoundly defamiliarized. Serge Kaganski argues that Denis and Godard render *Trouble Every Day*'s "vaguely urban terrain as if it were an African savannah"; an atavistic landmass that Dumont configures more directly.[38] *Twentynine Palms* indeed obsessively cuts away to extreme long shots of desert landscapes and the modern minutiae that litter them: wind turbines, distant roads, crumbling buildings, railway tracks. Both films and both filmmakers often eschew figures and figure movement at all, focusing repeatedly instead on physical aspects of the setting, directing us to contemplate opaque or (increasingly) vaguely menacing objects of contemporary urban scenery, such as blank walls, hotel fixtures, electricity pylons, or accumulating piles of garbage and city detritus.

While aesthetic design can make us strain to catch meaningful glimpses, it can also make us avert our eyes. Originally trained as a cinematographer at the Institut Lumière in Paris, and a self-described "image fetishist,"[39] Noé worked extensively as his own director of photography on *Irreversible*. (His collaborator was Benoît Debie, whose distinctive photography we will

Marcus is driven away by ambulance in an overhead shot from *Irreversible*

consider further in Chapter 4.) His crucial technical decision was to use predominantly a tiny, lightweight Minima camera to capture 360-degree regions of space around his characters, in vertiginous swoops, whirls, and gyroscopic spins. The effect recalls Michael Snow's *Back and Forth* (1969), a pioneering experiment in mapping out zones of filmed space. It also upsets, sometimes violently, viewers used to analytical editing and stable compositions. Always alert to newer technologies, Noé used a lengthy postproduction period and digital editing facilities to merge seamlessly disparate visual chunks, raw footage, into extended kaleidoscopic arcs of jarring motion. In consequence, scenes that are already disturbing, such as when the unconscious Marcus, beaten and apparently close to death, is driven off in an ambulance, are conveyed and amplified via a radical cinematographic design which asserts its stylistic presence, like the soundtrack, independently of events taking place. Vital sequences—some shot upside down, most unbalanced or arbitrary in their framing, many canted drastically off-kilter—segue into episodes of the camera being propelled through space, in extravagant loops and twirls. Melding digital and celluloid technologies, Noé's aesthetic design invokes avant-garde pioneer Brakhage's efforts to create a cinema of raw and unmediated perceptual intuitions. At times the impression is of free-form experiential data, wild and wandering visual patterns of light and darkness. In every sense of the phrase, *Irreversible* is hard to watch.

For all three filmmakers, however, the logic of such visual and aural schemes is highlighted during sexual encounters designed specifically to confront. Almost unbearable elements of proximity, scrutiny, and, above all, duration are endemic to the films' more graphic moments of sex-as-violation. During the underpass rape scene in *Irreversible*, for example, Noé's kinetic camera becomes suddenly and cruelly static. Instead of roaming flamboyantly and arbitrarily, it observes the struggling bodies of Alex and her attacker without moving, or pausing, or intervening, for an excruciating nearly nine-minute single shot—which may prove to be the most controversial long take in film history. And this motif of an extended take, typically framed in oppressively tight shot scales and set-ups without camera motion, is also the device of choice for Denis's sexual cannibalism scenes—such as when the imprisoned Coré wordlessly seduces and then slowly devours her would-be rescuer—as well as for Dumont's climactic depiction of sadistic male rape in a deserted desert gully.

Flesh, in all three films, is exposed to us within absorbing corporeal aesthetics. Compositions, typically extreme close-ups, dwell and linger on abstracted static shots or pans over goose bumps, writhing body parts, clumps of hair and naked skin. On the one hand, we see bodies displayed in emphatically nonsexual ways, repeatedly in the context of cleaning and hygiene: under flat fluorescent lighting in bathrooms, vigorously scrubbed in bathtubs, bathed in sprays from showers, reflected in washroom mirrors. On this point, Azoury aptly calls *Trouble Every Day*'s *mise-en-scène* a "refrigerated world."[40] But conversely—again these films exploit unpredictable reversals of style and narrative—these same bodies are then abruptly and graphically rendered visceral, or unconventionally sexualized. Denis jars us visually throughout *Trouble Every Day*, cutting, for example, early on from a sterile aircraft cabin interior to an abstract series of disjointed, wobbling handheld shots which seem to convey Shane's fantasy of a dying woman's corpse (his wife?), drenched not in water but in gore, with shallow focus blurring her smeared blood into a crimson haze. In the same way, from Katia's and David's extended stroll down a street in *Twentynine Palms*, Dumont without preamble cuts suddenly to a close-up of their violent, frantic sex in a motel room. As such protracted sequences unfold, moreover, the mix of the films' soundtracks, in contrast with elsewhere, suddenly becomes sparse, stark, and emphatically attuned to intimate bodily functions. The physical brutality is jarringly underscored by exclamations from the actors' vocal cords, which we hear pushed to grotesque breaking point: in ragged gasps, harsh sobs, and broken shrieks of pain. Human copulation, aggrandized and made primal by the style of all three films, reaches a brutish and guttural crescendo, as much a shattering release or explosion of energy as a sexual climax. The act of sex itself, in physical and cinematic form, becomes devoid of pleasure for both diegetic protagonists and their audience—an especially acute irony.

In the final analysis, this *cinéma du corps* is undoubtedly a vein of filmmaking that is difficult to appreciate objectively because it is so deliberately hard to watch, so deliberately hard to like. Far outside the mainstream, beyond the pale even of most art cinema made today, the work of Denis, Dumont, and Noé acquires such force that it leaves us stunned, affronted, and ultimately wary. The impact of such films, typically, is divisive. As Jean Bréhat, producer of *Twentynine Palms*, observes: "When someone is drawn to the film, it's in an excessive way—either people hate it and decry it, or they become fanatics. There's something really strong about it, it's never in between."[41] We must, however, move beyond such polarizing evaluations to understand the efforts, and ambitions, of this confrontational filmmaking to engage us, both in style and subject material. A hybrid cinema, merging high art intellectualism with low art body horror, these films exploit the cinematic medium in dazzling, coherent, and often unprecedented ways. Denis's summary of her conceptual goals as a filmmaker offers a perfect *cinéma du corps* rationale. She argues: "It's about exploring a formal design with which no one is familiar, the film itself offering a sort of immersion within aesthetic designs, taking us towards a more profound, more mysterious place."[42] Exploring sexuality and physicality at fascinating extremes, we should begin to consider this controversial strand of contemporary French cinema as having a rigorous, committed intensity akin to the avant-garde at its most dynamic and compelling—troubling every day, indeed.

In the Skin of Marina de Van

An alternative perspective on the *cinéma du corps* comes from the quite literal body of work of Marina de Van. Besides her progress as writer, actress, and director of short films, our focus here will be on de Van's debut feature, *In My Skin*, taking up both textual and contextual issues. Extending the *cinéma du corps* tendency, we will consider the impact of some of French cinema's leading institutions and figures, de Van's own testimony in a series of personal interviews, as well as, once again, her spirited self-presentation in the trade press as an ambitious, cineliterate debutant filmmaker. This methodology yields salient perspectives. If the *cinéma du corps* represents a form of contemporary avant-garde, then how and why might a young, first-time filmmaker manage her career to make such divisive films? Reversing the equation, what opportunities does this contested filmmaking model actually create?

Here, a defining context for de Van, vital to her career and the dynamism of the entire French cinema industry, is the role of the national film school system. Although the national French film school system is historically maligned

—derided by many icons, from the New Wave generation to Theo Angelou-polos to Christophe Gans—today it is a means for potentially rapid advance-ment, on- and off-screen. De Van's institutional encounters, in this light, proved professionally formative. After completing her baccalauréat with a literary emphasis, de Van briefly studied philosophy before applying to film school. In 1993, aged twenty-two, she enrolled in la Fémis, which since its creation in 1986 has replaced IDHEC as arguably France's most important film school. Housed today at the site of the old Pathé studios on the rue Fran-coeur in Paris, la Fémis is state-mandated to provide technical, cultural, and artistic training in the field of cinema and audio-visual media. The school is both particular in its admissions and demanding in its training—up to 1,500 applicants compete for just 40 annual openings, producing such notable graduates as Arnaud Desplechin, Noémie Lvovsky, and dozens more whose high profile careers inform French cinema, and this book.

La Fémis is best thought of as the domain of the elite, unapologetically selective, where students practice basic techniques, but are also led to be-come cineliterate innovators. It is, as a result, a source of filmmakers who are unfazed by the prospect of cinematic risk-taking. As Prédal argues, students at la Fémis "learn their craft, but above all are encouraged to create, to ex-press themselves, to develop their style: it is a school of artists more than professionals, those prepared to join the exclusive club of auteur-directors and not become mere metteurs-en-scène."[43] De Van's experience of la Fémis instilled her with belated creative direction, and in retrospect she considers its intensive yet inventive technical exercises, which culminate in six-month practical final examinations, to have directly motivated her full-time work in cinema. As she remembers it: "When I started out I couldn't do anything by myself, and if I hadn't been to la Fémis I wouldn't have done anything. You need great strength to direct, and I just wouldn't have had the courage. Paying my dues in la Fémis, I learned to work with finances, and also a crew, so I could do in a few years what people might take ten years to achieve else-where, because filmmaking is such a fight. I have to fight now, but now I'm stronger. For me, la Fémis was a pleasure, with great teachers."[44] Inspired by this environment, de Van saw herself as not merely a trainee, but rather as someone actively directed to carry out textual *research*. Subsequently, in her experiments behind and before the camera, as writer, director, and actress, de Van began to conceive of film as the means for startlingly intimate studies— artistic diagnoses—of the body, often her own, on-screen. De Van pursued the disjunctive capacity of film, its ability to divorce psychology from physi-cality by displacing the body of a real person into abstracted images. In what amounts to another declaration of *cinéma du corps* principles, in her work de Van conceived simultaneously how she wanted to treat a fissure between mind and body, while also, in so doing, probing the limits of her cinematic repertoire. As de Van analyzes this conception process:

> I was drawn to the subject because of the feeling that the body could become a stranger, that there might be a distance between consciousness and the life of the body. . . . And there was the idea that the main character, this girl, could try to investigate these sensations. So the challenging aspect was one of my main motivations, the key. But even in my short films there is always this problem: How to explore something that I don't know how to represent cinematically, how to convey these feelings, with always the constant threat of failure. . . . And I'm drawn to do this with images, using cinema — as opposed to, for example, theater, which I don't like. I need something spectacular, which excites my eyes, which I can't just see in the street.[45]

As Carrie Tarr points out somewhat dryly, these textual self-explorations extend to roles that de Van perhaps felt she could not impose on someone else.[46] (De Van's own deceptively simple premise was that, "More than being an actor, I wanted to film myself.")[47] All these points of departure led initially to a pair of shorts made while de Van was taking classes: *Bien sous tous rapports* (1996) and *Rétention* (1997), both of which, in their unflinching material and style, very much reflect the unusual technical and creative liberty endorsed by la Fémis. *Bien sous tous rapports* concerns a young woman, played by de Van, who is disturbed by her parents while attempting to perform oral sex, and then, bizarrely, instructed closely by them on how to improve her technique. *Rétention*, also enacted by de Van herself, depicts a young woman who becomes neurotically obsessed with her own physicality, exploring the contours of her form, preoccupied with her bodily functions, eventually refusing to discard any waste products from her own body.

These early ventures synthesized de Van's creative interest in the filmed — hence, stylized and dysfunctional — body. The shorts also gave de Van exposure and allowed her to network. In 1997, upon her formal graduation, in keeping with school tradition, all of the student films were shown publicly, a screening at which François Ozon, another la Fémis graduate, was present. Ozon's response to de Van's shorts was instant excitement. Struck by her direction, theme, and performances, he on the spot declared her to be his feminine double, a perfect match for his filmmaking sensibility, and so invited her to work with him. Thus followed a fruitful symbiosis, an informal yet concentrated creative partnership characterized by de Van as "fed day by day through our discussions . . . about murky and difficult engagements with the body."[48] De Van took lead roles in Ozon's *See the Sea* and *Sitcom*, collaborated as scriptwriter on the former and *Criminal Lovers*, then cowrote for him *Under the Sand* (*Sous le sable*, 2000) and *8 Women* (*8 Femmes*, 2002). Out of these encounters came a series of successful psychodramas, many of which link to the emergence of the *cinéma du corps* charted earlier in this chapter. *See the Sea*, for example, follows the festering psychosis of Tatiana, a young wanderer, performed in a glacial deadpan by de Van, who becomes sexually and emotionally fixated upon a young mother, whom she eventually lacerates and murders. *Sitcom*, a pitch-black comedy, situates de Van's character at the epicenter of an imploding bourgeois French family; she paralyses herself from the waist down after a failed suicide attempt, yet still attempts physical sensation through acts of sexual sadomasochism. Both of de Van's roles, in addition, are scripted and performed for long periods in silence, making her abrupt violent and sexual outbursts seem less tied to psychological motivations. A gap emerges, once again, between mind and body.

Like the work of other filmmakers attuned to the *cinéma du corps*—the insidious cyber-pornography conspiracy in Assayas's *Demonlover*, the rape-revenge course of Noé's *Irréversible*, the bloody bouts of sexual cannibalism in Denis's *Trouble Every Day*—much of Ozon's noncomedic work with de Van represents sociosexual deviance through acts which are horrifically, but above all physically, criminal. These are films about violence perpetrated on others, rendering victimized bodies as objects subject to graphically brutal urges. At the (amicable) conclusion of her collaborations with Ozon, however, de Van's work systematically inverted this motif, exploring dysfunctional physicality that manifests through violence turned instead on *oneself*, on one's own body. What emerges, in style and content, is perhaps the most incisive statement yet of the *cinéma du corps*—de Van's embodiment of corporeal malaise through self-mutilation.

In My Skin has its origins in an accident that de Van had as an eight-year-old, when a car ran over her right leg. The limb was left horrifically wounded, the rough edge of a snapped bone protruding through its flesh and skin. Years later, de Van recalls things from remarkable distance: "I felt no sense of panic, no pain, even though I should have passed out. I saw my leg as just another object, a deformed object . . . a scrap. . . . Later, at school, my scars became a kind of game. My friends and I amused ourselves by sticking them with needles, because my skin had become numb there. I felt proud, but at the same time this insensitivity was frightening."[49] From this childhood experience, and, later, her formative work in cinema, came de Van's motivations as a filmmaker. She challenges a basic cinematic convention that treats bodies on-screen as the means for character formation: as physically active, outgoing

Esther (Marina de Van) in the final sequence of *In My Skin*

and functional, more often than not traditionally attractive, and, crucially, the site of readable behavior from which derives overt psychology. Instead, de Van dwells on the body in and of itself, probing its nature as material substance, a sometimes compromised organic vessel or container.[50] Represented through de Van's camera, the body becomes matter abstracted from mind, the source of peculiarly remote sensation, or else, complete disassociation and passive disconnect.

An initially classical narrative, with strategic fissures that recall the approach of Noé, Denis, and Dumont, *In My Skin* concerns Esther, played by de Van. At a party, she scrapes open the calf of her right leg after stumbling on to exposed metal outside her host's house. Despite the severity of the injury Esther seems barely concerned, delaying her visit to the hospital (where a bemused doctor asks her, "Are you sure it's your leg?") and apparently feeling little distress. But increasingly she becomes fixated on the wounds. At home, she worries her sutures and reopens her cuts, much to the rising exasperation of her boyfriend, Vincent (Laurent Lucas). At her office, where she works as an international market researcher, Esther starts to tear at the leg itself, finding relief in widening her gashes and making them bleed. The self-mutilations worsen. At an important business dinner, Esther slashes her arm with a knife under the table, then digs her fork into the wounds, drifting apart from the conversation as her irritated boss looks on. To mask her self-inflicted abrasions from Vincent, Esther even stages a car wreck. So advanced does Esther's (self-)alienation become, that in the latter stages of the film, like *Persona*, the narrative breaks down. Esther isolates herself, and a series of graphic tableaux depict subjectively her violent explorations of her body. No specific contexts, or explanations, or resolution are granted, and the film ends with a repeated series of tracking close-ups of Esther alone in a hotel room, her body maimed but her face and emotions at least partly calmed.

At the center of *In My Skin*, de Van's Esther, like many of the stark and physically brutalized characterizations in the *cinéma du corps*, is an extraordinary feat of performance. De Van as writer-director obliges de Van as actress to enact scenes of complete physical exposure and extreme vulnerability, at times verging on humiliation. The subject of the film, unmistakably, is a protracted examination and systematic analysis of de Van's own body; its narrative is inscribed on to her flesh. Just after Esther's injury, for example, in an extended medium shot that is lit harshly to flatten her skin tones, the camera tracks over de Van's naked body as she inspects herself closely, obsessively, pinching and pulling at her oddly elastic skin while lying in a bathtub. Later, at a public swimming pool, a terrified Esther is accosted by a group of male work colleagues who grab her and drench her with water, causing blood to seep through her trouser leg, darkening her thigh area like a menstrual stain. It is suggestive to link such images to a feminist agenda, but de Van herself downplays this reading, insisting that Esther's estrangement is corporeal and not gender specific, an abstracting form of narcissism that craves tangible release.

Perhaps inevitably, some critics treat Esther/de Van's behavior as repulsive, a rather pessimistic reading. Tarr, for instance, characterizes it as a form of the monstrous feminine, deriving from Julia Kristeva an interpretation of deeds that are "images of abjection . . . [Esther] looks subhuman, even insect-like, as she sets about the cutting or brings her blood-soaked toes up to her blood-soaked face to wipe her eyes."[51] But de Van herself strenuously rejects this approach, citing audience reactions from numerous public engagements she made to support her feature's limited release; responses I can verify after a number of screenings I have curated. A more productive line of inquiry is to analyze Esther on-screen as active not passive, a sympathetic albeit traumatized human being rather than as a feminine grotesque. Certainly, *In My Skin* treads a fine line between stylistic immersion, replete with undeniably lyrical qualities, and offputting scenes of corporeal aversion. Again, in de Van's own testimony:

I really wanted the audience to be affected strongly. . . . What was most important for me was the emotion of her curiosity, of the anguish you can feel at your body's disconnection from you. It's a very human emotion. . . . Because my subject was in the material of the body I couldn't hide the blood, I couldn't hide the gestures, but even in scenes of incisions or cutting, I systematically avoided filming the knife plunging down, evoking violence that way. On the contrary, in scenes like the one where Esther licks at her cuts, I aimed for a kind of sensuality . . . while there was something very desperate in Esther's condition, there was also something very childish and childlike, especially in how she uses her mouth. At many of the screenings I attended, I did feel the audience was moved, but not in a negative or aggressive way . . . they had sympathy for her not as a sick person, but because they identified with her curiosity . . . that her nature was neither hysterical nor destructive.[52]

De Van's point about the childish nature of these violent acts, Esther's irresistible yet anarchic corporeal cravings, also recalls Vera Chytilová's *Daisies* (1966). This seminal yet still neglected proto-feminist film, more overtly political than de Van's work, is an avant-garde satire in which two characters named Marie roam destructively through a chaotic, often fast-motion landscape of cabaret bars, communist party feasts, train stations and the countryside, repeatedly attacking their own bodily images, on-screen, with scissors. Liberation and (self-)destruction uneasily coexist.

Such were the demands of Esther that de Van instilled herself forcibly with an impartiality about her own body, the film's raw material. For a year in advance she carried out actorly exercises designed to increase her objectivity and self-detachment: walking around in uncomfortable shoes, buying and wearing clothes that she disliked, growing her fingernails to awkward lengths, and so on. Closer to the shoot, she hired an acting coach, Marc Adjadj, to dissect her mannerisms, and reinterpret for her the physical nuances of the script that she herself had written. The end product is that de Van's acting technique drastically pares down her character's emotional range. More so than the roles with Ozon, she portrays Esther in a kind of becalmed withdrawal (with tiny deviations) that is austere, but strangely engrossing, at times faintly tragic. Even in scenes of acute physical crisis, when Esther literally turns on herself, de Van allows herself only flickers of facial response, a neutrality that does not crave sympathy from the viewer. In the throes of graphic traumas — hands and fingers stab, fingers make incisions, blood oozes and congeals — de Van's eyes and face often remain neutral or completely glazed, in stasis, betraying only an eerie calm.

While de Van resists certain broader interpretations, *In My Skin* does trace Esther's plight to the personal costs of careerism and late-phase capitalism. As Jacques Mandelbaum suggests, there is an "opposition of the individual body and of the social body, a backlash against the fragmentary corporatization of humanity."[53] Thus, the film's opening frames are divided in half, with color filters, as views of faceless modern buildings, office blocks around la Défense, offer soulless establishing shots. These banal, functional concrete structures, moreover, preface a *mise-en-scène* of Esther's own body arranged over an office console, as if she herself is part of the furniture, a business appliance, physical extensions of an enterprise. Like Sciamma in *Water Lilies*, de Van makes an understated point about the stunted psychological growth of young women inhabiting brutalist architecture. *In My Skin* is also a feminine counterpart to Jean-Marc Moutout's equally dispassionate *Work Hard, Play Hard* (*Violence des échanges en milieu tempéré*, 2003), which similarly opens in the confines of la Défense, about a young (male) executive trainee whose personality morphs as he masterminds the downsizing of a regional production center. (Unlike Esther, Moutout's protagonist suffers moments of anguish but ultimately prospers implacably: getting a promotion, going on a climactic beach vacation, and replacing his single-mother girlfriend with a less moralistic companion.)

Throughout, *In My Skin* underlines ironically that as Esther rises professionally, she unravels personally and physically. After she is promoted, Esther's colleague Sandrine (Léa Drucker), her only confidante, abruptly abandons her—failing pointedly to help when she is assaulted at the swimming pool. The motif of professional/personal disjunction also emerges in *In My Skin*'s pivotal sequence—a set piece widely admired by critics—which takes place during an abortive business dinner, as Esther tunes out of the facile professional dialogue (about that contemporary corporate cliché: Western expansion into burgeoning Asian markets) and de Van reveals her literal disembodiment with a shot of Esther's severed forearm, a life-like prosthesis, lying on the table in front of her. (A similar albeit less overt device is used in Pierre-Olivier Mornas's *As if Nothing Happened* [*Comme si de rien n'était*, 2003]), when a terminally ill character's uncontrollably shaking hand is framed by itself, separately, as if divorced from the body to which it nominally belongs.)

Indeed, *In My Skin*'s narrative trajectory exposes the lack of social surroundings that might safeguard Esther against such drastic physical decline. Such materials link de Van's film again to the alienating social contexts of the *cinéma du corps*, in which husbands, wives, and lovers prove inadequate, supportive family units are strikingly absent, corporate hierarchies involve themselves not at all, and forces of authority or government fail to intervene. This anxiety about absent or fragmented communities in some ways reflects contemporary France, which has become increasingly marked by social solitude. National census data confirm that in the early twenty-first century 31 percent of all French households now consist of a man or woman living alone, 18.5 percent female versus 12.5 percent male; nearly a third of France's domiciles are now not cohabited.[54] More troubling is the fact that single-inhabitancy is on the rise. In 1990, the average number of people per French household was 2.57; by 2030 it is projected to dwindle to 2.1, an 18 percent decline.[55] The issue of single occupancy is regularly highlighted in the French press, it must be said, when natural disasters like summer heat waves or flu outbreaks lead to dead bodies being discovered days later; these are human beings alone when most at risk. On-screen, by extension, devoid of the civilizing contexts of collective society, human behavior in the *cinéma du corps* is typically reduced to its most primal, atavistic instincts. Esther, an iconic *cinéma du corps* protagonist, is left socially isolated, personally traumatized, and dangerously by herself.

Coupled to this is a central paradox of *In My Skin*, that Esther's increasingly violent ruptures are grounded in the familiar and everyday. In contrast to David Cronenberg's *Crash* (1996) — a cited influence on *In My Skin* and an assigned film at la Fémis,[56] referenced by Esther's own abortive car accident — de Van avoids connecting self-mutilation to obvious deviance or body horror. Unlike *Crash*, *In My Skin* depicts neither a nocturnal underworld of social outcasts, nor a shared conspiracy of self-abuse drawn from pent-up nihilism and rage. Instead, Esther exists in a blank, impassive diegetic world. Her days are spent hunched over a computer monitor, surrounded by paper clips and reports, busy with data entry, punctuated briefly by stressful exchanges at work and home. When Esther cuts herself for the first time, crouched in an office archive, de Van pointedly cuts away to yet more shots of sterile glass skyscrapers, the oblivious la Défense cocoons. Moreover, while Esther's actions offer unstated responses to a numbing routine, they typically take place in bathrooms or bedrooms, as extensions of conventional rituals like grooming, cleaning, and self-examination, the same sensuous trajectory of *Trouble Every Day*. Over the course of *In My Skin*, Esther's behavior moves her simply and undramatically from self-scrutiny to self-injury. As de Van suggests, furthermore, in contrast to the world around her, these self-explorations are arrestingly intimate, showing "a kind of tenderness and curiosity, a softness and sweetness in the way Esther touches her own skin and blood."[57]

There is more, however, to both *In My Skin* and the *cinéma du corps* than social diagnostics. Like many of its related contemporaries, *In My Skin* is in part an experiment in lyrical cinema. At pivotal moments of Esther's condition, the film attempts to convey perceptual experiences directly on-screen; it deploys poetic aesthetic techniques, sensory impressions that stylistically outrun and strategically overwhelm its narrative. De Van, a self-declared formalist like Denis, prepared comprehensively in this context. She shot ex-

Split-screen framing during Esther's self-mutilations in *In My Skin*

tensive stylistic tests of each and every shot on digital video before exposing any celluloid, storyboarded meticulously, outlined arrays of editing options in advance, and met repeatedly with her cinematographer, Pierre Barougier, to develop framing, lighting, compositional, and optical effects. The results are formidable, sometimes again recalling the work of Brakhage—particularly *Dog Star Man* (1961–1964)—as well as, more recently, the abstracting and/or non-representational stylistic devices which inform *Irreversible, Sombre, Trouble Every Day*, and many other *cinéma du corps* texts. In another remark that connects directly to *cinéma du corps* practice, de Van describes her conceptual project as trying, "to privilege eye and mind . . . to enter into [Esther's] perceptions and emotions to create a deeper association with her intimate and sensorial experience."[58]

Such immersive formal strategies induce profound, and profoundly alienating, cinematic sensations. Just before Esther's climactic breakdown, for example, as she flees from an urban environment that suddenly registers as claustrophobic and threatening, de Van's stylistic design becomes radically amorphous. On the soundtrack, the aural balance and tone shift abruptly, rendering the noise of beeping supermarket check-outs and bustling, chatty shoppers as muted, discordant, and obscure. The image jumps between fast and normal motion, with passersby blurring past Esther in distorted point-of-view shots. The camera racks focus unevenly, as planes of color, bright light, and texture collide and juxtapose. Most jarringly of all, the film then shifts to a three-minute split-screen sequence of paired handheld images that represent Esther's state of withdrawal. Twinned shots move us inexorably from the banal (images of groceries, plastic bags, furniture, a hotel room interior) to the corporeal (swathes of blood, gouged flesh, ravaged body parts). The design hints at Esther's recoil and collapse, but its effects extend beyond this, becoming a pure cinema of nonrepresentational collage. Olivier de Bruyn calls the outcome a "poetics of pain";[59] de Van links the split-screen device to a wounding of the screen itself, the frame bisected, our perceptual vantage point cut asunder. From a synthesized and socialized physical whole, at this point of (non-)narrative climax, Esther is left a raw, chaotically subjective perceptual composite.

Building from such elements, a focal point of both *In My Skin* and the *cinéma du corps* arises from its impact on the spectator. Much of the hostility directed at these films centers on their ability to shock, to disturb, and consciously displease their audiences. But why need this effect be considered in wholly negative terms? So long theorized and conceived of as an entirely passive recipient, a pair of eyes and ears in thrall, the spectator of the *cinéma du corps* is instead a profoundly active participant. Set before *In My Skin* and its contemporaries, our role is challenging but exhilarating. We are compelled to assemble narrative across dissonant ellipses and omissions; we are confronted with performances at their most raw and visceral; we are experientially subsumed by virtuoso stylistic practices, engaged by abstract, perceptual cinematic data. Those I interviewed after watching *In My Skin* spoke of the experience as having been neither easy nor instantly enjoyable, but rather as unexpectedly rewarding, satisfying in large part *because* of the demands exerted by de Van. Here, again, the *cinéma du corps* is cognitively stimulating, unexpected, and uncompromising, brutally direct.

Memoirs of Matter: Diane Bertrand's *The Ring Finger*

As we have seen already, the *cinéma du corps* works through bodily tableaux: exacting physical encounters conveyed by vivid cinematic designs. In this light, a little discussed yet equally memorable part of this filmmaking is that alongside its violent sequences are more beatific, luxuriantly corporeal set pieces. In *Irreversible*, for example, there is the protracted long take through a translucent shower curtain of Marcus and Alex kissing each other, drenched and naked, roaming in their bathroom and through their apartment, the relaxed, good-humored rhythms of this most intimate behavior built around the improvisations of Cassel and Bellucci, a married couple off-screen. Most critics, in the same vein, resist the more sensuous, even innocent qualities of Esther's self-directed passions during *In My Skin*. But this lyrically immersive aspect, the equation of fleeting tenderness with compromised materiality, an idea invoked vehemently by Denis, de Van, and others, is undeniably central. Hence, a final test case for the *cinéma du corps*—a concluding defense and prospect for its artistic possibilities—is that its physical representations actually epitomize film as a medium, its capacity to distill corporeal ephemera, making permanent that which passes, fixing on-screen what is merely transitory. This evanescent world of the body is what concretizes the *cinéma du corps*. Its affinity is for what resonates, lingers on, after transient states of physical harmony and/or duress.

Pursuing this, a poignant counterpart to the more assaulting components of the *cinéma du corps* cycle is Diane Bertrand's *The Ring Finger*, a graceful, enigmatic, yet almost totally overlooked recent French film. *The Ring Finger* is based on a novella by Yoko Ogawa, who is, with Haruki Murakami, Japan's most internationally acclaimed contemporary fiction writer; both are often described as magical realists. In an unspecified time and place, *The Ring Finger* follows Iris (Olga Kurylenko), who works on the production line at a lemonade bottling plant. On the job, she gashes open her ring finger on broken glass, her blood welling onto the bottles that hurtle past, a piece of her body lost to the factory's industrial cacophony. Echoing Esther in *In My Skin*, Iris is both stunned and energized by her body's sudden exposure. Leaving her job, she relocates to a port town and becomes the assistant, and soon the detached lover, of a naturalist (Marc Barbé). He runs an institute that archives objects for its clients, items that represent, or embody, permanent repositories of memory. These specimens, however, signify destitution and a need for catharsis as much as nostalgia: like three decaying mushrooms that grew on the ruins of a woman's burned-down home; a kidney stone that nearly proved fatal; or, for another customer in mourning, a musical score composed by a lover days before he abandoned her.

Like much of the *cinéma du corps*, *The Ring Finger* alternates between the drab everyday, stasis, and moments of abrupt agitation or tension. The film records Iris's repetitive secretarial tasks (filing, conducting interviews, collecting and organizing specimens) as well as incidentally fantastic asides: silent visits from a boy who may or may not exist; rumors that her predecessors all vanished; a pair of shoes Iris receives from the naturalist that will eventually entrap her, she is warned. The film ends with a self-destruction, or self-abstraction, as ironically purifying as Esther's. Here, Iris wordlessly prepares her own scarred finger as a sample, descends calmly to the naturalist's laboratory in the institute's depths, opens its doors, then disappears as a burst of bright white light fills the image.

From a literary perspective, Ogawa's work is well suited to the ambivalent registers of the *cinéma du corps*. Her highly cinematic texts create a *mise-en-*

Iris (Olga Kurylenko) holds up a physical sample in *The Ring Finger*

scène of entropy that is paradoxically poetic. Held in thrall to defining moments from their past, Ogawa's characters cling to totemic objects or after-echoes of visceral sensations. These recollections are strong, all-consuming, yet they do not liberate; Ogawa's memory specimens are part symbiotic, part parasitic, enslaving the hosts that bear them. *Dormitory*, a companion tale to *The Ring Finger*, describes a woman drawn back to her deteriorating old college lodgings, managed by a triple amputee whose physical decline parallels the crumbling building. Prefacing the story, Ogawa reflects on the materiality of experience, the unsettlingly tactile weight of memory. This model, slipping between detailed reportage and bodily sensation, not only characterizes Bertrand's techniques in filming *The Ring Finger*, but also the insistent, abstracting intricacies of corporeal style we have traced among its *cinéma du corps* contemporaries. After an unexpected sound triggers a mental flashback, Ogawa's first person narrator recounts its "quaking, a current, even a throb. . . . I attempted analogies: the icy murmur of a fountain in winter when a coin strikes the bottom; the quaking of the fluid in the inner ear as you get off a merry-go-round; the sound of the night passing through the palm of your hand still gripping the phone after your lover hangs up. . . . But I doubted these would help anyone understand."[60]

On-screen, *The Ring Finger* reduces psychology to pieces of physicality, memories entirely configured by matter. Much of the film consists of languid studies of objects that are poised, like their human owners, in suspended animation, held up for cinematic scrutiny. In microcosm, the motif emerges in Bertrand's opening sequence. At the institute, a young burn victim removes her mushrooms from a silver box and places them in the naturalist's custody—they are all that remain in the aftermath of the fire that destroyed her home and past life, leaving scars that ravaged her right cheek. As piano music plays through the opening titles, Bertrand expressively saturates these objects, befitting their status as weirdly beautiful, hypnotic embodiments of trauma. Organic pieces that float captive in a test tube, the chunks tumble slowly through space, bathed in light, strangely timeless now, enveloped in liquid and clouds of bubbles. From these images we move into more ethereal patterns of light and darkness, gradually discernible as glass, parts of the bottles on a busy factory production line. Introduced for the first time, Iris then cuts her finger open on one jagged edge, recoiling in dismay, and the film's formulation is complete: impersonal things as lyrical incarnations, personalities constrained by vulnerabilities of the flesh, matter over mind.

Following this psychological logic, and in keeping with the asocial parameters of the *cinema du corps*, *The Ring Finger* treats people as (usually nameless) phantom entities, drones of the numbing present, going through the motions of daily routines, defined, if at all, by the labors they perform. Such figures include the naturalist, a hotel keeper, a shoe cleaner, dock workers, and an aging telephonist who lives in the institute. Long stretches of silence punctuate their comings and goings. Even the identity of Iris, almost always on-screen, is largely opaque, motivated only by her flight from her initial injury, her loveless but sexual relationship with the naturalist, and the understated tie she has with a sailor who shares her hotel room, sleeping there while she works by day, with whom she never speaks. Instead of showing readable human beings operating in a functional society, *The Ring Finger* and the *cinéma du corps* boil down the world to corporeal processes, vestigial connections forged through one iconic bodily act, which is then embodied (or imprisoned) here within one iconic relic. Iris and the naturalist begin a sexual relationship in an old bath house deep within the institute — he undresses her, penetrates her, then interrogates her about a specimen of her most horrific experience — yet their coupling is more sinisterly consummated by the red shoes he obliges her to wear. A second montage, of close-up fragments of their entwined body parts, does show a more nominally erotic encounter. But when Iris is asked by the shoe cleaner about whether she loves the man who gave her the shoes, she replies: "I'm only sure of the feeling of not being able to leave him."

Elsewhere, Bertrand traces this deadened capacity for spontaneous feeling through an abstracting, mechanized *mise-en-scène*. Iris inhabits atavistic spaces that cocoon her, like Esther's workplace in *In My Skin*, the nocturnal Parisian netherworlds of *Irreversible* and *Trouble Every Day*, and the despoiled wilderness of *Twentynine Palms*. Bertrand shows Iris in motion through landscapes of almost Gothic industrialization, condensing the last two centuries into an ambiguously threatening backdrop, economically barren. Endlessly,

Iris dwarfed by the industrial landscape in *The Ring Finger*

Iris comes and goes over rusting metal bridges, past decaying warehouses and wind turbines, through hollowed-out wharves whose only signs of life are the laborious movements of cranes, their hanging hooks (one of which she swings on during a bizarre fantasy sequence) and drowsily chugging cargo barges. When Iris arrives at the docks for the first time, famished and exhausted, a foreman waves her away with a symbolic brush-off: "No, it's too dangerous here, no work—go away."

To amplify the sense of alienation, Bertrand resorts to set-ups with extremely long lenses, condensing the on-screen spaces, blurring or merging Iris's body into the meshes of these grey, claustrophobic panoramas. Occasionally, moreover, Bertrand sexualizes the industrialized urban corridors. Iris abandons her rendezvous with the sailor, the only personal (and entirely non-corporeal) relationship she cultivates, when she sees him being approached by a bar hostess. At one point, more pessimistic still, Iris ventures through a red-light district, daubed with graffiti, past rows of prostitutes on display like over-lit shop window dummies; she is alternately intrigued and horrified, finally catching the eye of one girl who regards her blankly, imploringly. Scenes like these offer one culmination of *The Ring Finger* and the haunting social diagnoses of the *cinéma du corps*: people are objects, objects are people.

As we have seen, then, *The Ring Finger* explores how material things come to embody memories, repositories for corporeal exchanges that are unavoidable, that cannot be left behind. Extending this idea, we can equate the *cinéma du corps* itself with encounters that are indelible, both on- and off-screen. Critical testimonies, my own included, confirm the experiences of the actual *screening events*, as well as the materials of films like *Irreversible*, to be literally unforgettable. On this point, the contested but undeniable long-term impact of the *cinéma du corps*, some critics are especially forceful, ambitious about the status of these films. Marie-Noëlle Tranchant, analyzing *The Ring Finger* and relating it to its peers, traces this type of cinema's emerging importance as a continuation of France's cultural heritage. She argues: "One can, perhaps, be disconcerted and dubious when faced with such a bizarre cinematic object, but it encompasses what Baudelaire loved to discover in a painting or poem: *A sum of ideas and reveries.*"[61]

Tranchant's reflection moves us to the issue of the *cinéma du corps'* cultural and artistic revival. Without doubt, the phenomena we have outlined here have either loosely influenced or directly galvanized an assortment of inventive, exciting filmmakers. These stylistic and thematic principles now inform the careers of both women and men, French directors and those of other nationalities, newcomers fresh from la Fémis and veterans long acclimatized to the slings and arrows of festival filmmaking. This chapter began by exploring some of the best-known practitioners of the *cinéma du corps*, but to this ongoing tendency can also be linked fellow participants including Bertrand Bonello, Laurent Bouhnik, Jean-Claude Brisseau, Olivier Dahan, Xavier Giannoli, Christophe Honoré, Didier le Pêcheur, Robert Salis, and others. The list grows, as does its catalogue of achievements, its emphasis on cinematic and artistic experimentation.

More broadly, French film culture, historically so often the impetus for major developments in world cinema, is today once again of central significance. Nowadays, assertions about the irredeemable banality or even terminal decline of modern filmmaking abound. As cinema consolidates itself in the twenty-first century it does so under fire—the medium is routinely declared past its prime, infantilized, over-reliant on CGI spectacle, sucked dry by the demands of cautious global media conglomerates, and, more insidiously, called stylistically formulaic and without innovation in both the mainstream and festival circuits alike. To such ubiquitous discourse, the *cinéma du corps* offers a sharp rejoinder. A generation of contemporary French filmmakers, those discussed in this chapter notably included, is clearly rising to this challenge. Assertive in its radical techniques and startlingly—albeit disconcertingly—creative in its design, the *cinéma du corps* conveys forcibly its provocative materials, these fraught on-screen treatments of the body that evoke new levels of perceptual engagement from the viewer. As Olivier Joyard suggests, indeed, this group is collectively approaching "what may well be the next frontier of cinema."[62] From film schools to film festivals and beyond, with its *cinéma du corps* French filmmaking has found a distinctive new cutting edge.

CHAPTER THREE

Popular Cinema, Pop-Art Cinema

Most accounts of recent French cinema gloss over or disparage its popular sector;[1] they also assume that the mainstream is completely disconnected from the more artistically respectable, hence widely studied, realms of auteur filmmaking. This chapter engages with these inherited notions, disputing both. In the first place, of course, France's film mainstream is the fulcrum of its industry's battle to retain its domestic market share, combating American imports, and its fluctuating success headlines the CNC's annual reviews.[2] In this competitive context, popular French cinema is defined by its commercial attractions: an affinity for genres (principally the comedy and the policier or crime thriller); its use of France's dynamic indigenous star system; and, crucially, its ability to target the interests of local audiences while occasionally adopting aspects of mass cinemas abroad, thinking globally. Besides this mass-oriented template, however, there is the more severely neglected phenomenon of French pop-art cinema. The relationship between France's popular and arthouse filmmaking has in contemporary times evolved, as fractious and frequently oppositional, yet in an increasing number of cases, fascinatingly symbiotic. This is a new generation of filmmakers rejecting the traditional French dichotomy of auteurs creating high art versus *metteurs-en-scène* cranking out broad entertainments. Energetic and productive dialogue is ongoing across these rival camps.

In fact, French pop-art cinema today calls for revision, if not complete overhaul, of the paradigm that lingers, like so many others, from the New Wave era. The hereditary mantra is summarized by Susan Hayward and Ginette Vincendeau, who suggest of this late 1950s period that the "success of the *politique des* auteurs . . . and the films of the New Wave drove a wedge between 'auteur' and 'popular' cinema."[3] Famously, in print and on-screen, the *Cahiers* cohort declared France's commercial cinema to be ossified, so terminally impersonal that it was time for artistic revolution. Although the idea that the New Wave broke outright with the 1950s mainstream has been overstated ever since, and is itself ready for review,[4] the notion of a French popular and intellectual film division nonetheless gained widespread currency, and persists. As we will discover, although orthodox antagonisms still exist between French cinemas high and low—the distinction has even been exacerbated by recent hyper-commercial production trends—the conversation no longer ends there. While French popular cinema has itself developed apace in the twenty-first century, the emergence of a pop-art cinema, a fruitful coalition of textual means, is now inspiring many of France's most skilful and cineliterate filmmakers.

French popular cinema is characterized by its market orientation, a bottom-up ideology that appeals to the sensibilities of a broad audience. This can manifest on-screen through ribald humor that embraces mainstream culture and skewers elitism. Take, for instance, the assertive model of mass film that begins Laurent Baffie's *Car Keys* (*Les Clefs de bagnole*, 2003). Baffie, known for cultural satire and candid camera pranks on French television, plays himself, pitching his script to luminaries such as Claude Berri, Dominique Farrugia, and Alain Terzian. As Baffie outlines his premise—one man's search for lost car keys, which ninety minutes later turn out to have been in his left trouser pocket all along—the film's style is deliberately unsophisticated: its focus shifts erratically, a make-up artist wanders in and out of shot, the soundtrack is acoustically uneven, and digital videography makes the image fuzzy and overexposed. Playing up its lowbrow mindset, *Car Keys* also offers ironic juxtapositions of *mise-en-scène*. Baffie's pitch lurches further into self-parody ("Yes, it's an adventure, it's a quest, his rite of passage, an allegory!") while the camera picks out totems of filmic prestige behind the producers' desks: framed posters of modern auteurist classics like Michael Haneke's *The Piano Teacher* (2001) and David Lynch's *Mulholland Drive* (2001), festival trophies from Europe and North America, Berri's sculpture of a *cinématographe*, and Farrugia's face inserted into a still from *Citizen Kane* (1941). Unsurprisingly, Baffie fails to win these financiers over. When he is then rebuffed by a gallery of France's leading actors, a quip from Jean Rochefort sums up the film's manifesto as a self-consciously worthless *divertissement*. Directly to camera, Rochefort airily dismisses Baffie with the line, "I've worked with the greatest; I can't work with the lowest!"

While the opening of *Car Keys* defiantly—gleefully—resists sustained interpretation, it nonetheless invites conclusions about popular French film. This would appear to be an unabashedly scurrilous cinema, abandoning all cerebral pretensions. Following Baffie's logic, these films win audiences, not awards; they are incomprehensible to the critical and professional academy; they are self-evidently artless and ephemeral. Ambushing high culture has, furthermore, become something of a trademark for the mainstream French artisan. Consider the title sequence of Jan Kounen's *Dobermann* (1997), in which an animated attack dog urinates on the opening credits, before an abrupt cut takes us to a lavish wedding ceremony in the Notre Dame cathedral. This recent vogue for profaning the sacred may well have begun with Jean-Jacques Beineix's seminal 1980s *cinéma du look* films, especially *Diva*, a thriller about the spectacular, violent chase after a recording of a virtuoso opera performance. Five years later, Beineix made the dichotomy even more explicit in *Betty Blue*, whose infamous opening shot tracks slowly, inexorably, into a close-up of Zorg (Jean-Hugues Anglade) and Betty (Béatrice Dalle) having vocal and passionate sex on a bed over which hangs a reproduction of the Mona Lisa. As brash as they are blatant, Baffie, Kounen, Beineix, and likeminded contemporaries take their skirmishes with high French culture — the bedroom versus the Louvre; visceral thrills and bodily functions versus spiritual contemplations — to the point of stereotype and caricature.

Just as self-confident, however, are the methods of pop-art filmmakers. These ambidextrous figures flit nimbly, but far more sympathetically, back and forth between cultural registers high and low. Mainstream pleasures permeate the rarified materials of the arthouse, as popular and intellectual paradigms interconnect, complete osmosis, on-screen. A case in point is Jean-Michel Ribes's *Musée haut, musée bas* (2008; literally *High Museum, Low Museum*), adapted from his own popular stageplay. The film juggles dozens of characters played by dozens of stars in a chaotic fictional museum, the Malraux. Witticisms about pompous museum habitués mingle with jokes about bourgeois artistic tastes, with a more serious undertow about the politics and materialism of official French culture. Ribes's set pieces balance satire and slapstick: beleaguered male attendants protest that they no longer desire their wives and girlfriends after being surrounded by aesthetic female splendor all day (they congregate out of desperation in the mammoth exhibit); workers lugging crates in the basement mimic the poses of figures in canonical paintings; illegal immigrants arrive from Africa in boxes, to the horror of a management that prefers more "authentic" Third World artifacts; we enter a blank room in which nonplussed but quickly pretentious guests become an avant-garde artist's happening; and there is a café which serves desserts in the form of modern art masterpieces. Shortly after a scene in which a flustered minister is asked to speak about an exhibition consisting of dozens of giant photos of penises, the film ends as a quasi-thriller, as the museum sinks during a massive rainstorm. The final scenes of exodus and destruction, augmented by CGI, move so far from the arena of high art as to recall *Night at the Museum* (2006) and its similarly broad Hollywood sequel. An emblematic pop-art creation, *Musée haut, musée bas* relies upon an intellectual's fertile knowledge of art history for its cultural spoofing; yet this elitist mindset is suffused by the farcical mentality of someone like Baffie, an anti-arrogance artisan. Here and elsewhere, the pop-art filmmaker looks down, grand and sophisticated, but also looks up, pugnaciously.

Prompted by figures like Baffie and Ribes, this chapter discusses contemporary French cinema's popular and pop-art agendas, rethinking the generative force of this enduring low-versus-high equation. We start with four representative genre films and the stars that embody them: Vincent Cassel as Jacques Mesrine in the gangster epics, *L'Instinct de mort* (2008) and *L'Ennemi public no. 1* (2008); and Jean Dujardin in the comedy spy hits, *OSS 117: Cairo, Nest of Spies* (*OSS 117: Le Caire, nid d'espions*, 2006) and *OSS 117: Lost in Rio* (*OSS 117: Rio ne répond plus*, 2009). Building from these popular case studies, we can map the contours of French mainstream cinema, also defining how it diverges from the more radical trends in France's arthouse community. Key here is the recent proliferation of producer-centered, Hollywood-oriented genre filmmaking—most notably the rise of the twenty-first-century French blockbuster—and the extent to which popular French film has become more attuned to international styles and mass conventions; while, conversely, auteur filmmaking oftentimes now survives as oppositional, even counter-cinema.

As counterpoint to all this, we continue by examining the conditions in which France's popular and art cinemas exist as a point of mutual intersection rather than binary division. We will formulate this pop-art template through a series of test cases, initially Valeria Bruni Tedeschi's features *It's Easier for a Camel . . .* (*Il est plus facile pour un chameau . . .*, 2003) and *Actresses* (*Actrices*, 2007). Qualifying the conventional low-versus-high film art model, Bruni Tedeschi emblematizes a segment of contemporary French cinema, inventively cineliterate, interweaving elements of mass-oriented and intellectual cultures. As a result, Bruni Tedeschi's work is representatively hybrid: with a disconcertingly fluid and picaresque approach to narrative design; a multifarious address to the viewer with a comic yet staunchly progressive, feminist approach; a playful use of multimedia; a fierce yet elusive, even contradictory set of political agendas; and, above all, a dexterous conception of film style. In broader terms, Bruni Tedeschi not only highlights the pop-art model, but also its viability as a fertile middle ground in the crowded marketplace of French cinema today. Echoing this, we should then consider a suite of pop-art filmmakers—whose work is either neglected (Robin Campillo, Serge Bozon) or misunderstood and controversial (Olivier Assayas)—who model this exhilarating trajectory, tailoring it to their own needs, altering the old battle-lines of French film culture, from above and below.

Man in the Dark: Vincent Cassel in Jean-François Richet's
L'Instinct de mort and *L'Ennemi public no. 1*

Since the late 1990s, Vincent Cassel has become arguably French cinema's most iconic performer and readily exportable leading man. Cassel's highest profile work so far, the two-part biopic of notorious gangster renegade Jacques Mesrine, *L'Instinct de mort* and *L'Ennemi public no. 1*, directed back-to-back by Jean-François Richet, shows French cinema at its most consummately popular: textually astute about its star and generic materials, commercially aligned to both regional and global audiences. The two films — the first released in France in October 2008, the second a month later — gained 2.3 million and 1.5 million admissions respectively, winning three Césars between them, including Best Actor and Best Director. The films follow Mesrine's turbulent life story: from brutal origins in the French army during the Algerian war, to his rise under Paris ganglord Guido (Gérard Depardieu), his pseudo-Robin Hood crime sprees (robbing banks but never the poor; generously rewarding members of the public who aided his getaways), his exile in North America and Canada, a series of incarcerations and memorable jail breaks (after one escape he actually returned to try and rescue his former comrades), his self-styled media reign as France's anarchistic Public Enemy Number One, and his violent death at the hands of the French police on November 2, 1979. (The police left his bullet-riddled corpse uncovered for over an hour, as if gloating publicly, it was widely claimed at the time.) *L'Instinct de mort* opens with Mesrine's final moments, gunned down in his BMW in broad daylight in the Porte de Clignancourt district of Paris, before flashing back to depict events chronologically. Reflecting this, the two films were actually shot in reverse script order, over nine months, as Cassel progressively lost forty pounds, morphing from bloated kingpin to lithe hoodlum on the make. Significantly, the details of Cassel's self-imposed physical transformation, and the fact that the entire production was tailored to his process, were integral to how the two films were promoted. Clearly, the versatility and commitment of Cassel as star, as much as Mesrine's gangster infamy, was the life blood, the main cultural asset here.

While Mesrine biopics might seem of interest primarily to French audiences, their production was resolutely large scale and international. As director, Richet had based his career on two quintessentially French projects, the urban banlieue drama, *Ma 6-T va crack-er* (1997), and the tortured multi-racial romance, *De l'amour* (2001), before migrating to Hollywood as a genre director for hire, remaking John Carpenter's *Assault on Precinct 13* (2005). In this doubled capacity, a director's popular ambitions within both

French and American film industries, Richet reflects a growing contemporary tendency. Alongside Richet, producer Thomas Langmann was similarly adept in filmmaking across national boundaries. The son of industry veteran Claude Berri, Langmann began as an actor in France then moved to America as a production assistant, working on the sets of *The Godfather, Part III* (1990) and Steven Soderbergh's *Kafka* (1991; produced by Langmann's uncle, Paul Rassam). Preferring the more hands-on role of the American producer, Langmann invented himself as a hypercommercial creative and financial participant. Just thirty-six years old, Langmann came of age with *Asterix at the Olympic Games* (*Astérix aux Jeux Olympiques*, 2008), the third entry in the popular series which he inherited from Berri, who promoted him from associate producer. The Asterix deal was formative: Langmann credited himself as both producer and codirector, and it was the most costly French film to date at 78 million euros (its 6.8 million admissions placed it just outside the top twenty French box office in the first decade of the twenty-first century). On the Mesrine project, Langmann was just as commercially ambitious, raising a 45 million euro budget from French, Canadian and Italian sources, then basing the shoot in France, Spain, Algeria, Canada, and the United States. Taking the distinctively French properties (just like the beloved Goscinny-Uderzo Astérix comic books) of Mesrine and the policier,[5] Langmann rebranded his films to international distributors as *Bonnie and Clyde* (1967) and *Scarface* (1932; 1983) revisited; the films were eventually released widely across Europe, Asia, and Latin America, and in limited engagements in North America. As Langmann described his pitches and approach, "I'm not worried about France, since it's a hot subject here, but abroad we can't sell it as a movie about Mesrine; we have to promote it as a thriller."[6]

Central to Mesrine's mass appeal, though, on-screen and off, is the presence of Vincent Cassel. Langmann trumpeted in interviews a truism repeated by critics ever since—these films would be the ultimate star vehicle. So why put Cassel at the center of an expensive mini-franchise aiming at local and international popularity? To quantify Cassel as a cultural commodity, we should begin by analyzing how his stardom is understood in mainstream circles. A photo-feature on Cassel in the September 2009 *Première* magazine gives an ideal vantage point. Analyzing the actor in interview, the piece identifies what makes Cassel (along with Marion Cotillard) contemporary France's strongest screen export. The first reason, related to the fervor over the *cinéma du corps* we saw in the previous chapter, is, simply, that he starred in *Irreversible*. To Cassel, Noé's iconic film "was my international visa . . . everyone's seen it: Soderbergh, Cronenberg, Heitor Dhalia [who directed Cassel in *A deriva* (2009)] also."[7] *Première* next notes Cassel's linguistic flair (he is fluent in French,

English, Italian, and Portuguese); his celebrity marriage to Monica Bellucci (a regular collaborator whom he met on the set of *L'Appartement* [1996]; he subsequently learned Italian "out of love"); and his skills at consistently negotiating advantageous deals on domestic and international productions. (Cassel has also worked a number of times as his own co-producer.)

Most pivotal to Cassel's stardom, however, Gérard Delorme concludes, is his unparalleled breadth as an international performer. Certainly, Cassel is char-ismatically at home playing demented villains as well as kinetic heroes — he usually gravitates, more distinctively, towards grotesques which embody both extremes, unevenly, at once. In this light, Cassel's star persona grew from his role as Vinz (i.e. himself)[8] in 1995's *Hate*, a gun-toting would-be gangster, a loquacious and childlike anti-hero who craves violent outlet for his pent-up, partly justifiable rage. From here, Cassel's work encompassed an unhinged, gay Russian criminal (in *Eastern Promises* [2007]), an outlandish French *bon vivant* cat burglar (*Ocean's Twelve* [2004] and *Ocean's Thirteen* [2007]), a tripped-out cowboy (*Renegade* [*Blueberry*, 2004]), an intractable secret agent (*Agents secrets* [2004]), and decadent degenerates both foppishly aristocratic (*The Messenger: The Story of Joan of Arc* [1999], *Brotherhood of the Wolf* [*Le Pacte des loups*, 2001]) and vulgarly working class (*Birthday Girl* [2001], *Read My Lips* [*Sur mes lèvres*, 2001], *Sheitan* [2006]). On the point of social class Cassel's screen personality is particularly conflicted. Known for portraying underclass lowlifes, Cassel's own background was quite privileged, as the son of noted actor Jean-Pierre; some of Cassel's earliest work included dubbing Hugh Grant's middle-class comedy turns into French.

In sum, Cassel on-screen is expansively ambiguous, a mesmerizing leading man routinely flavored by psychosis. Far more incautious than his Hollywood counterparts — Tom Cruise's modest risks as a cynical hitman in *Collateral* (2004), say, or Mel Gibson in *Payback* (1999) — Cassel is an old-fashioned *monstre sacré* reinvented for modern audiences. Just as Cassel begins inevitably to charm us, so too does his violent sociopathology lurch into view — the reverse, of course, also being true. A highly representative Cassel screen minute begins the network narrative *Le Plaisir . . . (et ses petits tracas)* (1998). The film fades up to an extreme close-up of Cassel, lurking in gloom, passionately kissing the mouth of a brunette (she breathes, "You're not like the others, I could tell as soon as I saw you") whom in a single take he lovingly appraises, caresses, then garrotes. Cassel endlessly cultivates variations on this enthralling and unbridled creature of excess, an unfettered id, a man in the dark consumed by devouring desires. This screen personality even defines Cassel's 2009 ad campaign for Yves Saint Laurent, modeling their new fragrance, La Nuit de l'Homme (Man's Night). In the still, reproduced worldwide online and in

Multiple Vincent Cassels in the title sequence of *L'Instinct de mort*

glossy magazines like *Vanity Fair*, Cassel, wearing a wrenched-open tuxedo, the knuckles of his left hand gripping powerfully a mahogany chair leg, is shot in evocative, high contrast chiaroscuro. While two glamorous women, eyes shut and mouths open, close in on him from alongside and above, Cassel glares at the camera, imperious and arrogant, almost vampiric, reveling in his control over those under his sway: the two women—and us, his audience.

Langmann's self-promotional claim, that Mesrine would be Cassel's quintessential starring role, is indeed borne out by the design of both *L'Instinct de mort* and *L'Ennemi public no. 1*. Mesrine, a criminal narcissist famed as the man of a thousand faces, allows Richet to reflect on the ambivalent, chameleonic repertoire of France's leading male star-performer. If this is a star vehicle, then Cassel is in the driving seat right from the start, as *L'Instinct de mort*'s opening features an extended montage of geometric split-screens to represent Cassel-Mesrine furtively (or, more accurately, defiantly) leaving his Paris hideout.[9] Much later, we learn that Mesrine is under police surveillance; for now, we simply see an unfolding gallery of Cassels enacting what proved to be Mesrine's final public spectacle. All Cassel—shown singly, doubly, in triplicate, and times six—has to do is walk down the street, get into his BMW with his lover Sylvia (Ludivine Sagnier), and drive off. But *L'Instinct de mort* draws out this banality into nearly five minutes of expressive actorly minutiae. Cassel's dominant performance traits emerge: a meticulous spate of tics, his body and feline features kept in constant motion, each twitch hinting at volatile energies barely contained. Here, Cassel (disguised in curly wig and voluminous goatee) swaggers down the street, bouncing on the balls of his feet like a boxer, hitching his belt and sniffing the air, pinching the bridge of his nose, squinting suspiciously from side to side, clenching his jaw muscles as he glowers at the world around him. Multiplied by the split-screen image windows, Richet showcases Cassel's staccato micro-actions from varied but concurrent points of view. Occasionally, Richet even inserts footage from slightly divergent takes — the strutting Cassel gets to perform part of the scene in different ways *simultaneously*. In effect, *L'Instinct de mort* crafts the showiest of star-entrances, a simple stroll turned into a balletic *mise-en-abyme* of physical display, a dazzling Eisensteinian set piece that invokes Cassel's four years of teenaged training as a circus acrobat and street performer.[10]

Building from this, Richet's films carefully conflate Mesrine's and Cassel's split personalities[11] as they relate to policier archetypes. Like distant echoes of Jean-Paul Belmondo's early gangster roles, in *Classe tous risques* (1960), *Le Doulos* (1962), *Crime on a Summer Morning* (*Par un beau matin d'été*, 1965), and especially *Breathless*, Cassel plays Mesrine as an ambitious but essentially petty thug, a self-serving crook prone to flashes of grandeur, a showy romantic but occasional vicious misogynist. The audacious depravity begins with the young Mesrine's first organized crime — a housebreaking, during which he successfully convinces his wealthy victims, who return home unexpectedly, that he is actually a detective inspecting the crime he has himself just committed. Both Mesrine films delight in these constant dramatic and character reversals. Perhaps the most shocking about-face comes in *L'Instinct de mort*, a popular film which unsurprisingly revels in violent spectacle, with a scene in which Mesrine abruptly sticks a loaded pistol into the mouth of his first wife, Sofia (Elena Anaya), to whom he has been previously devoted, after she threatens to warn the police about his new lapse into robbery. A startling upwards tilt discloses that the assault is watched all the while by Mesrine's unblinking young son. Both films, indeed, obsess over how the sins of the father are visited upon the male next generation.

In similarly authentic screen mobster fashion, Richet highlights the cynical horseplay that prefaces Mesrine's most sadistic rages.[12] During a taxi ride with Guido, for instance, Mesrine makes booming racist jokes about Arabs before he stabs and buries alive Ahmed (Abdelhafid Metalsi), an immigrant pimp who has beaten Mesrine's girlfriend, Sarah (Florence Thomassin, a woman Cassel stalks in *Le Plaisir . . . [et ses petits tracas]*). Passionate yet animalistic, Cassel-Mesrine is at one point symbolically branded by Guido, his generically mandated policier mentor, as "un chien sans collier" — a dog without a collar. Even Mesrine's name directs us repeatedly back to this star-character's schizophrenic doubling. First of all, it has two pronunciations, *Mess-reen* or *May-reen*, the latter being Mesrine's preference, which he confirms at the start of both films — to a nurse in *L'Instinct de mort*, to an interrogating cop in *L'Ennemi public no. 1*. (The diminutive *Mess-reen*, phonetically a sneer, is favored by those unsympathetic to Mesrine's rise, as was actually

Jacques (Vincent Cassel) and Jeanne (Cécile de France), lovers on the run
in Monument Valley in *L'Instinct de mort*

the case among law officials and European television reporters in the 1960s
and 1970s.) A second connotation of Mesrine's name offers another formative contrast in *L'Instinct de mort* — to his supportive but ultimately ineffectual
parents he is *Jackie*; to his new adopted father figure, Guido, he is emphatically *Jacques*.

Reviving but mitigating the anti-high art taunts of *Car Keys*, Cassel's role
in the Mesrine films also reflects a fundamental trait of France's popular cinema. This we might call its cake-and-eat-it syndrome. That is, despite the
raucously politically incorrect sensibility of much mainstream French film,
ostensibly opposed to the powers-that-be and to sanctified high culture,
these films usually deploy strategic ideological disclaimers, often mediated by
humor. These are qualifying points of self-contradiction or ambivalence, a fa-
cetious nod towards acceptability or even nominal redemption for what might
appear incorrigibly antisocial materials. The split Cassel-Mesrine figure is a
perfect example of this process. At the end of *L'Instinct de mort*, for instance,
after we have witnessed (at exorbitant length) Mesrine victimized and brutalized in jail, a caption reports how his plight soon shed light on the appalling
penal system from which he broke free. (The real-life Mesrine did, bizarrely,
become a symbol for left-wing intellectuals like Jean-Paul Sartre, successfully
campaigning against solitary confinement in France.) Put on trial, in another
grandstanding Cassel moment, Mesrine rails against the corrupt French ju-
diciary system — the key to a criminal's handcuffs, he cries, can be bought
for 300,000 francs! Besides these superficial social tracts, *L'Instinct de mort*
arouses sympathy for Mesrine's nascent criminality by linking it to his weak
father, a Nazi collaborator during the Occupation. Like the archetype of James
Dean's matronly, apron-wearing dad in *Rebel Without a Cause* (1955), popular

film culture sees the roots of delinquency in paternal lapses and the historical failures of patriarchy. Mesrine, furthermore, even pays his dying father a Sunday hospital visit; asked why, he quips, "Well, all the banks were closed." (Here occurs yet another intertextual Cassel reference, widely spotted by critics, that Vincent's own father was initially cast as Mesrine Senior, before in an ironic twist he too succumbed to cancer, in April 2007.) Mesrine ends up sobbing over his father's body, a bad boy who just craves forgiveness.

A final point about the Mesrine films is that they underline French popular cinema's plans to entice audiences both local and global. Consciously epic, Richet uses the gangster genre as a commentary on modern French history, which he distills, and exports, in palatable shorthand. Here, Richet echoes Sergio Leone's *Once Upon a Time in America* (1984), whose gangland context is the modernizing United States across half of the twentieth century; and also Kinji Fukasaku's *Battles Without Honor or Humanity* pentalogy (1973–4), a tabloid-style crime exposé of the violent repressions of Japan's postwar era. (Christophe Barratier uses the same model in *Faubourg 36* [2008], molding France's turbulent Popular Front era into the setting of a traditional backstage musical.) Thus, punctuating *L'Instinct de mort* are passing asides about France's political development, from the shame of Mesrine's father's (French) World War II disgrace, to the Algerian colonialist debacle that "creates" Jacques's violent tendencies, to television updates about de Gaulle's increasingly contested social reforms.

Alongside these authentically French materials—after buying his first BMW, Mesrine boisterously belts out Edith Piaf's "Je ne regrette rien"—Richet interposes more international features, a multi-genre travelogue. Banished to North America, Mesrine goes on the lam with Jeanne (Cécile de France); their 1969 arrest, billed as the fall of "Bonnie and Clyde," is set to Dolly Parton's "Stand by Your Man," a brief lovers-on-the-run interlude shot in Monument Valley in Arizona. (To the angry American cops, Mesrine protests: "French! Touristes!") Hiding out in England for Mesrine's quasi-political awakening in the 1970s, London gets a similar gloss, its tourist landmarks paraded to The Clash's "London Calling." The city of Montréal, rewarding Langmann's Canadian investors and the potential viewers they represent, receives the same picture postcard treatment. By the end of the film, moreover, after the first protracted jailbreak set piece (another distinct sub-genre added to the mix) is reported by Canadian newspapers like the *Montréal-Matin*, the vast wilderness of Canada's northeastern landscapes reflects, climactically, Mesrine's newfound determination to become a neo-Western outlaw. Shot with a hand-held camera in a remote forest, framed through a car window smeared with a murdered sheriff's blood, Mesrine pledges to remain: "Dehors ou mort"—

freely at large or dead. Before *L'Instinct de mort* cuts to black, this final line, self-consciously portentous, is a gangster's coming of age, his commitment to embrace a life of crime. We can, however, also take the quip as reflecting the Mesrine project overall, its need to spread its commercial impact as far afield as possible, aggressively winning over audiences not just in France, but across the globe.

A Little Sean, a Lot of *Conneries*: Jean Dujardin in Michel Haznavicious's *OSS 117: Cairo, Nest of Spies* and *OSS 117: Lost in Rio*

While Cassel-Mesrine takes the world by force, another French popular icon, Jean Dujardin, plans on global domination through comedy. Indeed, Dujardin's best known star franchise, the inept secret agent OSS 117 series, reminds us, as we saw keenly with debutant cinema in Chapter 1, that much contemporary French cinema is primed for travel, a valuable means of raising France's international profile. On the North American front, a leading event in this context is the annual City of Lights, City of Angels (COLCOA) film festival, housed in the Directors Guild of America headquarters on Sunset Boulevard, Los Angeles. By its thirteenth series, in 2009, COLCOA had become a major Franco-American event. Managed full time since 2007 by the remarkably named François Truffart, a U.S.-based cultural attaché whose embassy acts as principal sponsor, COLCOA is tailored to American film industry professionals (writers, directors, exhibitors, agents, journalists, and especially distributors), as well as local cinephiles, and, in a clever effort to foster francophilia, over 2,000 students, invited in from a dozen Los Angeles County high schools.

COLCOA's activities reflect French cinema's twin ambitions abroad: commercial momentum, cultural appreciation. Occupying three theaters, COLCOA stages a (seemingly requisite) First Feature Award, flies in leading French stars and filmmakers for panel discussions, and screens looped packages of French movie trailers free of charge. Most attention focuses, however, on the festival's gala premieres of high status French productions—films either recently acquired by American distributors (in 2008, Music Box Films celebrated its purchase of *OSS 117: Cairo, Nest of Spies*)[13] or else yet to find American buyers. Tactical always, COLCOA screens the latter films just after, or even concurrently with, their French release (on April 24, 2009 it hosted the international premiere of *OSS 117: Lost in Rio* only a week after its Paris debut), followed by extravagantly catered wine-and-cheese receptions to woo possible suitors. Judged by its programming, confirmed by Truffart's annual editorials, COLCOA's goal is to put the diversity of French cinema in the shop window: from the upper echelons of the arthouse, to the broader fare of the popular mainstream, to the pop-art productions that incorporate facets of both. In 2009, for instance, within hours of each other COLCOA showed *Musée haut, musée bas*, *L'Instinct de mort*, and *Séraphine* (Martin Provost's much-vaunted, César-winning artistic biopic). The same year, Truffart argued for the breadth of achievement of French filmmaking across "all kinds of films, features and shorts, and particularly comedies, a genre that largely prevails over this program. Two other trends . . . [are] the number of films about women and/or written and directed by women, and the virtuosity of a new generation of French filmmakers to revitalize the genre movie, particularly the thriller."[14]

Prompted by Truffart, our attention turns now to the popular OSS 117 comedy franchise, so central to successive COLCOA festivals. In the first place, the OSS 117 films are highly proficient star vehicles, as emblematic of contemporary French screen comedy as *L'Instinct de mort* and *L'Ennemi public no. 1* are to Cassel and the French crime thriller. Even compared to Cassel's fast popular ascent, Dujardin's rise to cultural celebrity was meteoric. Today one of French cinema's highest paid and most consistently bankable stars, Dujardin's career hinges upon two elements: his matinee idol good looks and capacity to play the male romantic lead on the one hand, interwoven or strategically undermined on the other with his background as a vaudevillian, a skilful spoof artist with the anarchic comic energies of a perpetual adolescent. In the latter vein, Dujardin emerged as part of the comedy quintet Nous C Nous, a café-concert troupe based at the Carré Blanc theater, in Pigalle, near the Moulin Rouge, and, perhaps fittingly, next to André Breton's old surrealist haunt on rue Fontaine. On stage, Nous C Nous's repertoire featured pop-culture parodies, ranging from vacuous boy bands to Hollywood neo-classics (their best-loved skits, some revived on YouTube, include pastiches of *The Godfather* [1972], *Star Wars* [1977], and *Alien* [1979].) On the small screen, Dujardin's career took off when casting director Isabelle Camus spotted him on a TV talent show, M6's *Graine de star*, then assigned him in 1999 to the France 2 series, *Un Gars, une fille*, about an affectionately wrangling couple, Jean and Alex (Alexandra Lamy; both actors actually left their long-term partners to marry, in 2003), which ran successfully for five seasons.

After 2002, backed aggressively by his agent, Annabel Karouby, Dujardin pursued film roles exclusively. Following a handful of walk-ons or largely supporting roles—Dujardin even cameos as one of the multitude who scoffs at Baffie in the *Car Keys* opening—he was second-billed in 2004's *Mariages!*, a romantic comedy-ensemble drama about multi-generational couples seen by over two million paying customers. The following year, Dujardin broke through on his own terms with *Brice de Nice*, based on his erstwhile Nous C Nous sketches. This was an effervescent comedy about an airhead would-be surfer, fixated upon *Point Break* (1991), a cult figure among locals, who paddles endlessly through the becalmed Mediterranean waters in search of the perfect wave. *Brice de Nice* attracted 4.4 million viewers, the surprise hit of 2005, cementing Dujardin's persona as a child-like romantic lead, beguilingly self-involved, arrested in his development. Like Cassel, Dujardin is liable to act out on-screen, but his tantrums are comic, rather than violent, meltdowns. Indeed, besides his roles as Brice and OSS 117, Dujardin is now best known as Octave in *99 francs* (2007; an adaptation of the Beigbeder novel discussed in Chapter 2), a self-absorbed ad executive, emotionally stunted, who in one defining scene feeds, purely for kicks, a line of cocaine to the office hamster; and as the hero of the live-action version of cartoon Western gunslinger *Lucky Luke* (2009). To define Dujardin's stardom, a recent *Studio* feature comments provocatively that, unlike the majority of France's resolutely prideful film actors, Dujardin actively embraces the role of deliriously unselfconscious mediocrity, an unsophisticated buffoon with no redeeming qualities, who does not learn from his mistakes. As James Huth, director of *Brice de Nice*, suggests, Dujardin on-screen is: "Sympathetic [yet] simple . . . a beautiful big kid."[15]

While playing OSS 117 is an extension of Dujardin's stardom, it is also a measured comic deconstruction of a French mainstream cultural fixture. Agent 117 of the Office of Strategic Services (a French ancestor to the CIA; the 117 tag was traditionally given to the head of its Research and Analysis branch), otherwise known as Hubert Bonisseur de la Bath, was actually created in 1949 by popular writer Jean Bruce, the adopted name of Jean Brochet, predating Ian Fleming's James Bond by four years. Published in the Fleuve Noir espionage series, Bruce's hero, twenty-eight years old in his debut case, *Tu parles d'un ingénue*, is a straight-laced masculinist fantasy figure, even more zealously nationalistic than Fleming's alter ego. On-screen, OSS 117 first appeared in 1956's *OSS 117 n'est pas mort*, directed by Jean Sacha. While this initial film was a relative failure, Bruce's novels remained beloved: twenty million copies of the nearly one hundred OSS 117 sequels had been sold by Bruce's death in 1963 (somewhat ironically, given his famous hero, he crashed his Jaguar). Three months before the writer's fatal accident, however, following the international success of *Dr. No* (1962), Bruce's French superspy was resuscitated for another five, more successful, film vehicles. On the page, though, the OSS 117 hits kept coming, as Josette, Jean's widow, published a further 143 novels until her death in 1985; after that, her children wrote several dozen more, the last of which was published in 1992.

In the twenty-first century, OSS 117 began a new life as a mainstay of contemporary French cinema's most reliably popular genre, the comedy. Ten years after the final book, *OSS 117 prend le large*, François and Martine

Bruce began discussions with Nicolas and Eric Altmayer, a team of comedy producer brothers, with an eye for reinventing their franchise as a modern, knowing pastiche. (The escalatingly lucrative Austin Powers movies paved the way for what proved to be a quick sale.) The Altmayers appointed a writer, Jean-François Halin, a director, Michel Hazanavicius (largely on the basis of his co-directed cult film *Grand détournement* [1993], which, like *Dead Men Don't Wear Plaid* [1982], subversively re-edited Hollywood genre films), and, after the impact of *Brice de Nice* (which they produced), a lead—Dujardin. Capitalizing on their star's screen reputation as a ludicrous macho man, an attractive romantic fool, one early advert for what became *OSS 117: Cairo, Nest of Spies* immediately propelled Dujardin towards his principal target: the classical Bond films and their first, most robustly chauvinistic, leading man. The tagline proclaimed, "OSS 117: It's a little Sean, a lot of *Conneries* [crass stupidity]."[16] Enthusiastically backed by Gaumont, the Altmayers's distributor and main coproducer (which had also funded the 1960s OSS 117 films), *Cairo* was ambitiously budgeted at fourteen million euros for production (it eventually cost two million less) and two million for promotion. Released on over 600 prints (the standard gauge of saturation booking in contemporary France), *Cairo* drew 2.3 million admissions in 2006, ranking it sixteenth in the yearly chart. Its sequel, *OSS 117: Lost in Rio*, received a nearly doubled budget and achieved a rare feat for a follow-up—greater success, with 2.5 million admissions, the seventeenth biggest hit of the year. Further installments have already been commissioned of what is now one of France's most well known and consummately realized comic properties.

Just like Cassel's shop window placement in the Mesrine films, the OSS 117 vehicles are painstakingly tailored to their main commodity, Dujardin himself. (Far more so than Hollywood filmmakers with four times the budget, contemporary French mainstream directors know how to marshal their resources.) The star entrance of *Cairo* is particularly brazen. We open in lush black-and-white, a format ideally suited to Dujardin's poise between classical homage and classical kitsch, a man whose every hearty deed gains maximum attention. Dujardin, this new OSS 117, stays immaculately groomed no matter how action-packed or taxing the circumstances; modishly dressed in a never-ending series of slate grey wide-lapelled suits; his side-parted coiffure slicked stylishly down; his chiseled face, never far from a smirk, posed and made-up to accentuate its jutting square jawline. (This physical package Dujardin claims to have based on his own father as he looked in the 1950s, a cinephile who intermingles in his son's memory with the Hitchcockian heroes they watched together; Cary Grant in *North by Northwest* [1959] seems to be an immediate citation.)[17] A caption places us in Berlin, 1945, as a deliberately flimsy model airplane takes to the skies. On-board, a Nazi officer shoots his inferior for sleeping on the job, before a burst of turbulence slides his gun away. It is retrieved by the pilot, leaping from his cockpit; a tilt moves us lingeringly up from his leather jackboots, to the gun he now tosses from hand to hand, to his handsome facial features kept in shadow. The figure quips dryly, "Perhaps you're looking for this?" as a sting of music rises on the soundtrack. The Nazi, realizing he has been robbed of his secret V2 rocket plans, wails, "Who are you?" In response, the pilot—for it is indeed Dujardin—strides into close-up, tossing his cap behind him, pencil-thin mustache twitching, smug grin broadening, as he growls in a masculine baritone: "OSS 117, at your service." Depositing the German colonel through the open plane door with his boot, Dujardin flexes his eyebrows, retorts, "Thank you for flying OSS 117 airlines," and returning to the cockpit, offers the first of many excessively drawn-out, self-delighted guffaws of patronizing laughter. Our star, and correspondingly our film, could not be more pleased with themselves.

As we saw previously with the Mesrine films, an impulse in popular French cinema is to sketch a historical overview simply as a dramatic backdrop, a gloss of events in glib shorthand, context merely for the (often ill-gotten) gains of roguish yet appealing heroes. Even more emphatically in the OSS 117 films, history is a sitcom, the world is Dujardin's oyster. Time passes purely to supply snapshots of agent 117's privileged pursuits, an unstoppable alpha male, patriarchal agent of French colonialist adventures around the planet. Spanning World War II in *Cairo* to the first rumblings of Vietnam in *Rio*, OSS 117 always has his way. Here, like the cake-and-eat-it syndrome of *L'Instinct de mort* and much commercial French film—hedonistic spectacles rather desperately redeemed by dashes of irony or self-parody—both *Cairo* and *Rio* constantly tread a fine line between spoofing the masculinist paradise of the invincible superspy, and indulging him (and, implicitly, younger male audiences) in his retrograde passions. The rituals of the spy thriller—sexual escapades with glamorous yet treacherous women; loyal but disposable local sidekicks; battles with uniformed henchmen who cannot aim; the unmasking of nefarious conspiracies which climax in explosive travelogue set pieces—implacably play out, off-set marginally (just barely, but deftly) by Dujardin's and Hazanavicius's arch or exaggerated mannerisms. In *Cairo*, taking place in 1955, deliberately (according to Halin) just before Morocco, Tunisia, and, eventually Algeria claimed independence from France, 117 travels from Nazi Berlin to luxuriant Rome, then heads to Egypt to disrupt an extremist faction seeking liberty from Western manipulations. The main joke of *Rio*, set twelve years later, in 1967, is that despite the waning of French colonialist powers and the rise of countercultural backlash, 117, embroiled in a hunt for neo-

The problem with Arabic
is it's hard to read.

Agent OSS 117 (Jean Dujardin) and Larmina (Bérénice Bejo), with mismatched rear projection, in *OSS 117: Cairo, Nest of Spies*

Nazis, is unable to grasp, or simply finds it irrelevant, that the world around him has forever changed.

Like the opening of *L'Instinct de mort*, its catwalk of Cassels striding down the street, the exhibition of excess, licentious leisure, is key to OSS 117's popular appeal. *Rio*, like its predecessor, opens on a representative spectacle, fractured or deflated by strategic self-ridicule. The guest of honor at a raucous sixties party in full swing, Dujardin swaggers downstairs, fashionably late, whiskey in hand. A decade after his *Cairo* jaunts, our agent now appears a few pounds heavier, a little more jowly, his sideburns grown out—in other words, he perfectly replicates the slightly past-his-prime Sean Connery, tempted back to the Bond role after a four-year hiatus, in *Diamonds are Forever* (1971). But even if his suits are now louder, time has done nothing to inhibit 117's masculine prowess. In the exact same split-screen multiple framings of *L'Instinct de mort* (a purely ostentatious device used whenever 117 changes location, or in real terms goes on a new holiday), Dujardin, the only male present, is set upon delightedly by no fewer than twenty Asian women (we open in the "Orient" evoked by Hazanavicius's stylized ski chalet set) with whom he dances under the opening credits. After performing a magic trick, `117's next sleight-of-hand is to see off five gun-wielding assassins (whose vengeful relatives return throughout the film) then pounce upon the sole remaining female survivor. Sheer wanton gratuity, intentionally contrived, is the film's only saving grace here.

A few scenes later, we see the same bait-and-switch pattern. Back in his Paris base of operations, 117 learns that France is being blackmailed by an evil South American wrestling impresario, who threatens to expose the names of every Frenchman who collaborated with Nazi Germany. (In response, with

OSS 117 eyed up on the high dive board in *OSS 117: Lost in Rio*

his trademark furrowed brow, a small mind animatedly toiling for clarity, Dujardin deadpans, "Didn't General de Gaulle say that all of France resisted?") From here, 117 is dispatched to the Copacabanca Palace hotel in Rio; he soon emerges pool-side where he is immediately eyed up by twenty-six bikini-clad admirers, most of whom get cutaways or point-of-view shots to ogle his muscular torso. Here, on the brink of yet more sexist and/or racist outrage, *Rio* knowingly pulls its punches, descending its male-centered spectacle into emasculating farce. Bouncing on the high dive board, condescending smile in place, 117 lopes into position—but then freezes, aghast, as a flashback reveals how years earlier he once dropped his trapeze partner during a circus routine, afflicting him with permanent vertigo. Our hero is forced to retire to a sun-lounger, drowning his sorrows in martinis. *Cairo* provides a similar counterpunch to 117's heterosexist missions. This is the homoerotic subtext to his quest to avenge a fallen fellow agent, his old male partner, with whom, in another send-up flashback, he plays swing-ball and frolics through the surf on a deserted beach. The two end up intertwined, laughing incessantly in joyful abandon, like a restaging of the famous Burt Lancaster-Deborah Kerr love scene in *From Here to Eternity* (1953). *Rio* repeats the same bisexual deflection; after 117 takes LSD and has group sex with hippies on a beach, the rest of the film is punctuated by uneasy encounters with the man with whom he shared his most unforeseen intimacies.

Venturing further on to the tightrope, the OSS 117 films also broach political materials. This new travesty sets 117's extremist conservative viewpoint against a similarly caricatured leftist-libertarian perspective. The ribald tone begins in *Rio* when 117 is told to make love not war—he replies, affronted, "But both are possible!" From here, in the course of both films, 117 manages to: prevent Cairo's early morning Muslim call to prayer (with an off-screen act of violence); interrupt a neo-Nazi dinner date fundraiser in Rio; energeti-cally hail the future prospect of Israeli-Nazi peace; greet a female counter-intelligence expert with, "Nice to have such a pretty secretary . . . call me when you have to carry something heavy"; and celebrate his success at the end of *Cairo* by leaving confidently to sort things out in Iran, where "they really ap-preciate Westerners." On the touchy subject of Franco-American relations in the 1960s, 117 ponders aloud to Bill Trumendous, his CIA counterpart (a car-toonish equivalent of Bond's American friend, Felix Leiter, played here by Ken Samuels as a burlesque of Eddie Constantine), "And you, dear Bill—so South America interests the CIA now?" (Trumendous later betrays the cause with the barb, "I always got the feeling that we were only allies when you ask us to liberate you.") Among all these political charades, the most characteristically convoluted (France herself must also be mocked) comes when 117 is quizzed about Brazil's oppressive government: "But what do you call a country with a military leader, a secret police, one TV station, and State censorship?" 117's retort, his ubiquitous enlightened stupidity, is: "I call it France, miss, and not just any France—the France of General de Gaulle!"

The OSS 117 films, indeed, rely on these hallmarks of popular French cin-ema: a frantic series of back-and-forths, brutishly tactful diversions, broad comic subversions undercutting or mediating otherwise unappetizing vul-garities. So precocious is the double-stepping—just like Baffie's in *Car Keys* —that at times it turns into rather frenetic self-reflexivity. For the modern popular French filmmaker, after all, the best source of wit is to recycle gar-ishly the clichés of old mainstream hits. Early in *Rio*, for example, when two contacts mistakenly call him double-one-seven (thereby veering too close to Fleming's famous 007 moniker), Dujardin snips tetchily, "No, just one-seven." Many times, in the same way, 117's increasingly outlandish action set pieces hijack Hitchcockian tableaux: the Nazi-hunting plot from *Notorious* (1946), the track-and-zoom up a staircase from *Vertigo* (1958), and for *Rio*'s climax—as our hero finally apprehends his foe on top of Rio's giant *O Cristo Redentor* statue of Christ—a more sacrilegious version of *North by Northwest*'s Mount Rushmore finale. In terms of visual style, equally, Hazanavicius care-fully mimics the aesthetics of old spy films, the washed-out hues of leached technicolor prints shown too often on TV, as well as overtly mismatched rear projections for his obligatory car chases. (The films were also shot primarily with a 40mm lens, so as to replicate Hitchcock's favored depth of field from the late 1950s.) For the second unit location footage of Rio itself, the direc-tor goes so far as to swipe actual footage from one of *Rio*'s obsolete 1960s predecessors: stock images of Brazil in *Furia à Bahia pour OSS 117* (1967). The final touch is *Rio*'s end credits, which replay 117's vacation footage, shots we have seen him taking during his mission on an 8mm camera. The film thereby wraps up with 117 happily riding off into the sunset on a giant orange swan pedallo, a mock-up postcard rendition of which is included with the DVD. Beaming with carefree abandon, a grown man with the indiscreet appetites of an empowered teenager, OSS 117 here becomes a quintessential ambassador for popular French cinema at its most successfully outrageous — desperate to offend, desperate to ingratiate.

States of the Art: From *Brice de Nice* to Claire Denis

Flaunted by the antics of Mesrine and OSS 117, befitting the swagger of Laurent Baffie and his peers, French popular cinema is indeed enjoying a contemporary resurgence. Expensively assembled by hands-on producers, attuned to highly marketable stars and genres, commercially viable in France but also beyond its borders, films from *L'Instinct de mort* to *OSS 117: Lost in Rio* reveal a branch of French film craft that is accessible, resilient, and, in its own way, textually ingenious. Clearly, however, the point of origin for this recent tendency is the creative-business model developed since the 1980s by Luc Besson. Based initially on iconoclastic, youth-angled *cinéma du look* hits like *Subway* (1985), *The Big Blue* (*Le Grand bleu*, 1988), and *Nikita* (1990), Besson designed and made famous an aggressively commercial production aesthetic, changing his home industry forever. Returning now to the case of Besson will allow us to extend the reach of our analysis of popular contemporary French cinema.

In principle, Besson is a pre-New Wave throwback, modeling himself after mainstream professionals like Gilles Grangier, an expert 1950s genre director for hire, rather than intellectual mavericks like Truffaut. Since his earliest days working up through the ranks, indeed, Besson has always preferred the job description of *metteur-en-scène* to the mantle of auteur; while his work as writer, director and producer is now intentionally international, embracing popular genres and markets from France, America, and Asia. Single-mindedly, Besson prefers the multiplex to the cinemathèque, deriding France's predisposition towards high film art as well as the Cultural Exception protectionist defense infamously used by the French against the United States in the 1993 General Agreement on Tariffs and Trade (GATT) talks. Besson's dedication to delivering unpretentious entertainments to as many people as possible does have something of a sociopolitical motivation. In 2006, in the pages of *Première* (one of his few favored forums), Besson was drawn into a diatribe against the top-down French establishment. He argued: "For nearly a half-century we've been ruled by *énarques* [graduates of the *Ecole nationale d'administration*, i.e. France's political elite], so for nearly fifty years our country has gone further into debt, growing poorer, while unemployment's gone up and the gap between social classes has widened. Government *énarques* govern among themselves, for themselves, they know nothing about the people in the streets."[18]

Besson's iconic status and feisty egalitarianism have come to embody major paradoxes of French cinema: its need to reconcile artistic and industrial imperatives, to nurture its domestic film culture while replicating, or even directly partnering with, Hollywood's economic incursions. Neither a Hollywood convert nor quite a Gallic subversive, Besson views cinema, in Rosanna Maule's account, as "a narrative form of expression and entertainment . . . [yet whereas in Hollywood] any creative purpose remains subordinated to industrial and commercial considerations, for Besson creativity and style have primacy."[19]

Besson's beliefs, and their mass contemporary dissemination, culminated in 2000 when he founded EuropaCorp with Pierre-Ange le Pogam, a veteran executive from Gaumont. (The duo first collaborated on *Subway*.) Operating without state subsidies, in itself a declaration of intent, EuropaCorp's domain now extends to film production (domestic and international), distribution and TV rights sales, and a digital postproduction facility in Normandy called Digital Factory. In addition, EuropaCorp runs divisions dedicated to DVDs and video-on-demand, music production, licensing and cultural by-products (notably for Besson's *Arthur* brand), book and graphic novel publishing, music publishing, and advertising. Listed on the stock exchange in May 2007, EuropaCorp is ambitiously global and expansionist. One-third of its films are produced in English, and one-third of its revenues come from film tickets and DVDs sold outside France. To safeguard his profit margins, Besson keeps his staff and production overheads lower than those of his American rivals, striving for independence whenever possible. For his annual production slate of around ten films, Besson employs a stable of in-house directors (Louis Leterrier, Olivier Megaton, Pierre Morel, Aruna Villiers), promoted from within, or else hired from the commercial domain of advertising or music videos.

As we saw with Mesrine and especially the OSS 117 property, a franchise mentality is now vital to France's commercial film mainstream. Here again, EuropaCorp's commercial instincts blazed a trail; its core principle long being the cultivation of highly profitable cycles, mainly its *Taxi* (1998; 2000; 2003; 2007), *The Transporter* (2002; 2005; 2008), and animated *Arthur* (2006; 2009; 2010) series. But the company's most unprecedented success, a new role model, was its 2008 project *Taken*, an unlikely but fast-moving action thriller starring Liam Neeson as an ex-spy rescuing his kidnapped daughter from Eastern European racketeers. *Taken* was shot entirely in Paris, mostly in English, directed by Morel, cowritten by Besson; it ended up grossing $145 million in North America and $224 million worldwide, nearly six times its original production cost. (*From Paris with Love* [2010], EuroCorp's follow-up, yielded less immediate returns in North America.) *Taken*, however, was an event which returned Besson to the global stage, fresh eyes turning to the question of EuropaCorp's theory and practice. A studious manager, intermittent director but very active writer-producer, Besson was interviewed in *Variety* in 2009 (an increasingly rare public statement) and asked to quantify his methods. He replied: "We make films we'd watch with passion and without shame. . . . We make a conscious effort on a daily basis to keep thinking as producers and not as movie moguls."[20] So forceful is Besson's grass roots commercialist ideology, and so lucrative the results, that to some eyes his work still assaults directly the artistic identity of French cinema itself.[21]

Whatever the debates over his merits, Besson has inspired converts and transformed French cinema. As Charlie Michael observes, in Besson's wake[22] has arrived a vigorous series of "popular genre films that feature special effects and glossy production values . . . for those of us accustomed to thinking of French cinema as a low-budget, philosophical alternative to Hollywood, the past few years might have been a bit disorienting."[23] The kind of genre films at issue, moreover, feature high production values and broad commercial appeal but diffuse cultural specificity, flitting between traditional French forms (mainly comedies and policier thrillers), Asian templates (imported crews and stars alongside martial arts motifs), and Hollywood generic packaging. Notable breakthroughs here are action spectaculars like Besson's *The Fifth Element* (1997)—still France's biggest export success, grossing $265 million worldwide—*Brotherhood of the Wolf* (*Le Pacte des loups*, 2001), *Crimson Rivers* (*Les Rivières pourpres*, 2000), *Renegade*, and the *Taxi* and *The Transporter* cycles. These blockbusters target international audiences as much as domestic demographics, while their increased budgets and marketing costs derive from an institutional climate in which escalating private investment has disproportionately boosted French super-productions.[24] Between 1993 and 2008, in fact, the number of French films produced annually costing over ten million euros (the CNC's most expensive category) rose from three to thirty-five. In the same period, yearly investment in French cinema went up from 475 million euros to just under 1.5 billion euros—a 314 percent growth.[25]

In the light of EuropaCorp's paradigm and its many imitators, notably Langmann and the Altmayer brothers, to some respondents certain products of popular French cinema are no longer really French. Isabelle Vanderschelden, for example, suggests that the proglobal production formulae of films like *Brotherhood of the Wolf*, *Renegade* and especially Jean-Pierre Jeunet's *A Very Long Engagement* (*Un Long dimanche de fiançailles*, 2004) are best understood as transnational texts. Vanderschelden calls such productions reliant on "international strategies . . . on a production and textual level, deliberately blending nations and cultures . . . recycling and appropriating traditional genre films, resulting in mainstream popular films not limited to the French market."[26] More specifically, transnationalism can be detected in the interconnected financial entities that produce films like *A Very Long Engagement*, that are controlled by American interests (in this case, Warner France acting merely as a regional subsidiary), yet still campaign (with intense controversy and ultimate failure) for French funding programs from the CNC.[27] To other scholars, transnational features arise from intermingled multi-national formal features: casts from different countries, border-crossing plots, stylistic mimicry of Hollywood methods by non-American film cultures, and so on.[28] The transnational model is extended by Marwan Kraidy, who studies the impact of globalization not purely as hegemonic cultural exertion, a pattern of dominance and submission, but rather as a system of give-and-take, or international cultural communication. Alongside Kraidy's test cases from Latin America and Hong Kong, French cinema relates closely to his template of hybridity as "the cultural logic of globalization . . . [offering] foreign media and marketers transcultural wedges for forging affective links between their commodities and local communities . . . hybridity conjures up an active exchange that leads to the mutual transformation of both sides."[29]

Whatever the terminology used to describe them, the spread—and renovation—of internationalized, export-friendly genre films has begun apace in middle- to low-tier productions, on a scale unparalleled in French cinema history. Besides the more iconic blockbusters listed above, the twenty-first century in France has produced spy thrillers (*Agents secrets* [2004], *Secret défense* [2008], *Espion/s* [2009]), heist and caper movies (*Dobermann*, *The Nest* [*Nid de guêpes*, 2002]), erotic thrillers (*Corps à corps* [2003]), martial arts epics (*Kiss of the Dragon* [*Le Baiser mortel du dragon*, 2001]), conspiracy thrillers (*Tell No One* [*Ne le dis à personne*, 2006], *The Key* [*La clef*, 2007]), big game comedy escapades (*Safari* [2009]), medical conspiracy thrillers (*Qui a tué Bambi?* [2003]), many animated features and science-fictions (*Peut-être* [1999], *Immortel [ad vitam]* [2004], *Renaissance* [2006], *Eden Log* [2007], *Chrysalis* [2007], *Dante 01* [2008]), a slew of grisly serial killer films (*Le Plaisir . . . (et ses petits tracas)*, *Cette femme-là* [2003]), and the more familiar sight of France's old generic mainstay, policier procedurals (*Gangsters* [2002], *36 Quai des Orfèvres* [2004], *Le Petit lieutenant* [2005], *Go Fast* [2008], *MR 73* [2008], and *Gardiens de l'ordre* [2010]).

Proximate to these, and perhaps more peculiar, is the phenomenon of once venerated film categories being—depending on your perspective—reinvented for a broader audience, or, alternatively, vulgarized beyond repair. Banlieue cinema provides a vivid example. Carrie Tarr praises this cycle for its social activism, quasi-documentary studies of marginal demographics and French urban spaces which create "representations of conflict highlighting . . . individual problems of identity and integration."[30] But one of the more high profile recent banlieue films in France is the shamelessly exploitative, science fiction/buddy cop/martial arts fantasy *District B13* (*Banlieue 13*, 2004), a EuropaCorp coproduction cowritten and coproduced by Besson and directed by his protégé lieutenant, Morel. (Its obligatory sequel, *Banlieue 13: Ultimatum*, appeared in 2009.)[31] Similarly, the once renowned heritage genre, hailed by Phil Powrie as "the hegemonic French cinema of the 1990s,"[32] has manifested anew in violent, fast-cut, youth-oriented form via films like *Brotherhood of the Wolf*, and the CGI mystery spectacular *Vidocq* (2001), arguably the world's first entirely blue screen-shot film, whose success led to its director, Pitof, being hired by Warner Bros. for their (ultimately ill-fated) sub-franchise spin-off *Catwoman* (2004).

Not all popular French cinema has such international aspirations. In fact, the backbone of the film market in France remains the performance- or troupe-driven comedy, lesser known abroad but essential to the national industry retaining its indigenous home audience, the perennial target of a majority market share. In this vein the benchmark has been recently set, of course, with the unexpected supremacy of *Bienvenue chez les Ch'tis* (2008), which with 20.4 million admissions became the most popular French film of all time, beating the forty-year record of *La Grande vadrouille* (1966). Although much analysis focused on the impossibility of its regional humor, a fish-out-of-water comedy of a southern postal manager relocating to live among northern hicks, being comprehensible for international audiences, the film did get a limited global release, as *Welcome to the Land of the Chtis*. But in general terms, in the decade since 2000 the French box office has been consolidated by comic stars and the careful development of comedic franchises. Most prominently this includes the *Astérix* series (crowned by *Astérix et Obélix: Mission Cléopâtre* [2002], which before Dany Boon's *Ch'tis* breakthrough was the highest-grossing twenty-first-century film in France, with over 14.5 million tickets sold),[33] *Les Bronzés 3: Amis pour la vie* (2006; fourth[34] with 10.3 million admissions), *La Vérité si je mens! 2* (2001) (fifteenth; 7.5 million), *Camping* (2006) (thirty-sixth; 5.4 million; a very popular sequel was released in 2010); as well as one-off comedy hits like *The Closet* (*Le Placard*, 2001) (thirty-eighth; 5.3 million), and, of course, *Brice de Nice* (fiftieth; 4.4 million).

While such comedic properties are ubiquitous on-screen and in the popular French film press, however, they tend to receive only piecemeal international distribution, and almost never reach the key North American market. Even on DVD, such comedies are typically released without English subtitles, reflecting excessive trade caution about the perceived insularity of lowbrow French slapstick, as well as a self-imposed limit on the international circulation of French cinema at its most mainstream.

Along the commercial spectrum outlined here, this extraordinary wave of popular French cinema, and its clear departure from traditionally refined French film art, has been greeted with palpable agitation within the industry. Predictably, to the intellectual analyst, typified by the enduringly pro-auteur polemicists at *Cahiers du cinéma*, such Franco-Hollywood products reveal a deep-seated artistic banality. To others more sympathetic to the Bessonian approach, particularly in the pragmatic popular press of magazines like *Studio* and *Première*, the films are a welcome sign of French commercial acuity. More broadly, as Anne Jäckel has demonstrated from an industrial perspective, the conventional idea of French production models as ossified, narrow, or traditionally nationalist is simply no longer apt. Jäckel instead argues for the strength in depth and range of France's funding protocols, which encourage coproductions, support for marginal or activist filmmakers who are not even necessarily French, and a strong transnational commitment. In fact, the French model is a highly multi-functional one, in which "the commercial aspect of a film policy that allows mergers between French and foreign companies and encourages the production of large-budget pictures to compete with 'American' blockbusters is derided by the proponents of a more cultural approach to the film and audio-visual industries."[35] A similarly optimistic industrial summary has come from David Kessler, director of the CNC, who in *Libération* offered a tentative redefinition of the national production landscape based upon the impact of *Taxi 2, Yamakasi* (2001), *Brotherhood of the Wolf*, and the twenty-first-century revival of mass French filmmaking. Kessler declared: "This is a revelation: it demonstrates the popular potential of our national cinema, contrary to the fatalist discourse that we've been hearing for too long. . . . This success shows us the principal force of French cinema: its diversity."[36]

Extending Jäckel's and Kessler's points about this diversification process, we should note its equal applicability to the auteurist cinema for which France is more traditionally recognized. For as France's popular cinema has broadened its appeal through a profusion of international formulae, the French arthouse sector has consolidated its (national) identity by, conversely, specializing so much as to risk alienating even its minority audience. Central to this trend is the rise of the contemporary *cinéma du corps*, discussed in the previous chapter. As we saw there, this mode of cinema uses narratives about sexuality and physicality stripped of all romantic connotation, set in atavistic diegetic spaces—frequently the criminal or leisure underworlds of Paris— whose asocial denizens commit acts of corporeal desperation. *Sombre*, for example, depicts a wandering puppeteer carrying out a series of random sexual assaults while roaming rural France; *Intimacy* deconstructs a nonemotional yet explicitly carnal relationship set in the suburbs of London; and *L'Histoire de Richard O.* features its hedonistic eponymous protagonist (Mathieu Amalric) videoing, interviewing, and carrying out sex acts (some unsimulated) with a variously unbalanced suite of women, one of whom inadvertently kills him. Beyond its challenging subjects, however, it is the stylistic ambitions of the *cinéma du corps* which more forcibly affront its viewers. These nihilistic films are often lyrical to the point of abstraction, psychologically opaque, spatially elliptical, lacking stable narrative unities and legible film form. The interlinked work of *cinéma du corps* filmmakers—Bertrand, Denis, de Van, Dumont, Noé, Grandrieux, as well as a growing list of international directors—galvanizes an art cinema whose severity supersedes its predecessors.

Throughout France's *art et essai* community, moreover, even in projects less directly confrontational than the *cinéma du corps*, there is often a commitment to self-reflexive, rarefied design. Stylistic experimentation is an increasingly accepted practice among veterans and first-timers alike, while open-ended, puzzle box narration—the hallmark of 1960s modernism, made famous by Alain Resnais and Michelangelo Antonioni—is once again in favor. Consider the opening sequences of two recent debut features, which contrast sharply with our earlier, mainstream examples. Lucile Hadzihalilovic's *Innocence* fades up to an out-of-focus, fast motion blur of bubbles and dank green organic matter in motion, as a deep rumbling noise reverberates on the soundtrack. The shot is completely abstract, nonrepresentational yet arresting, one of the most unexpected openings in recent world cinema. Similar in its disorienting approach, albeit with legible imagery, is Siegrid Alnoy's *She's One of Us* (*Elle est des nôtres*, 2003). Her film begins with a clicking sound, never situated, followed by a quotation from Dostoyevsky's "The Dreams of a Ridiculous Man," and a medium close-up of a windswept woman's face, neutrally composed. She vanishes, revealing a distant, out-of-focus figure crossing a remote mountainside. Accompanying but not matching the images is a loud clap of thunder and the rasping sound of a woman's gasps for air.

The radicalism of these openings—suggestive of a non-narrative, associative perceptual sampling—is echoed in different ways by Hadzihalilovic's and Alnoy's more senior arthouse contemporaries. Reverse or splintered storytelling is a particular anti-mainstream approach of choice. In *5x2*, François Ozon uses backwards narration to invert ironically the demise of a couple, beginning with their divorce proceedings and ending on an idyllic yet forlorn long take, shot at sunset, of them walking blissfully out to sea on holiday in Italy. Here, walking off into the sunset together comes to mean a bourgeois couple's inevitable break; this is intimacy with a shrinking time frame, an unhappy happy ending. The same effect-and-cause plotting adds bleak poignancy to the rape-revenge course of Noé's *Irreversible*, which climaxes near its start when the wrong culprit is murdered, horrifically, in an underground nightclub. More self-conscious still is Chéreau's devastating *Gabrielle* (2005), an adaptation of a Joseph Conrad novella which also dissects an unraveling marriage, between a wealthy publisher, Jean (Pascal Greggory), and his disaffected wife, the eponymous Gabrielle (Isabelle Huppert). Chéreau, in fact, employs traditional Brechtian alienation effects to abstract us from his unfolding drama: alternating color with black-and-white, breaking its action into subtitled chapters, disrupting its flow with freeze-frames, and, most intriguingly, superimposing unspoken lines of dialogue on to the screen. (The caption "Stay!" appears, for example, when Gabrielle pauses on the brink of leaving a disrupted party; is this Jean's tacit command or a wife's unspoken social imperative?) At times, indeed, *Gabrielle*'s disjointed design and opulent but arid chateau *mise-en-scène* recalls that high water mark of screen modernism, *Last Year at Marienbad* (*L'Année dernière à Marienbad*, 1961). But such bewildering, bravura stylistic means are quite typical within the twenty-first-century French arthouse.

In this context, beyond *cinéma du corps* films like *Trouble Every Day*, Claire Denis remains a galvanizing figurehead for France's arthouse community. Her international celebrity advanced even further, if possible, in the wake of *35 Shots of Rum* (*35 Rhums*, 2008) and the postcolonial parable, *White Material* (2009). The former film in particular, conceived by Denis as a systematic homage to Ozu, her main cited artistic source, and especially his *Late Spring* (1949), is rife with high film art flourishes. A multiracial, multigenerational network narrative, *35 Shots of Rum* lingers over observational and behavioral minutiae, preferring wisps of narrative suggestion (a retiring train driver's mounting depression; a father's conflicted impulse to encourage the independence of a daughter he relies upon) to emphatic disclosures or classical unities. The film's masterful opening, for instance, is a wordless[37] seven-minute montage, propelling us sequentially around the outer rail network of Paris, among travelers, as dusk gathers gently into night. Lyrically, Denis here instantiates her themes of urban rootlessness at society's margins, the fluid national identities of immigrants, attenuated family groups, their unstated longings, and the impromptu communities of endlessly commuting workers.

If Denis acts as France's leading art cinema statesperson, then so too does her career reflect certain continuities within French high art film culture. The ceaseless festival profiles of the venerable New Wave generation—Godard's *Film socialisme* (2010), Resnais's *Wild Grass* (*Les Herbes folles*, 2009), Rohmer's *The Romance of Astree and Celadon* (*Les Amours d'Astrée et Céladon*, 2007), Varda's *The Beaches of Agnes* (*Les Plages d'Agnès*, 2008)—are obvious throwbacks here. There is also the cultural shadow still cast by Marguerite Duras, a legacy that manifested anew in Michelle Porte's adaptation of her 1962 novel, *L'Après-midi de Monsieur Andesmas* (2004). Porte's film is arguably contemporary France's most refined, old-fashioned piece of art cinema. Except for fleeting flashbacks, it takes place—at a stately pace—on top of a remote forested hillside near a southern French village, lavishing attentions on the textures of its rural landscape: verdant and golden foliage, the sweeping gusts of the Mistral, the relentless afternoon heat. Plot is provided piecemeal with little or no direct exposition. The eponymous Andesmas (Michel Bouquet, nearly eighty when he played the role) reminisces about his beloved daughter, Valérie (Anne Isserman), but his wistful memories are offset by those of an unnamed local woman (Miou-Miou, another senior screen notable), whose husband Valérie allegedly stole. Doting daughter or manipulative adulterer—which is Valérie, whom we glimpse only through other people's reflections? Porte and Duras accommodate both viewpoints in tandem, portrayals which contradict but also fascinatingly intersect. In sum, from the *cinéma du corps* to its more traditionalist contemporaries, the relative health of France's auteurist community, at least artistically, is clear. Moreover, while the French mainstream has now globalized and become attuned to the masses as never before, such practices are assertively countered by France's auteurist vanguard. While some voice unease that these refined arthouse practices risk commercial alienation,[38] alternatively, as one *Cahiers du cinéma* editorial argues, the stylistic buoyancy of French art cinema seeks collectively nothing less than "to stake out the contemporary avant-garde."[39]

The Eye of a Needle, a Pie in the Face: Valeria Bruni Tedeschi's *It's Easier for a Camel . . .* and *Actresses*

As we have seen, the practices of contemporary French popular and arthouse filmmaking can be distinct, oppositional. But this is not the whole story, and our attention turns now to the overlooked tendency of contemporary French pop-art cinema, a middle course created from connections between these low and high cinemas. Fresh, revisionist analysis is due the traditional separation of the mainstream from the arthouse—the long-standing cliché, revived in the opening scene of *Car Keys*, that French cinema either competes with Hollywood and befriends audiences, or else wins prizes and creates scholarly art. Our contrary point of departure here is that many French filmmakers now derive international visibility, textual charisma, and artistic identity through shifting permutations of the popular and the intellectual. What the example of Bruni Tedeschi and other pop-art filmmakers reveals is that high and low French filmmaking today exists productively, compellingly, in a state of cultural flux.[40]

Bruni Tedeschi's background and professional experiences might make her seem predisposed to high art and an auteurist agenda. The daughter of a prominent industrialist and a concert pianist, Bruni Tedeschi moved to France at the age of nine when her family was targeted by the extreme left Red Brigades in Italy during the early 1970s. Based subsequently in Paris, Bruni Tedeschi began what can only be described as a glittering career—today, she is indisputably a leading light of French cinema. Initially, Bruni Tedeschi trained as an actor at the prestigious Théâtre Nanterre-Amandiers, working with Patrice Chéreau, who chose her for the lead of his screen adaptation of Chekhov's *Hôtel de France* (1987). Based upon this performance, she went on to collaborate with a who's who of France's filmmakers: in Jacques Doillon's *L'Amoureuse* (1987), Diane Kurys's *La Baule-les-Pins* (1990), Laurence Ferreira Barbosa's *Les Gens normaux n'ont rien d'exceptionnel* (1993)—for which she won the Most Promising Actress César—Noémie Lvovsky's *Oublie-moi* (1994), Claire Denis's *Nénette et Boni* (1996), and Claude Chabrol's *Au coeur du mensonge* (1999). After 1998, Bruni Tedeschi supplemented her acting work with periods of writing, beginning with a series of semi-autobiographical dialogue scenes and narrative fragments. These she read to Lvovsky, who helped her develop the script of what eventually became her debut as co-writer-director.

It's Easier for a Camel . . ., the resulting film, depicts the fantasies and tribulations of Federica (Bruni Tedeschi), an émigré Italian and frustrated playwright living in Paris. Federica feels guilty about her inherited wealth, for which she repeatedly seeks counsel from a priest (Pascal Bongard). His advice to her is the biblical adage that it is easier for a camel to pass through the eye of a needle than for a rich man to enter the kingdom of heaven. Romantically, Federica not only lusts after the flustered curate, but is also distractedly torn among three other men. There is her socialist history teacher boyfriend Pierre (Jean-Hugues Anglade) who seeks marriage, her married ex-lover Philippe (Denis Podalydès) who seeks adultery (and who may actually be a figment of Federica's imagination), and an unnamed Man In The Garden (Yvan Attal) who lunches with his son in the park outside her apartment on the rue Renoir. In her family relationships, Federica is also under pressure. As her ill father (Roberto Herlizka) begins a terminal decline, Federica falls out with her jealous younger sister Bianca (Chiara Mastroianni), her mother (Marisa Borini, Bruni Tedeschi's actual parent), and her wayward younger brother Aurelio (Lambert Wilson). Little is resolved in any of these meandering plotlines, and the film ends as the father's body is returned to Italy by plane.

When *It's Easier for a Camel . . .* was released, in April 2003, it ended up attracting over 400,000 admissions — a respectable mid-range hit, in keeping with its pop-art status. Its deliberate dissonance, moreover, was noted by many critics, occupying a range of cultural strata. In *Les Inrockuptibles*, France's leading and quite serious pop culture magazine, Jean-Baptiste Morain suggested that, "the first film of Valeria Bruni Tedeschi is at once tender and mean-spirited, serious and light-hearted, balanced and chaotic, just self-deprecating enough not to be antipathetic, just narcissistic enough not to be sympathetic."[41] In the more venerated *Positif*, Francoise Audé, Philippe Rouyer, and Claire Vassé concurred with Morain's perspective. Audé noted that Bruni Tedeschi's "story continues to accumulate contradictions," while Rouyer and Vassé observed how the film strategically "balances different registers . . . [and] ruptures in tone."[42] In *Le Point*, Olivier de Bruyn, too, underlined the discordance of *It's Easier for a Camel . . .* which he traced to a schizophrenic relationship with the art cinema mode itself. De Bruyn claimed that in form and content Bruni Tedeschi's film was "triggered by a contemporary French cinema landscape doomed too often to minimalist introspection and existential reasoning. . . . However the script makes no secret of its connection to the true vocation of the cinéaste."[43]

Building from this critical consensus, we can situate Bruni Tedeschi's hybrid project more concretely within a pop-art template. David Bordwell offers a salient international context, writing about the popularization of radical technique in contemporary Hong Kong cinema. The resulting mêlée, Bordwell suggests, derives from highly refined, occasionally modernist features that are conscripted into a generic, stylistically engaging cinema. As Bordwell reflects: "In commercial film, experimentation is usually not anarchic messing about but self-conscious craftmanship. . . . Driven by competition, contrariness, or just the urge not to repeat oneself, the ambitious artisan presses against tradition, testing how far one can go while still playing by the rules of the game."[44] Ultimately, then, the goal is to render avant-garde idiosyncrasies into legible form, staving off the viewer's consternation while refreshing the materials of mainstream entertainment. A core principle of this pop-art cinema, in France as well as Hong Kong, is the need for its practitioner to sustain commercial

An animated Federica (Valeria Bruni Tedeschi) in *It's Easier for a Camel . . .*

viability but also directorial distinctiveness, to synthesize revitalized popular product from the esoteric approaches of the arthouse. Distilling low art from high art—or vice versa—the pop-art filmmaker can have it both ways.

In its narrative design, *It's Easier for a Camel . . .* certainly offers a skittish, yet skilful, mixture of arthouse solemnity deflected by mainstream self-mockery. Opening without any exposition or backstory, the film shifts between Federica's pampered childhood in Italy and her contemporary worries in Paris, intermingled with comic visions and cartoon skits. Using straight cuts without any temporal or subjective cues like dissolves, Bruni Tedeschi wanders playfully among her diegetic strands. This creates a stream-of-consciousness cinema, blending moments of youthful nostalgia, present-day malaise, and hypothetical projections of implausible victories, all varying wildly in mood. Significantly, the film also provides a running commentary about its own artistically erratic status. Federica labors over her writing throughout the film, and at one point she pitches a play to a would-be backer and cultural avatar, just like Baffie in *Car Keys*. The scene in which Federica meets the prominent theater director here takes place twice, with multiple conclusions. Initially, this pompous figure (who describes airily his season of Brecht, a Kundera adaptation, and an *Uncle Vanya* revival) fervently thanks Federica for existing, then deluges her with praise for her script's popular appeal: "When I read your play I cried twice—twice!—and laughed too." Second time around, though, the director now turns on the same material from a mass audience's standpoint, attacking its intellectual pretensions and morose self-involvement: "It's heavy, it's sad. . . . The real problem is that it depresses me; I don't do depressing."

Throughout the narrative, moreover, Bruni Tedeschi flits between the low-brow and the highbrow, while plot points accrue whimsically, disrupted by this inconsistent style. Near the opening, diegetic piano music continues as we cut from a cartoon of Federica struggling to push a camel's backside through the eye of a giant needle, to Federica pirouetting at her ballet class, through jump cuts of her silver Jaguar speeding across the center of Paris. Within scenes, events collide or are interrupted. One apparent flashback even begins with the adult Federica leading herself, as a child, in a stately dance through the Italian family home. Another sequence, more perplexing still, careens from a flashback (the young Federica at the Luna Park fair in Italy), to a possibly imagined recent encounter with Philippe in a café, to an outlandish pop-Freudian fantasy of her dressed as his daughter, climbing nervously into bed with him and his wife.

On the one hand, Bruni Tedeschi embodies here the mainstream director's broadly humorous sensibility, a self-directed insult comic, poking fun at Federica's solipsism and the stunted emotional growth of a poor little rich girl. (At times Bruni Tedeschi's self-loathing antics even recall Hazanavicius's and Dujardin's OSS 117 movies.) But on the other hand, Bruni Tedeschi also creates a complex subjective portrait of a stalled but active protagonist, a female-centered deconstruction of a woman in crisis. To do this, moreover, she adopts the experimental instincts of international art cinema. Like Ozu, she elides or subtends pivotal encounters in favor of observational minutiae; like Resnais, she reverses temporal flow and mixes truth with fiction. Jean-Michel Frodon analyses energetically the cinematic mélange that develops, which "takes off from its joyful contempt for the rules of genre . . . [enjoying] the most invigorating freedom, a madness which unsettles — including those within the drama — all systems of storytelling and description."[45]

Within such open formal conflicts, *It's Easier for a Camel . . .* interweaves features of French culture both high and low. In a mainstream vein, the film opens with the seemingly requisite establishing shots that — especially in popular comedies — showcase on-screen a travelogue iconography of Paris. Under blazing sunshine, we see Federica drive down the Champs-Elysées, towards the Eiffel Tower (under which is superimposed the title caption), alongside the Jardin du Luxembourg on the left bank, and on past tourist landmarks guaranteed to please international audiences. Bruni Tedeschi also cites a range of performance artforms across a broad cultural spectrum. Federica attends several times a Guignol puppet play, dances an extended accordion polka on a nighttime date with Philippe beside the Seine, takes ballet classes, goes to the opera with Pierre, tumbles through a circus routine ("I am the grande trapéziste!") to amuse her hospitalized father, and sits entranced

Federica's phantom pregnancy and fantasy lover, The Man in the Garden
(Yvan Attal), in *It's Easier for a Camel...*

through television variety shows as a youngster. (Sophie Fillières's excellent pop-art feature *Gentille* [2005] is similarly polycultural, moving rapidly at one point from a psychoanalysis session to a street performer fire-breathing.) Bruni Tedeschi uses multimedia to achieve similar aesthetic diversity. The film's animated asides—Federica grappling with the eponymous camel, a crowd cheering her writing, stars dancing in the night sky while she kisses Philippe—amplify the fantastic aspects of the live action, echoing the devices of both auteurs and mainstream comedians. Federica's cartoon reveries at once mimic the dancing Volvo logo imagined by Claire Denis's traffic-bound protagonist in *Friday Night* (*Vendredi soir*, 2002), as well as the high-speed CGI-animated car chase projected by Baffie in *Car Keys*.

More multifarious than mainstream artisans, Bruni Tedeschi still shares their suspicion for elitist culture and the sacrosanct, which she deflates with earthy wit. Religion is a particular target. While Federica waits for her unwitting priest confidante to finish a traditional baptism ceremony, for example, a voice-over cuts through the service; his earnest entreaties to avoid sin are heard, but with hearty sexual yearnings also pronounced apparently from the pulpit. "I want to take you," the curate whispers huskily, as if directly to his watching admirer, "from behind." Later on, Federica is urged by Bianca to commit to both Pierre and the institution of marriage, and Bruni Tedeschi stages the scene with Federica perched on the toilet, dismissing the idea out of hand as she gets up to wipe her genitals. (Bodily functions, it must be said, appear far more often in contemporary French cinema than in its prudish North American counterpart.) In its pop-art approach to politics, *It's Easier for a Camel . . .* is equally evasive. The uneven tone is set near the start when Bruni Tedeschi has Pierre bellow socialist anthems and lines from "L'Internationale" — "The world has a new foundation: we were nothing, we shall be all!" — from the window of Federica's luxury car as they pause in traffic near the jewelry district of the Place Vendôme. (One passerby, perhaps an extra, whoops in delight at the sentiments.) Yet later, during a lavish tea with Federica's mother, the same character is given a long speech in which he talks movingly of his father, ruined by thirty years of ten-hour days on the production line. Class conflict and political tensions, like gender roles and money, are issues for Bruni Tedeschi worthy of sympathy and scorn, thoughtful reflection but also satirical contempt. Everything and nothing is sacred.

Actresses, Bruni Tedeschi's follow-up feature, not only engages on its own merits, but also offers a charismatic extension of the pop-art dynamic unfolding in French film today.[46] Second time around, more critics recognized Bruni Tedeschi's sophistication, the deft cross-purposes of its playful pop-artfulness. Olivier de Bruyn, clearly a fan, outlined a series of keywords in *Le Point* to describe her mixed business, describing Bruni Tedeschi as a "delicious fantasist" with "ironic, painfully humorous, gently melancholic" inclinations.[47] Marie-Elisabeth Rouchy followed suit, pitching *Actresses* as a "risky conjugation" of materials, citing Bruni Tedeschi's own testimonial-rationale: "I enjoy canceling out conventional barriers, life and death, the past and the present, childhood and adulthood. . . . Let's say, in any case, that these barriers aren't as clear as all that."[48] Isabelle Regnier in *Le Monde* worked the idea further, analyzing what she called Bruni Tedeschi's process of *élaboration*. Here, Bruni Tedeschi and Lvovsky, her collaborator again, first write a conventional narrative, a screenplay structured around improvised scenes, then proceed to attenuate and bifurcate their text through "protracted work, which can take three or four years, which splinters the film's reality, extending it between the domain of spectacle, or of art."[49]

Echoing its predecessor, *Actresses* is a quasi-autobiographical approximation of Bruni Tedeschi herself, self-deprecating auteur. The writer-director plays Marcelline, cast as the lead role of Natalya Petrovna in a troubled production of Ivan Turgenev's *A Month in the Country*. (*Actresses'* text-within-a-text and theater setting, the Théâtre des Amandiers, both come from Bruni Tedeschi's own past, her apprentice years with Chéreau and a disastrous moment in her career when she could barely find work and was herself fired as Natalya on the brink of opening night.) Marcelline, just past forty like the woman who plays her, is a successful actress who craves a private life, and, most of all, a child. Distanced from her highly judgmental Mother (Marisa

Grand piano as comic prop: The title caption of *Actresses*

Borini, Bruni Tedeschi's actual parent again) and Aunt (Simona Marchini), Marcelline has fleeting relationships with her pretentious but ineffectual director (Mathieu Amalric), and her equally narcissistic junior co-star, Eric (Louis Garrel). Coming apart at the seams, Marcelline is visited, apparently, by the specters of her dead father and boyfriend, then eventually the phantom figure of Natalya herself (Valeria Golino) who protests Marcelline's wavering ability to portray her. Alongside Marcelline is Nathalie (Lvovsky), the hapless director's assistant, whose efforts to seduce her indifferent boss — he responds with a breezy "I'll think about it" — ironically bring her closer to her henpecked husband ("I don't do theater; I'm in real estate"). The film ends, unresolved of course, as Marcelline flees the show, mid-performance, chased by Natalya; she swims down the Seine to the strains of Glenn Miller's "In the Mood," which Marcelline's swimming instructor has earlier suggested will improve her technique.

A pop-art manifesto is set out in the opening shots of the film, a wonderfully emblematic set piece. In a low angle wide shot, we see a crane hoisting a grand piano into the air between a row of opulent, historical apartment tenements. Bruni Tedeschi's name and the film's title are superimposed on to the piano as it arcs erratically across the frame, spinning barely under control above the road. By now, insistent car horns and bicycle bells, the sounds of irascible but unseen traffic, fill the air. Next, we see Marcelline's Mother and Aunt observing from an upstairs window, as a stressed deliveryman yells up from the street that their piano is ready. While the enormous instrument hovers ominously, just missing their glass windows, the two women bicker, deciding finally that the piano is meant for the floor below. "Look!" the Mother suggests, "It seems alive, like an elephant!" "Don't shout," the Aunt retorts, "I've got earache." The point of all this, acutely distilled, is that this icon of high culture, an ornate and obviously expensive grand piano, is here reduced to a clumsily handled bulky object, the source of foolish spectacle, a slapstick comedy unfolding before an at best disinterested audience.

Throughout the film, Bruni Tedeschi thrives within the multiple registers and shifts of tone that characterize the pop-art film. One highlight, another iconic moment, comes as the cast gather for a postrehearsal meal in the theater. Marcelline arrives late, trying to catch the waiter's eye. Prone always to unasked-for introspections, she murmurs ruefully to the assembled table: "No one answers me tonight, everyone's deaf, I'm like a fish in a bowl." Nathalie, glaring, responds bitterly: "People work—you're not the center of the whole world." Here, just as *Actresses* seems poised at a point of serious critique, the sympathy-contempt motif that follows Federica in *It's Easier for a Camel . . .*, Bruni Tedeschi deftly punctures the mood. Without preamble, the neglectful waiter stumbles over a diner's leg, causing him to fall and hurl a cream pie into Marcelline's face from point blank range. Intellectual slapstick breaks out again, high and low cultures exploding together like curdled dessert.

While this gag comes across as wildly unexpected—the diners seem more shocked than amused by Marcelline's sudden, perhaps warranted pie to the face—in *Actresses* Bruni Tedeschi takes these pop-art ruptures further, condensing them at times across rapid-fire, tonal lurches of cutting. Editing itself becomes an efficient means of pop-art juxtaposition: broad or uncomfortable physical humor, a staple of the mainstream, deflates but is also suffused by the earnest subjective yearnings of a traumatized heroine, that mainstay figure of the arthouse. Early on, for instance, Bruni Tedeschi lingers in close-ups on Marcelline's faltering pleas in church before a Virgin Mary effigy ("Holy Virgin, give me a husband . . . and I will renounce . . . fame"); then via a straight cut summarily takes us to her lying on the obstetrician's table, legs in stirrups, vaginal examination in progress. Moments later, as Marcelline rambles about her need to have a child so late in life (her obstetrician soon quips that it is her husband, upstairs, who is the psychoanalyst), Bruni Tedeschi jump cuts to her character throwing up extravagantly as she walks down the street, her white projectile vomit almost drenching a passerby. Better still, later, comes an intertextual jolt, as Bruni Tedeschi cuts from a passionate stage love scene between Marcelline and Eric, to our heroine racing through a downpour, in total disarray, to confront a priest, again played by Pascal Bongard, as if coerced to reappear from *It's Easier for a Camel . . .*. As the priest recoils from her, appropriately wary, she begs him: "Give me a child! . . . Like a gift—I thought giving was part of Christian life?"

Taken seriously, *Actresses* comments on the life of the mind and the body, the ego versus the heart, careers undermining domesticity, spiritual needs at war with physical needs. (When one rehearsal breaks down after Marcelline stalls over which hand Natalya would use to open a door, the director yells at his truculent cast: "I want bodies, not psychology!") But conversely, simultaneously, Bruni Tedeschi mocks her own textual pretensions in raising such questions in the first place. In this vein, another pop-art edit breaches a long take in which Marcelline and Eric share a night bus ride home, wondering intimately whether they love each other on stage or in reality. Before fleeing, Marcelline confesses, "I kiss you, I love you. . . . You're my prince, you're my love in a play, not in life." Cut—to Marcelline sharing a rowboat with her Mother and Aunt, who argue furiously and wrestle off their seats, narrowly avoiding capsizing into the lake. From grand passion in art, the film staggers to petty strife in actuality.

So disconcerting are these pop-art shifts—Louis Guichard calls them "paradoxical antidotes"[50]—that at times they veer closely to an aesthetic of distraction, the film interrupting itself, its own train of textual thought. Several times, in fact, *Actresses* resorts to shots that conflict internally, pop-art materials contrasted within a single set-up. A foregrounded line of action, typically a pompous monologue or conversation, is set off in the frame against an incidental piece of physical business or understated moment of low comedy. One such design is a static long shot, lasting a minute, in the theater canteen. Here, Natalya's on-stage spouse, Islayev, broods screen left about coping with his (very minor) role: "No one really notices me," he reflects sadly to himself, "I'm the husband." And on this point he is clearly correct: while Islayev wallows in self-doubt, Bruni Tedeschi provides equal space to an unidentified extra, screen right, who attracts our attention by devouring a bowl of spaghetti, twirling the fronds on his fork, speed-feeding himself while spraying meat sauce. A psychological crisis, internal beliefs under chronic strain, shares space in Bruni Tedeschi's cinema with a man messily stuffing his face with pasta. Jacques Tati would have appreciated this motif, and you cannot pay Bruni Tedeschi's pop-art cinema a higher compliment than that.[51]

As an emblem of French pop-art cinema, however, the case of Bruni Tedeschi is instructive beyond her direction of two bravura features. In addition to its capacity for textual invention, pop-art cinema today grants professional opportunities, especially for international distribution and exhibition. In recent years, this type of filmmaking is programmed perennially by the expanding range of middle-rank film festivals, such as Moscow, Boston, Stockholm, Chicago, San Sebastian, Los Angeles, and London. Bruni Tedeschi's debut, following this trajectory, won at the 2003 Tribeca Film Festival awards for Best Emerging Filmmaker and Best Actress. *Actresses*, even more elevated, won the Jury Prize at the 2007 Cannes Film Festival. Such institutional endorsement also extends to the prestigious North American market. *It's Easier for a Camel . . .*, in this context, was chosen for the 2005–6 *Tournées*, a package of films offered to American schools and universities by the French American Cultural Exchange (FACE), a partner of the Cultural Services of the French Embassy in the United States, cosponsored by the CNC and the French Ministry of Foreign Affairs. As an official *Tournées* selection, *It's Easier for a Camel . . .* was designed to screen as part of locally organized French film festivals. In effect, Bruni Tedeschi's film was promoted as an artwork too sophisticated for the multiplex, but more palatable for audiences than radical French arthouse fare. In this category, Bruni Tedeschi joins the ranks of contemporary pop-auteurs like Yvan Attal, Jacques Audiard, Maïwenn le Besco, Christian Carion, Sophie Fillières, Christophe Honoré, Cédric Klapisch, Patrice Leconte, and a host of others. Raising the profile of French cinema abroad, occupying a dynamic cultural middle ground, this pop-art French cinema combines low art with high art in fresh and productive ways. Perhaps Bruni Tedeschi herself sums up this cinematic template, and its diverse appeal, most succinctly. Asked by an interviewer whether *It's Easier for a Camel . . .* was a mainstream comedy or a lofty tragedy, she replied: "I prefer it when these two elements are put intimately side-by-side: it seems to be me that there's actually nothing stronger than that."[52]

The Zombie Body Politic: Robin Campillo's *They Came Back*

Through the gates of the Saint-Louis cemetery they come, a stream of the living dead. Electronic tones pulse as these undead legions advance through deserted streets, apparitions with shuffling feet, faces turning from side to side, uncannily impassive. Abruptly, the camera cuts into a leftward tracking shot, much closer to the shambling crowd, revealing the walking bodies to be weirdly unmarked by death, their glazed expressions and sleepwalker's gait the only clues that something is terribly wrong. The horde's measured progress takes it unimpeded into the surrounding town. Cars are abandoned as motorists stop in awe, passersby come to a bewildered halt, occasional individuals, picked out with a long telephoto lens, falteringly approach the lumbering zombies. From these strange scenes, we move to a town meeting in progress, as anxious citizens call for action. To them, and the viewer, a sober announcement is made: "Initial estimates, which however remain very vague, have stated that more than 70 million women and men have returned into the world . . ."

These scenes, taken from the opening of Robin Campillo's *They Came Back* (*Les Revenants*, 2004) are some of the more quietly disconcerting in recent world horror cinema. It is crucial to note, however, that such images are far from unusual among today's French filmmakers. For within the wholesale commercial proliferation of contemporary French cinema, horror in particular has seen an explosion of interest and investment. This genre, historically the most denigrated but most profitable of all, was until recently quite marginal in France, typified only by a small number of early shorts (such as Abel Gance's 1912 *The Mask of Horror* [*Le Masque d'horreur*]), Maurice Tourneur's *La Main du diable* (1943), the classical works of Henri-Georges Clouzot (most famously *Les Diaboliques* [1955]), Georges Franju's *Eyes Without a Face* (*Les Yeux sans visage*, 1960), and, less reputably, Jean Rollin's 1970s softcore vampire erotica. But in a burst of recent activity, a group of young French filmmakers has created what Réné Prédal calls "*le cinéma gore.*"[53] Recently this comprises lower-budget productions that mimic Hollywood sub-genres: slasher or stalker films (*Deep in the Woods* [*Premenons-nous dans les bois*, 2000], *High Tension* [*Haute tension*, 2003], *Inside* [*A l'intérieur*, 2007], *Vertige* [2009]), vampire dramas (*Les Morsures de l'aube*, 2001), supernatural thrillers (*Maléfique* [2002]); high horror camp (*Bloody Mallory* [2002]), zombie-policier hybrids (*La Horde* [2009]), and macabre suspense films about backwater psychopaths and sadistic torture chambers (*Sheitan* [2006], *Ils* [2006], *Frontière/s* [2007], *Martyrs* [2008], *Humains* [2009], *The Pack* [*La Meute*] [2010]).

In response to these productions, one critic suggests that "we can begin talking about a viable, exciting rebirth in French horror film,"[54] but, as elsewhere, this pop culture phenomenon is not limited to France's borders. The visceral appeal of new French horror, especially to a youthful demographic, has translated extremely well to a global scale, with wide DVD distribution of these titles evident as far afield as Latin America and Asia. Revenue from these films has also predictably led to international opportunities for their more successful directors, in the form of Hollywood horror films crewed by French émigrés. Like echoes of Jacques Tourneur's work for Val Lewton's RKO unit in the 1940s, these Franco-American B-movies now include: Mathieu Kassovitz's *Gothika* (2003), Christophe Gans's adaptation of the video game franchise *Silent Hill* (2006), David Moreau's and Xavier Palud's *The Eye* (2008), Eric Valette's *One Missed Call* (2008), and Alexandre Aja's remake of Wes Craven's *The Hills Have Eyes* (2006), followed by *Mirrors* (2008) and *Piranha 3-D* (2010).[55] Remarkably, in the early twenty-first century there are more French filmmakers at work in the North American film industry than at any time since the mass filmmaking exodus of World War II and France's Occupation. And it is horror cinema—vulgar, graphic, shamelessly derivative yet undeniably potent—that has propelled these young French directors to Hollywood.

Belying its status as arguably the least elevated genre of all, this French horror renaissance in some cases has proved a fascinating context for pop-art cinema. Here, like Bruni Tedeschi, Campillo might seem an unlikely candidate. His career is intimately linked to realist political filmmaker Laurent Cantet, with whom he cowrote *Time Out* (*L'Emploi du temps*, 2001), *Heading South* (*Vers le sud*, 2005) and the Cannes Grand Prize-winner (breaking a twenty-one-year gulf between French recipients), *The Class* (*Entre les murs*, 2008). (Campillo also edited all these films, along with Cantet's other feature, *Human Resources*). Cantet's films (in which Campillo's contributions have received little fanfare) are decisive moments in contemporary French cinema, high-water marks for a kind of overt leftist political discourse prized by many film critics and scholars. *Heading South* aside, Cantet and Campillo's methods are largely naturalistic, favoring nonprofessional actors (just one recognized performer in *Human Resources*; none in *The Class*), little or no nondiegetic music, and understated and dramatically flattened screenplays that avoid inflated denouements. Cantet's and Campillo's plots, however, are nonetheless very calculated probings of social faultlines. *Time Out*, for example, is the factually based story of a white collar worker, recently fired, who maintains the illusion of ongoing work to his credulous family and associates; *The Class* derives from the autobiography of a struggling junior high school teacher, whose experiences were distilled through a year's worth of improvisations in which the cowriter/instructor, François Bégaudeau, played himself. To scholars such as Will Higbee and Martin O'Shaughnessy, Cantet epitomizes French cinema's potential for political activism, a committed social inquiry in which these "social-realist melodramas intriguingly place their social crises at the heart of the societal norm—an indication, perhaps, of just how profoundly the socioeconomic malaise of the 1990s has affected virtually all levels of contemporary French society."[56]

What, then, of the horror film's role in Campillo's directorial debut, the supernatural as a facet of political discourse?[57] One precursor, conceptually at least, is a tendency within the Japanese New Wave of the 1960s, epitomized by the work of Kaneto Shindo, an atom bomb documentarist whose elliptically gruesome thrillers, *Onibaba* (1964) and *Kuroneko* (1968), deconstructed masculinist myths of the samurai genre, while also linking Japan's patriarchal social order to its ruinous hunger for war.[58] Part of the effort to resuscitate more respected horror auteurs, certainly, rests on the claim that

The dead awake: The opening sequence of *They Came Back*

figures like Shindo and George Romero, working in North America, inter-
rogate the dysfunctionality of capitalism via horrific social breakdowns that
are allegorical.[59] (Writing in *La Croix*, Genviève Welcomme acclaimed *They
Came Back* as a "fable . . . the return of the dead, an archaic theme, as old as
humanity.")[60]

In this light, Campillo's approach to zombie film iconography is to remove
all traces of the format's customary gore and graphic violence, designing instead a vestigial thriller that is indirectly affecting, beautifully sinister rather
than visceral or confrontational. On-screen, Campillo's pop-art negotiation
is to obey generic mandates — a horror film that horrifies — but also to represent more insidious, intangible social polemics: ageism, inequality in the
workplace, and the all-encroaching, bureaucratic forces of governmental and
corporate authoritarianism.

With sobering detachment, *They Came Back* follows a sudden two-hour
outbreak in which millions inexplicably return from their graves, emerging
on the streets with no trace of decomposition or decay. (In one interview,
Campillo stated: "I have no idea why the dead have come back. . . . I wanted
to put elements of the fantastic on an equal footing with things that are very
concrete.")[61] As with traditional horror films, the supernatural world has clear
rules: only those deceased in the last ten years return, meaning that two thirds
of the zombies are over sixty years old, and only ten percent under forty. To all
intents and purposes these zombies are physically intact, although scientific
research finds their body temperatures to be five degrees below normal, and
that they suffer, variably, from a kind of aphasia that means they only partially
understand their un-bereaved relatives. More peculiar is their decreased need
for sleep; many of the zombies return to work nocturnally, or else walk the
streets to congregate silently after dark.

The government's response to the situation, citing United Nations regulations (this is apparently a large-scale epidemic, although our focus remains on one small town), is to bypass safety protocols and mass produce a drug, Lithanol, to control the undead, while the army commandeers community centers as internment camps. Soon, spy satellites and observation balloons monitor the undead's movements at all times, night and day. All these methods situate the dead as refugees in their own home town, narcotized victims of a Big Brother State. And, underlining this imagery of drugged, enforced mass relocation (although the undead offer no initial resistance), the return of these reanimated people soon instills social crises: not all loved ones are welcomed with open arms, families are uneasily reconciled with altered ex-members, while the zombies' impaired brain function prevents their professional reintegration. Like illegal immigrants relinquishing rank and status, in *They Came Back* returning architects become production line machinists, politicians labor as soup servers; the zombie population is a working underclass. (Most of the dead are retired, Campillo notes, but the State can no longer afford their pensions and needs their labor.) But all that the returned seek, as we are told by the Mayor in a voice-over that is at once chilling and sympathetic, neatly conveying the film's ambivalence, is: "In short, the right to resume their lives."

Campillo balances the broader social ramifications of his narrative with specific character test cases; both are framed in a highly unsettling stylistic template that is measured, neutral, almost beatific for all the unnatural events shown on-screen. The widescreen frame is in almost constant motion, tracking and panning around the streets and between interactions that are often obscured by windows, blinds, and glassy apertures. More distinctive still, the film's ever-present minor-key synthesized tones render the flow of events constantly unnerving: dinner in a canteen with meals served by a blankly staring returnee, army troops patrolling a dormitory whose inhabitants need no rest. The film's most effective dramatic reversal, a pop-art device par excellence, is that as the film unfolds Campillo makes the zombies behave predictably and calmly, while the pillars of their community, the normal alive, act like unbalanced threats. The horror of the film is this inversion: like veterans of war or social outcasts, the zombies lay bare our unstated group hypocrisies, our petty self-interests and fears of trauma or difference. The intangible tension which permeates *They Came Back* — like one scene of a returnee, Mathieu (Jonathan Zaccaï) regarding neutrally (longingly?) a park filled with playing children — and our constant expectations of violence are reflected back on us, an audience's knowledge of countless horror clichés turned into unthinking social prejudices. And most arrestingly of all, Campillo takes no editorial position, judges neither side.

Soon, moreover, it is hard to tell the populations apart. One particularly poignant plotline has the unnamed Mayor (Victor Garrivier) unable to accept his returned wife, despite her efforts at normalcy, and the two are reconciled only after his death from stress and heart failure. *They Came Back*'s nominal lead, Rachel (Géraldine Pailhas), a grieving widow, just as ironically, is initially unable to bear the revival of the husband, Mathieu, whose loss supposedly triggered her depression. When she does, belatedly, resume their physical relationship, she drifts apart from her work, becomes distanced from her career and abandons her other relationships. The most shocking sequence of all, a zombie film invoking domestic and parental violence in memorable deadpan, involves a married couple whose young (undead) son's offputting activities — his sluggish motion lags him behind other children playing catch; he increasingly wants to rejoin his undead comrades for companionship after dark — leads them to lock him in their apartment, jailing him at home, while he scratches pitifully at the door and windows. Worse, as the father protests and the mother coolly proffers Lithanol, the boy quietly, in measured steps, falls over their balcony, crumples on the ground, then stiffly walks off into the night. They watch him go.

But Campillo reserves a final, viscerating about turn for the film's closing sequences. Again the pop-art filmmaker has it both ways, effectively exploiting generic mainstream materials while also permeating them with the ambiguities of the arthouse, the textually familiar undercut by the troublingly opaque. After carefully marshalling the viewer's sympathies, recasting the undead by way of social prejudices, workplace exploitation, ageist intolerance, and the simple fear of the unknown, the film abruptly shifts course. In the final scenes, the returned apparently retaliate: explosions break out around the town, terrorism is implied, before the ubiquitous troops finally, inevitably, respond by opening fire on their undead targets. Some of the returnees calmly disappear into sewers underground — including a neutrally composed Mathieu, much to Rachel's anguish — but more are gunned down, slaughtered, their doubly dead corpses removed by bus, or conveyed by stretcher to the graveyards from whence they came. For a film that engages so many contemporary paranoias, this highly moving climactic imagery is suggestive of nothing less than Holocaust or genocide.

In the very last sequence, though, Campillo strategically breaks his own diegetic logic again, denying the plausible supernatural the film has elsewhere insisted upon. The troops abandon the bodies on top of their erstwhile graves, and we now — bizarrely — see the lined-up bodies, many of which are recognizable characters, simply disappearing, as if wished away, vanishing from collective view. Now the electronic score recedes to naturalistic silence and *They Came Back* concludes on a devastating shot that resists closure and explanation: Rachel posed in medium close-up, staring at her blank reflection in a mirror, rubbing away the condensation from her shower. The shot is held, she blinks once; cut to black. So open as to recall high art Antonioni modernism from the 1960s, the film here seems to demand an allegorical interpretation, yet it also remains utterly grounded in the horror film particularities of its preceding conception and design. A moody zombie flick; a caustic intellectual inquiry into social injustice and exclusion—both the dual facets of Campillo's project are present and intact, individually coherent; yet both also forcefully coalesce into something else, something distinctively new. In broader terms, moreover, Campillo's film demonstrates the potential of French pop-art cinema to revitalize the viewing experience, making the known unknown. *They Came Back* revives profoundly our interest in ingrained conventions, reheated cultural leftovers, invigorating what are clichéd mainstream materials. Like the horror subject itself, Campillo brings things back from the dead.

Instruments of War: Serge Bozon's *La France*

As we have seen, a major part of the pop-art cinema model is to interconnect textual devices high and low, defamiliarizing both. In this context, the work of Serge Bozon is an apt example of how unclassifiably refreshing such filmmaking is. Bozon, a film critic affiliated with *La Lettre du cinéma*, designed *La France* (2007), his third film, as on one level a traditional genre exercise. It is set in 1917, a World War I film about the plight of eleven young soldiers, led by their doleful Lieutenant (Pascal Greggory), all of whom, it turns out, are deserters with diminishing hopes of survival. Besides this dramatic backdrop, *La France* focuses on a young woman, Camille (Sylvie Testud), living in a remote village in the northeast of France, whose young husband François (Guillaume Depardieu) is a recent conscript. After receiving a curt, dismissive letter from him—"Camille: Don't write to me, I don't want to hear your news, you won't see me again"—she cuts her hair, disguises herself as a soldier, and sets off in dogged pursuit. Soon, she discovers the wandering platoon, and persuades them to accompany her on this apparently futile search. Both of these plotlines, the plucky seeker heroine rushed into danger alongside a doomed battalion, are already near cliché, so clearly do they derive from popular lore.

Indeed, at first glance *La France* is highly compatible with the heritage of World War I on-screen; Bozon cited in many interviews his belief that the war film was the last classical genre left in contemporary French cinema. In this light, *La France* is a direct thematic descendent of early landmarks such as

Camille (Sylvie Testud) finds François (Guillaume Depardieu) in *La France*

Abel Gance's *J'Accuse* (1919), Raymond Bernard's recently re-released *Wooden Crosses* (*Les Croix de bois*, 1932), Jean Renoir's benchmark *La Grande illusion* (1937); as well as classical Hollywood war films like Raoul Walsh's *Objective, Burma!* (1945) and Sam Fuller's *Merrill's Marauders* (1962). Bozon also openly acknowledged the central motif, World War I as the advent of truly dehuman-izing mass conflict, reworked in successful contemporary films such as *The Officer's Ward* (*La Chambre des officiers*, 2001), *Merry Christmas* (*Joyeux Noël*, 2005), and *Les Fragments d'Antonin* (2006). A *cinéma du corps*-derived case, the deadpan yet graphic horrors of Bruno Dumont's more abstract, unnamed war in *Flanders* (*Flandres*, 2006) is another proximate case. Colliding with these approaches, though, is a film of which *La France* is an acute pop-art deconstruction—Jean-Pierre Jeunet's *A Very Long Engagement*. This film, the transnationalist test case we considered earlier, is an expansive, internation-ally successful wartime epic about Mathilde's (Audrey Tautou) pursuit of her lost fiancé, Manech (Gaspard Ulliel). But where Jeunet's production is com-mercial in the most calculated sense—in its opulent production design, its beguiling visual style, its trite sense of humor, its cloying use of Tautou's waif star persona—Bozon's is schizophrenic and anachronistic.

La France abounds with pop-art devices: an array of stylistic ruptures and tonal oscillations, a hybridity of citations, its textual revivals of low and high cultures. There is initially the sheer oddity of the performances: stylized and deliberately stilted, overtly choreographed, emphatic yet uncommunica-tive, recalling the arthouse severity of Robert Bresson and his contemporary converts Céline Sciamma and Eugène Green. Here and elsewhere, *La France*'s expressive balance is disruptive, unharmonious. Something is amiss even in the opening shot, as Camille and a group of village girls descend from a hilltop (she has promised them signs of their absent menfolk) in offputting geometry, holding then breaking their static poses, lined up on the horizon, to scatter over a 45-degree arc in peculiar syncopation, arms all held out at right angles, broken by Camille inexplicably falling to the ground and lying prone. In the second scene the process continues, as Camille's unnamed sister (Cécile Reigher) reads François's intercepted letter aloud, solicitous then abruptly scornful, greeted only by an evasive neutrality from Testud as Camille, who busies herself, offering no direct rejoinder, making her bed as all hope for her married future is taken from her. The traditional, audience-friendly stakes of war epics, an emotionally direct melodrama of war-torn lovers like Jeunet's, are dissipated, while easy identification is avoided. Even basic issues of diegetic logic are clouded: Why is the sister so inconsistent, then pernicious? If Camille is so unaffected by the brusque letter, why does she abandon her life to seek François?

Developing this uneven opening, *La France* soon foregrounds a series of pop-art manipulations. Cryptic stylistic devices—Jean-Marc Lalanne's term is "bizarre protocols"[62]—impinge upon the film's diegesis. The first method, obvious even to a non-technician, is the abrasively murky quality of the actual image. Working with his sister, Céline Bozon, a graduate of la Fémis and Jean Paul Civeyrac's long-term cinematographer, Bozon chose for his film stock Kodak 5299, normally used as an intermediate during postproduction, a type of celluloid he claimed had never been used for actual shooting. The Bozons describe the results as an "aquarium aesthetic,"[63] in which every-thing and everyone looks to be underwater. Alternately, we might say that this is a film which literally takes place in the fog of war.[64] On-screen, *La France*'s color scheme is drastically muted: verdant greens manifest as sallow off-greys, sunlight turns into pondwater; while the light itself is rendered as slightly opaque, oppressive, even tactile, making Camille and the soldiers' slow progress across the countryside seem even harder work. By contrast, for the night scenes, the Bozons favor extremely bright spotlights and strong key light set-ups. In the scene where Camille flees her village after dark, for instance, avoiding the soldiers who prevent her first escape attempt, her body, the buildings, and even the surrounding woodlands are bathed in vast pools of harsh, almost fluorescent direct glare. The aesthetic itself is a witty pop-art inversion: day is night, night becomes day.

More assertive still is *La France*'s most audacious feature—these soldiers perform music on instruments, and sing.[65] Four times in the film's highly

The doomed battalion, their weapons turned into musical instruments, in *La France*

attenuated, picaresque narrative (Jacques Morice describes it as "an auda-cious military road movie which resembles nothing known")[66] the recruits, without preamble, break into song. As the troupe stands or sits in tableaux, battered instruments appear from nowhere (a dirty clarinet, guitars fashioned from cans, two wooden xylophones, an accordion, and two stringed devices) and a performance begins. A defiantly idiosyncratic technician again, Bozon insisted that all the numbers had to be composed for the film and performed live, recorded digitally on twenty-five microphones, sixteen of which were wireless. While citing the musical is nothing new in contemporary French cinema—from Ducastel's and Martineau's Jacques Demy homage *Jeanne and the Perfect Guy* (*Jeanne et le garçon formidable*, 1998), to Ozon's *8 Women* (2002), Honoré's New Wave retrospective *Love Songs* (*Les Chansons d'amour*, 2007), and Maïwenn le Besco's outlandishly self-reflexive documentary-musical *Le Bal des actrices* (2008)[67]—Bozon's performance inserts seem peculiarly disjunctive in the context of a joyless narrative about death and war. Even when the lovers are reunited at *La France*'s climax, a potentially romantic culmination, after the couple has made love, François abruptly lists his dead comrades, staring into the night sky, before a brief caption tells us that our group of deserters "never reached" their destination.

A key issue, raised by the songs especially, is Bozon's relationship with Brechtian style. Are these alienation effects, textual schisms, the means for direct political commentary and audience empowerment? Again, the answer for the pop-art director is yes and no; an unsettling gap between high and low film culture opens up. So disruptive are *La France*'s numbers that they might recall the high art Brechtian methods of Godard and Oshima: the famous direct address and metatextual, political self-reflexivity in films like *Two or Three Things That I Know About Her* (*Deux ou trois choses que je sais d'elle*, 1967) and *Night and Fog in Japan* (1960), revived in films like *Gabrielle*. Here, however, the devices are but vestigial traces, textual fissures positioned as performative entertainments, ambiguous breaks bracketed off from the otherwise pessimistic action.[68] All four of the songs do obliquely relate to the textual issues at hand. The quasi-folk lyrics, evoking emotional turmoil but poetically abstract, indirectly comment on bleak wartime (they are often sung from the distressed perspective of "I, the blind girl"). Bozon also makes diegetic concessions: the non-professional musicians make mistakes and strike wrong notes; their instruments are made from ugly and broken detritus (Bozon insisted that they be made from materials appropriate to the era, like a Dogma production designer). Clearly, on-screen and under Bozon's challenging direction, this is music produced under great duress. But on the other hand, most strikingly, no commentary is ever made about the fact that these are deserters fleeing both French and German troops, desperate to remain hidden, allied with no one (even a local farmer's family, initially sympathetic, turns on the hapless group), yet they are made to proclaim their presence on the battlefield so overtly. The third number even takes place in a cave, ostensibly as the troupe avoids German patrols. As a representative pop-art motif, singing songs in the trenches ultimately becomes an absurdist statement. The songs are neither funny nor romantic, best thought of as a hopeless exclamation of collective solidarity, ironically appropriate in the terminal confines of the First World War.

Like that of many contemporary pop-art filmmakers, Bozon's work evades critical assimilation; were it not so studied, the effect might be described as playful. In some ways, *La France* creates another paradoxical dichotomy, like Bruni Tedeschi's and Campillo's—here, that of intimate, persistently optimistic sentiment (Camille's capacity for unstinting love, the soldiers' fragile creation of a musical ensemble, imperfectly beautiful songs offered up into the air) versus a brutally indifferent world at war. Either way, the critical reception of *La France* interrogated Bozon for his many provocations: the reasoning behind his title, *La France*, invoking the country itself; and an explanation for the musical segments which neither cohere with a plausible diegesis nor the war genre so meticulously observed otherwise. While Bozon was thoughtfully skittish about these subjects, he was most specific, and articulate, on relating both issues to what we have characterized as France's textually dynamic cinema of pop-art materials. In fact, Bozon asserted himself as a pop-art spokesman. In *Libération*, he declared: "I love changes in register, as it's better to do things which affect us the most, even though they may be perceived as idiosyncrasies. . . . [France's best contemporary cinema] has a taste for this mixture of tones, of genres. . . . Moreover, at the risk of sounding like a megalomaniac, I just wish we could get rid of this horrible break: *art et essai* versus commercial cinema."[69] Here, like many of his professional contemporaries, the main war Bozon wages is with the old-fashioned notion that French cinema must keep its mainstream and intellectual film materials apart.

Better the Devil You Know: Olivier Assayas's *Demonlover*

Deceptively tranquil, *Demonlover* opens in a luxury airplane cabin interior. We are in what is obviously executive business class: the window shutters over the plush leather seats are all closed, a low hum drones in the background, internal lights are dimmed, while small blue fluorescent beams illuminate the central aisle, the only color accents among the greys and whites of this neutral space. After a pause, a stewardess walks carefully through the shot towards the cockpit, retrieving an empty water bottle. Her dark pink, ersatz Asian uniform is as blandly institutional as the company-issue blankets covering the sleeping passengers. Cut to a steadicam shot moving briskly forwards, as we gradually encroach on generic business patter ("In short, I think that negotiations are well underway . . ."), to which a young woman, a secretary, attends, scrawling in shorthand. Another cut reveals in long shot that these are the only people awake. Seen by no one except a nondescript businessman, rows of television monitors above the comatose bodies show silent images of explosions, fire and diving bodies, a formulaic Hollywood spectacular in progress. The plane flight continues.

This prefacing scene of *Demonlover*, typical among Olivier Assayas's contemporary films *Boarding Gate* (2007) and *Clean* (2004), sets up an instantly recognizable *mise-en-scène* of twenty-first-century globalization. We could be absolutely anywhere on planet Earth here, high above international waters somewhere, nowhere. Beyond the fragments of French dictation, nothing differentiates the polyglot nationalities of the passengers or the cabin crew. We don't know the time, or time zone, in which these banal events take place. Instead, this is an hermetically enclosed, transitional non-place, far removed from borders on the ground and any sense of locality or context. The elite businesspeople traverse international space, a hyper-capitalist deal is struck, while a lavish mass media thriller, barely noticed but ubiquitous, plays out before a slumbering audience, as if it is the flow of violent images which keep

Diane (Connie Nielsen) in the office in *Demonlover*

it tranquilized, numb. *Demonlover* highlights its engagement with what we saw earlier as a transnational screen model. As David Thompson suggests, "Assayas achieves his own updating of that French glossiness that in the 1980s was disparagingly dubbed the cinéma du look. . . . [The film] plays in an emotionally anaesthetized, dystopian mode that could be called 'steel-and-glass cinema': cinema set in the recognizably contemporary urban world but framed and shot in such a way that it becomes detached, not unreal so much as irreal, bordering on science fiction."[70]

Demonlover, which will never again be as serene as its opening shots, is a pop-art treatment of these late-phase capitalist motifs. At first glance — although the film's public premiere, at the 2002 Cannes festival, produced an angry backlash — *Demonlover* presents as a slick thriller about mass media and corporate conspiracy. The opening scene turns out to be a flight in progress between Tokyo and Paris; its passengers are the Volf Corporation, finalizing a lucrative distribution contract with a Japanese media company, TokyoAnime. Diane (Connie Nielsen, part of Assayas's international cast) inveigles her way into the negotiations, poisoning the bottled water of her boss, Karen (Dominique Reymond), and alienating her put-upon assistant, Elise (Chloë Sevigny). The Volf group form a partnership with an American company, Demonlover, headed by brash executive Elaine (Gina Gershon), which has vague links to an S&M torture porn website, Hellfireclub. By this point, *Demonlover* is already convoluted, but two thirds of the way through it collapses into strategic, terminal incoherence. Diane turns out to be a double agent for Demonlover's rival, Mangatronics, and kills Elaine after a lengthy scuffle that also leaves her unconscious. When Diane comes to, all trace of the violence is gone, and preceding characters, relationships and plotlines have altered. (The structure recalls David Lynch's *Mulholland Drive*, although no critics gave Assayas the benefit of the citation.) Now, Elise appears to be a senior executive, Diane's subterfuge has been somehow exposed, while her relationship with a colleague, Hervé (Charles Berling), becomes sexual as well as professional. In its final stretch, *Demonlover* is even more confrontational: Diane's date with Hervé becomes an ambiguous rape, during which she shoots him in the head and kills him. Worse, after fleeing the Volf organization, Diane eventually ends up a prisoner of the Hellfireclub group, and the film concludes with her posed on its website, the sexual plaything of an indifferent American teen, who finishes his homework while her agonized face is frozen on his computer monitor.

The ambiguous multiple registers of *Demonlover*'s pop-art palette are everywhere reinforced — from the aggressive features of the *cinéma du corps*, to the pulp genres of international cinema at its most debased. Assayas's film is a deconstructed thriller that only erratically thrills, trafficking in images of sexual commerce and cyber-gratification that are too grotesque to gratify. Sleek and dense with detail, *Demonlover* is also arid, overt about the sinister undertones of the global commerce it represents. Even after we leave the plane cabin, *Demonlover* lingers in neutral, technologized spaces (stark office boardrooms, luxury hotel suites, designer nightclubs, barely personalized penthouses), while the film explores, without flinching, the compulsions of violence and commercialized sexual exchange that fund such impersonal opulence. This is accentuated aesthetically by Assayas and his cinematographer, Denis Lenoir, who interspersed DV with 35mm during postproduction, whiting out and overexposing their stocks to cast a ghostly, pallid sheen over the bustling imagetrack. *Demonlover*'s diegetic worlds, as much as their virtual reality counterparts, intermingle abstractly, are troublingly indistinct. In the scenes of Diane and Hervé inspecting the TokyoAnime facilities, for instance, the interiors are so diffused with a heavy, grey-blue hue that the workplace resembles nothing less than *La France*'s suffocating aquarium aesthetic. Similarly, as Elise paces through the blank halls of the Volf Corporation's headquarters to a meeting with Diane, the hospital-like walls seem to merge with the flooring; the human form of her ghostlike body hangs oddly suspended in space, bound to nothing. Assayas's customary lack of establishing shots further disrupt the viewer's equilibrium; his scenes merge together in medias res, with shots conveyed by a constantly moving medium close-up steadicam, unhinging our grasp of time and space. The most notable set piece in this context, admired even by *Demonlover*'s most ardent detractors, occurs when Diane and Hervé visit a Tokyo nightclub. Under an aural mix of beats, guitar strums and rumbles, the ensuing collage, a demented music video, batters us with syncopations of close-up neon flashes, go-go-dancers bouncing on a stage, strobelights picking out bits of dancers' bodies, shapes and textures devoid of context. (At times, in its design, *Demonlover* is a true companion film to *Irreversible*.)

Just as vividly unbalanced was *Demonlover*'s reception, within which the film's pop-art leanings became apparent again. The source of fierce critical infuriation, at times rage, Assayas's film provoked both mainstream respondents expecting a conspiracy thriller that abides by logical generic conventions (the irony being, of course, that the thriller is inherently implausible), as well as analysts who expected auteurs like Assayas to stick to his career course, making films that conform to intellectual type: like a coming-of-age story (*Cold Water* [*L'Eau froide*, 1994]), cinephile homage (*Irma Vep* [1996]), socially conscious heritage film (*Les Destinées* [2000]), extended domestic drama and ode to the Musée d'Orsay (*Summer Hours* [2008]), or epic biopic (*Carlos* [2010]). Breaking the trust of both walks of cinematic life, low and high, *Demonlover* was greeted with disbelief. The tone, and diagnosis, is summed up by Olivier Père, who suggests that: "Cinéaste of the contemporary, plugged into fashions and trends in cinema, [Assayas] plunges the spectator into a universe that is anxiety-laden and artificial. . . . His taste for experimental 60s cinema collides with new visual forms, which lack morality yet are also beautiful: images of manga and of cyberculture, but also scenes of pornography and murder."[71] One particularly scathing critique of *Boarding Gate*, from an American perspective, also epitomizes the reception of Assayas's recent filmmaking. Beyond the issue of evaluation, the consternation arises from films that conform to neither commercial nor intellectual mandates; many critics cannot countenance the pop-art dichotomy. In this case, the frustrated critic complained/praised that Assayas's film: "[Is] one of the most sophisticated, beautifully textured, soulfully acted shitty erotic thrillers ever deserving of a straight-to-video release. Much like Assayas's previous effort, the equally gorgeous, aloof cyberthriller *Demonlover*, *Boarding Gate* is a French cinéaste's *idea* of what a slick, jet-setting contemporary suspense film might look like, not a satisfying execution of same."[72]

As far as mainstream critics are concerned, the pop-art confluences in Bruni Tedeschi's work ultimately create a self-mocking, hence satisfying tone. For Bozon and Campillo, too, the mixed materials are perceived to be unsettling but in keeping with the feverish states of social conflict they depict. But Assayas's more provocative fusions, close in some ways to the highly fragmentary work of Honoré, are more overtly designed to confront such tastes: with the most arthouse and characteristically French of materials (linked back to the *cinéma du corps*), interspersed with devices that are utterly globalized, lowbrow, and banal (a corporate paranoia thriller laced with charmless erotica). Occupying territory at the most inconsistent, incoherent, scattershot end of the pop-art continuum, Assayas, it seems, cannot win.

In conclusion, the fraught case of *Demonlover* boils down the pop-art equation to its fundamentals. Clearly, as represented by the range of projects analyzed here—from Bruni Tedeschi to Campillo to Bozon to Assayas—the pop-art model extends from the engaging (comedic breaches of style and tone, a flippant self-awareness, open design that charms) to the decisively agitational (contradictory and excruciating amalgamations, vicious political enquiries, open design that repels). At one extreme of this continuum, *Demonlover* raises the basic question of justifying, or understanding, the pop-art template's existence. How does such a gratingly incongruous film come into being, get produced, position itself within French and international film culture? Right from its conflicted conception, *Demonlover* echoed the torrid business affairs about which it obsesses on-screen; its creation befitting the split purposes of a filmmaker like Assayas, engaged with cultural practices both exactingly highbrow and sordidly disreputable.

Even as a treatment and script, *Demonlover* was shaped by pop-art frictions. In the first place, the project came from writing that was critiqued, then encouraged, by Assayas's reading group, perhaps the most illustrious such gathering in France, consisting of Claire Denis, Jacques Fieschi (a la Fémis professor and cowriter of *Savage Nights*, *Sade* [2000], and *Nathalie . . .* [2003]), and Emmanuèlle Bernheim (cowriter of *Friday Night*, *5x2*, and *Les Invisibles* [2005]), the President of the la Fémis entrance examination board). On the other hand, *Demonlover*'s script also built on Assayas's fervent belief that certain recent Hollywood thrillers are not only the most powerful treatments of global capitalism, but also the most brutally modern films to have been produced in any context. Pored over by intellectual auteurs, yet assembled from the wreckage of films like John Carpenter's *They Live* (1988), David Fincher's *Fight Club* (1998), Tony Scott's *Enemy of the State* (1998) and Michael Mann's *The Insider* (1999), *Demonlover* was the product of Assayas's diverse cinephilia, a remnant of his career at *Cahiers du cinéma*, as writer and editor, between 1979 and 1985. As Aurélien Ferenczi remarked dryly about this offputting mix of conceptual sources: "Unexpected references from such a cinephilic perspective . . ."[73]

Ferenczi's point is doubly well taken, for even Assayas's position as a working cinéaste is conflicted. While Assayas embodies that quintessential French filmmaking role—the cineliterate cinephile, on the record declaring that criticism must permeate practice—he is also openly skeptical about the auteur theory and the principle of individualistic artistic seclusion that it engendered, particularly in the wake of institutional changes during and after the New Wave. As Rosanna Maule argues, Assayas's ideas were emblematized by a 1983 essay he contributed to *Cahiers*, in which he protested, "The premise of auteur-oriented cinema—that is, a subjective conception of cinema—has unfortunately inspired a generation of self-absorbed filmmakers, alienated from film spectators and too comfortable in their reliance on public subsidies to worry about the reception of their films."[74] This position is the legacy of Assayas's earliest writings in the 1970s and 1980s, right through to contemporary interviews in which he defended *Demonlover* on the grounds that it *deliberately* violated norms of the mainstream and the arthouse, attacking the safe cocoon in which conventionally assembled films leave the viewer.[75] This is, by result, a filmmaker dismissive of auteurist self-indulgences who, ironically, resituates his work by way of the (confounding) intentions of its maker. Ambivalent about the auteur label, as appreciative of classicism as modern arthouse filmmaking, drawn to mainstream artisans (notably George Lucas) as much as international iconoclasts (Andrei Tarkovsky, Hou Hsiao-Hsien, Ingmar Bergman), Assayas's pop-art compulsions problematize the very role of critic-turned-filmmaker, arguably France's most influential cinematic export.

As an end product, too—befitting both the pop-art formula and the era of digital proliferation it depicts—*Demonlover* challenged production norms and ended up existing in multiplying textual versions. With a budget of 6.4 million euros, *Demonlover* was neither a superproduction nor a microbudget *art et essai* venture. This fact, coupled to its unappetizing subject materials, led to its rookie Elizabeth Films producers, Edouard Weil and Xavier Giannoli, shopping the project around most of France's funding sources. This piecemeal approach intermittently paid off (with funding input secured from television channels like France 2 and M6, along with an international affiliate of Studio Canal, independent investors and by deferred costs agreed to by the LTC laboratory), but also broke down (it was denied an *avances sur recettes* grant, while Canal+ backed out on the grounds that its budget exceeded the 5.34 million euros ceiling imposed by the State for the channel's obligatory domestic production investments). Even after *Demonlover*'s production was cobbled together, moreover, its textual form never stabilized. Today, there are at least four separate versions of Assayas's film; none of them approaches unity. After its disastrous 2002 Cannes premiere, Assayas recut *Demonlover* for its brief theatrical release, eliding or pixellating the most graphic sex scenes from its live action and anime segments. He then revised it again for its first two DVD releases, which varyingly include portions of the earlier footage. Even on its second region 1 DVD release, by the now defunct Palm Pictures, extra footage was ambiguously appended, in the form of an Easter Egg code, accessed via a five digit sequence included in the packaging, which reveals additional bonus materials from the mocked-up Hellfireclub website.

From its origins to the present moment, years after its first appearances on-screen, it is as if *Demonlover* never quite knew exactly what it wants to be, who it wants to be seen by, how far it wants to push its textual agenda, how deeply it can sustain its premise to confront but also engage an audience. Regardless of its eventual status as a cult film that still inspires passions, and walk-outs, *Demonlover* and its dogged director in many ways epitomize the pop-art template that galvanizes aspects of French cinema today. These are films, most of all, that undermine easy classifications, inherited critical assumptions, the outmoded model that French cinema is *either* highbrow or lowbrow, esoteric or popular, that it cannot explore both approaches at once. Since the late 1950s, when the New Wave filmmakers first declared their break with ossified mainstream norms, critics have continued to endorse this conceit, that a gap had forever opened between France's commercial cinema, down below, and a self-consciously artistic elite, up above. Old habits die hard, but this comfortable cinematic division, which was only ever partly true anyway, has lost its relevance. As far as French cinema goes, the rules have decisively (and perhaps thankfully) changed. Fluently idiosyncratic, at times close to chameleonic, filmmakers such as Bruni Tedeschi, Campillo, Bozon, and Assayas form a kind of impromptu vanguard, a motley crew of inspired textual iconoclasts. From pies in the face to pop songs in a war zone, politicized zombies to poisoned designer Evian bottles, these wonderfully disconcerting films remind us that vexation, and unpredictability, can still play defining roles in the contemporary cinematic experience.

CHAPTER FOUR

Feminine Cinema

*Toscan du Plantier, the
president of UniFrance,
says that French cinema
"will be saved by women."
This may just be a* formule,
*pretty words, I don't know.
But I do think that maybe
the way we shoot a scene
of two people making love
is pretty different.*

TONIE MARSHALL,
director of *Venus Beauty
Institute (Vénus beauté
[institut]*, 1999)

Concerning the rights of its female citizens, France
has often lagged behind its Western neighbors.
Reflecting this, a catalog of France's belated efforts to enfranchise women is usually cited by both
Anglo-American and French feminists. There was
the so-called "first wave" of feminist intervention,
symbolized by the 1949 publication of Simone de
Beauvoir's *The Second Sex*, coinciding with women
finally getting the right to vote in 1944, then having
their equal status with men written into the 1946
and 1958 French Constitutions, which initially offered more theoretical than tangible support. A second phase of pro-female social overhauls emerged
in the 1960s and 1970s, for many catalyzed by the
widespread role of women in the mass civic protests of May 1968. Henceforward, French women
began to gain control over their bodies and their
fertility, through the legalization of contraception
(1967), the decriminalization of abortion (for a five-
year trial run under the 1975 Veil Law; then permanently in 1979), and the right to terminate unwanted
pregnancy under the national health care system
(1982). During the same period, women in France
also made social progress: the right to obtain paid
work and open bank accounts (1965), jurisdiction
over families becoming a parental instead of just a
paternal power (1970), and the right to divorce by
mutual consent (1975).

More recently, debates about women's position
in modern France reignited in the aftermath of the
1989 French Revolution bicentennial. Attention
focused on French women's lack of institutional
parité, the infamous statistic that France had the

Lola Doillon directs her cinematographer, Romain Lacourbas, on set for *Et toi, t'es sur qui?*

lowest proportion of women in political office than any European country except Greece — in 1995 just 5 percent of those in public office were women, versus a 53 percent female electorate. As many historians observed, here the great inconstancy of the French Republic came into view once again: that France is underwritten by the notion of a universal model citizen defined by neither gender nor ethnicity, yet the French state will, under public pressure and often reluctantly, occasionally legislate for the needs of its more marginalized constituents. Feminist writer Geneviève Fraisse memorably describes this as France's *vertige identitaire*, identity vertigo.[1] In response to the *parité* campaign — which gained political traction after a proequality manifesto was published in *L'Express* in 1996 — the French government enacted sweeping political reforms. In June 2000, this culminated in changes to articles 3 and 4 of the Constitution, officially requiring a 50/50 gender split among the candidates offered by parties for election. With tougher financial penalties enforced by a 2007 addendum, the law had a clear impact at local and regional levels; but while it remains popular among the general population, the quota system certainly offered no miracle cure for gender inequality. In real terms, moreover, the *parité* mandate punishes the smaller political parties less able to pay the fines levied for a lack of female candidates, as happened during the 2002 and 2007 French elections, which raised the proportion of female members of parliament by merely about 10 percent.

What remains is an intriguing, pivotal paradox about contemporary France, which ricochets between the most reactionary and the most forward-thinking contexts for women's advancement. As Roger Célestin, Eliane Dalmolin, and Isabelle de Courtivron remark, highlighted by the *parité* case, France is unavoidably a country in which the situation of women is "broadly integrated into the fabric of national discourse. . . . [France could] change from one of the most backward societies in terms of women's representation in the political sphere into one of the most progressive in this same area — at least in *theory*." [2] So while many obstacles remain, the actions of contemporary French women do have the capacity to secure recognition, sometimes acclaim, and, most important of all, change. As this chapter will discuss, nowhere is this pattern of embattled yet vibrant female agency in France more visible than in its cinema. The point is confirmed by no less iconic a figure than writer-director Catherine Breillat, who stated in 2008 that: "Today the film industry is perhaps the one place in France where parity exists between the sexes." [3]

Already we have seen in incidental fashion the work of prominent women film practitioners. In Chapter 1 we considered France's unprecedented slew of women debutants — some of whom were targeted by film schools like la Fémis seeking *parité* in their enrollments — whose work shared commonalities and was celebrated in unison, yet diverged quite widely in treating the materials of the first film. Chapter 2 discovered the pivotal role of more agitational female film artists within France's *cinéma du corps*, ranging from the seminal and well-known efforts of Breillat and Denis, to emergent figures like de Van and Bertrand, all keen to push the boundaries of France's arthouse and avant-garde environments. In Chapter 3, equally, we saw the impact of Bruni Tedeschi, as actress, writer-director and figurehead, to the new multi-registers of France's pop-art cinema. Retaining these women's ongoing careers as a guiding context, this chapter will engage more systematically with the issue of what is termed here a feminine cinema.

Surveying broadly, we can make interrelated claims about the contemporary French situation. One interesting point of departure is that among France's filmgoers, between 1999 and 2008, women made up on average 52 percent of the national audience, versus 48 percent men. [4] In terms of production, another overarching perspective is that women are today thoroughly (if still somewhat unevenly) integrated across the expansive spectrum of French cinematic practice, from the center-stage of the mainstream to the fringes of more experimental circles. This situation is embodied by Diane Bertrand, whose career encompasses *cinéma du corps* creations like *The Ring Finger*, but also the spritely Karin Viard star vehicle, *Baby Blues* (2008), a comedy about the (ultimately unresolved) dilemma faced by an upwardly mobile female executive — either taking a promotion in New York City, or having a baby with her long-term boyfriend in Paris. While conditions are by no means ideal (we will soon encounter the entrenched professional sexism faced by the debutants of Chapter 1), more opportunities exist now for more women in more walks of cinematic life than ever before. Extending our preceding case studies and the women at their epicenters, we can sketch the continuum of this strength in depth.

Highest profile is the commercially buoyant output, often consisting of comedy-dramas, of well established figures: Josiane Balasko, Laetitia Colombani, Anne Fontaine, Nicole Garcia, Agnès Jaoui, Noémie Lvovksy, Coline Serreau, and Danièle Thompson. These filmmakers share the distinction of having made films which reached over a million theatrical viewers (a standard gauge of commercial success), regularly placing their work in France's yearly top box office lists.[5] The ranks of such female writer-director celebrities, the so-called millionaires, are newly joined by Isabelle Mergault, whose *Je vous trouve très beau* (2006), about the relationship between a Romanian mail-order bride and an irascible French farmer, attracted 3.5 million filmgoers, the eighth most successful film in France that year; it won her the Best First Film César. Mergault's follow-up, *Enfin veuve* (2007), again about a mismatched marriage, had 2.2 million admissions, ranking it thirteenth in annual box office. Meanwhile, way off at the other cinematic extreme, closer in budget and unorthodox design to France's more avant-garde film creations, there is the representative career of someone like la Fémis graduate Laetitia Masson. Working in digital video on radical, self-reflective autobiographical essay-films, Masson's work is exemplified by the wittily self-lacerating tale of a struggling filmmaker poised on the brink of selling out, and creatively imploding, *Why (Not) Brazil? (Pourquoi (pas) le Brésil*, 2004).

Uniting many (but not all) of these recent films by women is what we might call simply a female-centered approach, if nothing else defined by a major protagonist who is a woman, and a plot that focuses on her interests and desires, and the challenges of realizing them. Already, with some caution, we can isolate a feminine instinct towards the sheer *depiction* of issues pertaining to women: films which probe and oftentimes undermine gender clichés; films about female identities within the roles of wife, daughter, mother, and so on; films presenting women in some form of opposition to men; films which glean drama from settings rife with gender and social inequalities (multigenerational families, hierarchies in the workplace, etc.). An unsung point of genuine progress in contemporary French cinema is that such female-centered materials, usually portraying women of all ages, upbeat yet pragmatic, are no longer hard to find on-screen. Some of these works, in fact, attract large audiences — a nice antidote to the largely male-centered forms of popular cinema we studied in Chapter 3. Today, indeed, feminine subjects appear in French films that are culturally unexceptional — mainstream products with valuable qualities, works not to be patronized — as well as the more idiosyncratic avenues of auteur cinema.

Take the recent example of Laetitia Colombani's *Mes stars et moi* (2008). Colombani's film, a relatively well-received and mainstream comedy (with over 300,000 admissions), follows George (Kad Merad, unexpectedly now one of France's leading stars), a cleaner at a talent agency who sneaks access to the schedules of three film stars, Solange Duvivier (Catherine Deneuve), Isabelle Séréna (Emmanuelle Béart) and Violette Duval (Mélanie Bernier). George is domestically isolated except for an enormous pet cat (which he puts in feline therapy, then occupies the sessions with his own neuroses) so he insinuates himself into the lives of "his" leading ladies, with destructive results. Mid-way through the film, however, the female trio fights back against their stalker. Violette has her film crew empty George's house, ostensibly staging a "Meet the Fans!" event, and rain ruins all his furniture; Isabelle has her jealous boyfriend terrify George within an inch of his life; best of all, Solange steals George's prized possession, his Smart Car (and the idea of Catherine Deneuve deigning to drive such a vehicle in itself makes *Mes stars et moi* worth watching). By the film's conclusion the quartet is reconciled, but clearly George has been reinvented as a man. He learns to express his feelings, gains respect for his estranged wife and daughter (who give him a second chance) before — with no apparent irony — the film ends with George credited for showing all of France that these three women stars are still box office champions. There is nothing too revolutionary here — just a female-written, -directed and -centered film, something that is now far more common in France than anywhere else. The point is made more starkly obvious versus North America's enduringly male-dominated cinema, attested by the mild critical furor that greeted the gently feminist subtext of Nora Ephron's *Julie and Julia* (2009). Platitudes aside, Kathryn Bigelow winning Best Director at the 2010 Oscars for *The Hurt Locker* (2009) simply raises the question as to why it had taken eighty-three years for a woman to be so honored in North America.

Staying in touch with women directors and popular French film, there is the similar and still more successful case of Lisa Azuelos's *LOL (Laughing Out Loud*, 2009). Azuelos's comedy-drama, very female focused, in fact proved something of a cultural phenomenon: with 3.6 million admissions, it was the third most popular French film of 2009, released subsequently in no fewer than five different DVD editions. A sprawling network narrative of teens and their fractured adult families, *LOL* primarily follows the brittle but loving relationship between Anne (Sophie Marceau) and her daughter, Lola (Christa Theret; in essence reprising her role from Doillon's *Et toi, t'es sur qui?*). To broaden the appeal of the adolescent cinema we explored in Chapter 1, Azuelos's film parallels the fumbling explorations of high schoolers with those of their more jaded parents. The links are often acute, like Lola smoking a forbidden joint with her cousin in her bedroom while their parents, downstairs, do the same thing themselves; or when Anne and Lola both lose their virginity on the same night (it is Anne's first sexual experience after a protracted divorce). At its best, *LOL* depicts poignantly the well-intentioned but fraught mother-daughter bond, at one point even relating it to the transgenerational impact of feminism in France. Contrasted with her warm but more conservative mother (who broods that the house "needs a man"), the forty-year-old Anne is horrified to learn of Lola's recent experiences with sex and drugs, struggling to reconcile her own feminist activist past with her worries as a single parent: "When you see your little one heading off to lead the life of a liberated woman, it's much harder to accept. . . ." (Less commercially oriented, Julie Lopes-Curval's *Mères et filles* [2009] traces this same grandmother-mother-daughter relationship arc.) Although typically dismissed by the cinephiles of *Les Inrockuptibles* and the leftist political analysts (often chauvinistic) at *Libération*, films like *LOL* are now reliable parts of contemporary French cinema. They are clearly palatable to mass audiences, yet are thoughtful about French women's social situations, sympathetic about the pressures on their lives at home and at large.

What films like *Mes stars et moi* and *LOL* ably demonstrate is that today many French women filmmakers are simply going about their business, finding audiences, working in an industry accommodating them on an unprecedented and increasingly proportionate scale. Returning to the notion of feminine cinema, though, there are important historical and conceptual matters linked to this process of women reclaiming their stake in filmmaking. Since women have been so long excluded from the means of film production, so often relegated to the position of passive objects on-screen, to many respondents, feminist or otherwise, film as a medium has long been equated with a male-centered or outright misogynistic viewpoint that makes its products inherently regressive. Through a series of representative case studies, this chapter uses the French example to analyze the methodologies of women filmmakers engaged with this crucial issue. We will consider films that feature the female-centered depictions above, but that also explore concertedly the *stylistic vocabulary of feminine cinematic design*. The central matter, then, is to understand the nature of such films as profoundly open and polyvalent, initiating a debate about alternative screen representations: the stylistic means, the textual repertoire, the internal conundrums and even contradictions, the polyphonic devices from which a nonhegemonic, nontraditional mode of cinema might derive. Our point of departure becomes those filmmakers embracing a multifarious, editorially sophisticated, at times radically expressive set of cinematic materials. On these terms, contemporary French feminine cinema embodies France's enviable position as harboring the most productive and extensive population of women working in cinema anywhere in the world, past or present.

Broaching the Screen Feminine: Christine Carrière's *Darling*

Christine Carrière's third feature, *Darling* (2007), distills key issues about contemporary feminine French cinema. The film is an adaptation of Jean Teulé's popular 1998 novel, a partly fictionalized account of the life of his cousin. Its protagonist is an almost perversely stoic woman whose abusive long-term relationships, initially with her parents, farmers who despise their daughter's ambitions, and subsequently her husband, an emotionally unstable truck driver, eventually lend her a battle-worn dignity, even grace. On-screen, the woman in question is Catherine Nicolle (Marina Foïs, who was nominated for a César), whose dreams of escape from a rural life and the prospect of marriage to a farmer lead her to begin CB radio conversations at night, under the name "Darling." During these chats she comes into contact with Joël (Guillaume Canet), with whom she has a sexual relationship. Soon the couple marry, although his violence and infidelities leave her emotionally as well as physically assaulted on a daily basis. Despite the abuse, Catherine refuses to seek outside help, but her family splinters anyway and her three children are taken into foster care. The film ends, though, with the quartet briefly reunited, windswept, sitting beside a motorway as she names the brands of trucks that surge past. A caption reports that the real life "Darling" now has a secure job, and hopes of rebuilding her life despite having lost custody of her children.

Never a more ironically titled film, *Darling*'s unremittingly bleak subject area, its incisively female-centered content, creates an overtly feminist text. Aspiring to authenticity, the film intervenes into the life of a brutalized woman cast adrift by French society, whose families fail her, who endures humiliations through indomitable willpower alone. Certainly by its final stages, Car-

X-rays and the body: the title sequence of *Darling*

rière's film is a powerfully literal, physically direct treatment of Catherine's appalling life experiences, a woman set against the world. For our purposes, however, *Darling*'s bravura opening segment, a bookending thesis statement, offers an additional, broadly representative point about the especially cinematic engagements of feminine filmmakers in France today.

The opening in question embodies a textual approach to open form, a disorienting yet affective design—elliptical, inconclusive, verging on stylistic abstraction, mercurial but evocative. Under the film's titles, Carrière cuts across a series of black-and-white stills. These objects initially appear obscure, until we realize that they are X-rays of body parts, arranged in extreme close-up under glaring hospital lighting, a few arranged by a disembodied hand. Some of the images are so overexposed that they actually are illegible; some are recognizable as parts of bones like a skull, ribs, and back vertebrae; whereas others, implausibly, seem to be organic materials like leaves and flowers. Others, stranger still, manifest as unreadable swathes of red, white, and black, indistinct shadows, poetic corporeal traces, quite beautiful despite the pessimistic context. For Carrière's own "un film de" graphic—as with Bruni Tedeschi's billing in *Actresses* appearing on the swinging grand piano, French directors use their names as textual motifs as much as credits—the image is more arresting still. Her shot is another collage of scientific data interwoven, or juxtaposed, with more pronounced lyrical forms: the vestigial pattern of a staring eye in delicate purple, the upper left curve of eyelashes in black, outlines of the top of a blueprint, and, at the bottom of the frame, what looks like a network of blood vessels, or a muscle juncture.

At first, this array of shots might seem merely to establish internal images of Catherine, very briefly hospitalized, a patient being studied. This might even broach the conventional discourse of women on-screen as passive, medicalized, prone to hysteria. But then Carrière cuts to a long shot of the attending physician, ostensibly checking the results of the X-rays, and we see that most of the preceding images are not on the doctor's board, are not, in fact, diegetically present. What *Darling* creates, in consequence, is the pivotal motif of a doubled and expansive cinematic approach: the empirical data of a woman's body, on the one hand, set alongside abstract stylistic patternings, a more nondiegetically poetic rendering, on the other. Here in this collage are bones versus flowers; a physical diagnosis versus an interrogation of a state of mind; the component parts of a body versus the female consciousness it houses; scientific examination versus access to an offset or displaced subjectivity. Omniscience is denied.

The effect is amplified as the credits end and the sequence continues, finally taking us to Catherine, the film's focal point. A minute of screen time has elapsed now, under heavily percussive nondiegetic music, and Carrière cuts to shots that situate us more concretely in a medical environment, as a white-coated professional, Dr. Lemaire (Christian Ruché), glances from the slides to the waiting woman in the next room, their apparent source. Into a telephone, he gives a suggestive yet incomplete account of Catherine's trauma, a litany of her physical conditions: "Head injuries, internal hemorrhaging, intestinal blockage. . . . Signs of old wounds as well as new ones. . . . I don't know how she survived it." The analysis continues and Carrière cuts to shots of Catherine in the adjacent space, but holds back from showing her directly and continuously. Instead, we first see Catherine off-center in a long shot, framed from behind and to the left as she sits besides CT scan equipment. Next, in profile, another long shot is of her sitting facing right, in a different room, sipping from a cup, her body rendered hazy through the thick privacy glass of a medical exam suite. Then we get a medium close-up, the woman's facial features still vague through the glass, the cup raised back to her lips. At last, the doctor completes his phone call, but by now he discovers that his patient has vanished, the only sign left of Catherine a spilled cup she has abandoned on the floor.

Yet another example of a masterfully compact statement of intent, a micro thesis, *Darling*'s opening defines a cinematic train of thought proximate to many female filmmakers at the cutting edge of their profession. Challenging and stylistically open, Carrière's sequence, and the film that ensues, yields powerful but partial insights about its complex central female protagonist. While the condition of the female body is candidly dissected on-screen, the broader rhetorical and textual position conveyed by the film is abstract, inconclusive. The film withholds while simultaneously making things evident; the limits of *Darling*'s representations raise searching questions about its own materials, issues about which the film refuses to editorialize in trite or didactic ways. Here, Catherine is a victim who neither seeks nor desires help, a tormented idealist who keeps blazing her own course, a beaten invalid who retains agency. In close-up, the corporeal processes of her body are laid bare yet also made mysterious, lyrical, and elusive. In many ways, indeed, the intricacies of this protagonist embody the polyvalent qualities of contemporary French feminine cinema, as well as the evocative yet exacting stylistic means by which it is configured. This *Darling* connotes proximity and intimacy, while also highlighting the specter of diegetic violence, a troublingly inhospitable and unaccommodating world on-screen. These textual multiplicities augment and stylistically reconceive what might otherwise have been a bombastic or reductive introduction. As Foïs herself describes Carrière's approach to directing actors, creating a world on-screen, and handling her audience: "She explains nothing."[6]

To Have It, or Not: Concepts of the Feminine in French Cinema

The fractured images of Catherine's body and mind in *Darling* prompt our more direct engagement with contemporary French feminine cinema. As we have seen, beyond the initial issue of female-centered depictions, there is the cinematic equation itself, a reconception of the stylistic materials through which more progressive feminine representations might develop. Also at issue is the problem of trying to delimit a feminine cinematic format at all. For many critics and filmmakers, the term can be a misleading misnomer, destructive not productive. Consider Marina de Van's response when asked about her relationship with other female filmmakers in France, her investment in a broader women's cinema movement. Caustic yet articulate, de Van replied: "No, I always think of myself as an individual, as different from another woman as another man. Maybe in real life I have more links with women, but as an artist I don't feel a connection, especially. I don't identify with the term 'women's cinema' or 'feminine cinema.' It can be a way of treating certain artists as a minority, or of marginalizing them."[7]

Clearly, there is some justice to de Van's position, a warning which has been widely echoed. Unintentional or not, the risk of marginalizing female directors rises when they are treated in abstraction, as a list of cherry-picked auteurs — say, from Alice Guy to Maya Deren to Chantal Akerman to Jane Campion — whose films exist apart from, isolated from, any evolving continuum of film practice. One response, discussed earlier as a principle woven into previous chapters, is the need to situate women filmmakers across the whole spectrum of contemporary French filmmaking, within the fabric of mainstream conventions as well as the more oppositional sectors of art cinema and the avant-garde. The fact that women now permeate substantial areas of French filmmaking becomes, then, a shaping context but also a rhetorical platform from which to build. Contemporary France, in this sense, offers the best test case yet to study the capacity of women to integrate within, but also affect, a dynamic film industry and culture, as active agents rather than marginal traces. (A secondary aspect to this is the role of female *film critics* within France's cinema culture, cited in this book as frequent advocates for the women whose work we have encountered.)

Without leaving de Van's comments behind, this indifference or hostility to a term that can falsely suggest inclusiveness, the paradigm of women's filmmaking in France has nonetheless received a growing amount of attention. How and on what terms has French cinema arrived at this state of greater gender parity? From the outset, feminist scholars such as Françoise Audé, Carrie Tarr, and Brigitte Rollet provide useful inroads, especially in their overarching claim that the 1980s and 1990s saw nothing less than the beginnings of a larger-scale women's cinema in France. Looking ahead, Emma Wilson's claims are crucial, too: not only that "women directors are set to cut to the quick in French cinema," but also that to understand these new cinematic materials "scholars must move beyond auteurist and more thematic and genre-based approaches."[8] New methodologies for a new feminine cinema—the prospect is unexpectedly pressing.

Among its respondents, French women's filmmaking coalesces around paradoxes: the qualified advances this form of cinema has made, the drawbacks to its successes, the limits possible to its further gains. Tarr and Rollet declare in the first words of their highly influential survey, *Cinema and the Second Sex*, "Women's filmmaking in France is a source of both delight and despair."[9] They note that the situation has, inarguably, revised in women's favor: from the dearth of female representation in the early 1950s, the industry moved from single digit percentages of women in the 1980s, towards about a fifth in the 1990s. Today, women are at times responsible for a third of all films produced in France.[10] In 2007, to take a recent annual sample, according to official CNC data women directed 24 percent of all French features produced, nearly a quarter, a rather modest year by recent standards, yet still four times the percentage of female directors in the same year in the United States.[11] However, for a cultural industry founded upon the auteur principle, Tarr and Rollet argue, France remains less willing to celebrate the achievements of its newer generations of female film professionals, Claire Denis and Agnès Varda notwithstanding. As Ginette Vincendeau has observed in a related claim, the dominant auteur model fragments any collective approach mustered by women filmmakers, as well as, ironically, excluding individuals from any canonical and often institutional appreciation. Vincendeau suggests: "French women cannot experience their practice in any other way than as auteurs, thinking that they are doing very well out of this individualistic game, whereas very often they are being 'had.'"[12]

Tarr and Rollet's conclusions, their theoretical compromise, is to classify the "major themes and issues which women directors have chosen to work with."[13] As a result, shaped around a dichotomy taken from preexisting treatments of French cinema ("Personal films" versus "Genre films"; the striated model that French filmmakers produce only arthouse curiosities or popular films, a premise this book contests), Tarr and Rollet itemize the sub-issues depicted by female directors en masse. Their tropes are principally: adolescence and coming-of-age, domestic formulations (the couple, the family), socialization; and then feminine inflections of genres like comedies, road movies, policiers, and heritage cinema. In the final analysis, *Cinema and the Second Sex* remains a groundbreaking study for both French- and English-language scholarship, but it has perpetuated a methodological gap still recurring today. The key question is unasked and unanswered: What are the *cinematic* means by which feminine cinema is conjugated; how do its central practitioners engage (or subvert) the medium conceptually and stylistically?

Other scholars offer ways into the perplexing and, it seems, evasive subject of these active yet overlooked women within recent French film practices. Françoise Audé, updating her work in 2002 with the compendium *Cinéma d'elles 1981–2001*, attempts a similarly exhaustive model in the vein of Tarr and Rollet. Audé's point of departure is more political, framed by the early 1980s: how "after twenty-five years of the power of the Right, the arrival in 1981 of a leftist majority was not the signal for a break, nor hardly forward progress," but that this moment did create, befitting the statistical rise of women entering the film industry, certain "modes of establishment"[14] of French film feminism. Retaining the same oppositional framework of low versus high art, Audé singles out the breakthrough texts of Coline Serreau's *Three Men and a Cradle (Trois hommes et un couffin*, 1985) in the popular sector, and Varda's *Vagabond (Sans toit ni loi*, 1985) as its arthouse counterpart. From here, Audé outlines more broadly the formats to which women became most drawn (the policier, comedies, documentaries, quasi-activist "social fictions"), into which she inserts snapshots of iconic females. Audé also preserves space for more esoteric analytical categories, most strikingly the "habits" of women directors, their thematic tropes about masculinity, sexuality, morality, desire, and deviance. By way of conclusion, ultimately an auteurist, Audé presents an elite taxonomy: seven filmmakers whose "originality and ambition . . . overwhelms and reinvents a cinema which is sometimes timid or suffocated by constraints and compromises."[15] The women Audé canonizes are: Breillat, Dominique Cabrera, Denis, Jeanne Labrune, Masson, Sandrine Veysset, and last but not least, Varda. (A useful footnote to Audé's book is an article she published in *Positif* that addresses the phenomenon of "actrices cinéastes," women performers becoming directors, excelling in both capacities, materials that we considered in Chapter 1.)[16]

Responding to the now undeniable scale of French women's cinema, subsequent scholars have nuanced these accounts. Guy Austin notes France's historical lack of academic feminist activity—in particular, the absence of psychoanalytical *Screen* theory, derived from Laura Mulvey, as it affected Western scholarship in the 1970s and 1980s, and, to a lesser extent, informed filmmaking practices. As a result, Austin argues that "these women embrace a sense of diversity and individualism born not of feminism but of the *auteur* tradition in French cinema."[17] This methodology, isolationist more than broadly conceptual, then informs sections on "avant-garde auteurs" Marguerite Duras and Varda, popularists like Kurys and Serreau, and selected marginal figures like Breillat, Denis, Claire Devers, and Martine Dugowson. Rosanna Maule offers a slightly oppositional perspective, suggesting that recent authorial practices in France, especially in regards to women, have challenged preexisting notions of the auteur, an inherited term that fails to account fully for women. She argues that: "Female authorial practices developed in this context since the 1980s prompt a rethinking of the notion of women's cinema as a type of agency . . . [which] purposely ignore[s] sexual difference and gendered identity as binding and limited concepts."[18] As evidence for these engaging claims, however, Maule limits herself to just the self-conscious mannerisms of Denis (her collective production strategies, her postcolonial focus, her intertextuality), a curious approach given Denis's well-documented status as arguably second only to Varda in the feminist film canon.

More wide-ranging, Emma Wilson's 2005 essay, "*Etat Présent*: Contemporary French Women Filmmakers," draws together the threads of this contested field of inquiry. Charting the activities of UniFrance, Wilson notes the rising trend of female-authored films screened at its major annual "Rendez-vous du cinéma français" sales event, held each January at the Grand Hôtel in Paris (which in 2009 was attended by 350 distributors and 120 journalists from around the world). Other institutional contexts confirm Wilson's theme of consolidation and growth. English-language monographs, she points out, published by Manchester University Press in the United Kingdom and the University of Illinois Press in the United States, now consciously target a greater representation of female filmmakers: from Varda and Denis (inevitably) to Serreau, Diane Kurys, Duras, and others. (Again the auteur complex precludes sustained attention to newcomers, as well as more versatile pop-art filmmakers like Bruni Tedeschi.) Wilson also uses Prédal's studies of recent French film as a critical barometer, revealing a shift from token entries about women to a wider dissemination of female-directed works throughout such accounts. Lastly, Wilson highlights the abiding importance of the Créteil International Women's Film Festival, founded in 1978 and designed to showcase (and encourage) women at work in the film industry. Wilson's final conclusion is a call to arms that this book seeks to address. On the challenges of keeping pace with the impact of French women filmmakers, Wilson states: "Criticism might seek to find means to track such films in their moments of metamorphosis and rupture, their new transitory and transitional modes."[19]

Besides these scholarly engagements, women's filmmaking now consistently attracts more interest in France's mainstream and trade presses. A series of recent events catalyze this broadening continuum of responses to a new feminine French cinema. During the summer of 2007, to take one recent reference point, more than a dozen first-time women directors released theatrical features in Paris. As Chapter 1 indicated, five of these eventually monopolized, in another extraordinary moment for female directors, the César Best First Film nominations.[20] But alongside that quintet came other female directors, with films including Fassio's *Je déteste les enfants des autres*, Nadine Labaki's *Caramel* (2007), Danielle Arbid's extraordinary *Un Homme perdu* (2007), Audrey Estrougo's *Regarde-moi*, and Cheyenne Carron's *Ecorchés* (2007), among others. This neatly presented a vanguard of activity, a cultural package, the kind of overt tendency to which pop-cultural critics habitually attend.

An unexpectedly strong reaction came from *Première*, a magazine that apparently for its commercial survival had favored American film products since its 2006 relaunch. However, in August 2007, over a cover still of Ludivine Sagnier, its "Girl of the Year," the *Première* editors commissioned a feisty and ambitious piece billed as: "Enquiry: The feminine revival of French cinema." (This train of thought recalls Tonie Marshall's provocative sound-byte at the start of this chapter, a subtext of Chapter 1, that women renew French film.) Inside the issue, Stéphanie Lamome declares boldly how, "Forty years ago, you could count the number of female cinéastes on the fingers of one hand. Today there's a whole new generation of women directors seizing celluloid."[21] Backing up these rallying remarks, Lamome cites Jackie Buet, founder of the Créteil festival, and a widely quoted spokesperson for women's film rights. Buet's comments add sociopolitical fuel to the fire, also returning us to the protracted *parité* controversies: "We're coming out of a fifty-year battle for women's rights. In France, like in other Latin countries, it's still hard for a woman to put herself forward, including politically, which is most striking during the election process. But this is changing. . . . We've always had this tendency to indoctrinate young girls with a form of self-censorship, engendering certain passive values. Today, though, a new generation seems to be taking things in hand."[22]

Building from this, Lamome applies Buet's points to the French film profession's ingrained sexism, using eyewitness testimonies to characterize the glass ceiling, fractured but intact, that hinders the rise of women. Although the historical reluctance of established producers to back female directors has changed, asserts Carron, many women report the patronizing attitudes they encounter in the business, especially among male-dominated crews and technical staff, and worst of all among camera operators, their alleged right-hand men. (Estrougo reports, for instance, the chauvinistic "stylistic reflections" of being told, "It's great to make a film when you're so young — and, moreover, you're a girl!")[23] Le Ny continues by suggesting that gender disparities in salaries and budgets are still in place, but that she and her colleagues take heart from the profiles achieved, and sustained, by figureheads like Varda, followed by Breillat and Denis. On this point, the influence of the Varda-Breillat-Denis trio as feminist icons, activists on- and off-screen, Lamome echoes Wilson by concluding that great as these past achievements have been, the collective strength of women filmmakers today is their forward momentum, towards a greater diversity of subject areas and approaches, inspired by but not bound to female-centered materials per se. As Buet confirms, twenty-first-century female cinéastes are no longer merely fly-by-night debutants pursuing the intimacies of adolescence, domesticity, and gender relations (Tarr's and Rollet's primary tropes). Instead, the reach of feminine cinema extends not only to larger political and social concerns, but also to the provocative and challenging means of these films' conception and formal execution. In the same vein, as Buet contends, the key point is this feminine cinema's stylistic ambition and focus upon minutiae: "Unlike men, women have never been afraid to film banality, time passing, duration."[24]

In the wake of the *Première* dossier, other film publications followed suit, again using the 2007 advent of women directors as a preface to a broader assessment of the contemporary scene, or simply as a prompt to address the emergent careers of women filmmakers more frequently. This was notably evident in *Le Film français*. The increasing presence of women became particularly clear, for instance, in one of the paper's regular features, the *Le*

Film français "on the sofa" group interview, staged in the luxury Paris Fouquet's Hotel, in which five or six professionals (usually directors and actors), all with new films in release, lunch together, share a group photo, then pitch their project to the trade press readership. To take just one issue, in September 2007, much was made of Audrey Estrougo's (diminutive but assertive) presence on the sofa alongside heavyweight directors like Jean-Jacques Annaud and Damien Odoul; she not only led off the interview, but her personal essay was printed first in the article.[25]

In similar fashion, *Studio* magazine's December 2007 annual special issue (typically designed to commemorate the preceding year) took the Best First Film César all-female sweep as its cue for an appraisal of women in the film industry. Béatrice Toulon's report, "Girls' Time," celebrated the achievements of the young quintet by signaling its place among a growing constellation of established female practitioners: Maïwenn, Ferran, Emmanuelle Bercot, Lvovsky, Bruni Tedeschi, Jaoui, and so forth. Toulon's conclusion reiterates the notion of a generational shift among female filmmakers; and, concomitantly, the critic's need to look ahead, focusing on the scope of stylistic particularities broached by women directors, and not backwards, simply citing their thematic feminist links to Varda. In Toulon's formulation: "The fact is that these girls have things to say. . . . Not directly inspired by their elders . . . this isn't just a 'women's cinema' or just an intimist cinema. . . . If Woman, as Aragon put it, is the future of Man, then could She be cinema's present?"[26]

Among these recent professional events devoted to French women filmmakers, one particular series marked a kind of cultural culmination, the female cinéaste as a preeminent force. And despite a certain ambivalence we have seen about the baggage of canonical feminine directors, it is perhaps apt that the spotlight returned to the pioneering career of Agnès Varda, on whose work an intensity of scrutiny burned brighter than ever. Firstly, between June and October 2006, Varda staged a multimedia installation, "*L'Ile et elle*," at the Fondation Cartier Pour L'Art Contemporain, her third such venture in this latter phase of her career, following exhibitions at the Venice Biennale in 2003, and another at the Galerie Martine Aboucaya in Paris in 2005. As Kelley Conway observes, critical reactions to *L'Ile et elle* verged on rapture, with one prominent analyst hailing Varda as nothing less than a national treasure. More success soon followed. After the Fondation Cartier exhibition, Varda edited a highly prestigious collection of essays devoted to her showing, soliciting essays from illustrious writers such as Raymond Bellour, Dominique Païni (ex-head of the Cinémathèque Française and the Centre Pompidou), and Laure Adler (who had between 1999 and 2005 been the director of the France Culture national radio station). Next, topping even this scale of recognition, in January 2007 Varda was commissioned by the French government to design a multimedia art installation commemorating *les justes*, those citizens responsible for sheltering Jews during the Holocaust, an event staged and televised live at the Panthéon mausoleum, hosted by Jacques Chirac himself. Varda's creation, *Les Justes*, comprising more than three hundred photos as well as four short films, in essence celebrated her already groundbreaking career as the world's leading woman filmmaker and a ubiquitous role model for female cinéastes in France. As Conway concludes: "One can scarcely imagine a more forthright expression of approval for Agnès Varda and her work from the realm of official culture. . . . In short, in case anyone had any doubt whatsoever, Varda has been canonized."[27]

In sum, the presence of women in French cinema, the debates they have inspired, the notion of feminine filmmaking as a continuum not a sidelined trajectory—all these have become clear in recent years. In response, recalling our earlier *Darling* test case, we can pursue the question of the *cinematic and stylistic* agendas common to this contemporary French feminine cinema, its capacity to create a textually progressive design and less orthodox or patriarchal relationship with the viewer. A number of feminist writers offer helpful theoretical contexts. In her recent survey of feminist cinema, Geetha Ramanathan gives a relevant, quite revisionist frame. Instead of a monolithic counter-cinema, Ramanathan suggests, deft women filmmakers instead pursue a wide range of aesthetics, different templates "that emerge as a consequence of a shift in the strategies of representation . . . visual, aural and narrative strategies that attempt to bypass extremely restrictive cinematic constructions."[28] Confluent with this, the feminine cinema model that emerges in France is not one of rigid or dogmatic didacticism, but rather a fundamentally open system, with multifaceted options encompassing radical impulses alongside reconfigured features from the commercial mainstream. Kate Ince recognizes this "new focus on the complexity and difficulty of women's individual experiences that cinema is just as well placed to convey, thematically and formally."[29]

Echoing this idea, especially in the work of debutant women filmmakers, Tarr and Rollet note the recurring motifs of childhood and youthfulness (evident even in films not explicitly about coming of age), which on the one hand is a conventionally "appropriate" domain for women's cinema, but on the other foregrounds "the perceptions of child or adolescent protagonists whose experiences are normally marginal and marginalizing, which has the potential to challenge hegemonic adult modes of seeing and displace the fetishistic male gaze of dominant cinema."[30] This idea, then, is the crux of contemporary feminine French filmmaking—the creation of a stylistic repertoire to circumvent or short-circuit an outmoded, closed-off, dogmatic cinematic logic. Mary Gentile suggests that the goal is "to provide multiple viewpoints within the text itself, and multiple vantage points for the viewer/interpreter . . . since women have been and are in a marginal position with regard to the discourse and values of society, it is to be expected that they will be among those who come to this plurality of vision and expression."[31] Alison Butler reiterates this idea—that women's filmmaking "is always an inflected mode, incorporating, reworking and contesting the conventions of established traditions."[32] Drawing on the work of philosopher Luce Irigaray, Caroline Bainbridge also calls for a "feminine cinematics" of decentered and nonprescriptive enunciative structures, playful experiments in inconclusive screen representations which convey a disruptive, unstable, ultimately empowering relationship with the viewer.[33]

Most ambitious of all, perhaps, is the assessment of Geneviève Sellier, who underlines the subversive potential of contemporary French feminine cinema. In the polyphonic scope of their work, Sellier contends, women filmmakers today have the ability to collapse France's ingrained elitist and popular cultures, dismantling their patriarchal value systems, disseminating and normalizing the female-centered materials we saw in texts as disparate as *Mes stars et moi* and *Darling*. (Sellier's essay was written before Bruni Tedeschi's directorial career began, but this idea seems perfectly attuned to the pop-art forms in both *It's Easier for a Camel . . .* and *Actresses*.) To Sellier, such cinema not only unifies women filmmakers of all political stripes, but also underpins the newly empowering diversity of recent French film. Indeed, Sellier is convinced of the sheer breadth of viewpoint, hitherto inconceivable, now available to women on-screen. She argues: "On one end are those whose gaze is (consciously or otherwise) oriented by traditional 'female' values of compassion, generosity, altruism, and the desire to be loved; on the other are those who use cinema as a tool of rebellion against the patriarchal, macho order. Between these two poles we can find all the possible variations, including the most contradictory ones imaginable."[34] No wonder that so many of these films feature female protagonists in fascinating states of uncertainty and growth, inhabiting diegetic worlds that constrain but do not contain, embodied by provocative and lyrical modes of film form. While this contemporary French feminine cinema is not necessarily utopian—far from it—it can be textually progressive, enigmatic, and frequently profound.

School's Out: Lucile Hadzihalilovic's *Innocence*

Hadzihalilovic's *Innocence* showcases some of the professional methods, the stylistic principles and open narrative and perceptual experimentation that sustain such a rich strain of cinema. In the first place, Hadzihalilovic—born in Lyon, France but raised in Morocco—was shaped by the French film school system. Hadzihalilovic graduated in 1986, as la Fémis replaced IDHEC (l'Institut des Hautes Etudes Cinématographiques) as the official elite state school, directly supervised by the Ministère de la Culture. Both institutions (IDHEC very belatedly; its successor from its inception) prioritized the recruitment of women, and la Fémis (which now often boasts gender parity in its direction track)[35] today emblematizes how women's cinema in France has progressed. Ambitious, state-funded, hiring active and acclaimed filmmakers for its instructors, la Fémis is a leading example of how France continues to devote artistic and logistical resources to subsidize its national cinema, and its most talented prospects, including women. Indeed, while much discussion focuses on the high profile means by which the French state intervenes to safeguard its cinema—its policies of trade regulation and annual quotas, its support of annual grant programs and production investment tax write-offs, its constant monitoring of television and film economies—less attention is given to France's institutional commitment to a cutting-edge film education, encouraging new generations of students-turned-filmmakers. Hadzihalilovic's impact is in part a product of this protectionist program. As Vincendeau confirms, moreover, the arrival of Hadzihalilovic "is testimony to the vitality and diversity of female filmmaking in France, where more than a third of movies are made by women (something of a world record)."[36]

Hadzihalilovic's nascent career was indeed shaped initially by the product of her graduation from film school: the short, *La Première mort de Nono* (1987). After this, she formed a long-term collaboration with Gaspar Noé, editing his *Carne* (1991) and its sequel *Seul contre tous* (1998), producing the latter, then in 1991 setting up together a production company, Les Cinémas de la Zone. In 1996, with Noé as cinematographer, Hadzihalilovic wrote, produced, edited, and directed another short, *La Bouche de Jean-Pierre*, funded by Canal+, which played on the *Un Certain Regard* Cannes panel, then was selected for other festivals including Avignon, Clermond-Ferrand, Montréal, and Toronto. Described by its filmmaker as a homage to Roman Polanski's *Repulsion* (1965) and *The Tenant* (1976), the short film is "an ordinary, everyday story, rather gloomy and pessimistic, told through the eyes of a nine-year-old girl."[37] The girl, Mimi (Sandra Sommartino), is sent to live in a claustrophobic *habitation à loyer modéré* (HLM) apartment after her mother tries to commit suicide, where she is at once compelled and horrified by her aunt's sexual interactions. Child abuse is implicit, parental neglect more explicit, and the film ends with Mimi taking sleeping pills to copy her mother.

Subsequent to this early phase of her career, Hadzihaliovic's *Innocence* was

A coffin arrives at the school in *Innocence*

released in 2004. As we shall see, it exemplifies a pivotal segment of France's contemporary cinema: a conceptually bold and widely traveled debut feature, made by a female graduate of a French film school, received with acclaim and some lingering notoriety. *Innocence* takes place during a year in the life of an unnamed girls' boarding school,[38] situated in a dense forest in an unspecified time and place, although aspects of its Victorian *mise-en-scène* suggest the *fin-de-siècle* past. The film follows the rituals of the girls' lives: their daily regimes of classwork and exercise, their grooming and deportment, their warm interactions with two school teachers, Mlle Eva (Marion Cotillard), a ballet instructor, and Mlle Edith (Hélène de Fougerolles), a scientist and biologist. The pupils, ranging from six- to twelve-year-olds, live in units arranged by seniority, marked by the color of their hair ribbons. The film begins with the arrival of a new recruit, Iris (Zoé Auclair; a nonprofessional like the majority of the cast), and ends with a group of graduates arriving, unnerved but energized, into an apparently contemporary outside world. Much of the film centers on Iris and the two older housemates with whom she forms attachments: Alice (Léa Bridarolli), who becomes disillusioned and escapes over an exterior wall, never to be mentioned again; and Bianca (Bérangère Haubruge), part of the graduating group, who, in the film's final shot, we see playing in a city fountain, meeting for the first time on-screen a boy of her own age.

Befitting this polyvalent text, the international reception of *Innocence* was enthusiastic but conflicted. Most critics noted Hadzihalilovic's blend of citations, among a wide spectrum of media with mixed cultural status, high and low. There is the film's expressionist source novella, *Mine-Haha, or The Corporeal Education of Young Girls* (1888), by German writer Frank Wedekind (more famous for his *Pandora's Box* [1904] play); as well as international cinema texts, such as Jacqueline Audry's *Olivia* (1950), Peter Weir's *Picnic at Hang-*

ing Rock (1975), Victor Erice's *Sprit of the Beehive* (1973), and Dario Argento's *Suspiria* (1977); the work of photographers Sally Mann (who attracted lasting controversy for exhibiting nude stills of prepubescent children, including her own offspring) and Bernard Faucon (known for inserting child mannequins into images of natural idylls); as well as classical painters, from Belgian Léon Frédéric to Franco-American Mary Cassatt. Beyond the pronounced intertextuality, however, there was little consensus about the unity of *Innocence* at all — except a consistent defense of its director against charges of encouraging pedophilia.[39] Vincendeau traces the film's neutrality to its "ability to mix everyday realism with the uncanny . . . the arrival in a coffin of young Iris is followed by scenes showing the girls' ordinary activities — playing, tying ribbons in their hair, swimming in the river."[40] Vincent Ostria echoes the idea of obscure, blurred categories, noting the film's "very abstract gothicism where horror and the fantastic are barely suggested, no more."[41] More polemical critics, such as Isabelle Regnier, propose a purely allegorical reading of a textually "suffocating atmosphere" that critiques patriarchy while offering a "relatively sterile equivocation."[42] But most respondents side with Arnaud Schwartz's open-ended perspective: "It's a first film, free and strange, sometimes disturbing, which evades right away any efforts to label it."[43]

At the level of narrative design, *Innocence* is indeed pervaded with ambivalence and ambiguity; its narration is restricted and elusive, without a fixed editorial position. Loosely built around the activities of school days, the film shifts repeatedly to sequences of elemental natural splendor, either in stand-alone segments without people present, or else in measured tracking movements that remove the camera from the children, as if the frame simply wanders away from humanity. In this way the film consolidates its innocent perspective, connecting the girls' pursuits to shots of unspoiled flora and fauna, seasonal transformations of the woods, birdsong, and close-ups of animals at large. At times this compositional logic approaches a statement about biological processes and growth — the fledgling children set beside images of butterfly pupae, a cast-off snake's skin, leaves and flowers budding then erupting into life — and more rarely the appearance of caged mice, pinned butterflies, and stuffed birds in Edith's classroom suggests a loaded commentary about the girls' confinement. But the majority of the natural asides *are* unsituated, purely lyrical sensory details, verging on abstraction, linked, if at all, as an organic pacing or rhythmic counterpoint to the often cryptic human behaviors. As Wilson suggests, "*Innocence* lets this play of scale, this disorientation, this intrusion of one set of images into another, match and be molded by the changing shapes of its subjects and the diversity of sizes and senses entrapped here."[44]

In keeping with its liminal narrative, *Innocence* mutes its narrative payoffs and limits any overarching cause-and-effect. Related to Buet's earlier points about female cinema's embrace of minutiae, Hadzihalilovic's principle here is the passing of time, and incidental observation. Plot points accrue but are appropriately small scale, quiet, deflated by their lack of duration and resonance. There is, for example, the abrupt annual arrival of the school's headmistress (Corinne Marchand; a witty inversion of her iconically feminist lead role in Varda's *Cleo from 5 to 7* [*Cléo de 5 à 7*, 1961]) to preside over the selection of a girl, after lengthy review, based on her arcanely well proportioned body mass and poise, for immediate graduation. One hapless student, Laura (Olga Peytavi-Müller), tries to flee in a boat but drowns; her recovered body is burnt in a pagan funeral pyre, then never referred to afterwards. The eldest girls, we see later, perform before graduation a strange costumed pageant in butterfly costumes; the demographic, gender, and motivation of its silhouetted (but paying) audience are never fully revealed. Elsewhere, the intense but indirect hearsay of the girls' conversations communicates a set of rules: that no leave from the school is allowed, no families visit, and a rumor that its staff of elderly domestics are all failed escapees.[45] Iris, the audience's surrogate, asks questions—what lies outside the walls of the grounds? where do the seniors go at night? where is her brother?—that go unanswered. Alongside the more legible school rituals, moreover, are events that defy logic and quite subliminally propel the film into a fantastic realm: the spectacle of new students arriving in coffins (as if they have died in the outside world, or been given up and relinquished by their parents), glimpses of an underground train network and obscure machinery, the secret passages that line the school building, the buzzing electric lights that hang in the woodlands, the bizarre subterranean rumbles that rise periodically on the soundtrack in place of music.[46]

The fundamental openness of *Innocence*, and ultimately the film's engagement with the viewer, is amplified by Hadzihalilovic's conception of film style. Consider *Innocence*'s elliptical opening, an emblematic passage. For ten seconds there is no image at all, before credits appear in flickering gothic typeface, as we hear faint pulses of industrial reverberation. A slow fade-up brings a medium close-up of a coffin with a star-shaped grill mesh, apparently in transit in an underground railway. The credits continue over black, while the distant roars of unplaced noise, louder now, echo again. The first extended use of the imagetrack comes with *Innocence*'s bravura opening set-piece. These are two long takes, interrupted by the film's title card, of unplaced, barely readable organic debris: the camera initially situated in pure abstraction, with shallow focus blurring the moving matter into a cloudy, dim, dank mass. Circular outlines gradually become visible as bubbles; there

Lyrical abstractions in the opening images of *Innocence*

are swirling waves of darker algae green and flashes of sallow white; the camera's velocity and position are unclear. All the while the cavernous booming continues, from far-off machinery to organic immersion. The second shot is more representationally readable as underwater photography; our vantage point nears the surface from some depth. Successively, next, the film cuts through a series of natural tableaux (the surface of a babbling stream and the white noise of water, trees, birdsong, clearings in a wood) and only gradually, almost reluctantly, moves to areas of habitation (underground tunnels, a passageway, dim hallways, a children's classroom with tinny gramophone music, then a room in which we see the earlier coffin resting on the floor). It takes six-and-a-half minutes before the first human character enters, frame right, in the form of a young, booted pair of legs. Nearly eight minutes pass without dialogue, and *Innocence* remains at times arrestingly silent. (Its concluding segment, equally ambitious, also consists of eight minutes with no conversation.)

This opening is stylistically assertive yet absorbing, close to abstraction, echoing the work of other French women filmmakers, like the first segment of *Darling*. It also cites quite directly, in conception and content, the lyricism of avant-garde pioneer Stan Brakhage, most closely *Mothlight* (1963), which consists of thousands of frames of organic detritus, moth parts, twigs, and leaves, edited together into a rush of perceptual data. As a declarative opening for *Innocence*, fundamental to the film's title, the passage situates Hadzihalilovic by way of Brakhage's famous tract, "Metaphors on Vision," which envisioned film as a means to recapture an infant's idealized, presocial vision: graphic texture and materiality rather than defined objects organized in space. As Brakhage theorizes, "Imagine an eye unruled by man-made laws of perspective, an eye unprejudiced by compositional logic, an eye which does not respond to the name of everything but which must know each object encountered in life through the adventure of perception."[47] Echoing this principle, Hadzihalilovic has declared of her work, in addition to her very confrontational *cinéma du corps* creations with Noé, that "we both like the experience of film to work visually, sonically, physically, rather than through words."[48]

To be sure, Hadzihalilovic systematically foregrounds style itself, with compelling formal exercises that also broaden her cinematic palette, drawing upon sources from both mainstream and arthouse cultures, configured in enigmatic, even contradictory ways. From a minimalist or documentary impulse, Hadzihalilovic and her director of photography, Benoît Debie, shot *Innocence* in Super 16 using no artificial lights or three-point set-ups except the tiny lamps we actually see on-screen. At the opposite end of the cultural spectrum, however, the duo exactly followed the popularist methods of Jean-Pierre Jeunet — notoriously his colorized, sanitized Paris in *Amélie* (2001) — by using digital postproduction to heat up and oversaturate color hues, particularly verdant greens, auburn browns and burgundy reds. The results are strikingly autumnal, bold yet subdued, with a level of visual opacity associated with Claire Denis's work with Agnès Godard. Debie's imagistic habits, indeed, making light itself fetid and tangible, a diffuse yet resplendent gloom, underpin his films for Noé and Hadzihalilovic. (The aesthetic is also evident in *Vinyan* [2008], his collaboration with Fabrice du Weltz, an insidious thriller about a couple searching for their lost son in the jungles of Burma, which like *Innocence* opens on swirling shots of weirdly abstract aquatic patterns.) Throughout *Innocence*, moreover, Debie's stylized aesthetic uses a cinemascope frame favoring static compositions, longer shots and longer takes — a distanced, formalist staging of the film's peculiar diegesis that blends unstated horror with materials from children's fiction.

This motif of school life, specifically drawn from young adult literature, is another facet of *Innocence* that reconfigures Western European popular culture. Hadzihalilovic herself notes the influence of enduringly popular English school literature, especially the Malory Towers novels of Enid Blyton.[49] Proximate too is the long-lasting *Madeline* series by Ludwig Bemelmans, set in a French boarding school, and similarly concerned with rituals and repetition. *Innocence*'s cyclical structure, its school-bound narrative of the fantastic and the everyday, also, inevitably, recalls the Harry Potter franchise, especially the abiding structure of a secret portal to a child-oriented realm, like Hogwarts School being accessed by magic express train, or, in C. S. Lewis, the kingdom of Narnia reached through the back of a closet. Closer to home, *Innocence* also connects to a slew of recent French hits from the same boarding school milieu, such as the ghost story and Virginie Ledoyen vehicle, *Saint*

Ange (2004), and the hugely successful *The Choir* (*Les Choristes*, 2004). Added to this, of course, is the resonance of contemporary French horror cinema and the *cinéma du corps*, as well as a narrative design that mirrors the Hollywood A-film *The Village* (2004).

Hadzihalilovic's design culminates in her finale, a highly representative open conclusion that in my experience leaves audiences confounded but energized, unsure what to think. Descending beneath the school one last time, Bianca and her fellow graduates exit the underground theater then pass through the dripping tunnel network. With Edith and Eva, the girls board the subterranean train and depart. The journey proceeds, and *Innocence*'s final couplet of lines are spoken: Bianca asks, "What will happen to us?" and Eva replies, deadpan, that "One thing's certain—you'll forget us very quickly." Time passes (as Buet noted earlier, women directors tend to preserve these neutral temporal advances) and the train rattles on, lights flickering, towards an unknown destination; minor key strings are briefly heard, muffled, on the soundtrack. A cross-cut returns us momentarily to the school, where another recruit arrives in a coffin. Finally, though, Hadzihalilovic shows the girls ascending from the train into a vast but nondescript terminus. One shot, inert yet poignant, shows the two teachers in medium close-up as they stand and observe, absolutely without expression, as their charges leave them behind. Are these women regretful, nervous about the fates of the departing class? Or are they confident about their ex-students, satisfied with their instruction?

As a final transition, Debie exposes an image directly into the blazing sun, a flourish and homage to the celebrated cinematographic motif of Kazuo Miyagawa for Kurosawa's *Rashomon* (1950). (The visual citation is also thematic, evoking Kurosawa's paradigmatically open text, its multiple perspectives within a courtroom drama that has no verdict.) With this burst of bright light, shown directly for the first time in *Innocence*, we see the girls arrive in a central courtyard before a vast concrete building. Apparently, we are in contemporary France; a disclosure that resituates, intensifies the peculiarities of the film's preceding events. (Unlike *The Village*, Hadzihalilovic offers no rationale for her temporal malapropism.) Alone and without adult supervision now, Bianca and her group climb into one of the fountains, removing their socks and boots. In another drastically overexposed shot, Bianca moves to the fountain's base, smiling directly at the camera as it arcs through the streams of water. Next, in shots that are whited out almost completely, Bianca gazes at a boy who joins her in the water, grinning and splashing; a medium shot of him is the first and only unobscured male face in the entire film.[50] A long shot, taken from above, moves us above the fountain, before we return to the rumbles and abstract water imagery on which *Innocence* began. Fade to black, as the noise recedes, before a title card and dedication to Noé wrap up the film, which has no end credits. Here, *Innocence* stops rather than concludes with another of its ambiguous doublings. Does this climactic sequence make us think of lambs to the slaughter, home-schooled naifs belatedly exposed to a world in which they cannot thrive, or survive? Or are they butterflies emerging from pupae, fierce and sensorially engaged individuals, empowered and unafraid to respond to the world and to the opposite sex? Regarding these questions, Hadzihalilovic in one interview offered a point about her artistic influences that extends to both *Innocence* and the feminine cinematic trajectory it distills. She declared: "There is no final explanation, just a lot of possibilities."[51]

Innocence, as we have seen, embodies a vanguard of debutant cinema: made by women, profoundly cineliterate, indebted to France's varied walks of cinematic life. In Wilson's analysis, Hadzihalilovic should be hailed for her "revelatory first film, *Innocence*, [which] intrudes on our images of childhood, renewing them, opening us to the sensory perceptions of children, their bodily impressions as they encounter themselves with others in strange new incarnations."[52] In equal measure, *Innocence* gives a concerted textual response to David MacDougall, whose *The Corporeal Image* concludes that there is a general poverty of cinematic representations of children and non-adult subjectivity. MacDougall's summary, in fact, provides another rationale for Hadzihalilovic's achievements: "If any overriding reason exists for filming children, it is to rediscover their complexity—to give them the respect due to persons living in themselves rather than our conceptions of them, and to put ourselves in a better position to learn from them."[53] In this, *Innocence* fully conveys the intensity of its title, through the meticulous freshness and diversity of its cinematic methods, its stunning maturity, the productive ambiguities of the responses it evokes, and, most impressively, the qualities of contemporary French feminine cinema that it ably represents.

As a corollary to this, *Innocence* shows the professional opportunities for French women filmmakers, especially those alert to the prospects of international distribution and exhibition. As we have already seen with debutant and pop-art filmmakers in France, these kinds of films are ideally suited for the expanding range of middle-rank film festivals, such as Amsterdam, Boston, Chicago, Moscow, and San Sebastián. Like many of her colleagues, Hadzihalilovic, and her film, especially profited in this regard. During *Innocence*'s festival run in 2005, she won Best New Director at San Sebastián, the Bronze Horse best film award at Stockholm (where Debie won Best Cinematographer), and the FIPRESCI (International Federation of Film Critics) prize at Istanbul. Such institutional recognition subsequently gave Hadzihalilovic privileged access to the prestigious North American market. *Innocence* was chosen for the 2006–7 and 2007–8 *Tournées* Festival, a package of films made available via $180,000 worth of competitive grants to American schools and universities by the French American Cultural Exchange (FACE), partnered with the Cultural Services of the French Embassy in the United States, the CNC, and the French Ministry of Foreign Affairs. As an official *Tournées* choice, *Innocence* was offered to local, grass-roots French film festivals organized by schoolteachers and university instructors, promoted as a culturally appropriate product for subsidized export from France. In this category, Hadzihalilovic joins colleagues including Bruni Tedeschi, Julie Lopes-Curval, and Eléonore Faucher, women who are all now forging long term careers in feature production. The resurgence of French cinema, with its invigorating prospects for women filmmakers, continues.

Human Resources: Two Films by Siegrid Alnoy

Echoing the open designs of Hadzihalilovic and other contemporary woman filmmakers, Siegrid Alnoy's early short, *Our Children* (*Nos enfants*, 1999), epitomizes these polyphonic techniques. The film opens on a shot of an empty child's stroller in a hallway. We hear unsituated voices talking to the infant in question; one cries out, then two women, Pascale (Jocelyne Desverchère) and Frédérique (Mireille Roussel), are seen leaving the building. From here we cut to the duo on a bench, joined in medium long shot by a third woman, Stéphanie (Sasha Andrès), evidently their crony. Rain falls and the three women chat energetically, sharing hot bread and (inadvertently) a container of breast milk, discussing the routine of being mothers to their unruly, unconventional kids—one is too thin; another has no appetite—who apparently are playing together off-screen. The trio laughs uproariously, pausing occasionally to chide an unseen offspring. ("You know you're going to traumatize him, yelling like that!" comes a quick reprimand.) Four jump cuts and a strange insert shot of Stéphanie staring blankly into space are the only jolts amidst the scene's lively flow.

Suddenly, however, our perspective alters. Spatially, Alnoy disrupts proceedings through an axial cut, revolving us 180 degrees, moving to a backwards tracking shot that retreats from the trio, shown now from behind. We then hear a stern, authoritarian woman's voice addressing the group, who shrink guiltily in their seats as white-coated attendants converge. One of the doctors demands: "Which of you took this stroller? You know very well it belongs to one of the mothers visiting today." Stéphanie is led away, at first sadly then desperately, and we infer that rather than being mothers resting happily in a park these are inmates in an institution, child-snatchers not caregivers. Alnoy zooms into the real mother reunited with her son, while off-screen a voice cries "No!" hysterically, and Stéphanie turns, horrified, to watch the boy being taken away. The last shot, even more perplexing, shows the young child himself screaming, as if he has actually just been parted from his mother, who is not the woman standing beside him. Cut to black, the credits roll, but the film is not yet over. Now we hear two gunshots, the boy calling for his mother, before on the soundtrack begins a series of whispered parental commentaries, confessions that seem at once nondescript and sinister: "He won't stop making noise with his toys"; "I think they've taken my other children swimming"; "Children are like birds"; "That's enough, now you need to listen."

Clearly, there is little diegetic coherence here. *Our Children*, whose title now feels very incongruous, starts out with everyday banalities, lurches towards implications of insanity, then retreats back to where it ostensibly began. Is this an allegorical, blackly comic treatment of motherhood? An ambiguous game with the viewer, who is led down the garden path then shoved into the undergrowth? Equally, it could all be taken as Alnoy juxtaposing two enduring feminine stereotypes—the figure of the dutiful mother, transformed abruptly into a violent and hysterical invalid—that clash together, overlap, disintegrate. As the film's voice-overs continue, decreasing in volume, right through to the film's final copyright credit, *Our Children* creates a highly engaging *mise-en-abyme* of multiple perspectives, mutually viable yet contradictory meanings. Like many of her female contemporaries, Alnoy's interest as a filmmaker is in an open text: she baits and switches then baits again.

On this point, we can turn to Alnoy's debut feature, *She's One of Us* (*Elle est des nôtres*, 2003). In the first place, this film broaches one particularly striking facet of contemporary feminine French cinema—an aesthetic of gender inversion. This model, somewhat ironically, recalls the famous tactic of Charles Lederer, working with Howard Hawks to remake *The Front Page* (1931) and update the Ben Hecht-Charles MacArthur play, *His Girl Friday*. What happens dramatically when you switch the sex of Hildy Johnson, changing a main protagonist from a man into a woman? In the context of recent French cinema, a spate of gender inversions underlines the sophisticated self-awareness among women writer-directors. There is, for example, Magaly Richard-Serrano's autobiographical *On the Ropes* (*Dans les cordes*, 2007). This is a boxing film, arguably the most masculinist of all genres; a number of critics even compared its fight scenes, some favorably, to Martin Scorsese's *Raging Bull* (1981). In Richard-Serrano's hands, however, the boxing milieu becomes the context for an increasingly bitter domestic fall-out and pugilistic rivalry between two women: a trainer's daughter, Angie (Louise

Szpindel), and his niece, Sandra (Stéphanie Sokolinski). In the same vein, Estrougo's *Regarde-moi* reworks the male-centered format of banlieue cinema, foregrounding the approach by framing the film's first half from the boys' perspective, then repeating her time frame but from the vantage point of the girls. Veteran Josiane Balasko uses the same principle in *A French Gigolo* (*Cliente*, 2008), which reverses *Pretty Woman* (1990), as Balasko's protagonist, the wealthy but disaffected Judith (Nathalie Baye), embittered after a divorce, begins a commercial/sexual relationship with Marco (Eric Caravaca), who, it turns out, has a struggling family and troubles of his own. (Almost incidentally, Balasko derails one of Western culture's most inexplicable taboos: an older, sexually active woman paired with a younger, receptive man.) The gender inversion model even shapes recent women's French fiction, notably Marie Darrieussecq's very well-regarded *Pig Tales* (*Truismes*, 1996), about a sexually exploited masseuse who inexplicably becomes a pig,[54] invoking, of course, Gregor Samsa's transformation in Kafka's *The Metamorphosis* (1915). In sum, this aesthetic of inversion reflects a more systematic shift than the one Tarr and Rollet first envisaged, rather tentatively, as a strategy in which female filmmakers "have appropriated mainstream male-oriented genre filmmaking . . . by inserting a point of view informed by a feminist (or at least a woman's) awareness."[55]

In *She's One of Us*, Alnoy's use of the inversion aesthetic most clearly relates to *Time Out*—although Alnoy and her film also inflect Dumont's male-focused work—by transposing Campillo and Cantet's narrative of an ominously calm but disenfranchised office worker, who in the face of redundancy clings to a charade of his middle-class position at all costs, to the case of struggling temp Christine Blanc (Sasha Andrès again). Alnoy's protagonist, in keeping with her last name, increasingly connotes a stark or troublingly blank identity. *She's One of Us* (the title comes from the French version of "For He's [She's] a Jolly Good Fellow," referring more to someone joining a drinking game) follows Christine as she inexorably rises through the ranks of an anonymous industrial business. Initially Christine is on the margins, tenuously employed in that least forgiving of female careers, a part-time secretary, pathetically eager to befriend her temp agency boss, Patricia (Catherine Mouchet). Abruptly, *She's One of Us* then ruptures textually after Christine suddenly, brutally kills Patricia at a swimming pool, beating her to death with a fire extinguisher, just like the murder Pierre carries out in *Irreversible*.

Now, inexplicably, Christine's female identity evolves while her social fortunes rise. After hours of laborious driving lessons, Christine finally gets her license: she is mobile and at liberty. Next, she becomes the dominant partner in a conventional heterosexual couple—her often mentioned but

Absent present: Christine Blanc (Sasha Andrès) in *She's One of Us*

absent boyfriend (when asked by her mother why he never appears in any photos, Christine replies that he's always behind the camera) finally materializes, taking his place as a generic, subserviently loving companion. At work, Christine turns into a fast-tracked, full-time executive, envied by her colleagues. (At this stage, her red two-piece business power suit, a costume Christine wears almost constantly, becomes appropriate to her social and professional rank.) The film in its final portions opens yet more fissures in its own narrative: Christine for no reason abandons her job along with her besotted ex-colleague Eric (Eric Caravaca), but then is finally arrested by the police, before, in another startling about face, the last shot shows her sitting in a patrol car at night, alone, possibly awaiting recapture, but apparently free to move forward, if she so chooses, again.

In a number of interviews, Alnoy espoused what she called a "hallucinatory aesthetic" in which, like the pop-art manipulations of *La France* and *They Came Back*, *She's One of Us* conveys a jarring world of people nominally alive but psychologically bereft, another form of the dead awake. Far more affectively disorienting than *Time Out*, *She's One of Us* is a purgatory in which, as Alnoy puts it, "Work is a sickness, it empties us of our creative powers and turns us into ghosts. . . . Today, we identify ourselves on the basis of our jobs—that's not living, it's merely functioning."[56] Throughout her film, Alnoy sets up internal contradictions that befit such a numbing, inhospitable, dehumanizing environment. Even the film's title, in both the original French and its English translation, conveys this clash between a distinctive individual and an enclosing mass: *Elle est des nôtres*, *She's One of Us*—like *Our Children*, the possessive or inclusive term is ultimately threatening, incarceration, something to be resisted.

The same principle of disunity and internal estrangement permeates Alnoy's *mise-en-scène*. Most obviously, she chose to shoot *She's One of Us* in the Rhône-Alpes region, in the southeast of France but north of its more recognizable Mediterranean coastline. This, instead, is an area where hyper-industrialized areas coexist with rugged mountainous landscapes, modern strip malls sprawl in the shadow of wilderness peaks, and suburbs encroach on verdant hillsides. Everywhere Alnoy's camera roves, the organic is set alongside the corporatized industrial. In the establishing shots that punctu-ate the film, tracts of forestlands and foothills loom on the distant horizon but most of the film takes place in urbanized steel-and-glass units: offices lit with sallow fluorescence, endless rows of enclosing cubicles, teeming but sterile canteens, impersonal conference rooms like those of *Demonlover* and *In My Skin*. (Several shots of these office interiors are even deliberately out of focus, as if the *mise-en-scène* is so uninspiring, so unavoidably depress-ing that Alnoy cannot quite bring herself to rack focus.) Alnoy develops this contrast further, moreover, through the repeated motif of Christine reentering the outlying zones of natural splendor, wandering through the countryside in unplaced, abrupt insert shots that pointedly breach her continuity editing, the otherwise efficient succession of images that place her within profes-sional milieus. Another irony, though, is that even when Christine escapes to the wild, standing above waterfalls or paused frozen amidst the terrain, the unchanging blank expression on her face, her robotic stasis, bespeaks a lost capacity to experience the world around her, to feel anything but alienated distance. Like Jean-Marc Moutout's *Work Hard, Play Hard*, a film about an idealistic business graduate who inexorably sells out, it feels as if there is just no prospect either of professional fulfillment or domestic harmony, no balance however your career advances.

She's One of Us defamiliarizes the spaces around Christine, making her twin roles as socially marginal temp (before the murder) and socially domi-nant executive (after) puzzlingly connected. Whatever her rank and position, the film suggests, Christine does not belong; there is, moreover, nothing tangible to belong *to*. Christine drifts, is constantly in motion, her blank face and body reappearing from place to place ubiquitously, like a glazed contem-porary flâneur; but she is also framed disjunctively on-screen, a figure that is out of sorts, perennially out of place. Often, Alnoy and her cinematographer, Christophe Pollock, push extreme shallow focus or shoot their lead actress through apertures and opaque screens, like a translucent bus shelter, thick panes of blurring glass, or angular, modernist window frames. More intrusive still, Alnoy's favored device is to bisect bodies on-screen, lopping off heads or cutting torsos abstractedly in half. When Christine and Patricia adjourn one meeting, for example, Alnoy stages the scene with neither woman's head in shot; their banal conversation about cars ("Me and mechanics: my boyfriend loves his new Xsara") does not originate from human mouths, it seems, while the focal point of the frame becomes a red office chair, mid-ground center, and a commuter bus that sweeps along the road outside. (Following Alnoy's other gender inversions, Alnoy here distantly recalls Tati's *Play Time* [1967], and Monsieur Hulot's abstract wanderings through a modernist cityscape in which objects and people interchangeably compete for space.) The trajectory is taken to a bizarre extension after Christine's boyfriend returns/materializes, and the two share non-intimacies redolent of the *cinéma du corps*. Framed from knee to waist, we see the couple beside a bathtub filling loudly with water. They undress and stand in the tub, apart, with only their midriffs, thighs and genitals visible. Alnoy holds the shot for twenty-eight excruciating seconds, with no motion, before finally the two bodies approach—and then she quickly cuts away to Christine asleep in bed, face down. This is arguably the most abstract, least erotic sex scene in recent world cinema.

Tracing this back to the feminine cinema model, Alnoy's interest is clearly in privileging a woman's point of view, scrutinizing Christine's erratic behaviors and antisocial inclinations, while situating her actions within a dysfunctional diegesis. Although marginalized and expressively blank, Christine is stylistically privileged and curiously empowered; nothing and no one can stop her. While the rhythm of this modern world is clearly off, it still marches to her particular—omniscient?—beat. Here, Alnoy's approach is again compellingly open and nonjudgmental—at times she is more free form than Hadzihalilovic. Often, *She's One of Us* recalls Godard's radical experiments in *My Life to Live* (*Vivre sa vie*, 1962), focused on Nana (Anna Karina), another socially excluded female protagonist, in a film that explores different permutations for staging scenes cinematically, as much as it plays out the actual scenes themselves. Abandoning norms like shot-reverse shot and continuity editing, how else might you piece together Christine's interactions? One particularly stylized sequence shot couplet, in which Christine wins (of course) 1,000 euros from a scratchcard given her by her colleagues, cuts only after an unsettling delay from a drawn-out long take of the animated group, excited by their boss's win, to Christine's non-reactive face in medium shot: she says not a word, does nothing, but basks in their adoring glow. Elsewhere, another motif comes as Christine sits alone in a mall, and the camera spins full circle, panning 360 degrees around the space this woman (now triumphantly?) occupies. Systematically, the course of Alnoy's camera, its textual vectors, is

Dehumanized spaces: A conversation focused on a red office chair in *She's One of Us*

utterly configured to Christine's presence: the image is framed above her, in the office adjacent to her, putting her out of focus frame center (when she is first interviewed about the murder), tracking before her, tracking behind her, showing her in silhouette, nearby and far distant, endlessly pursuing new screen configurations of this unknowable *her*.

Alnoy's stylistic intricacies, Christine's viewpoint centralized within a world correspondingly deranged, also link *She's One of Us* to a close literary relative, Céline Curiol's novel *Voice Over* (*Voix sans issue*, 2005). In this book, Curiol's nameless young woman protagonist, a disembodied announcer at the Gare du Nord train station, fixates romantically on a man while careening through encounters in an almost unrecognizable Paris cityscape, with a demoralized African immigrant, a transvestite bar performer, an experimental photographer, and others. At once subjectively present and objectively detached, bound to a particular mind yet corporeally meandering, *Voice Over* juggles multiple renderings of the same events, different versions of vignettes delivered as crisp yet poetic, vaguely menacing fragments. Leaving a café, our female narrator conveys the moment as: "She walks along suspended above her regular footsteps, fascinated by the ease of her movements."[57] When the woman runs frantically to catch a train, we get the truly extraordinary sentence: "Her métro pass isn't in her bag, her métro pass is in her bag."[58] During a métro journey, as She watches a young father interact with his little girl, Curiol recounts the events as: "She feels as if she's watching two similar scenes at once. The first tender, that of a little girl expressing her affection for her father, the second that of a father, turned into a man again, holding his prey down on his knees."[59]

Paul Auster, the book's champion on its North American release, describes Curiol's style in ways that echo the texts analyzed in this chapter. Auster argues that *Voice Over*: "moves with the emotions of her character, from the precise, clinical tone of an empirical observer to the opulent, disjointed streams of thought assaulting a mind in the grip of hallucinations."[60] The textual poise, in other words, is elegantly omniscient yet peculiarly disjunctive, reveling in a bravura expressivity while underscoring its own omissions and limitations. In the final analysis this creates a stylistic *mise-en-abîme*, a stream of incompatible textual positions, parameters which open up representational possibilities while delimiting any prospect of closure. Without a sturdy vantage point there's no end in sight here, no horizon at all.

Fissures: Alanté Kavaïté's *Ecoute le temps*

A domestic violence victim's unfathomable determination; a group of school children living in the past but also the present; mothers as tender caregivers as unhinged criminals; a professional loser on her path to boundless supremacy—such are the materials of contemporary French feminine cinema. This vein of filmmaking engages us through female-centered subjects, incisive social diagnoses conveyed through stylistic resources that are open, discursively turbulent, discomfiting yet undeniably invigorating. So much modern film and media is predicated on the belief that it must *tell us what to think and feel*, normalizing a preordained view of the world, that these films, conversely, are just conceptual fresh air. Looming in the background, moreover, is the fertile breadth of French cinema, a culture industry that ranges from audience-pleasing mass genres to unclassifiable experiments, texts which afford women an array of models for cinematic redeployments, subversions and inversions. These are the means of what Sellier calls "the polyphonic approach."[61]

Alanté Kavaïté's *Ecoute le temps* (2007) is one of the more adventurous examples of this contemporary feminine cinema. Much of its impact comes from the sheer blatancy of its inversion aesthetic, its efforts to derail the more self-absorbed, crass, male-centered components of conventional French cinema. (Kavaïté's film also creates an intriguing extension of pop-art cinema.) *Ecoute le temps* starts out initially as a psychological thriller, a traditional whodunnit potboiler with hints of the supernatural. Its protagonist, Charlotte (Emilie Duquenne), is a sound engineer working on location when she learns of the murder of her estranged mother (Lumila Mikaël). Returning to her unnamed rural home village, Charlotte is ostracized as an outsider; most of the locals hated her mother, rumored to be a witch. Charlotte soon encounters suspects for the crime: Bourmel (Etienne Chicot), the town's corrupt mayor who is busily fighting pro-organic campaigners; one of the ringleaders, Julien (Mathieu Demy), a farmer and her mother's ex-lover; and Jérôme (Bruno Flender), a mentally disturbed neighbor with a repressed sexual appetite for both Charlotte and her mother. Charlotte's investigations continue, and she stumbles upon the unsolved disappearance of a local nine-year-old boy some time earlier. Most of the film, though, unfolds as Charlotte sets up her equipment in the front room of her mother's old house and obsessively records. (The film's title translates literally as *Listen to Time*.) Without explanation, she hears sounds from the present intermingled with voices from the past; temporal and spatial breaks move us backwards and forwards as the mystery unfolds and the house itself begins to collapse around her.[62]

Kavaïte's generic backdrop draws from the French mainstream at its most commercially acute. Two strands converge here. First, *Ecoute le temps* revives an abiding French cultural fixation: a *cinéma rural* about city slickers (usually Parisians) going back to basics, learning truths about themselves in timeless rustic backwaters. This cycle often manifests as comedies, like the story of a disillusioned young urbanite taking on a decrepit farm in Christian Carion's hit *The Girl from Paris* (*Une Hirondelle a fait le printemps*, 2001); the still more popular tale of a postal office manager banished to the hinterlands in *Bienvenue chez les Ch'tis*; or innumerable films about extended families and friends taking (invariably tense) countryside vacations, such as *Je déteste les enfants des autres* and *Our Precious Children* (*Nos enfants chéris*, 2003). Alternatively, the *cinéma rural* trope also underpins contemporary French films about the evils awaiting those foolish enough to venture beyond the Paris city limits: *Ils*, *Sheitan*, *Frontière/s*, and the other horror films we encountered in Chapter 3. (A blackly comic version combining both elements might be Dominik Moll's *With a Friend Like Harry . . .* [*Harry un ami qui vous veut du bien*, 2000]); the widespread influence of Dumont's *cinéma du corps* depictions of latent rural savagery is also obvious.)

The second of Kavaïté's sources, less immediately promising, is the highly masculinist contemporary suspense thriller. Nowadays, this hypercommercial template inflects French cinema's predilection for bourgeois melancholia (which we saw in Chapter 1) in the form of a young, male seeker hero righting domestic wrongs, fighting to reintegrate his family unit and, typically, bail out his errant wife. This is the modern French action film as a reassertion of patriarchal obligations and rights. Deft, effective, often politically dubious and at the very least entirely male-centered, such thrillers number some of French cinema's biggest recent hits. These include EuropaCorp's *Taken*; Guillaume Canet's *Tell No One*, about Alex (François Cluzet), who is embroiled in a murder investigation as he seeks his wife, who has resurfaced eight years after her apparent death; and Guillaume Nicloux's less lucrative *The Key*, which follows Eric's (Canet) descent into interfamilial warfare as his dead father's urn turns out to be filled with drugs. A supremely potent case of the male-oriented domestic thriller is Fred Cavayé's *Pour elle* (2007), nominated for a César Best First Film award. *Pour elle*, built on riveting performances from its leads, has Julien (Vincent Lindon) risking life and career to free his unraveling wife (Diane Kruger) from prison after she is falsely jailed for murder; the film ends with the family group, father, mother and son, reunited after fleeing to an unspecified tropical location.

Besides having its roots in mainstream film culture, the final part of the film's web of allusions, a key factor in its feminine design, comes from farther afield—Thierry Jousse's 2005 *cinéma du corps* film *Les Invisibles*. This piece of art cinema, cited in Chapter 2, also focuses on an obsessive-compulsive sound technician, Bruno (Laurent Lucas), an electronic artist who samples everyday noises then weaves them into avant-garde soundscapes.[63] Bruno's acoustic compulsions create, however, an archetypically male counterpoint (or counterpart) to Charlotte. Jousse's protagonist fixates on a disembodied female voice on a nocturnal chat-line, a woman who becomes his anonymous sexual partner then disappears, leading Bruno into an underworld of Parisian sex clubs, before he discovers climactically that she is a mother with a young daughter. In effect, *Les Invisibles* represents Bruno's self-gratifications versus two versions of femininity, stereotypically constructed as unknowable-sexual or domestic-maternal. Conversely, in *Ecoute le temps*, Charlotte's labors are a conduit to self- and social knowledge, restoring her family's name, dispelling the town's hypocrisies, painstakingly reconstructing the past, fleshing out rather than caricaturing the role of mother. This was, it turns out, a witch whom most of the hostile townspeople actually sought out for her clairvoyant advice; she was murdered for confronting Julien about his ethical responsibility for the missing boy he had run over and accidentally killed. Essentially, then, in the guise of a domestic thriller, Kavaïté crafts a feminine cinema out of male-oriented texts like *Les Invisibles* and *Tell No One*. In broader terms, as Sellier suggests, work like Kavaïté's treats sympathetically "the solitude of independent women . . . [while equally] these films challenge the narrative mode inherited from the New Wave, with a narcissistic, solitary (male) figure, an alter ego of the author, at the center of the story, a formula still used by Assayas or Desplechin."[64]

How do Kavaïté's female-centered materials coalesce with her cinematic execution? In the first place, the film's title sequence creates, just like *Innocence*'s experimental preface (and Brakhage citation), the motif of an abstract, transient space, depicting cinematically a wild or natural state devoid of human intervention, a pure and untainted aesthetic ideal. To frame the film, Kavaïté and her cinematographer, Dominique Colin, first immerse their camera in a dense and viscous liquid, with clusters of bubbles rising to the surface. A suite of handheld shots, desolate but beautiful tableaux, moves us through what is revealed to be a network of hot springs thronged with mineral deposits. Pockets of gas erupt to the surface through vents in the rock-face, colorful accretions ring water-blasted pools, the jutting textures of stones form subterranean patterns, gusts of wind drift sand across the landscape. Metallic greys mingle with stark yellows blurring into copper oranges. Two minutes in, Charlotte's arm, holding a boom mike, enters the frame, as she attentively records the sounds of these earthly processes, immersed in her work, oblivious to her waiting crew. Besides the sheer minutiae embraced here — Charlotte's technology (like Kavaïté's filmmaking) poised in harmony with the organic world — Kavaïté makes explicit a subtext of both *Innocence* and *She's One of Us*. This is an undertone of feminine ecocriticism, films that bear witness to man-made (social) contaminants and how they degrade the environment. Fascinatingly incidental to the rural murder mystery, the vestiges of the domestic thriller and the *cinéma rural* that structures *Ecoute le temps*, is the accumulation of acts of pollution which Charlotte observes: toxic fertilizer spills and run-offs, chemical byproducts dumped in the countryside, the ruin of fresh water supplies, a legacy of guilt denied by everyone around her.

In keeping with the polyvalent features of feminine French cinema, Kavaïté creates strategic ruptures, oppositional registers, in her text. (During the successful international festival run of *Ecoute le temps*, from Santa Barbara to Belfast to Shanghai, it traveled on occasion under the title *Fissures*.) During its early sequences, after Charlotte occupies her mother's house, *Ecoute le temps* begins as an old-fashioned procedural policier, focusing on the ritualistic behavior of worn-out investigators and a rogue's gallery of hostile local suspects, all steeped in a stifling *mise-en-scène* of dank rural decay. When Charlotte is interrogated by two policemen about her mother's past habits, for instance, Kavaïté plays the whole scene as her protagonist makes tea, reaching down a cup, finding the teabags, cutting between these banal preparations and the weather-beaten cops' disinterested questions. Soon after, Charlotte visits the funeral parlor, and in long shot Kavaïté holds on its two proprietors' sullen lack of response, a scene punctuated all the while by the death rattle of a screw wrench being turned over and over again. On one train of thought, *Ecoute le temps* revels in these concrete, empirical details: factual data, the forensics of the case, the textures and flavors of this unsavory setting. Alongside these,

Charlotte (Emilie Duquenne) in *Ecoute le temps*

however, the film dwells on unsituated lyrical asides, the same ambiguous visual refrains we saw in *Innocence*, *Darling*, and *She's One of Us*. Before the police visit, there is a context-free shot of a curving road, lined with dormant trees, vanishing into a descending mist. More suggestive still is the image that precedes the two uncooperative morticians: an out-of-focus broken window in the foreground, with Charlotte's face in close-up behind it; her eyes flicker behind a spider's web of refracted light, the fractured glass resembling a mental contusion or the onset of physical disintegration. The shot also makes Charlotte look as if she has a halo.

The most pivotal, protracted scenes in *Ecoute le temps* — Charlotte using her equipment to reconstruct her own past and her mother's last days — probe this discrepancy between the objective-knowable and the subjective-inexplicable. Having set up all the dramatic conventions and implied conspiracies of a domestic thriller, *Ecoute le temps* becomes in real terms an *in*action film. Unlike the long, physical, male-instigated set pieces of *Tell No One* (Alex fleeing the police through the Paris rush hour) and *Pour elle* (Julien breaking his wife out of hospital), Kavaïté's film derives largely from Charlotte's drifting stream-of-consciousness, the never-rationalized aural incidents she records, which we, as viewers, see. Time and space distort — some of the images are plausibly flashbacks, others come from moments at which Charlotte was not present. Many seem complete, while others are inconclusive in both duration and chronology. Each scene fragment is apparently cued by the microphone's location, shots intercut with Charlotte marking the floor with chalk, suspending lengths of string that soon fill the room with a matrix of interlinked strands, like a physical manifestation of a mind, a cerebral cortex. From this, we get plural points of view from different time periods with shifting emotional currents: Charlotte as a girl happily playing cat's cradle with her mother; nervous

Charlotte's web: The matrix of the past reconstructed in *Ecoute le temps*

locals visiting to have their futures told; young Charlotte's growing frustration with her "abnormal" parent, her father, and (later) Julien interacting with her mother in a state of desire and unease. Like the pop-art manipulations of Bruni Tedeschi, Kavaïté weaves a kaleidoscope of fantasies, breakdowns, hopes, and passions.

Kavaïté also echoes Alnoy and Curiol in that she depicts events-in-progress while openly reflecting on their construction, giving alternative or even contradictory conclusions about what her scenes actually represent. Glimpses of the past coalesce with the diegetic present; characters and dialogues intersect in dazzling permutations. One scene cuts abruptly from Charlotte pedaling on her bike to an empty seat in her front room. Across the table, Charlotte listens on her headphones and records; in the next shot Jérôme appears in the empty seat, and while a shot-reverse shot pattern implies that she somehow sees him, we next hear the mother's voice offering tender advice about introverted isolation that seems to be directed to both of them simultaneously: "Try to find something to do outside work. . . . Open up to others, meet someone." Cut back to Jérôme standing up, walking around the table; the camera pans to reveal the mother seated; he tries to kiss her and is rebuffed. (Several of Charlotte's reimagined sequences, it must be said, end or collapse on a moment of male intrusion or threatened violence.) While the false implication of Jérôme's guilt is more usual thriller material, Kavaïté also seems to draw an oblique connection between the wrong suspect and Charlotte herself, two close childhood friends who have both withdrawn into a solipsistic, understated despair.

The final point about *Ecoute le temps* is that ultimately it satisfies all the forms it inhabits. The film works as a meticulously compelling murder mystery (which Charlotte inexorably solves), as an indictment of petty (male) authority and the degradation of the French countryside, as a moving reflection on the frictions between mothers and daughters, as a questionable, even schizophrenic portrait of a troubled and grief-stricken state of mind. (Many of the peculiar behaviors, even some of Charlotte's, might be explained by the belated revelation that toxic chemicals have leached into the village's water supply.) *Ecoute le temps* ends, perhaps appropriately, with a coda that inverts its opening. While the film begins with Charlotte's mother accidentally running over a deer — a bad omen, she predicts to her horrified daughter, for what will come — it closes with Charlotte, tranquil now, stopping her own car to walk, apparently seeing another wild deer regarding her behind trees off in the distance. Is this a further fantasy or wishful projection? An ironically lyrical final touch for a film that is both poetic and harshly claustrophobic? An optimistic hint about the natural course of things resuming, an abiding echo between past and present, mother and daughter? Before Kavaïté cuts to black, her last shot is of Charlotte standing completely still; her face is an absolutely static, blank, reflective yet inexpressive mask. As always in contemporary French feminine cinema, there are no easy answers.

Prospects for Contemporary French Feminine Cinema:
Ça brûle and *Toi et Moi*

In keeping with a feminine cinema which revels in multifarious designs, we conclude with two endings that pointedly distort or subvert closure. The first final segment comes from Claire Simon's *Ça brûle* (2006). Simon, a professor at la Fémis as well as an active filmmaker, often makes documentaries, like *Mimi* (2003), but *Ça brûle* is an intimate fiction, typical within the female filmmaking we have surveyed in that it deals with a troubled adolescent, Livia (Camille Varenne, making her debut), and the rising emotions of her first serious romantic desires. Set in a village in the south of France, *Ça brûle* opens as Livia is thrown from her horse and is found, unconscious, by Jean (Gilbert Melki), a local fire fighter. She is intensely attracted to him, although Jean is merely friendly towards her; he is married and a father. At first glance, Simon's film invokes obvious feminist traits: it is aligned to a socially marginal young woman, on-screen virtually always; it links the complexities of her personal needs and failures to a compromised domestic milieu (Livia's mother and father are separated and she has no close parental influence); and the film systematically inverts the traditional male gaze, the motif of passive women's bodies arranged for scopophiliac male consumption on-screen, that is so often attributed to mainstream cinema. This last aspect is obvious, for instance, during a scene where Livia calls Jean on her cell phone, and spies on him, fixated yet unseen, as he takes her call while working, sweating and stripped to the waist, atop the roof of a nearby house.

But there is more to *Ça brûle* than just female-centered depictions. Less ubiquitously polyvalent than films like *Innocence*, *She's One of Us* or *Ecoute le temps*, *Ça brûle* nonetheless adopts the open, lyrical feminine cinema treatment for strategic effects; a book-ending treatment that revises our impression of the surrounding film, as we saw with *Darling*. The model is clear during the film's final segment. In a nihilistic fit of pique, Livia starts a fire to punish her cell phone, which has no messages for her. The moment is obviously symbolic of Livia's thwarted passions — her pyre soon burns a nearby pair of praying mantises, mating while the female bites the head off her male. The fire quickly spreads to consume the nearby countryside, sweeping all before it. (The scenes of the blaze, rousing wild animals to mass panic, are so dynamic, shot to capture the simultaneous primal beauty and terror of forest fires, that they recall Terrence Malick's and Néstor Almendros's harvest scenes in *Days of Heaven* [1978].) Jean, although alienated from Livia, nonetheless ventures deep into the advancing danger zone, by now an inferno, to rescue the young woman once more.

At this point, Simon inverts our anticipations of narrative closure, stylistic coherence, and, especially, editorial judgment about her (at best) blithe protagonist. Soon, Jean gets disoriented as he succumbs to the effects of smoke inhalation. Reversing their roles, it is Livia who eventually finds him, supine in the dust. In a highly ambiguous, tragically romantic reunion, Livia bends down to lie on him and in medium close-up he inexplicably pulls her close, making imploring eye contact, caressing her face tenderly. Livia tries to rouse him, but he stirs only feebly, wordlessly clinging to her, disconcertingly oblivious to the dangerous smoke billowing around them. Several minutes of screen time pass as the couple's movements subside. Death — apparently — comes as the two lie intertwined in close-up on the ground, reconciled like star-crossed lovers. The crackles of approaching flames grow louder on the soundtrack, while thickening smoke obscures the image. Now, Simon cuts to a sixty-second long take, replacing all diegetic sound with a distorted minor-key tone, as her mobile frame, wobbling, advances over blackened roads, drifting pockets of smoke, singed vegetation, through images of a wasteland with no humans present. This last shot is unplaced, oddly bracketed off and set apart from *Ça brûle*'s otherwise very naturalistic aesthetic, unconnected to anything or anyone in the diegesis. Livia's complexities — is she ultimately a victim, when her unsated desires are aggrandized like this? — prompt Simon to cut to black on these improbably beatific tableaux, scenes of unpredictable poetic force. Here, yet again, is also an ecocritical paradox: sumptuous devastation, a scorched earth that is part of the natural course of environmental renewal.

As in the work of le Besco, de Van, Doillon, Fillières, Sciamma, Bruni Tedeschi, Hadzihalilovic, Alnoy, Kavaïté, and many others among France's growing vanguard of highly adept female filmmakers, Simon's *Ça brûle* avoids simple verdicts and any sense of finality, preferring instead multiple permutations that unsettle both internal and external stylistic norms. This feminine cinema is alert to France's social and political fault-lines, gender inequalities, yet refuses any monolithic or didactic response; it admits contradictions, attenuating or tearing deliberate breaches in filmmaking conventions that are still so often homogenous and male-centered. Like the web motif in *Ecoute le temps*, these filmmakers weave together a matrix of citations from different cultural sources, complicating their meanings, creating new possibilities for feminine-centered representations on-screen. Neither triumphant nor defeatist, these films reflect on their female protagonists' social and personal actions as an ongoing struggle, empowering but tenuous, a work in progress. Befitting the embattled status of French women today, the feminist trajectory on which this chapter opened, the filmmaking sensibility here is meticulously enigmatic, with no pat viewpoints about the prospects of these women and the worlds they inhabit. From a range of professional perspectives, within the mainstream and far removed from it, female filmmakers in France today continue to explore the scope of this contemporary feminine cinema, the materials, ultimately, with which to create a more fluent and conceptually progressive cinema. In many ways recalling the achievements of key women pioneers before them, these filmmakers offer us films that are often profound, all the more so for being profoundly inconclusive. Regarding the thorny but essential question of women's rights to filmmaking, France in the twenty-first century, perhaps unexpectedly, may well be the best scenario to emerge in world cinema so far.

Julie Lopes-Curval's *Toi et Moi* (2006) offers us a fitting last take. The film follows a pair of half-sisters, Léna (Marion Cotillard) and Ariane (Julie Depardieu). The former is a professional concert cellist, painfully self-effacing, who enters into a fragile relationship with Mark (Jonathan Zaccaï), a fellow musician, from whom she eventually drifts apart. Ariane, who writes photo-novellas for a living, meanwhile does eventually find personal fulfillment, ditching her unreliable businessman boyfriend for the more attentive Pablo (Sergio Peris Menchota). On one level, *Toi et Moi* works as a rather mournful, female-centered romantic comedy. (In 2009, it was belatedly released on region-1 DVD to capitalize on the growing American interest in Cotillard; as we saw in Chapter 3, putatively France's most exportable female star.) Lopes-

Curval's ambitions, however, lie here but also elsewhere. To fracture her own generic set-pieces, she inserts into the drama a series of bizarre static tableaux, in which her characters become photo-novella characters, altering their personalities, commenting on the action, and making alternative decisions to those taken by their diegetic counterparts. By consequence, the photo-novella format, itself often dismissed as a despised feminine sub-culture, deliberately splits the *Toi et Moi* text into two, exploring fantasy hypothetical scenarios (possibly yet not definitively from Ariane's perspective) beside the events that actually take place. The device not only accentuates the two women's inner lives and creativity (music, photography, writing, cultures high and low) but also strategically opens up the text, turning the conventional dramatic parameters of the romantic comedy into a garden of forked paths, some taken, others not, the burdens of different choices coexisting poignantly alongside each other.

The back-and-forth pattern culminates in Lopes-Curval's beautifully effective (non-)ending. Two years after their emotional lives have diverged — Ariane's into motherhood and continued professional satisfaction; her half-sister's into troubled solitude — Léna emerges from a period of depressed withdrawal to rejoin her orchestra. During a rehearsal, she is awkwardly but tenderly reunited with Mark, who has since married another woman. *Toi et Moi*'s final doubled sequence is of Léna's successful new concert performance, watched by Ariane and her mother. The house lights fade to black and the recital begins. As the chamber music rises, Lopes-Curval cuts to the two women in the audience, observing Léna on stage with evident compassion and pride. Now, photo-novella stills of an alternative Léna are intercut with the concert in progress, as in an opulent hotel she re-encounters a different Mark, not married, seeking her company. The music continues as the couple embraces; he promises her, "Nothing can prevent us from being happy now." Here, *Toi et Moi* once again has it both ways, with an unhappy happy ending, an unspoken wish fulfilled by a stroke of imagination as fleeting, but moving, as the notes from Léna's cello. Lopes-Curval, one among many of French cinema's leading female talents, makes a self-reflexive joke about clichéd pop-culture romances, while simultaneously exploring the limits of a woman's personal agency and jurisdiction, the web of prospects that might potentially define what she really needs and wants. Contemporary French feminine cinema, a new approach for a new generation of women filmmakers, is powerfully alive to such confusions and contradictions, dreams and their corresponding realities.

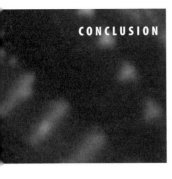

Instructive Cinephilia

FILM LITERACY AND LA FÉMIS

I think it's important in film school to have time to dream, like when you're a child. You need to dream, you need to have time to do your own research, and to be free to do your own films.

FRANÇOISE MARIE, director of *On dirait que* . . . (2007), graduate of French film schools L'Ecole Louis-Lumière and IDHEC

This book's interrelated strands, our conceptual survey of contemporary French cinema, reveal a cluster of textual and professional issues. Central among these, this conclusion iterates, is France's abiding cinephilia, a passion for film in all its forms. This contemporary cinephilia exists, though, not only as a staple of French critical *reception*, the traditional model, but also emerges as a recurring textual approach, cinephilia as an *active craft practice* permeating French cinema today. On the one hand, France's film culture is still shaped in many ways by a clear cinephilic impulse, an ideology that is obvious in the zealous engagements of critical studies, interviews, and analyses that we have encountered in previous chapters. But cinephilia also exists as a production process, a train of stylistic thought, a methodology instilled in French film schools, applied on-screen by committed and conceptually fluent film practitioners, modeled most overtly by critics-turned-filmmakers like Assayas and Bozon. The final section of *Brutal Intimacy* will pursue this concluding premise by defining this notion of cinephilia, relating it to the craft methods we have seen diversely at large in France. Next, it traces the model to the seminal pedagogical efforts of la Fémis, an influential source of French filmmaking, before offering, as an emblematic final case study, the example of Jean Paul Civeyrac. We close by reflecting on the French belief in the confluence of theory-pedagogy and actual filmmaking practice.

We have already seen extensively how contemporary French filmmakers routinely draw from an assertive stylistic palette. Even among mainstream directors, especially in comedies, there is often a pronounced cinematic self-awareness. We saw this, for instance, with Laurent Baffie's panoramic intertextual asides, the series of jokes that open *Car Keys*; and the obsessive cultural cross-referencing in both OSS 117 films. Throughout the French film industry, indeed, cineliteracy, as a craft practice, is rife. Roaming across the continuum of French cinema, as we have done, considering especially the work of pop-art artisans and the more experimentalist fringes, we can see an even more sustained emphasis on sophisticated, cinematically self-conscious design, films diverging from a more functional or expositional mode in favor of abstracted asides, flourishes of lyrical obscurity, materials that are densely cinematically charged. Even though much contemporary French cinema is quite classical and textually unified, it nonetheless returns compulsively to these bravura moments of cinematic rendition, alternatives to a mainstream global cinema that still derive from Bordwell's seminal formulation of classical Hollywood as "an excessively obvious cinema."[1]

Consolidating the findings from our previous case studies, we can gauge more fully this applied, active cinephilia. This is the notion, to restate, that contemporary French filmmaking is defined, either strategically or ubiquitously, by stylistic virtuosity for its own sake; among a population of filmmakers seeking more abstrusely expressive design elements, a kind of sensually intense, even rhapsodic textuality. Contemporary French cinema is flavored through these cinephilic moments by filmmakers *on-screen* as well as by critics *in print*. We can characterize this trajectory as an acutely overdetermined or excessive design, filmmaking that flaunts its cinematic affinities. Again, while much French cinema still works towards classical goals — narratives legible to a broad viewership, using techniques that are diegetically unified — there is widespread recourse to alternative stylistic features, patterns of textual virtuosity, overt declarations of cineliterate art. In other words, we must account for the fact that many contemporary French filmmakers align themselves, either in passing or in principle, with an excessively *non*-obvious cinema.

The concept of cinephilia, a zeal for cinematics, is therefore salient to our conclusions about contemporary French cinema, the state of its art. Two major studies, Antoine de Baecque's *La Cinéphilie: Invention d'un regard, histoire d'une culture 1944–1968* (2003), in French, and Christian Keathley's *Cinephilia and History, or The Wind in the Trees* (2006), in English, are foundational for us here. The primary model set out in both accounts is historical, proximate to the work of André Bazin, who argued that true cinematic analysis emerged from "the total art of the watching of films."[2] From Bazin's roots as an *animateur* and host of ciné-club discussions emerged his school of film criticism, a founding principle of *Cahiers du cinéma*, giving rise to the auteurist passions of the New Wave generation, a group committed to making the kinds of films that they themselves loved to watch. In a pivotal sense, then, it is the particular ardor of film engagement that is at issue, a deeply felt conviction among certain respondents about the inherent value of a relatively young medium, of cinema's capacity to excite fervent critical energies. As de Baecque frames his own essayistic inquiry: "We can attempt to define a history of the history of cinema . . . the constitution of a public around animated images . . . the cultural legitimation of a production and an activity that was for a long time held in contempt . . . all these themes are at the heart of the work of those dedicated to cinephilic rituals, implemented in ciné-club networks between the 1940s and 1960s and in film publications."[3] From this systematic approach, de Baecque and Keathley contend, came the study of film itself: the advent of specialists in cinema history and historiography, the rise of the discipline of auteurism and textual analyses in publications and academic forums alike.

Cinephilia exists, then, as a historical tendency—the course towards a more rigorous critical scrutiny of cinema that was popularized in the 1950s. It concomitantly emerges as a particular form of spectatorial practice, an especially intense, keenly felt attendance of the unfolding moving image itself. David Bordwell describes one particular path towards cinephilic proclivities: "The cinephile loves the *idea* of film. . . . The pious will call Cinema a holy place, the secular will see it as the treasure-house of an artform still capable of great things."[4] In terms of cinephilia as a moment-by-moment process, Keathley suggests it is: "The fetishizing of fragments of a film, either individual shots or marginal (often unintentional) details in the image, especially those that appear only for a moment. . . . Whether it is the gesture of a hand, the odd rhythm of a horse's gait, or the sudden change in expression on a face, these moments are experienced by the cinephile who beholds them as nothing less than an epiphany, a revelation."[5] What Keathley refers to is a kind of sensorial abandon to the pleasures of an apprehended image, often shorn of context, sometimes shorn of everything except delight in textuality itself, the stylistic minutiae of life, distilled, on-screen. George Toles echoes this principle of serendipitous viewing fixations, arguing that "the film lover pursues the apparently incidental, throwaway element in order to discover, on closer inspection born of intuition or feeling, how the inconsequential is essential—a possible key to the whole design."[6] When de Baecque follows this same trajectory, he ruminates more transcendently that from a cinephilic perspective, an instinct felt sharply among French critics since the 1910s, the ultimate question is whether through cinema, "Can one learn to see?"[7]

To contemporary historians of such habits, cinephilia is usually perceived to be in decline. From Keathley's American perspective, and even to a lesser extent de Baecque's French perspective, cinephilia is quite simply not what it used to be. To the former writer, indeed, whether it is through the growth of psychoanalysis in academia, a doctrine that preaches suspicion about the beguiling textual logics of filmmaking, or else the spread of cultural studies, approaching texts largely as symptomatic of broader shaping political and social forces, cinephilia has been marginalized, cast into doubt, made incidental. Conversely, certain cinephilia advocates, notably Malte Hagener, Marijke de Valck, and Thomas Elsaesser, contend that the practice thrives still on the international film festival circuit. As Liz Czach puts it, "With the decline of other screening opportunities and venues, the film festival has emerged as a privileged site for big-screen, art cinema cinephilia."[8] Debate about modern cinephilia continues, reflected perhaps most sharply by the rise of specialist DVD and digital boutique restoration houses like Criterion in the United States, Masters of Cinema in the United Kingdom, and Blaq Out in France. These outfits cater in large part to home media cinephiles, producing re-released film masterworks, accompanied by audio tracks of academic lectures and ancillary critical materials, conferring the ability to dwell obsessively on newly remastered images from canonical texts, with scholarly discourses appended at the touch of a remote control. Especially among the lively online communities of specialist BitTorrent collectives and sites like criterionforum.org, where enthusiastic textual analyses intermingle with glee about forthcoming releases (or even speculation about them), modern cinephilia, aligned to the small screen and the intellectual intimacies of DVD, seems robust indeed.

Returning to the case of contemporary France, however, it is evident how neglected cinephilia is as an *active* principle, a shaping textual concern among so motivated directors. This cinephilic approach affects filmmaking practices; it is not just a facet of critical reception. In the sympathetic French environment—central to what my introduction called France's cinema ecosystem—this cinephilic tendency can indeed seem ubiquitous. It certainly unites the wealth of our previous case studies: their meticulous, often obsessive attendance to textual minutiae, the frequent recourse to aesthetic abstractions, lyrical incidentals that outrun or overwhelm the functional needs of sustaining narratives on-screen. These are cinephilic moments inserted either as narrative asides or bracketing textual accents, passages that are usually wordless, often found in title sequences. Or, alternatively, these segments are highlighted for their own value as expressively dense, stylistically overdetermined film renderings, kinetically vivid exercises placed for like-minded *col-*

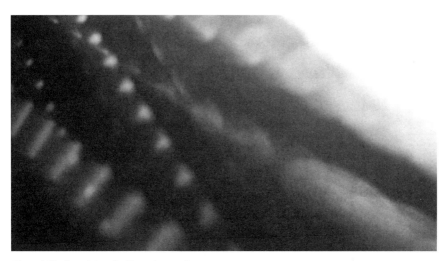

Cinephilic flourishes in *Dans les cordes*

leagues, as well as critics, to admire, emulate, and outdo. Cinephilic moments like these, moreover, encourage or even directly solicit the cinephilic gaze described so eloquently by Keathley and Toles, an appreciative apprehension that we must extend to interested filmmakers as well as interested critics. In sum, this contemporary cinephilia, on- and off-screen, is key to the vitality of French film, now perhaps more than ever.

Elements of cinephilic practice are rife in French cinema, from the dazzlingly intricate title sequence/star entrance of *L'Instinct de mort* to *The Ring Finger*'s bloodied bottling plant montage sequence. The more you look for cinephilic episodes, the more contemporary French examples you find. There is, for instance, the opening of *On the Ropes*, a film mentioned in Chapter 4. An otherwise naturalistic film about boxing and domestic rivalries fades up on an almost monochrome medium shot of its female protagonist lying supine, staring directly at the camera. The camera itself is in motion, it wobbles; traffic sounds reverberate beside a strangely diffuse but insistent tone on the soundtrack; passing car headlights cast yellow beams that backlight the woman's upper body and strands of her hair; no practical information is conveyed about where, when, or, indeed, with whom, we are. Richard-Serrano's first cut takes us to another (point of view?) shot of a translucent material blowing in the wind, highly tactile, perhaps a curtain, lined with fronds of black stitching, over which pools of white illumination rove, back and forth, back and forth, as the focus racks gently and the soundtrack builds aural density. The third shot pushes in closer still, an abstract kaleidoscope of bright and dark textures, graphic contours of lines in space that closely resemble

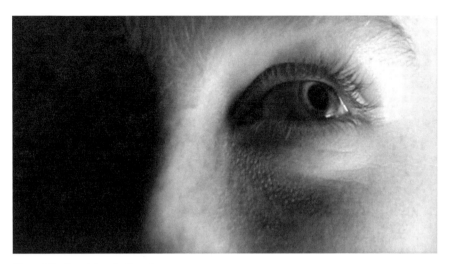

Cinephilic flourishes in *Sequins*

strips of celluloid. At this point, dissolving to a hazy shot of Paris awakening at dawn, we get Richard-Serrano's "un film de" credit, a filmmaker staking proud ownership over the cinephilic features that precede, as much as the narrative that ensues.

Or there is Eléonore Faucher's *Sequins* (*Brodeuses*, 2004). This film centers on a young woman, Claire (Lola Naymark), pregnant but single, alienated from her parents, employed by an older woman (Ariane Ascaride) to make embroideries. Stylistic exercises punctuate Faucher's text, a debut feature linked to those we saw in Chapter 1. One provocative cinephilic flourish occurs as Claire gets her first — terse — instructions from her new colleague, and starts work. Faucher cuts, jumping in space and time, adjusting her expressive register from the literal to the connotative. On-screen appear extreme close-ups of mother-of-pearl sequins, glittering shapes, interwoven with netting in extraordinary shallow focus, a technical feat which Faucher amplifies through minutely executed racked planes of focus, perfectly diffused key and natural light sources, and graceful arcs of her mobile camera. Aural strokes from a solo violin, soon joined by others in piercing treble, underscore the thrust of the sequence — its stylistic musicality, the labor of work but also images of creation as song. We crosscut from the fabric's sheen to extreme close-ups of Claire's face, in partial shadow, starkly rendered with an abstracting (and non-naturalistic) sheer black background. The treatment foregrounds the delicate grooves in the skin around Claire's eyes, worry-lines prematurely acquired, yet also symptoms of her enraptured concentration, alongside the wisps of her thick red hair, the curvature of her eyelids, the home-made virid-

Cinephilic flourishes in *A Christmas Tale*

ian headscarf she wears while working. Back we go to extreme close views of disparate parts of the embroidery, its delicate reflections now intimately linked to the shapes of Claire's own body, this figure interwoven, literally and figuratively, with a beautiful tapestry being born before our eyes, a matrix of materials and its artist.

Consider, equally, a passage near the opening of Arnaud Desplechin's *A Christmas Tale* (*Un Conte de Noël*, 2008). The film focuses on Junon (Catherine Deneuve), a matriarch with bone cancer in urgent need of a marrow transplant from a compatible donor, whose eccentric and divided extended family gather for Christmas. Part of the family's history is recounted with silhouetted marionettes, stick figure shadows moving above grainy footage of faded photos, zoom in and outs over abstract forms from X-rays and children's paintings, out-of-focus home movie footage, and an unsituated shot of a tiny theatrical proscenium. Then we meet Junon herself, bustling about the family house, making breakfast; a series of dissolves moves us sinuously from her apparently functional body, to steam from a kettle, wan beams of morning sunshine, and lines of photos of her children; but now the image loses definition as Junon leans back against the wall, breathing heavily, dropping her tray while axial cuts go in and out of focus, studying the troubled face from either side, quivering like the actress herself. While Desplechin represents something concrete here—Junon's illness; the brittle complex of individuals within this fragile family unit—the sequence itself is playfully evasive and evocative, almost deliriously focused on warm and cold textures, the vivid materiality of memories, the tactile dimensions of emotional and physical pain.

Or there is the ending of *In My Skin*, a film discussed in Chapter 2. Esther (Marina de Van) abruptly leaves the hotel room in which we have seen her self-mutilate, gaining release through disturbing yet intimate communions with the matter of her own body. Coinciding exactly with the crash of the slammed door, the rattle of the keys in its lock, de Van cuts the shot and returns us, in physical proximity but temporal discontinuity, to Esther once again lying prone within the room. Held in extreme close-up, the middle-right portion of Esther's face is posed slightly out of focus, as are, more overtly, the green patterns of the rearground hotel room wallpaper, its jade color swathes oddly interacting with the pigments of Esther's staring eye which unblinkingly regards the camera. Isolated piano notes, offset by muted percussions, accompany the frame's gradual movement, spinning away, as the camera at once tracks back and zooms out, elongating the on-screen space, adding depth cues but maintaining its claustrophobia, as more of Esther is revealed, confined to the bed in the room. Now de Van dissolves to repeat the same shot three times, underlining its artifice and abstractions, alerting the viewer to the image's purely graphic component parts: four juxtaposed zones of faded wall decoration, a violated but tranquil face, a cushioning mass of dark hair, the brown paisley patterns of the bedspread. In triplicate these materials are artfully arranged before us, this brutalized body cocooned in numbing motion, a form discovered in mournful stasis, a figure in calm repose at last. Cut to black.

La Fémis: Cinephilia Practicalities

All of our preceding examples, broadly representative of cinephilic moments in recent French cinema, come either from films made by la Fémis graduates, or else from productions derived from workshops with professionals connected to the school. This textual sampling is also confirmed by the dynamic and diverse impact of la Fémis alumni and teachers dealt with elsewhere in this book: from Noémie Lvovsky to Céline Bozon, Christine Carrière to François Ozon, Céline Sciamma to Marina de Van. What, then, of France's film school system as a catalyst in the values and habits of its contemporary filmmakers? The equation is the relationship between la Fémis and the approaches we have explored throughout this book, culminating most specifically in the practices of French textual cinephilia, a tendency we have seen often in our previous test cases, isolated now in this conclusion.

The first point to make about la Fémis is that it is a very neglected context to French cinema, peripherally mentioned by some French-language writers, almost completely ignored in English. But the full ambitions of la Fémis for its students, befitting its full title as L'Ecole Nationale Supérieure des Métiers de l'Image et du Son, emerge from its self-description as nothing less than "a complete technical, artistic, and cultural education in the field of cinema and the audio-visual."[9] In its current form, the school opened its doors in 1986, one of France's state school crown jewels, conceived, like its predecessor IDHEC, as the principal source of State-funded film education. In other words, la Fémis is a loose equivalent to FAMU in Prague, or VGIK in Moscow, or the BFI-sponsored National Film and Television School in London. In France, however, the government-sponsored film school system is divided into two: whereas l'Ecole Louis-Lumière is the major technical institution, la Fémis is designed to balance professional indoctrination with critical studies of the history of the medium, offering aesthetic immersion alongside technical pedagogy.[10] (One la Fémis student I interviewed said she lacked the scientific training to get into Louis-Lumière, so simply changed schools.) As described first hand by de Van herself, the school's ideology encourages its students to conceive of their studies as not just practical and technological, but rather a systematic process of "intensive artistic *research*."[11]

After a succession of different directors and locations, in the fall of 1999 la Fémis moved permanently to its current location at 6, rue Francoeur, in the 18th arrondissement of Paris. This is the site of the old Pathé film studios, the setting for a host of French classics, such as Robert Bresson's *Les Dames du Bois du Boulogne* (1945) and Marcel Carné's *Children of Paradise* (*Les Enfants du paradis*, 1945). (As Sylvain Monier points out wryly, it is the la Fémis students who are really children in paradise.)[12] Less frequently used for commercial cinema today, la Fémis nonetheless makes itself available for occasional productions, recently for Laurent Tuel's *Jean-Philippe* (2006), which was shot in the rooms of the school itself, not on its soundstages. Attended today, the school does seem like a remarkable throwback, a working studio complex, a hive of activity above and below ground, a logistically rich focal point of French film craft. During my recent visit, for example, as I was shown around I witnessed American exchange students from New York University carrying out light meter readings and sound tests, a cinematography class exposing 16mm footage, a film society event centered on a discussion of *Boys Don't Cry* (1999), carpenters building a new set, production designers dressing a stage, dozens of editors working on student film postproductions, and many other spectacles besides. La Fémis's resources, indeed, are formidable: nearly one hundred thousand square meters of space, twelve classrooms, dozens of offices and administration spaces, four soundstages with an average floor plan of 220 square meters, twenty-nine editing suites, an in-house laboratory and carpentry workshop, a library and videotheque, two mixing studios, multiple equipment rooms housing cameras of all formats, and, as a kind of culmination to the school's business, three technically cutting-edge screening auditoria: the Jean Renoir hall (170 seats), the Jacques Demy hall (60 seats), and the Alice Guy hall (20 seats).

Besides the superiority of its technical resources, there is the simple fact that la Fémis is excellently situated within Paris, a fixture of the city's film culture and professional scene. Conflating both points, one recent la Fémis graduate, Matthieu-David Cournot, attests: "You do feel like you're in a studio, you've got the electrical department, all the equipment's there, set construction, with training going on real sets. . . . It's beautiful and it's inside Paris, unlike so many other places like Louis-Lumière, which are in the suburbs. . . . One of the reasons why so many professionals come in is that it's convenient, they can come in while they're shooting."[13] Another bonus for the school is the fact that virtually next door, at 8, rue Francoeur, is the headquarters of the AFC (l'Association des Directeurs de la Photographie Cinématographique), which is the major trade organization for directors of photography in France. Each year, the AFC hosts its trade show within the la Fémis building, showcasing all manner of new wares, products, and sponsorship opportunities (partnerships exist with Kodak, Fujifilm, and Panavision, among others) in the fields of film and HD cameras, film stocks, lights, video monitors, and so on. To demonstrate these new technologies, a series of screenings is held, ranging from restored classics (for the March 13, 2008 show, for instance, Jean Cocteau's *Orpheus* [*Orphée*, 1950] had top billing) to contemporary French blockbusters. Annually, about 2,000 people attend these AFC–la Fémis events, from people in the upper echelons of the profession keeping abreast of their trade, to la Fémis trainees learning the basics.

Emblematized by this strong relationship with such a powerful trade organization, one mantra of la Fémis is its integration of critical studies with first hand access to equipment and practical training in the hands of working professionals, including the many successful graduates invited to return. Entry to the school is very restricted—and to la Fémis's detractors, elitist—with 1200–1500 applicants vying annually for around 40 open positions. (Prédal notes the school's success in attracting applications from women, even achieving parity in its direction track during many years of its operation, in part facilitating the kind of feminine aesthetic that we explored in Chapter 4.)[14] Three levels of grueling competition weed out the contenders. A professional panel assesses each candidate's creative dossier (first round), then grades their written or oral test for the stated area of interest (second round), before the la Fémis president convenes a jury and holds public interviews addressing all aspects of the would-be student's artistic goals and motivations, as well as his or her abilities to analyze closely an allocated sequence from a particular film (recent cases include Hou Hsiao-Hsien's *Good Men,*

Good Women [1995] in 2001, Chantal Akerman's *La Captive* [2000] in 2002, and Luis Buñuel's *Viridiana* [1961] in 2004). The average age of incoming students is twenty-three years old, five years more advanced than was the case with IDHEC. All of the students I spoke to had strong memories of the stress and commitment involved in simply gaining access to la Fémis, before their instruction even began.

Once a student has been accepted, training at la Fémis is drawn from seven different departments: direction, screenwriting, cinematography, sound, editing, production design, and set design. To these subdivisions la Fémis has added additional modules in scriptreading and editing (in 1992), a masterclass in European coproduction (2002), and an applied course in distribution and exhibition (2003). Most of the courses encourage teamwork and collaboration, cinema as the mutual practice of art. For the first year students receive instruction across all these related areas, then gravitate to a stated field of interest, which they study during their second and third years through analytical seminars, practical exercises, group works, and, by the fourth year, an exacting final project (the *travail de fin d'études*). In the first year, students start out on DV micro-shorts, moving towards group shorts (usually around ten minutes) on 16mm during years two and three, before completing their work, approaching graduation, by working with 35mm. Part of the la Fémis philosophy, across the board, is to balance a broad film education with a specific professional destination, the best of both worlds. As one recent graduate (ultimately of the cinematography division) summarized the process she encountered: "I never forget that within la Fémis I was able to experiment with 35mm cinemascope, the new Aaton 2 film stock, different ways of developing stock in the lab, steadicams, and even trying out being an actor!"[15]

Besides its on-site pedagogy, moreover, the school provides extracurricular assets, with close links to the BiFi (le Bibliothèque du film, France's national film library), the Cinémathèque Française, and other state academies for animation, design, and fine arts. In addition, la Fémis also emphasizes entrepreneurial activities and self-promotion. In the first place, the school has its graduates screen their final shorts before an audience of its distinguished alumni (Emmanuelle Bercot, Emmanuel Bourdieu, Sophie Fillières, Lvovsky, Masson, Dominik Moll, among others). This annual event facilitates networking, as does the school's promotion of internationalism via exchange programs with schools in countries as far afield as the United States, Canada, Australia, Germany, and the Philippines. Another productive culmination of la Fémis is its long-term record of placing its graduates on artistic or debutant panels at leading film festivals like Cannes; thirty-five ex-la Fémis students were credited on films that played there in 2006, for example. Assessments vary, but some estimates reckon that 90 percent of la Fémis graduates find eventual employment in the French film industry.

A major facet of the craft taught at la Fémis, part of its impact on the field, is the instantiation of cineliteracy, and, ultimately, cinephilia among its emergent professionals. In the first place, the importance of critical studies and film history to la Fémis inductees is almost immediately apparent. Upon entering the rue Francoeur building and approaching the main desk, rows of assigned books, published by la Fémis itself, are prominently displayed for the students to buy. Centered on the two most prestigious tracks, direction and scriptwriting, all la Fémis students must study extensive passages from key texts about cinema history and theory. For their screenwriting classes, students read Jean-Claude Carrière's (the ex-president of la Fémis) *Raconter une histoire*, a compendium of narrative analyses based on luminaries ranging from Homer to Shakespeare, to scripts or treatments by filmmakers such as Jean-Luc Godard, Andrej Wajda, Milos Forman, Luis Buñuel, and Volker Schlöndorff. Certainly a challenging lead-in for a newcomer student, Carrière's point of departure is: "What links the forms of the most ancient works of literature and the most recent works of cinema?"[16] Better yet, for their direction classes, la Fémis students analyze the teachings of that most infamous filmmaker-instructor, Sergei Eisenstein himself, in the form of his transcribed *Leçons de mise en scène*.[17] Translated from Russian to French by Jacques Aumont, the book is Vladimir Nijny's account of Eisenstein's intensive VGIK workshops, first published in 1957, an evocative connection between two leading world film schools, past and present.

Assigned textbooks are just the first phase of the school's pursuit of cineliteracy and cinephilia. At the library, second-year students are issued with another imposing document to accompany the rest of their instruction. This text is the work of Alain Bergala, film and television director, ex-editor of *Cahiers du cinéma*, and one of la Fémis's main pro-cinephile teachers. It is titled simply: "The 156 Films That You Must Have Seen: The List" (see Appendix). There follows a taxonomy of these so-called essential films, broadly representative of the canon (Eisenstein, Welles, Godard, Truffaut, Bresson, Tati, Mizoguchi, Ozu, Dreyer, Fellini, Varda, Hawks, Griffith) along with some interesting wild cards (Mambety, Grémillon, King Hu, Pialat, Melville, Naruse, Walsh, Hou); about a third of the titles come from French cinema. Under the list, moreover, Bergala issues a more emphatic call to arms, declaring his cinephile intentions, something he defines as both a mode of viewing and a production practice, equally vital preoccupations for any film professional-in-training. His first pitch is a mode of operation, the cinephilic habit: "156 films, that's one film a week for three years, which is a reasonable cruising speed. Nothing need stop you from carrying this out."[18] Next, Bergala advocates the especially intense cinephilic spectatatorial process, the need when watching films to have "really *watched*, meaning thought about, discussed, because watching something without letting it sink in isn't really watching something at all."[19] Finally, Bergala draws the two habits together into a decisive formulation of cinephilia, through which passionate viewing generates sophisticated filmmaking. He argues: "Watching a film, from which we learn about working in cinema, generates ideas, reflections, comparisons, aspirations, likes and dislikes about cinema. . . . [This lists aims] to instill a desire in everyone, from each film seen, to work out their ideas about this process. Without doubt, each trainee's notes about works from the past will become, in the long term, a vital tool for them to work out . . . the creative contours of their sensibility. And there is no great cinema, whoever is trying to make it, without a cinematic sensibility."[20]

In keeping with this cinephile mandate, la Fémis students become oriented, especially in their formative first two years, to the ideology that intensive film study yields an arsenal of practical devices, the means to make effective films. (The student who photocopied his list for me had dutifully worked through Bergala's canon, faltering only by the Rs.) Many of those whom I interviewed confirmed their cinephile habits, studying masterworks intensely both in and outside classes, habits which informed their eventual approach, the nuts and bolts of their conceptions of film style. Noémie Gillot, for example, one recent graduate, singled out among all her la Fémis experiences "the magisterial classes of Alain Bergala, which were among the most passionate I went to. . . . The first years of [la Fémis] study use lots of film screenings, and seminars on themes and encounters with cinéastes. . . . We referred back to these discussions when we were looking for a certain type of image or effect to replicate."[21]

Today, la Fémis graduates number more than 800 active film practitioners in France; the school's influence, and the dissemination of its methods, are catalytic forces, and growing, within contemporary French cinema itself. And it is active cinephilia, defined here as a minutely focused process of viewing and textual scrutiny, informing the stylistic ambitions of actual production *practices*, that offers one key way through which this tendency can be defined. The point is confirmed by Marc Nicolas, director of la Fémis, on the occasion of its twentieth anniversary, in 2006. In interview, Nicolas defended the school's cinephilic model on the grounds that: "My personal conviction is that great artists know the history of their art. . . . [la Fémis] offers a pedagogy of analyzing film which fills in any gaps in method. . . . I would even like to increase this form of teaching, days spent devoted to the history of the art, to augment further the practices of our departments."[22]

Ghosts of the Past: Jean Paul Civeyrac's *Through the Forest*

Drawing our conclusion together with a final extended case study, the work of Jean Paul Civeyrac represents the conflation of instruction with practice, with cinephilia the guiding force behind both activities. Having studied philosophy at the University of Lyon, Civeyrac entered la Fémis and graduated in 1991 by completing his short, *La Vie selon Luc* (1991), a Bressonian 16mm project about a young gay hustler, alienating friends and family as he stubbornly continues his cynical, money-oriented lifestyle. Five years later, Civeyrac returned with his first feature, *Ni d'Eve ni d'Adam* (1996), about a socially ostracized boy, Gilles (played by the nonprofessional actor, Guillaume Verdier), who has learning difficulties, yet is forced to survive on the streets. While the film was successful, Civeyrac then underwent a quite extraordinary career reversal: paring down his (already low) budgets, scaling back his crews, turning to high definition DV rather than celluloid, abandoning the realist mode of dramas set within urban fringes of Paris in favor of intimate and elliptical chamber dramas. His subsequent films, especially *Les Solitaires* (2000), *Fantômes* (2001), the short *Tristesse beau visage* (2004) and the minifeature *Through the Forest* (*A travers la forêt*, 2005), explore strikingly what François Bégaudeau calls, "Interior realism . . . representing the turmoil, thoughts, dreams, sufferings, and procrastinations of his characters."[23] Key to these second-phase works is that they interweave the diegetic past with the present, insisting not only on the coexistence of both temporal states, but also on the prospect of physical encounters between the spirits of loved ones who have died and the living partners who fixatedly mourn their passing. Civeyrac makes little or no textual distinction between fantasy and actuality, between moments from history and those occurring now, refusing to differentiate these conditions a priori. In his own words: "The past makes its way into the present, the present as if it was already past . . . if I'm going to isolate one or the other, I'll treat them in the same way."[24]

The point of departure to take with Civeyrac, cinephile-filmmaker, is that he remains an active instructor, promulgating his methods within the directing courses he is invited to give at his old school, la Fémis. In interview, Civeyrac has outlined the defining factors of his teaching philosophy, a fascinating insight into a facet of French cinema rarely if ever discussed, as well as situating precisely Civeyrac's own work as writer-director. The founding approach, of course, is the intertextuality of cinema, which for Civeyrac is less a process of cinephilia than just a basic operating principle, something inherent to filmmaking. Civeyrac's own work is a tissue of referentiality, from his kinship to Cocteau (*Les Solitaires*, about the intimate frictions between two brothers, one of whom is visited by his dead wife, is based on *Les Enfants terribles* [1950]; *Le Doux amour des hommes* [2001] repeatedly cites *Orpheus*); to his reverence for the fluid staging and blocking strategies of Lubitsch's 1930s Hollywood comedies; to his template of using close-up studies of faces as the means to depict psychological implosions, a trope acquired from Bergman, especially *Persona*.

Bringing this into the classroom, Civeyrac's model is film art as a continuum of formal interstices, cinema history as cinema present. The cinephilic moments we identified earlier, sensual citations of style, lyrical and even narratively abstracted textual treatments for which so many contemporary French filmmakers share an affinity, either in passing or wholesale. In essence, cinephilia defines the pedagogy Civeyrac pursues in his work both as active professor and active professional. He argues: "It's amazing to see [my students] become so exuberant, revealing their personalities, even if they don't listen to what I tell them. For me, la Fémis is an art school. I held onto that idea. I never teach how to direct a product, but how to develop personal works. . . . You read a lot of severe criticisms of la Fémis, claiming that it's isolated from the world of cinema. This is false because each year 50 percent of our professionals teach there, and 90 percent of its students find film work."[25] Here, Civeyrac's work reflects an extension of the cinephilic model, an ideology which permeates his career. It is evident, indeed, throughout the range of roles Civeyrac inhabits, the varied sub-occupations we have seen throughout this book as being so vital to active French filmmakers — their work as film students, film scholars, critics, interviewees, cultural activists, cinephiles, self-promoters, cultural entrepreneurs, writers, and vibrant film practitioners.

Civeyrac's films find consistent world festival exposure, but for most viewers, access to his work will come on home video. Even here, at the level of textual self-presentation, Civeyrac is positioned for cinephilic consumption, his materials collated for the connoisseur. In December 2005 Civeyrac's collected films were released in France by Blaq Out, the country's leading designer home media label, in an expensive, boutique bilingual edition clearly earmarked for international online purchase, promoted as such on the company's website. The Civeyrac dossier, eight films on three DVDs, was sumptuously packaged in a hard cover book, each page containing a disc, the whole thing postfaced with a Cocteau epigram ("Let me caress your cheek and your hair, let my hand learn your face by heart"). More unusually, the tome came with a DVD-ROM homage made by French multimedia artist, Grégory Chatonsky, in which key passages from Civeyrac's works are digitally sampled and rendered as a new whole. (The results recall a less manipulated, more sympathetic treatment than the works of avant-garde found footage artists like Bruce Conner and Martin Arnold.) Best of all, though, is an anecdotal encounter: I first tried to track down Civeyrac's bookset in Paris, at the Bibliothèque du film, only to find that two of its pages, hence two of the DVDs and six of the films, had been ripped out and stolen. This theft is possibly the ultimate symbolic act of Civeyracian cinephile devotion.

Turning to arguably Civeyrac's most representative work, *Through the Forest*, we can consider the particular textual aspects of this preeminent French cinephilic filmmaker at large. The film takes places in a series of ten long takes, mobile but uninterrupted sequence-tableaux. Highly ambiguous, the narrative centers on Armelle (Camille Berthomier), first shown awakening in bed alongside Renaud (Aurélien Wiik), who, it transpires, actually died some time ago in a motorcycle accident. Against the advice of her older sister, Bérénice (Alice Dubuisson), Armelle visits a medium with her other sibling, Roxane (Morgane Hainaux). But soon Armelle comes to believe that her lost lover has been reincarnated as another man, Hippolyte (Wiik again). After he rebuffs her, Armelle apparently takes an overdose of sleeping pills; the following tableau shows her pacing through Bérénice's apartment, oddly disaffected, reflected in mirrors, while her sisters sleep. Next, in the seventh segment, Armelle has seemingly returned from a two-day coma, but the diegetic world no longer coheres. In a café, before a bold crimson wall (the richest source of color in the whole film), Armelle interrogates Bérénice and Roxane about their tenuous romantic relationships—both are hastily engaged to fiancés they love unreliably—and her sisters at first protest, pause, then oddly acquiesce to her charges. A stranger proffers Armelle a cigarette, unprompted, while another lights it for her, also unasked. More dramatic—and supernatural or fantastical?—still, Hippolyte's girlfriend abandons him for no reason, before he accepts that he is indeed Renaud reincarnated, and reunites with Armelle in a highly stylized love scene. The film ends, however, with Armelle leaving her corporeal lover on a wooded hillside, lured away by Renaud's whispered call, vanishing into a dense band of trees as an unsettling minor refrain rises on the soundtrack.

Throughout, Civeyrac's design is overtly cinephilic, meticulously revivifying aesthetic fragments from past masterworks, augmenting his own stylistic virtuosity. (Marie-Noëlle Tranchant calls the results "beautiful obstinate poetry.")[26] Civeyrac's technical framework, ten labyrinthine long takes, is obviously an ode to Hitchcock's *Rope* (1948), reworked more recently in digi-

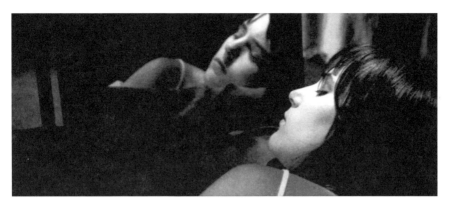

Armelle (Camille Berthomier) during 'Night,' the sixth sequence shot
of *Through the Forest*

tal form in another heavily cinephilic work, Alexander Sokurov's *Russian Ark*
(2002), a one take feature shot entirely on DV. (Civeyrac says of the long take
structure itself, a cinephilic approach par excellence: "The *plan-séquence*, it
rings out like a challenge, a demonstration.")[27] The other main source of textual derivation for *Through the Forest* is similarly exalted: Mizoguchi's *Ugetsu*
(1953), a film beloved by 1950s French cinephiles and generations since for
its confluence of long take compositions with supernatural subject materials.
Often, Civeyrac returns to Mizoguchi's most famous sequence shot, in which
Genjuro (Masayuki Mori) returns home to his ravaged village home, finds it
deserted, then circles back only to discover the miraculous phantom reap-
pearance of his dead wife, Miyagi (Kinuyo Tanaka). Panning right and left, the
camera maintaining its position throughout, Robin Wood hails this shot in
the language of a fervent cinephile. He argues that: "The *frisson* this moment
excites is due largely to the simple technical feat that there has been no cut,
no dissolve, no editing of any kind: the impossible has happened before our
eyes."[28] Hence, what is attractive to Civeyrac as a cinephilic filmmaker is that
the complicated logistics of a long take, the labors required to sustain the
sequence shot, offset, or counterbalance, the possibility of staging events that
are fanciful or supernatural.

In *Through the Forest*, Civeyrac embraces fully the cinephilic mode, developing the moments we have seen used by many French filmmakers as
textual accents or brackets into a fundamental design parameter. As such,
his conception of style is as dense as it is overt, lyrically abstruse to the point
of incomprehensibility. The textual qualities of DV are key to Civeyrac's
methods. Unlike most contemporary world directors, who resort to DV due
to fiscal or logistical necessity, Civeyrac is highly attentive to DV's aesthetic

particularities, especially its capacity to capture legible, or partly legible images in near-darkness, where it can aesthetically exceed even the fastest film stocks. On the *Through the Forest* shoot, Civeyrac would assemble his cast and crew after 4 p.m. only, favoring days with murky weather, so as to merge deteriorating daylight (his visible and tangible diegetic spaces) with the onset of dusk and gloom (invoking the abstract or intangibly supernatural). The process was amplified by Civeyrac's decision to shoot on DV, transfer to 35mm for theatrical screenings, then retransfer the celluloid print back to video for the DVD release. The end product is a highly diffuse rendering of human bodies and on-screen spaces, as the textuality of the digital format, aspects of its imperfect materiality, intermittent pixelations, and inconstant graphic resources are accentuated, its faltering means of reproduction laid bare, the technical invisible made arrestingly visible.

Consider *Through the Forest*'s first seven-minute long take, like those to come a stylistic thesis shot. The film opens with Armelle and Renaud slumbering, naked, in a bed. She stirs first as the camera tracks into her face; it retreats as she stretches, stands up, and inspects herself before a mirror. At this point the camera moves briefly behind a vase of two dozen white roses, an arrangement that neatly hides the man's face, which will remain gracefully obscured during the entire sequence. Traced out on-screen, *Through the Forest* clearly prizes the beautifully ornate, floral abstraction, above the drably functional. Later, we will surmise that it also conflates the former motif with fantasy and fantastical desires, and the latter with the humdrum everyday; the twist being that from Armelle's (and the film's) perspective, romantic imagination is a far more consistent and reliable realm than actuality. The point is amplified as Armelle now sings a song, accompanied like Bozon's soldiers in *La France*, by abruptly nondiegetic music, a strummed guitar. To intensify this trajectory, lyrical style as an intermediary between past and present, subjective and objective, Civeyrac turns to lighting, his favorite cinephilic element. Recoiling from the bright daylight she glimpses between the curtains (which, appropriately, in keeping with the properties of DV, whites out her face and the shot itself, an ugly flare of sallow), Armelle retreats to bed. Now, in the first of his many supernatural stylistic shifts, the on-screen light turns abruptly nocturnal (we hear a rumble of thunder but Armelle comments, with justification, that it's "incredible, it was sunny a moment ago, there weren't even any clouds"). All dialogue ceases, Renaud disappears, and Armelle herself becomes a spectral figure on-screen, only barely apparent as she walks back through her shadowy apartment, calling her vanished lover's name.

Here and elsewhere, Civeyrac flaunts the readable limits of his own image, in keeping with a film that refuses mediation between what is plausible, actually taking place, and what is imagined or supernatural.²⁹ (Many of *Through the Forest*'s critics struggled over which scenes are meant to be dreams, fantasies, or real; rather missing the point that Civeyrac refuses any such ontological logic, either from scene to scene, or even within continuous long takes.) Alongside the underlit DV, Civeyrac again cites Mizoguchi, especially his perverse predilection for staging important melodramatic moments with his actors' backs to camera and their faces hidden from view.³⁰ Often, Civeyrac similarly inverts this compositional norm, throwing his actors in the foreground into gloom, while conversely highlighting his backgrounds, making them richly visible, stark and white. In the fourth sequence, for instance, when Armelle confronts a skeptical Hippolyte then is consoled by Roxane, virtually the whole scene unfolds with the actors' faces in dark obscurity, while the college campus behind them is brightly lit by the waning afternoon sun. This process of aesthetic elision becomes a kind of cinephile joke; when Armelle fleetingly reveals her face, she puts on sunglasses.

As *Through the Forest* continues, the lyrically disjunctive forms of Civeyrac's approach develop. If fantasy and reality are interchangeable, mutually permeable, then Civeyrac at times attenuates his narrative entirely, in favor of pure passages of aesthetic abstraction. The sixth sequence, titled "Night," is one of the worst offenders for a spectator seeking diegetic unity. The shot begins with aural links as well as disconnections: we hear Armelle singing although her lips no longer move; the song instead continues from the preceding scene, some time earlier, after she has taken an overdose, contrasting with a telephone intermittently ringing, and fleeting nondiegetic music. In the foreground, a window frame bangs in the breeze, as it does so blacking the frame out completely, covering the camera. Now strident minor key strings rise on the soundtrack, while all three sisters pace through the apartment in silhouette. The trajectory builds towards purely graphic interplay: Armelle shown via her reflections in mirrors, a corporeal *mise-en-abyme*, then the bodies of our principal characters rendered as patterns of dark greyscale, a liminal *mise-en-scène* of gathering darkness, offering mere glimpses of recognizable things on-screen.

From a more rhapsodic perspective but the same point of departure, Civeyrac's ninth shot, "Pure Happiness," shows us Armelle and Hippolyte erotically intertwined before a translucent screen, framed by a suite of color filters and gentle camera movements, removed from any diegetic contexts. The motif is conveyed more ambivalently in the final shot, as Armelle retreats into a row of trees, her body disappearing by degree within the crepuscular forest, the frame dissolving into twilight and blackness. Armelle walks away, her body recedes, the image itself disperses. Civeyrac gives no obvious editorial grounds on

Armelle slowly disappears in the closing shot of *Through the Forest*

which to read this climactic moment, whether it is Armelle blissfully reunited with Renaud, albeit in fantasy, or else a kind of collapsing subjective vision, perhaps as the consciousness of our protagonist declines, as she hovers on the brink of death. Either way, visual style profoundly outpaces narrative, the cinephilic features of Civeyrac's cinema reviving films from the past while also embracing the aesthetic possibilities of a new medium, DV, a format that may herald as a major part of film's future. These final seconds of *Through the Forest* are dazzlingly conceptual and brilliantly rendered, the culmination of one of the more memorable films that recent French cinema has to offer. Recalling de Baecque's earlier formulation about cinephilia teaching us to see, Civeyrac foregrounds the act of viewing itself, challenging us by flirting with total illegibility, yet rapturously embracing the visual possibilities of cinema.

Just as Civeyrac's work frames the last section of this conclusion, so too does his testimony provide a final unifying perspective, resituating *Through the Forest* in the context of the diverse and dynamic modes of filmmaking we have now seen in contemporary France. In an interview about his cinematic process, Civeyrac recalled: "There's a phrase that Matisse said to Aragon, when Matisse had become a real old master: 'I have the feeling that I've finished elaborating my means of expression.' Now I'm no Matisse, but I had that sentiment with me for this film."[31] The career of an artist in summary—a lifetime's work with a medium in order to elaborate the means of its best expression. This is a model we can apply more broadly to contemporary French cinema itself, a configuring impulse behind its momentum forwards into the twenty-first century.

Whether it is work by men or by women, debutants or veterans, films drawn from a spectacular popular cinema, radical avant-garde experimentation, or unclassifiable pop-art amalgamations, French cinema today is constantly preoccupied with invention and reinvention, filmmaking connected to the past yet alive to the prospects of the future. These varied approaches sustain contemporary French cinema's richest asset — its scope and conceptual diversity. From mainstream films with flashes of lyrical dexterity, to arthouse creations derived from debased popular genres, French cinema today is a fascinating continuum of practice, perennially offering something for everyone. As articulated in this book, France's cinema is best thought of as a series of concentric circles, filmmakers operating in different contexts who are nonetheless mutually in conversation, either skeptically or sympathetically aware of the breadth of film around them. Heavily subsidized by the taxpayer yet often commercially acute, directed towards local audiences yet constantly poised for successful global export, French cinema can be a paradoxical enterprise. Its films are sometimes conflicted yet often catalytic, engagingly unpredictable, brutally intimate, the products of a major center of world film in the twenty-first century. Through all its varied avenues of activity, contemporary French cinema is united, above all, by its pursuit of elaborating ever more cinematic means of expression.

The 156 Films That You Must Have Seen

The List (SOURCE: La Bibliothèque de la Fémis, Paris; author's translation)

This list is not a list of prizewinners, neither is it a list of the 156 *best* films in the history of cinema. Its conception is something else. One hundred and fifty-six films, that's one film a week for three years, which is a reasonable cruising speed. Nothing need stop you from carrying this out.

What's the point of a list like this? A young man or a young woman who had watched (really *watched*, meaning thought about, discussed, because watching something without letting it sink in isn't really watching something at all) these 156 films would have a solid idea about what had come before them since cinema's inception. This list seems to us to draw up a range of essential works and filmmakers to see, in order to find one's way within a universe that you're preparing to enter.

The conception of this list is less historical (in the proper sense of the term) and more about cinematic culture. No painter could know the craft of every masterpiece that came before them. Same thing with cinema: What matters is knowing to the best of your ability what cinema is capable of at the height of its powers, of what forms this art can take.

Cinephilia has always been linked with a taste for generating lists, inasmuch as such lists are temporarily finalized, about which the aim is to generate impassioned debate. Every such list, by definition, is debatable. It sets out preferences, things in which we have a personal investment, about which we feel passionate. Everyone can get surprised or indignant about what's included or not included, about what's chosen or not. That is also the point of a list like this, to push someone to compare it with THEIR perfect list, to identify what are the most scandalous omissions, in their opinion. This debate facilitates a better configuration of one's own imaginary cinematic world, to understand more clearly the cartography of one's own personal taste.

This list also implicitly derives from the shaping perspectives of the present moment when it was created (2004), from a particular place (France), for its intended audience (students in la Fémis), with a reasonable amount of subjectivity. No one can talk about a perfectly rendered History of Cinema descending from the sky above. I have created this list with much hesitation, doubts, second guessing, helped by consultations with other department heads, but never in a spirit of compromise and consolidation. Bearing in mind all the input of other teachers at the school, I've tried to give it a broad coherence in keeping with my point of departure.

In no way either are these my *favorite* films, or even the most *accomplished* films of each filmmaker. The choice is more about what each film represents, how it embodies the particularities of its credited filmmaker, how it resonates with that filmmaker's own brand of music, how it relates to and is informed by the cinema and its potentially personal qualities. It's always more interesting for a beginner to discover filmmakers at the point of their true emergence, rather than when they have already established their mastery and are coasting. My choice here is always governed by what seem to me to be the most *productive* films for a contemporary beginner.

Picking *one* film by Jean Renoir, by Fritz Lang, by Orson Welles, or Godard is as absurd a task as picking *one* painting by Picasso in a century's worth of painting, especially for filmmakers who span radically different periods in cinema, for example the silent or sound Buñuels, or the European or American Langs. It's up to each individual to see that each film is but a simple indication, emblematic, and that it's never enough, for any canonical filmmaker, to see only one of their films.

French cinema gets the lion's share of this list because, after all, it's from this genealogy that most la Fémis students, whatever their department, will find their place and learn their job.

Watching a film, from which we learn about working in cinema, generates ideas, reflections, comparisons, aspirations, likes, and dislikes about cinema. Nothing is more volatile than these points of departure. And this is another function of this list: to instill a desire in everyone, from each film seen, to work out their ideas about this process. Without doubt, each trainee's notes about works from the past will become, in the long term, a vital tool for them to work out where they themselves stand, about their own likes and dislikes, the creative contours of their cinematic sensibility. And there is no great cinema, whoever is trying to make it, without a cinematic sensibility.

ALAIN BERGALA, September 12, 2004

Chantal Akerman *Jeanne Dielman* (1975)
Robert Aldrich *Kiss Me Deadly* (1955)
Woody Allen *Manhattan* (1979)
Theo Angelopoulos *O, Thiasos* (1975)
Michelangelo Antonioni *L'Avventura* (1960)
Dario Argento *Suspiria* (1977)
Olivier Assayas *Irma Vep* (1996)
Boris Barnet *By the Bluest of Seas* (1936)
Jacques Becker *Casque d'or* (1952)
Marco Bellocchio *Fist in His Pocket* (1965)
Ingmar Bergman *Summer with Monika* (1953)
Bernardo Bertolucci *The Conformist* (1970)

Bing Wang *West of the Tracks* (2004)

Bertrand Blier *Going Places (Les Valseuses*, 1972)

Frank Borzage *The River* (1929)

Robert Bresson *Pickpocket* (1959)

Jean-Claude Brisseau *De bruit et de fureur* (1987)

Tod Browning *Freaks* (1932)

Luis Bunuel *Un Chien andalou* (1928); *Viridiana* (1961)

Frank Capra *It's a Wonderful Life* (1946)

Léos Carax *Boy Meets Girl* (1984)

Marcel Carné *Daybreak (Le Jour se lève*, 1939)

John Cassavetes *Shadows* (1959)

Alain Cavalier *Thérèse* (1986)

Claude Chabrol *Les Bonnes femmes* (1959)

Youssef Chahine *Cairo Station* (1957)

Charlie Chaplin *Modern Times* (1936)

Souleymane Cisse *Yeelen* (1987)

Jean Cocteau *The Testament of Orpheus (Le Testament d'Orphée*, 1960)

Francis Ford Coppola *The Godfather* (1972)

David Cronenberg *Crash* (1996)

George Cukor *A Star Is Born* (1953)

Cecil B. De Mille *The Ten Commandments* (1956)

Jacques Demy *The Young Girls of Rochefort (Les Demoiselles de Rochefort*, 1966)

Brian De Palma *Dressed to Kill* (1980)

Raymond Depardon *San Clemente* (1982)

Giuseppe De Santis *Riso Amero* (1949)

Vittorio De Sica *The Bicycle Thieves* (1948)

Arnaud Desplechin *My Sex Life . . . or How I Got into an Argument*
    (Comment je me suis disputé [ma vie sexuelle]), 1996)

Jacques Doillon *Ponette* (1996)

Stanley Donen *Singin' in the Rain* (1952)

Alexander Dovzhenko *Earth* (1930)

Carl Dreyer *Ordet* (1954)

Marguerite Duras *India Song* (1974)

Julien Duvivier *Pépé le moko* (1937)

Clint Eastwood *Unforgiven* (1992)

Sergei Eisenstein *The General Line* (1929)

Jean Epstein *The Fall of the House of Usher* (1927)

Victor Erice *Spirit of the Beehive* (1973)

Jean Eustache *The Mother and the Whore (La Maman et la putain*, 1973)

R. W. Fassbinder *The Marriage of Maria Braun* (1978)

Federico Fellini *La Dolce Vita* (1960)

Abel Ferrara *Bad Lieutenant* (1992)

Marco Ferreri *Dillinger Is Dead* (1969)

Robert Flaherty *Nanook of the North* (1922)

John Ford *The Searchers* (1956)

Georges Franju *Eyes without a Face* (*Les Yeux sans visage*, 1960)

Sam Fuller *The Naked Kiss* (1964)

Philippe Garrel *Liberté la nuit* (1983)

Jean-Luc Godard *Pierrot le fou* (1964) *Histoire(s) du cinéma* (1998)

Jean Gremillon *Remorques* (1941)

D.W. Griffith *Birth of a Nation* (1913)

Sacha Guitry *Good Luck* (*Bonne chance*, 1935)

Howard Hawks *Rio Bravo* (1959)

Alfred Hitchcock *Vertigo* (1958)

Hou Hsiao-Hsien *City of Sadness* (1989)

King Hu *A Touch of Zen* (1970)

John Huston *The Misfits* (1961)

Otar Iosseliani *Farewell, Home Sweet Home* (*Adieu, plancher des vaches*, 1999)

Aki Kaurismaki *Drifting Clouds* (1996)

Elia Kazan *On the Waterfront* (1954)

Buster Keaton *The General* (1927)

Abbas Kiarostami *And Life Goes On . . .* (1992)

Krzysztof Kiewslowski *A Short Film about Love* (1988)

Stanley Kubrick *The Shining* (1979)

Akira Kurosawa *Seven Samurai* (1954)

Fritz Lang *Metropolis* (1926) *Fury* (1936)

Claude Lanzmann *Shoah* (1985)

Charles Laughton *Night of the Hunter* (1955)

Sergio Leone *The Good, The Bad and The Ugly* (1966)

Jerry Lewis *The Ladies Man* (1961)

Joseph Losey *Time without Pity* (1956)

Ernst Lubitsch *The Shop around the Corner* (1940)

Short films by the Lumiere brothers

David Lynch *Lost Highway* (1997)

Leo McCarey *An Affair to Remember* (1957)

Djibril Diop Mambety *The Little Girl Who Sold the Sun*
    (*La Petite vendeuse du soleil*, 1999)

Joseph Mankiewicz *The Barefoot Contessa* (1954)

Anthony Mann *Winchester '73* (1950)

Chris Marker *Sans soleil* (1983)

Marx Brothers *Monkey Business* (1931)

Jonas Mekas *Walden* (1969)

Georges Méliès Selections

Jean-Pierre Melville *Bob the Gambler* (*Bob le flambeur*, 1956)

Vincente Minnelli *Brigadoon* (1954)

Tsai Ming-Liang *The River* (1996)

Hayao Miyazaki *Spirited Away* (2001)

Kenji Mizoguchi *The Life of Oharu* (1952)

João César Monteiro *La Comédie de Dieu* (1995)

Nanni Moretti *Red Wood Pigeon* (1989)

F.W. Murnau *Sunrise* (1928)

Mikio Naruse *Older Brother, Younger Sister* (1953)

Manoel de Oliveira *Val Abraham* (1993)

Max Ophuls *Lola Montès* (1955)

Nagisa Oshima *Cruel Story of Youth* (1960)

Yasujiro Ozu *Tokyo Story* (1953)

G.W. Pabst *Loulou* (1928)

Marcel Pagnol *Angèle* (1934)

Pier Paolo Pasolni *Accatone* (1961)

Artavazd Peleshian Program

Pierre Perrault and Michel Brault *Pour la suite du monde* (1963)

Maurice Pialat *A nos amours* (1983)

Roman Polanski *Rosemary's Baby* (1968)

Michael Powell *Peeping Tom* (1960)

Otto Preminger *Laura* (1944)

Nicholas Ray *Johnny Guitar* (1954)

Satyajit Ray *The Music Room* (1959)

Jean Renoir *Boudu Saved from Drowning* (*Boudu sauvé des eaux*, 1932);
    The Rules of the Game (*La Régle du jeu*, 1939)

Alain Resnais *Night and Fog* (1955) *Muriel* (1963)

Jacques Rivette *Gang of Four* (*La Bande des quatre*, 1988)

Glauber Rocha *Black God, White Devil* (1964)

Eric Rohmer *La Collectionneuse* (1966)

Roberto Rossellini *Stromboli* (1950)

Jean Rouch *The Lion Hunters* (*La Chasse au lion à l'arc*, 1965)

Georges Rouquier *Farrebique* (1946)

Jacques Rozier *Adieu Philippine* (1961)

Martin Scorsese *Taxi Driver* (1976)

Douglas Sirk *Written on the Wind* (1957)

Victor Sjostrom *The Wind* (1928)

Jerzy Skolimowski *Moonlighting* (1982)

Josef von Sternberg *The Scarlet Empress* (1934)

Jean-Marie Straub and Danièle Huillet *From the Clouds to the Resistance* (1979)

Eric von Stroheim *Greed* (1924)

Andrei Tarkovsky *The Mirror* (1974)

Jacques Tati *Play Time* (1967)

André Téchiné *Wild Reeds* (1994)

Jacques Tourneur *Cat People* (1942)

François Truffaut *Stolen Kisses (Baisers volés*, 1968)

Tsui Hark *Once upon a Time in China* (1991)

Johan van der Keuken *De Platte Jungle* (1978)

Agnès Varda *Vagabond (Sans toit ni loi*, 1984)

Paul Vecchiali *Drugstore Romance (Corps à coeur*, 1979)

Dziga Vertov *Man with a Movie Camera* (1929)

King Vidor *Duel in the Sun* (1946)

Jean Vigo *L'Atalante* (1934)

Luchino Visconti *The Leopard* (1963)

Raoul Walsh *High Sierra* (1941)

Orson Welles *The Magnificent Ambersons* (1942)

Wim Wenders *Kings of the Road* (1976)

Billy Wilder *Kiss Me Stupid* (1964)

William Wyler *The Children's Hour* (1962)

Valerio Zurlini *Family Portrait* (1962)

NOTES

Introduction: The Contemporary French Film Ecosystem

1 Olivier Poivre d'Arvor, "Letter to Our American Friends," *Culturesfrance* newsletter (January 2008): 2.

2 Ibid., 6.

3 See Alan Riding, "Entr'acte: Next Lone U.S. Dissent: Cultural Diversity Pact," *International Herald Tribune* (October 12, 2005). http://www.iht.com/articles/2005/10/12/news/entracte.php. Accessed on October 24, 2008.

4 David Bordwell, Janet Staiger, and Kristin Thompson, *The Classical Hollywood Cinema: Film Style and Mode of Production to 1960* (London: Routledge, 1985): 388.

5 The case study is drawn from the annual financial summaries produced by *Le Film français*, as well as the useful production analysis published as "Producteurs: Premiers rôles ou figurants?" *Première* (February 2009): 74.

6 Michel Palméri, "Producteurs: Premiers rôles ou figurants?" *Première* (February 2009): 70–77. All translations from French are my own.

7 Quoted in ibid., 75–76.

8 Jonathan Buchsbaum, "After GATT, Has the Revival of French Cinema Ended?" *French Politics, Culture and Society* 23:3 (2005): 50.

9 Laurent Creton, *Economie du cinéma: Perspectives stratégiques* (Paris: Armand Colin, 2005), 259.

10 Sarah Drouhard, "Production cinéma: toujours plus d'argent," *Le Film français* 2873 (March 16, 2000): 9.

11 Sarah Drouhard, "Beau fixe sur la production française," *Le Film français* 3254 (March 28, 2008): 6.

12 Ibid.

13 "Texte prononcé par Pascale Ferran aux César 2007," in Le Club des 13, *Le Milieu n'est plus un pont mais une faille* (Paris: Stock, 2008): 313.

14 Ibid., 39.

15 Isabelle Vanderschelden, "The '*Cinéma du milieu*' Is Falling Down: New Challenges for Auteur and Independent French Cinema in the 2000s," *Studies in French Cinema* 9:3 (Fall 2009): 255.

Chapter 1. 5 x 1: Young Cinema and First-Timers

1 Réné Prédal, *Le Cinéma français depuis 2000: Une Renouvellement incessant* (Paris: Armand Colin, 2008).

2 Personal interview with Lola Doillon, October 23, 2008.

3 See Will Higbee, "Towards a Multiplicity of Voices: French Cinema's Age of the Postmodern Part II — 1992-2004," in Susan Hayward, *French National Cinema*, 2nd ed. (New York: Routledge, 2005), 315.

4 See Frédéric Gimello-Mesplomb, "The Economy of 1950s Popular French Cinema," *Studies in French Cinema* 6:2 (2006): 141–150; and Gimello-Mesplomb, "Le Prix de la qualité: L'Etat et le cinéma français (1960-1965)," *Politix* 16:61 (May-June 2003): 97–115.

5 See Tim Palmer, "An Amateur of Quality: Postwar French Cinema and Jean-Pierre Melville's *Le Silence de la mer*," *Journal of Film and Video* 58:3 (Fall 2007): 2–19.

6 CNC official self-description: http://www.cnc.fr/Site/Template/T11.aspx?SELECTID =968&id=566&t=3. Accessed October 7, 2008.

7 Charlie Michael, "French National Cinema and the Martial Arts Blockbuster," *French Politics, Culture & Society* 23:3 (Winter 2005): 57. See also Rémi Fournier Lanzoni, *French Cinema from Its Beginnings to the Present* (New York: Continuum, 2004), 196.

8 See Gimello-Mesplomb (2006), 142–143.

9 Source: UniFrance website, http://en.unifrance.org/corporate/our-activities/global-reach. Accessed October 9, 2008.

10 Source: http://en.unifrance.org/directories/company/325221/collectif-jeune-cinema-cinedif. Accessed December 4, 2008. See also www.cjcinema.org.

11 See Luc Moullet, "Césarienne/oscarification," *Cahiers du cinéma* 478 (April 1994): 38–39.

12 See Guy Austin, *Contemporary French Cinema* (Manchester: Manchester University Press, 2006), 119–120.

13 Ciment, "*Editorial: Première œuvres*," *Positif* 514 (December 2003): 3.

14 François-Pier Peilnard-Lambert, "Sacre et oublis," *Le Film français* 3245-3246 (February 1, 2008): 10.

15 Barbara Théate, "La Première fois de Lola Doillon," *Le Journal de Dimanche* (June 10, 2007). Note that many contemporary reviews come from dossiers assembled at the Bibliothèque du Film in Paris, which supply no page numbers and often lack complete citations. All page numbers are given where possible in this book.

16 In Emmanuèle Frois, "Lola Doillon, l'envol d'une enfant du sérail," *Le Figaro* (May 25, 2007).

17 Théate, "La Première fois de Lola Doillon."

18 Elodie Lepage, "Jeux d'été," *Le Nouvel Observateur* (June 14, 2007).

19 See Palmer, "An Amateur of Quality."

20 Richard Neupert, *A History of the French New Wave Cinema*, 2nd ed. (Madison: University of Wisconsin Press, 2007), 182.

21 Frois, "Lola Doillon, l'envol d'une enfant du serial."

22 Palmer, interview with Doillon.

23 Cécile Mury, "Les Années tchatche," *Télérama* (June 13, 2007).

24 Source: *Le Film français* 3248, February 15, 2008: 17.

25 Palmer, interview with Doillon.

26 As Doillon puts it, "I wanted a scene that encompassed (1) the presentation of the two girls and their differences in personality, (2) their way of talking, (3) the role of the camera, attached to these characters like a documentary, the length and scale of the shot underlining that they're interesting, important. To create this design, I immediately thought of the long take." (Palmer, interview with Doillon).

27 Using an intricately staged long take for a stylistic opener is, of course, a well-established tradition for the flamboyant director, most famously in *Touch of Evil* (1958), perhaps, a device homaged by, among others, Robert Altman in *The Player* (1992), and Paul Thomas Anderson in *Boogie Nights* (1997). Doillon's own long take was originally much longer, so long, in fact, that it unbalanced the first act of the film (Palmer: interview with Doillon). Doillon's full-length version, approaching four minutes, was included in the DVD version of *Et toi, t'es sur qui?*

28 Serge Kaganski, "*Et toi, t'es sur qui?* de Lola Doillon," *Les Inrockuptibles* (June 12, 2007): 44.

29 Mury, "Les Années tchatche."

30 http://www.tns-sofres.com/_assets/files/2009.10.06-ados-mobiles.pdf. Accessed October 8, 2009. Also relevant to *Et toi, t'es sur qui?* is the fact that among French adolescents, girls start cell phone use earlier (49 percent by the age of 12), and use mobiles 10 percent more often than boys. A statistic that received much press attention was that 15 percent of adolescents admitted to giving their cell phone number out online to someone they had never met in person.

31 Quoted in Lepage, "Jeunes pousses," *Le Nouvel Observateur* (June 14, 2007).

32 Lepage, "Jeux d'été."

33 Alison J. Murray Levine, "Mapping *Beur* Cinema in the New Millennium," *Journal of Film and Video* 60.3–4 (Fall/Winter 2008): 47. See also Carrie Tarr, *Reframing Difference: Beur and Banlieue Filmmaking in France* (Manchester, UK: Manchester University Press, 2005).

34 Palmer, interview with Doillon.

35 Mury, "Les Années tchatche."

36 See Charles Sowerwine, *France Since 1870: Culture, Society and the Making of the Republic*, 2nd ed. (New York: Palgrave Macmillan, 2009), 428–430. Notable among the revolts were the references to May 1968, frequently on websites whose slogans referenced the graffiti of France's most infamous wave of social protests.

37 Tanya Krzywinska, *Sex and the Cinema* (London: Wallflower Press, 2006), 31.

38 Like Doillon and many French first-timers, Sciamma's choice of title for her debut is striking yet, on reflection, cryptic. The original French name, *Naissance des pieuvres*, translates as *Birth of Octopi*, an analogy Sciamma likens to, "The birth of a monster inside you, in your stomach, which you didn't see coming and which grows really fast. It's desire, jealousy, spreading its ink, its tentacles . . ." (Jean-Marc Lalanne, "À cet âge-là, tous les desirs sont invivables" *Les Inrockuptibles* (July 31 2007): 57).

Alongside this is the metaphor of young girls as octopi: beautiful and graceful in water, clumsy and dysfunctional on land. Either way, the film's opening sequence, showing glimpses of girls grooming, dressing, and preparing for their swimming meeting, is intercut with shots of animated fronds, like tentacles, snaking across the frame. The purpose of this preface is less obvious for the English-language viewer. In several interviews, incidentally, Sciamma admitted to liking the English title equally, for its similarly organic, if less intrusive, connotations of natural development, blooming, and growth.

39 See the admiring write-up of François-Pier Pelinard-Lambert, "Jeunes talents à suivre," *Le Film français* (August 10, 2007): 5.

40 Marie-Noëlle Tranchant, "Sappho à la piscine," *Le Figaro* (August 15, 2007).

41 Lalanne, "*Naissance des pieuvres* de Céline Sciamma," *Les Inrockuptibles* (July 31, 2007): 58.

42 Elodie Lepage, "Le Dur métier de fille," *Le Nouvel Observateur* (August 16, 2007).

43 Lalanne, "À cet âge-là, tous les desirs sont invivables": 57.

44 Robert Bresson, *Notes sur le cinématographe* (Paris: Gallimard, 1975). Consider, as context, Bresson's famous opening declarations: "Rid myself of errors and accumulated falsehoods. Know my resources, make sure of them," and "The facility of using my resources well diminishes as their number rises" (15).

45 Lepage, "Le Dur métier."

46 Lalanne, "*Naissance des pieuvres.*"

47 Bresson, 51, 62.

48 Tranchant, "Sappho à la piscine."

49 Kuleshov's conception of cinematic art as maximally affective often manifested in back- and spotlit performers, whose gestures were expressively heightened by a simplified, pared-down, or black backdrop. See, for example, Porfiri Podobed's introduction as the eponymous lead of *The Extraordinary Adventures of Mr West in the Land of the Bolsheviks* (1923): under blazing side-light, beaming, clutching a dove in each hand. Kuleshov's theories are expounded in "Art of the Cinema," in Ronald Levaco, ed. and trans., *Kuleshov on Film: Writings of Lev Kuleshov* (Berkeley: University of California Press, 1974), 41–124.

50 Philippe Azoury, "*Pieuvres* comme un poisson dans l'eau," *Libération* (May 19, 2007): 22.

51 I thank David Bordwell for alerting me to this.

52 See Daniel Serceau, *Symptômes du jeune cinéma français* (Paris: Editions du cerf, 2008), 23, for a more negative conception of actors becoming directors. Serceau's premise is that the process is "a banality, a simple and mechanical consequence of a general aspiration for the title of director." I don't agree, and neither do I share Serceau's overarching position, that French cinema veers intrinsically towards a mediocre median position—a process somehow accelerated by its would-be auteur debutants—far from the heyday of great auteurs like Renoir, Ophuls, and Mizoguchi. Serceau's work seems paradoxically predisposed against the contemporary

cinema it ostensibly explores, replete with hazy analytical subcategories and an almost constant yearning for the past.

53 Isabelle Regnier, "Choisir un acteur a quelque chose de sacré," *Le Monde* (September 25, 2007).

54 Quoted in Axel Zeppenfield, "Mia Hansen-Løve's *Tout est pardonné* + Entretien," *Cahiers du cinéma* 627 (October 2007): 21.

55 Jean-Philippe Guérand, "La Femme aux deux visages," *Le Nouvel Observateur* (August 30, 2007).

56 See, for example, Donald Richie, *A Tractate on Japanese Aesthetics* (Berkeley: Stone Bridge Press, 2007).

57 Official data reported by INSEE. www.insee.fr/fr/themes/tableau.asp?reg_id =NATnon02326 and www.insee.fr/fr/themes/tableau.asp?reg_id=NATTEF02310. Accessed October 12, 2009.

58 Although she did not mention it directly, le Ny's script also links to the motif of terminal illness in French cinema, a recurrent dramatic feature in diverse recent films including *Savage Nights* (1992), *Son frère* (2003), *As If Nothing Happened* (2003), *Clara et moi* (2004), *Time to Leave* (*Le Temps qui reste*, 2005), *The Witnesses* (*Les Témoins*, 2007), *A Christmas Tale* (2008), and *Paris* (2008), among many others.

59 Stephen Holden, "'La Moustache': A French Mystery Plays With Notions of Conspiracy and Illusion," *New York Times* (May 24, 2006). http://movies.nytimes .com/2006/05/24/movies/24mous.html. Accessed on January 3, 2009.

60 A neglected part of the director's job, especially key to actor-filmmakers like le Ny, is the impact of casting. The nuances of *Those Who Remain* stem from le Ny's reprise use of the stars of Emmanuel Carrère's debut feature *La Moustache* (2005), a Kafkaesque tale in which Lindon plays a husband who shaves off his mustache, only for his wife (Devos) not to notice, to deny he ever had one, leading to his sanity slipping while their marriage bizarrely fragments.

61 Personal interview with Marina de Van, July 14, 2008.

62 Regnier, "Choisir un acteur."

63 Guérand, "La femme aux deux visages."

64 Phil Powrie, "Unfamiliar Places: 'Heterospection' and Recent French Films on Children," *Screen* 46:3 (Autumn 2005): 343.

65 The importance of short films to the first-time director is underlined by the testimony of David Thion, producer of *All Is Forgiven*, who was persuaded to assemble financing for the project after being impressed with Hansen-Løve's presentations, and also the flair evident in her early prefeatures. See Fabien Lemercieer, "A Slightly Puzzling Quality: Interview with David Thion." http://cineuropa.org/interview.aspx ?lang=en&documentID=79968. Accessed January 4, 2009.

66 In its multiple language formats and alternate casts, *Persepolis* becomes something of a best-case scenario for international circulation. Dubbing and redubbing an animated work allows for an audience-friendly translation of foreign content (the Iranian and European settings of Satrapi's biography) into nationally oriented

incarnations. The process is helped, of course, when the Iranian materials are performed by highly recognizable all-star casts: in France, with voices from Chiara Mastroianni, Catherine Deneuve, and Danielle Darrieux; and in America, from Sean Penn, Iggy Pop, and Gena Rowlands. Having it both ways, the American region 1 DVD included French and American versions on different audio tracks.

67 Anthony Bobeau, "*Persépolis* à la conquête des Etats-Unis," *Le Film français* 3225 (September 14, 2007): 9.

68 Patrick Caradec, "Deux nouveaux auteurs pour l'animation française," *Studio* 3245/6 (February 2008).

69 Satrapi's work, a woman's first hand testimony from a country notorious for censoring its female population and its creative ambitions, is part of a spate of such accounts published in the West to critical and popular success. Similar projects include Azar Nafisi's *Reading Lolita in Tehran: A Memoir in Books* (2003), Azadeh Moaveni's *Lipstick Jihad: A Memoir of Growing up Iranian in America and American in Iran* (2006), Nahid Rachlin's *Persian Girls: A Memoir* (2006), and Pardis Mahdavi's *Passionate Uprisings* (2008).

70 Ann Miller, *Reading* bande dessinée: *Critical Approaches to French-Language Comic Strip* (London: Intellect Books, 2007), 241.

71 Françoise Gaspard and Farhad Khosrokhavar, "The Headscarf and the Republic," in Roger Célestin, Eliane Dalmolin, and Isabelle de Courtivron (eds.), *Beyond French Feminisms: Debates on Women, Politics and Culture in France, 1981–2001* (New York: Palgrave Macmillan, 2003), 61–68.

72 Joan Wallach Scott, *The Politics of the Veil* (Princeton: Princeton University Press, 2007).

73 Caradec, "Deux Nouveaux auteurs."

74 Bernard Génin, "French animated films: it's cartoon time!" http://www.diplomatie .gouv.fr/en/france_159/label-france_2554/themes_3713/culture_3922/cinema _3925/french-animated-films-it-cartoon-time_7077.html. Accessed on December 4, 2008.

75 Quoted in "Etre une Iranienne libérée . . . ," *Télérama* (June 27, 2007).

76 Ibid.

77 Olivier Seguret, "L'Animation dans une nouvelle dimension," *Libération* (June 26, 2007).

78 Richard Neupert, "Kirikou and the Animated Figure/Body," *Studies in French Cinema* 8:1 (Spring 2008): 43.

79 Quoted in Olivier de Bruyn, "L'Iran en noir et blanc," *Le Point* (June 21, 2007).

80 Quoted in Eric Loret, "Etre persane," *Libération* (June 26, 2007): 68.

81 Hamid Reza Sadr, *Iranian Cinema: A Political History* (New York: I. B. Tauris, 2006), 234.

Chapter 2. The *Cinéma du Corps*

1 For my earlier treatments of this phenomenon, see Tim Palmer, "Style and Sensation in the Contemporary French Cinema of the Body," *Journal of Film and Video* 58:3 (Fall 2006): 22–32; and Palmer, "Under Your Skin: Marina de Van and the Contemporary French *Cinéma du corps*," *Studies in French Cinema* 6:3 (Fall 2006): 171–181.

2 Philippe Azory, "En écho aux photos de Jeff Wall," *Libération* (July 11, 2001): 6.

3 Frédéric Strauss, "Contre: Empesé," *Télérama* (July 11, 2001).

4 Serge Kaganski and Frédéric Bonnaud, "Tendre est la nuit: Entretien avec Claire Denis," *Les Inrockuptibles* (July 3, 2001). This was Denis' acerbic response to the charge that her films are overly aestheticized. Her rebuttal recalls Noël Burch's famous remark that stylistic parameters more directly shape the cinematic experience than narrative or interpretational functions: "Film is made first of all out of images and sounds; ideas intervene (perhaps) later." (Burch, trans. Helen Lane, *Theory of Film Practice* [New York: Praeger, 1973], 38.)

5 Denis, Dumont, and Noé, like most contemporary French arthouse filmmakers, are very well versed in cinema history, and in interview routinely cite more esoteric or experimental directors whose work combines abstraction with narrative. See, for example, Dumont's impromptu remarks about film art in Sébastien Ors, Philippe Tancelin, and Valérie Jouve, *Bruno Dumont* (Paris: Dis voir, 2001), 46.

6 A representative write-up is Richard Gianorio's "Le Vrai faux scandale", *France-Soir* (May 24, 2002).

7 See, for example, Guillaume Loison, "Ferme ta gueule!" *France-Soir* (May 25, 2002). The cries of "shut up" came, apparently, after one section of the audience volubly reacted to *Irreversible*'s extended rape sequence. Public screenings of *cinéma du corps* films I have attended or curated are seldom calm.

8 Richard Falcon, "Reality is Too Shocking," *Sight and Sound* 9:1 (January 1999): 11.

9 Olivier Joyard, "Sexe: La Prochaine frontière du cinéma," *Cahiers du cinéma* 574 (December 2002): 11.

10 Martine Beugnet analyzes some of the key films from a Deleuzian perspective in *Cinema and Sensation: French Film and the Art of Transgression* (Edinburgh: Edinburgh University Press, 2007).

11 See David Sterritt, "'Time Destroys All Things': An Interview with Gaspar Noé," *Quarterly Review of Film and Video* 24 (2007): 315.

12 Laurent Creton and Anne Jäckel, "Business 1960-2004: A Certain Idea of the Film Industry," in Michael Temple and Michael Witt (eds.), *The French Cinema Book* (London: BFI, 2004), 219.

13 For a strong summary of Breillat's career to date, see Kate Ince, "From Minor to 'Major' Cinema? Women's and Feminist Cinema in France in the 2000s," *Australian Journal of French Studies* 45:3 (September–December 2008): 284-288.

14 Philippe Rouyer and Claire Vassé, "Entretien François Ozon: La Vérité des corps," *Positif*, 521/522 (July/August 2004): 43-4.

15 Shirley Jordan, "Close-Up and Impersonal: Sexual/Textual Bodies in Contemporary Women's Writing," *Nottingham French Studies* 45:3 (Autumn 2006): 9. Jordan's excellent summary of the key works and their critical reception contains language, as in this citation, that transfers particularly well to the film style of the *cinéma du corps*, especially her ideas about notational determination and acts of exhaustive recording.

16 *Baise-moi* failed initially to get a visa certifying it as suitable for sixteen-year-olds and older (une interdiction aux moins de 16 ans). Public protests, with Breillat prominent, and an investigation by the Commission de la classification censorship board then led to the revival, for *Baise-moi* and subsequent releases, of France's eighteen-years-old-and-over certification, for films with "scenes of unsimulated sex and/or extreme violence." See Philippe Rouyer, "Sexe et classification: L'Interdiction aux moins de 18 ans fait son come-back," *Première* (April 2007): 66-67.

17 Carlos Pardo, "Crime, pornographie et mépris du peuple: Des films français fascinés par le sordide," *Le Monde Diplomatique* 2:00 (February 2000): 28.

18 Ibid.

19 Nicolas Schaller, "Les Nouvelles frontières du X," *Première* (April 2007): 58-67.

20 James Quandt, "Flesh and Blood: Sex and Violence in Recent French Cinema," *Artforum* 42:6 (2000): 24-27.

21 Will Higbee, "Towards a Multiplicity of Voices: French Cinema's Age of the Postmodern Part II—1992-2004," in Susan Hayward, *French National Cinema*, 2nd. ed. (New York: Routledge, 2005), 325-327.

22 Réné Prédal, *Le Jeune cinéma francais* (Paris: Nathan, 2002), 34.

23 Linda Williams, "Cinema and the Sex Act," *Cinéaste* 27:1 (Winter 2001): 21.

24 Ibid.: 29.

25 Linda Williams, *Screening Sex* (Durham: Duke University Press, 2008), 259-260.

26 Ibid., 273.

27 Ibid., 298.

28 See Sterritt, "Time Destroys All Things": 307. Noé's married stars, Vincent Cassel and Monica Bellucci, embarked on a systematic press campaign to defend *Irreversible* against its opponents. In one interview Cassel claimed that he actually *hoped* the film would get booed; at least this showed that blasé modern audiences were being forced out of their familiar viewing comfort zones. Richard Gianorio, "J'espère que le film sera hué. . . ." *France-Soir* (May 24, 2002).

29 Mark Kermode and Nick James, "Horror Movie," *Sight and Sound* 13:2 (March 2003): 20-24; Grégory Valens, "*Irréversible*: Irresponsible," *Positif* 497-498 (July-August 2002): 111-112; Philippe Rouyer, "*Irréversible*: Bonheur perdu," *Positif* 497-498 (July-August 2002): 113-114.

30 Serge Kaganski, "*Irréversible*," *Les Inrockuptibles* (May 15, 2002).

31 Jean-Pierre Dufreigne, "Elégance du cannibale," *L'Express* (July 12, 2001).

32 Jacques Morice, "La Scène de dévoration n'était pas prévue: Entretien avec Claire Denis, réalisatrice de *Trouble Every Day*," *Télérama* (July 11, 2001).

33 Scott Tobias, "Interview: Jane Campion." http://www.avclub.com/articles/jane-campion,33148/. Accessed October 16, 2009.

34 Jean-Marc Lalanne, "Comment aller toujours plus loin," *Libération* (July 11, 2001).

35 Quoted in *Twentynine Palms . . . off.*

36 Robin Wood, "*Irreversible* For and Against," *Film International* 5:3 (2003): 5.

37 Quoted in Lalanne, "Comment aller toujours plus loin."

38 Serge Kaganski, "*Trouble Every Day*," *Les Inrockuptibles* (May 22, 2001). See also Judith Mayne, *Claire Denis* (Chicago: University of Illinois Press, 2005), 110–120, for a useful discussion of "pulsating" space in *Trouble Every Day*.

39 Holly Willis and Kiino Villand, "Brutal Genius: Gaspar Noé Talks About his Latest Film," *Res* 3:3 (2003): 7.

40 Azoury, "En écho": 6.

41 Quoted in *Twentynine Palms . . . off.*

42 Jean-Michel Frodon, "Il s'agit de s'aventurer au-devant d'une forme," *Le Monde* (July 11, 2001).

43 Prédal, *Le Jeune cinéma français*, 39.

44 Personal interview with Marina de Van, July 14, 2008.

45 Ibid.

46 Carrie Tarr, "Director's Cuts: The Aesthetics of Self-Harming in Marina de Van's *Dans ma peau*," *Nottingham French Studies* 45:3 (Autumn 2006): 78.

47 Quoted in Philippe Rouyer, "Entretien Marina de Van: le corps-objet," *Positif* 502 (December 2002): 28.

48 Ibid.

49 Quoted in Philippe Piazzo, "'Le Film vient de mes émotions, pas d'un principe," *Le Monde*, (December 4, 2002): 35.

50 Here, de Van's work relates closely to the theories and practices of avant-garde filmmaker, Stan Brakhage, who became similarly dissatisfied with the cultural norm of treating bodies merely as means for character formation. In *Sirius Remembered* (1959), for example, Brakhage filmed the progressive decomposition of his dead family dog, a process of (artistic) grieving, but also the means to lay bare the physicality of a creature bereft of personality, exposing its matter and corporeal form. In Brakhage's own analysis: "I was coming to terms with the decay of a dead thing and the decay of the memories of a loved being that had died and it was undermining all abstract concepts of death." See Brakhage, *Essential Brakhage: Selected Writings on Filmmaking by Stan Brakhage* (New York: Documentext, 2001), 226.

51 Tarr, "Director's Cuts": 82.

52 Personal interview with Marina de Van, July 14, 2008.

53 Jacques Mandelbaum, "Dévoration d'un personnage sur l'autel du corps social," *Le Monde* (December 4, 2002): 34.

54 Source: www.insee.fr/fr/themes/tableau.aspreg_id=NATTEF02313. Accessed October 19, 2009.

55 Source: www.insee.fr/fr/ffc/docs_ffc/irsoco19.pdf. Accessed October 19, 2009.

56 See the conclusion for remarks about the artistic impact of cinephilia and viewing habits in la Fémis.

57 Personal interview with Marina de Van, April 3, 2005.

58 Personal interview with Marina de Van, August 26, 2004.

59 Olivier de Bruyn, "*Dans ma peau*: corps à corps," *Positif* 502 (December 2002): 27.

60 Yoko Ogawa, trans. Stephen Snyder, *The Diving Pool: Three Novellas* (New York: Picador, 2008), 110-111.

61 Marie-Noëlle Tranchant, "Conte insolite," *Le Figaro* (June 10, 2005).

62 Olivier Joyard, "Sexe: La prochaine frontière du cinéma," *Cahiers du cinéma* 574 (December 2002): 12.

Chapter 3. Popular Cinema, Pop-Art Cinema

1 A notable and welcome exception is Darren Waldron and Isabelle Vanderschelden (eds.), *France at the Flicks: Trends in Contemporary French Popular Cinema* (Newcastle: Cambridge Scholars Publishing, 2007). In their introduction, Waldron and Vanderschelden trace some of the recent, albeit tentative, efforts to treat French mainstream cinema as an object of study. The role of France's mainstream film press in the reception and culture of this popular cinema remains, it must be said, seldom acknowledged.

2 In 2008, much to the delight of the CNC analysts, France won, taking 45.7 percent of the market versus 44.5 percent for American films. Since 1999 French productions have claimed the annual majority proportion of national filmgoing just twice, in 2006 and 2008. http://www.cnc.fr/CNC_GALLERY_CONTENT/ DOCUMENTS/statistiques/frequentation_mensuelle/2008/frequentation2008 .pdf. Accessed November 5, 2009.

3 Susan Hayward and Ginette Vincendeau, "Introduction," in Hayward and Vincendeau (eds.), *French Film: Texts and Contexts*, 2nd ed. (London: Routledge, 2000), 6.

4 See Tim Palmer, "Paris, City of Shadows: French Crime Cinema Before the New Wave," *New Review of Film and Television Studies*, 6:2 (August 2008): 213-231. Godard's flagship creation, *Breathless*, has never been fully appreciated for its array of citations from the 1950s policier, in plotting and design, which are arguably as vital as its modernist innovations.

5 See Palmer, "Paris, City of Shadows" for a more systematic historical account of the policier, a genre which remains, alongside the comedy, France's most perennially popular format with audiences, but not necessarily with critics and scholars.

6 Joan Dupont, "Thomas Langmann, a hot young producer, with 3 new films," *International Herald Tribune* (January 24, 2008). www.iht.com/articles/2008/01/24/ arts/fmdupont.php. Accessed January 29, 2008.

7 Gérard Delorme, "Pourquoi Vincent Cassel est-il aussi fort à l'export?" *Première* (September 2009): 24.

8 Amplifying *Hate*'s self-reflexivity, a film in which all three stars have the same first

name as their characters, is the fact that during the central trio's ill-fated trip to Paris, visiting an acquaintance who owes them money, the name on the apartment block's door buzzer is clearly visible as Cassel.

9 The integrality of Cassel's body to the visual design of the Mesrine films is overt, and remains so. With Cassel on-screen virtually throughout, Richet wholeheartedly configures his style to his star: cutting on Cassel's motions, parading his passage with push-ins, pans and tracks, trailing adoringly behind or before him with an attentive steadicam. So total is the fusion of frame and actor that it recalls the consummate James Cagney-Warner Bros. star vehicles of the early 1930s, inventive yet laconic delights like *The Public Enemy* (1931), *Taxi!* (1932), *The Picture Snatcher* (1933), and *Footlight Parade* (1933).

10 Asked about his formative work at L'Ecole du cirque, Cassel recalled it having taught him, "A pleasure in physicality. I also did a lot of dance . . . breakdancing, capoeira. . . . I had no idea this would all end up helping me so much." Kruger Bros., "J'aime ça!: Entretien avec Vincent Cassel," *Première* (October 2001): 102.

11 The symbiosis between Cassel and Mesrine, movie star and underworld star, is exploited throughout. One perfectly dovetailed moment comes when Mesrine, in March 1977, tells his exasperated lawyer about his new publicity-seeking memoir, *L'Instinct de mort*, written in jail, upon which Richet's film is actually based. Cassel, smirking openly, quips: "You know, in the streets, I'm a real star!"

12 Here, Cassel's homages to the gangster leads of Martin Scorsese — mainly Robert de Niro in *Mean Streets* (1973) and Joe Pesci in *Goodfellas* (1990) — are especially clear. One foundational part of Cassel's persona is, of course, his restaging of the "You talkin' to me?" monologue from Scorsese's *Taxi Driver* (1976) in *Hate*.

13 *OSS 117: Cairo, Nest of Spies* proved a solid investment, well-reviewed, if somewhat bemusedly, in America, grossing over $300,000 but also programmed widely in regional film series, and very popular among audiences at, for example, the Seattle and Wisconsin film festivals.

14 Francois Truffart, "Welcome to COLCOA 2009," www.colcoa.org/2009/info/ welcome. Accessed November 23, 2009. See also, Bijan Tehrani, "François Truffart Talks About COLCOA 2008," www.cinemawithoutborders.com/news/130/ ARTICLE/1543/2008-04-04.html. Accessed November 23, 2009.

15 Thomas Baurez, "Hello Mr. Nice Guy: Phénomène Jean Dujardin," *Studio* (October 2005): 58. Dujardin returned the compliment four years later during interviews for *Lucky Luke*, on which he was reunited with his *Brice de Nice* director, suggesting, with affection, that Huth had the mentality of a rampaging twelve-year-old.

16 See Patrick Fabre, "7 Manches et des manchettes pour OSS 117," *Studio* (May 2006): 74-79, for a useful discussion of the project's origins, published by a magazine that consistently championed Dujardin's abilities.

17 Ibid., 78.

18 Ghislain Loustalot, "Ça aurait pu se passer comme ça . . . mais il a décidé de tout dire," *Première* (January 2006): 63.

19 Rosanne Maule, "*Du côté d'Europa*, via Asia: The 'Post-Hollywood' Besson," in Susan Hayward and Phil Powrie (eds.), *The Films of Luc Besson: Master of Spectacle* (New York: Manchester University Press, 2006), 26.

20 Quoted in Ali Jaafar and Elsa Keslassy, "France's EuropaCorp Strikes Gold," *Variety* (May 6, 2009). www.variety.com/article/VR1118003298.html?categoryid=3618 &cs=1. Accessed November 6, 2009.

21 See, for example, Susan Hayward, *Luc Besson* (Manchester: Manchester University Press, 1998).

22 The relative failure of Besson's own *Angel-A* (2005)—with just under 850,000 admissions in France, a modest release in the United Kingdom, and no United States distribution at all—after nearly six years away from directing, seemed to indicate that his popular touch was indeed best suited to the role of financier, writer, and promoter of young talent like Gérard Krawczyk and Morel. Besson's triumphant return to live-action direction came, however, in 2010, with the very popular release of *The Extraordinary Adventures of Adèle Blanc-Sec* (*Les Aventures extraordinaires d'Adèle Blanc-Sec*), based on the Jacques Tardi comic book, which had more than 1.6 million paid admissions.

23 Charlie Michael, "French National Cinema": 55.

24 Ibid.: 58–60.

25 Much of this investment boost has come from domestic financing: the 1993 figure of 475 million euros (retrospectively converted from francs) included 341.1 million French investment versus 133.9 foreign; by 2008 the proportion was 1,228.8 million euros French versus 266.7 million foreign. In other words, external investment doubled while internal investment rose by 359 percent. www.cnc.fr/CNC _GALLERY_CONTENT/DOCUMENTS/statistiques/par_secteur_FR-pdf/ ProductionCine190509.pdf. Accessed November 9, 2009.

26 Isabelle Vanderschelden, "Strategies for a 'Transnational'/French Popular Cinema," in *Modern & Contemporary France* 15:1 (February 2007): 37–38.

27 For an account of the contemporary French funding situation, of which *A Very Long Engagement* is arguably the most contested case, see Jonathan Buchsbaum, "The *Exception Culturelle* is Dead.' Long Live Cultural Diversity: French Cinema and the New Resistance," *Framework* 47:1 (Spring 2006): 5–21.

28 Among the burgeoning literature on transnational cinema, useful introductory entries include: Elizabeth Ezra and Terry Rowden (eds.), *Transnational Cinema: The Film Reader* (New York: Routledge, 2006), and Luisa Rivi, *European Cinema After 1989: Cultural Identity and Transnational Production* (New York: Palgrave Macmillan, 2007).

29 Marwan M. Kraidy, *Hybridity, or the Cultural Logic of Globalization* (Philadelphia: Temple University Press, 2005), 148.

30 Carrie Tarr, *Reframing Difference: Beur and Banlieue Filmmaking in France* (Manchester: Manchester University Press, 2005), 84.

31 Reiterating popular French cinema's constant need to face off low and high cultures

against each other, as we saw earlier with Baffie, Beineix, and others, *Banlieue 13: Ultimatum* opens on a long fight scene with a protagonist seeing off legions of enemies with a priceless Van Gogh painting.

32 Phil Powrie, "Heritage, History and 'New Realism': French Cinema in the 1990s," in Powrie (ed.), *French Cinema in the 1990s: Continuity and Difference* (Oxford: Oxford University Press, 1999), 2.

33 Source: CNC.

34 *Taxi 2* is fifth; home-produced product occupies six slots in France's ten highest grossing films of the first decade of the twenty-first century, including four of the top five.

35 Anne Jäckel, "The Inter/Nationalism of French Film Policy," *Modern & Contemporary France*, 15:1 (February 2007): 33.

36 Quoted in Michael, "French National Cinema": 61.

37 As we saw in Chapter 2, the films of Claire Denis are (with those of Philippe Grandrieux) contemporary French cinema's least talkative works, artfully preferring images and sounds to spoken words. At the other end of the spectrum, Danièle Thompson's films are among France's most dialogue-driven. *Le Code a changé* (2009), for example, features speech without cease for its entire opening forty-five minutes; during a large dinner party gathering (that contemporary French staple set piece), Thompson juggles five distinct conversations, often wittily intercut, at once.

38 According to CNC figures, admissions for films designated as *art et essai*, in itself a malleable and often contested term, fluctuated between 29.1 percent in 2000, to 34.5 percent in 2005, to 18.8 percent in 2007. Not only is the *art et essai* label no longer always apt textually, as this chapter argues, but such commercial reckonings fail to gauge the exposure of more specialist French cinema abroad. For a useful discussion about this and related issues, see Isabelle Vanderschelden, "The '*Cinéma du milieu*' is Falling Down: New Challenges for Auteur and Independent French Cinema in the 2000s," *Studies in French Cinema* 9:3 (Fall 2009): 243-257.

39 Olivier Joyard, "Sexe: la prochaine frontière du cinéma": 10.

40 Deidre Russell makes a connected point about the prospects for "personal" stories in popular film, and more autobiographical mass designs, in "Contemporary Trends in Personal and Popular French Cinema," in Waldron and Vanderschelden (eds.), *France at the Flicks*, 75-88.

41 Jean-Baptiste Morain, "La Grand trapéziste," *Les Inrockuptibles* (April 16, 2003): 34.

42 Philippe Rouyer and Claire Vassé, "Entretien: Valeria Bruni Tedeschi, la foi et la richesse," in *Positif* 507 (2003): 29.

43 Olivier de Bruyn, "Viva Valeria!" *Le Point* (April 18 2003): 109.

44 David Bordwell, *Planet Hong Kong: Popular Cinema and the Art of Entertainment* (Cambridge, MA: Harvard University Press, 2000), 261-262.

45 Jean-Michel Frodon, "L'Envol d'un film au mépris joyeux des lois du genre," *Le Monde* (April 16, 2003): 26.

46 Bruni Tedeschi's work even extends to a kind of pop-art promotion. To coincide with the release of *Actresses*, she appeared as part of *Studio* magazine's regular "Face aux lecteurs" ("Meet the readers") series. For this, filmmakers or stars spend a day in Paris with selected respondents, whose questions, like the essays in *Studio* itself, are a blend of gossipy banter and more systematic analyses. Judging from the texts and photographs, not all professionals enjoy this experience, but Bruni Tedeschi gave a strong performance, responding to questions about her film's autobiography, its title, the dedication to her brother (who died just after production finished), and how much she hated working with Steven Spielberg on *Munich* (2005). See Sophie Benamon, "Valeria Bruni Tedeschi face aux lecteurs," *Studio* (December 2007): 9–12.

47 Olivier de Bruyn, "Valeria compte double," *Le Point* (December 20, 2007): 66.

48 Marie-Elisabeth Rouchy, "Conjugations dangereuses," *Le Nouvel Observateur* (December 10, 2007).

49 Isabelle Regnier, "Une Génération qui puisse son inspiration dans l'autobiographie," *Le Monde* (December 26, 2007).

50 Louis Guichard, "Il est plus facile la deuxième fois?," *Télérama* (July 12, 2006).

51 Interestingly related to this reference, the 2008 Best First Film César nominee Ursula Meier, a self-declared pop-art filmmaker, said of her debut feature *Home* (2008): "I wanted to mix tones and genres, jumping from a dramatic scene to another one that's more burlesque. I kept in mind both Tati and Pialat." Quoted in Mathieu Loewer, "*Home*, a road movie in reverse." http://cineuropa.org/interview .aspx?documentID=84220. Accessed January 23, 2009.

52 Quoted in de Bruyn, "Valeria compte double."

53 Prédal's term is here taken largely as a point of departure; from *Le Jeune cinéma français* (Paris: Nathan, 2002), 97–98.

54 Donato Totaro, "*A l'intérieur*: A Rebirth of French Horror." http://www.offscreen .com/biblio/pages/essays/french_horror/. Accessed January 2, 2009. The sight of American fanboy fanzines and websites getting frantically excited about French films may just be a first in Franco-American cultural relations.

55 The trend continues outside the horror genre, as with the case of Richet, discussed earlier, and Florent Emilio Siri following *The Nest* with the Bruce Willis vehicle *Hostage* (2005). After *Gothika*, Kassovitz himself took this model to a kind of conclusion with the Canal +/Twentieth Century Fox international co-production *Babylon A.D.* (2008), a disastrous thriller, recut by his producers, which he subsequently disowned.

56 Will Higbee, "'Elle est où, ta place?' The Social-Realist Melodramas of Laurent Cantet: *Ressources humaines* (2000) and *Emploi du temps* (2001)" in *French Cultural Studies* 15:3 (2004), 248. See also Martin O'Shaughnessy, *The New Face of Political Film: Commitment in French Film Since 1995* (London: Berghahn Books, 2007).

57 A superficial link to the thoughtful politics of *They Came Back* is the opening sequence of the far less enlightened *Frontière/s*, of choppily edited footage of urban

riots, which sketchily invokes France's October 2005 banlieue riots, as well as the opening stock footage in Kassovitz's *Hate*.

58 See David Desser, *Eros Plus Massacre: An Introduction to the Japanese New Wave Cinema* (Bloomington: Indiana University Press, 1988), 120–122.

59 Robin Wood is a catalytic figure in terms of American cinema here, with work begun in his co-edited anthology, *The American Nightmare: Essays on the Horror Film* (Toronto: TIFF, 1979) and continued in *Hollywood from Vietnam to Reagan* (New York: Columbia University Press, 1986).

60 Geneviève Welcomme, "Les Morts prennent place parmi les vivants," *La Croix* (October 27, 2004).

61 Quoted in Jean-Pierre Lacomme, "A tombeaux ouverts," *Le Journal de Dimanche* (October 24, 2004).

62 Jean-Marc Lalanne, "*La France*," *Les Inrockuptibles* (November 20, 2007): 46.

63 See, for example, Mark Peranson, "Band on the Run: Serge Bozon's *La France*," *Cinemascope* 33. www.cinema-scope.com/cs33/int_peranson_bozon.html. Accessed January 11, 2009.

64 Céline Bozon's ingenious cinematography on *La France* recalls another great aesthetic pairing, Jean-Pierre Melville and Henri Decaë, notably their experiments with Eastman Color stock in *Le Samouraï* (1967) to diffuse and wash out the tonal range of primary colors. See Tim Palmer, "*Le Samouraï*," in Phil Powrie (ed.), *The Cinema of France* (London: Wallflower, 2006), 130.

65 The technique is already synonymous with Bozon's fledgling career. It was also used, albeit with more traditionally choreographed dancing, in his mini-feature *Mods* (2002), a film set in the 1960s, featuring archaic English pop songs (provided by late-1960s bands such as The Alarm Clocks, The Seeds, The Unrelated Segments and The Calico Wall), interposed within a plot about two soldiers attempting to revive their institutionalized brother.

66 Jacques Morice, "*La France* de Serge Bozon," *Télérama* (November 21, 2007).

67 Le Besco's film ostensibly documents the lives of France's leading female performers, from Jeanne Balibar to Charlotte Rampling, in which, playing "themselves," they mock their own personae. Karin Viard, for example, demands to be seen as more "ordinary" than her customary neurotic, over-achieving screen characters; le Besco duly shows her milking an uncooperative cow in a mock film-within-a-film for, of all people, Bertrand Blier. Wittily pop-art in her methods, alongside the day-in-the-life segments, le Besco inserts garishly designed nondiegetic song-and-dance numbers for her cast of female stars. *Le Bal des actrices* concludes with the women berating the actual film itself as an artistic shambles, as it devolves into le Besco's own navel-gazing and self-involved asides about balancing motherhood and filmmaking.

68 Less determinedly ambiguous than Bozon are several related pop-art films, which use popular genre materials to make more explicit political commentaries. Following the well-trod conventions of war films as coming-of-age narratives, Florent

Emilio Siri's *Intimate Enemies* (*L'Ennemi intime*, 2007) explores the fall-out from France's post-colonial war in Algeria during the 1960s. Serge le Péron's more successful *I Saw Ben Barka Get Killed* (*J'ai vu tuer Ben Barka*, 2005) recasts the political conspiracy surrounding the 1965 murder of Barka, a Moroccan dissident, as a fatalist policier as filmed by Jean-Pierre Melville: to a caustic jazz score, in a monochromal Paris, climaxing in the execution of its low-life protagonist in a dingy apartment that looks identical to Alain Delon's in *Le Samouraï*.

69 Didier Péron, " 'Une Cinéphilie un peu décalée,' " *Libération* (November 21, 2007): 37.
70 David Thompson, "Stop Making Sense," *Sight and Sound*, May 2004. Reproduced on http://www.bfi.org.uk/sightandsound/feature/238. Accessed January 15, 2009.
71 Olivier Père, "Les Seins de glace," *Les Inrockuptibles* (November 6, 2002): 71.
72 Scott Tobias, "*Boarding Gate*," *The Onion A.V. Club* (March 20, 2008). www.avclub .com/articles/boarding-gate,3040/. Accessed January 13, 2009.
73 Aurélien Ferenczi, "Embrouilles à Tokyo," *Télérama* (September 26, 2001). One of Assayas's favorite examples is David Fincher's *Fight Club* (1999), cited here and elsewhere, a highly regarded thriller among contemporary French critics.
74 Quoted in Rosanna Maule, *Beyond Auteurism: New Directions in Authorial Film Practices in France, Italy and Spain since the 1980s* (Chicago: Intellect Press, 2008), 88.
75 See, for example, Mark Peranson, "Reattaching the Broken Thread: Olivier Assayas on Film-making and Film Theory," *Cinema Scope*, 14 (Spring 2003): 30–39; and David Thompson, "Olivier Assayas Power Games," *Sight and Sound* (May 2004). Reproduced on www.bfi.org.uk/sightandsound/feature/260. Accessed January 16, 2009.

Chapter 4. Feminine Cinema

1 See, for example, Geneviève Fraisse, trans. Jane Marie Todd, *Reason's Muse: Sexual Difference and the Birth of Democracy* (Chicago: University of Chicago Press, 1994).
2 Roger Célestin, Eliane Dalmolin and Isabelle de Courtivron, "Introduction," in Célestin, Dalmolin and de Courtivron (eds.), *Beyond French Feminisms: Debates on Women, Politics and Culture in France, 1981–2001* (New York: Palgrave Macmillan, 2003), 3. Italics theirs.
3 Catherine Wheatley (trans.), "French Cinema Now: Unbelievable But Real: The Legacy of '68," *Sight and Sound* 18:5 (May 2008): 32.
4 Source:www.cnc.fr/CNC_GALLERY_CONTENT/DOCUMENTS/publications/etudes/ Evolution_du_Public_(1993_2008)_020709.pdf. Accessed November 5, 2009.
5 The club of what is sometimes referred to as *les millionnaires* notably includes: Balasko's *French Twist* (*Gazon maudit*, 1995, 3.8 million viewers); Colombani's *He Loves Me, He Loves Me Not* (*A la folie . . . pas du tout*, 2002, 1 million); Fontaine's *Coco avant Chanel* (2009, 1 million); Garcia's *The Adversary* (*L'Adversaire*, 2002, 1.1 million) and *Place Vendôme* (1998, 1.2 million); Jaoui's *The Taste of Others* (*Le Goût des autres*, 2000, 3.8 million), *Look at Me* (*Comme une image*, 2004, 1.6 million) and *Parlez-moi*

de la pluie (2008, 1 million); Lvovksy's *Les Sentiments* (2003, 1.2 million); Serreau's *Chaos* (2001, 1.2 million) and *18 Ans après* (2003, 1.5 million); and Thompson's *Jet Lag* (*Décalage horaire*, 2002, 1.1 million), *Orchestra Seats* (*Fauteuils d'orchestre*, 2006, 1.9 million) and *Le Code a changé* (2009, 1.6 million). Besides these canonized figures, there are a number of other millionaire French women filmmakers, who typically moved from either writing or acting to direction, often then taking on multiple roles, the same process we studied in Chapter 1. Since 2000 this list features Isabelle Doval (*Rire et châtîment*, 2003, 1.1 million), Valérie Guigabodet (*Mariages!*, 2004, 2 million; *Danse avec lui*, 2007, 1 million), Alexandra Leclère (*Les Soeurs fâchées*, 2004, 1.5 million; *Le Prix à payer*, 2007, 1.4 million), Valérie Lemercier (*Palais Royal!*, 2005, 2.8 million), Lisa Azuelos (*Comme t'y es belle!*, 2006, 1.1 million; *LOL (Laughing Out Loud)* ®, 2009, 3.6 million), Pascale Pouzadoux (*De l'autre côté du lit*, 2009, 1.8 million), and Géraldine Nakache (*Tout cequi brille*, 2010), 1.4 million).

6 Xavier Leherpeur, "Classe tous risques," *Le Nouvel Observateur* (November 8, 2007).

7 Personal interview with Marina de Van, July 14, 2008.

8 Emma Wilson, "*Etat présent*: Contemporary French Women Filmmakers," *French Studies* 59:2 (2005): 223, 220.

9 Carrie Tarr with Brigitte Rollet, *Cinema and the Second Sex: Women's Filmmaking in France in the 1980s and 1990s* (New York: Continuum, 2001), 1.

10 The figure is closer to 6 percent in the USA, according to the Women Make Movies collective. http://www.wmm.com/resources/film_facts.shtml. Accessed January 28, 2009.

11 The actual statistic is 42 features out of 186 produced in 2007, or 24.2 percent, as drawn from the CNC's statistical annual review.

12 Ginette Vincendeau, "Women's Cinema, Film Theory, and Feminism in France," *Screen* 28:4 (1987): 9.

13 Tarr with Rollet, *Cinema and the Second Sex*, 14.

14 Françoise Audé, *Cinéma d'elles 1981–2001* (Paris: Editions L'Age d'Hommes, 2002), 8.

15 Ibid.: 172.

16 Françoise Audé, "Actrices cinéastes, leur amour du jeu," *Positif* 495 (May 2002): 21–24.

17 Guy Austin, *Contemporary French Cinema: An Introduction* (Manchester: Manchester University Press, 1996), 82.

18 Rosanna Maule, *Beyond Auteurism: New Directions in Authorial Film Practices in France, Italy and Spain Since the 1980s* (Chicago: Intellect, 2008), 209. Maule's book suffers elsewhere from a lack of breadth, a rather abstracted theoretical approach to French cinema's buoyant diversity focused instead on a tiny group of infamous auteurs: Besson, Assayas, and Denis.

19 Emma Wilson, "*Etat Présent*: Contemporary French Women Filmmakers," *French Studies* 59:2 (2005): 223.

20 A less optimistic counterpoint is the fact that among the 2009 nominations for the Best First Film Césars, just one, for Ursula Meier's *Home* (2008), went to a woman. Le Club des 13, in keeping with their jaundiced diagnoses about French cinema, found the 2008 slew of acclaimed female debuts to be delightful but likely something of a false dawn. See Le Club des 13, *Le Milieu n'est plus un pont mais une faille* (Paris: Editions Stock, 2008), 13. The fact remains, however, that in the first decade of the twenty-first century, the Best First Film César was won four times by women: besides Satrapi, by Julie Bertucelli in 2004 for *Since Otar Left* (*Depuis qu'Otar est parti*), by Yolande Moreau in 2005 for *When the Sea Rises*, and by Isabelle Mergault in 2007 for *Je vous trouve très beau*.

21 Stéphanie Lamome, "Girl Power," *Première* (August 2007): 78.

22 Quoted in ibid., 78–79.

23 Quoted in ibid., 78.

24 Quoted in ibid., 79.

25 Anthony Bobeau, "Audrey Estrougo: '*Regarde-moi* n'est pas un documentaire sur la banlieue,'" *Le Film français* 3227 (September 28, 2007): 16.

26 Béatrice Toulon, "Le Temps des filles," *Studio* hors-série (December 2007): 75.

27 Kelley Conway, "The New Wave in the Museum: Varda, Godard, and the Multi-Media Installation," *Contemporary French Civilization* 32:2 (Summer 2008): 209.

28 Geetha Ramanathan, *Feminist Auteurs: Readings Women's Films* (London: Wallflower, 2006), 1.

29 Kate Ince, "From Minor to 'Major' Cinema? Women's and Feminist Cinema in France in the 2000s," *Australian Journal of French Studies* 45:3 (September–December 2008): 282.

30 Tarr with Rollet, *Cinema and the Second Sex*: 25.

31 Mary Gentile, *Film Feminisms: Theory and Practice* (London: Greenwood Press, 1985), 70–71.

32 Alison Butler, *Women's Cinema: The Contested Screen* (London: Wallflower, 2002), 22.

33 Caroline Bainbridge, *A Feminine Cinematic: Luce Irigaray, Women and Film* (New York: Palgrave Macmillan, 2008), 15, 48, 185.

34 Geneviève Sellier, trans. Margaret Colvin, "French Women Making Films in the 1990s," in Célestin, Dalmolin and de Courtivron (eds.), *Beyond French Feminisms*, 220.

35 La Fémis publicity, promotion, and student materials, accessible at lafemis.fr. Self-description viewed at http://www.lafemis.fr/index.php?rub=1. Accessed January 18, 2008.

36 Ginette Vincendeau, "*Innocence*," *Sight and Sound* 15:10 (October 2005): 68.

37 Damjana Finci, "*La Bouche de Jean-Pierre*." www.filmfestivals.com/cannes96/cfile29.htm. Accessed January 18, 2008.

38 For a related discussion about the role of preadolescent children in contemporary French cinema, see Phil Powrie, "Unfamiliar Places: 'Heterospection' and Recent

French Films on Children," *Screen* 46:3 (Autumn 2005): 341–352. Focusing on Nicolas Philibert's *Etre et avoir* (2002) and Christophe Ruggia's *Les Diables* (2002), Powrie also offers the sociodemographic context that France's birth rate has risen sharply over the last decade versus that of its European neighbors.

39 Emma Wilson, "Miniature Lives, Intrusion and *Innocence*," *French Cultural Studies* 18:2 (2007): 173.

40 Vincendeau, "*Innocence*."

41 Vincent Ostria, "Jupette infernelles," *L'Humanité* (January 12, 2005): 20. An interesting parallel film is the Brothers Quay's equally peculiar *Institute Benjamenta* (1995).

42 Isabelle Regnier, "Le Pensionnat des épouses dociles," *Le Monde* (January 12, 2005): 28.

43 Arnaud Schwartz, "La Secrète métamorphose du féminin," *La Croix* (January 12, 2005): 23.

44 Wilson, "Miniature Lives," 176.

45 Here *Innocence* offers a sly autobiographical self-reference, typical of debutant French women's cinema, as in films like Bruni Tedeschi's *It's Easier for a Camel . . .* and Maïwenn le Besco's *Pardonnez-moi* (2006). For the girls' housekeeper and cook, Madeleine, one of the elderly captives, is played by Hadzihalilovic's own mother, Micheline.

46 Hadzihalilovic, like her partner Noé, to whom *Innocence* is dedicated, is minutely attentive to the layering, timbre, and overall impact of sound design on the audience. Her term for the process is *le rumble*: "We use the English word to describe those sheets of deep sound" (in Romney: 36).

47 Stan Brakhage, "Metaphors on Vision," in *Essential Brakhage: Selected Writings on Filmmaking by Stan Brakhage* (New York: Documentext, 2001), 12.

48 Quoted in Jonathan Romney, "School for Scandal," *Sight and Sound*, 15:10 (October 2005): 36.

49 Ibid. Note also that in this context emerges another international facet of French cinema, its use of English culture and literary heritage. Leading examples include François Ozon's use of English writer Elizabeth Taylor's source novel for *Angel* (2007), and, more famously, Pascale Ferran's adaptation of the second version of D. H. Lawrence's book for *Lady Chatterley* (2006).

50 Interestingly, the original novella ends with another train of boys arriving at the same underground station as Bianca and her group. Hadzihalilovic's decision to remove the gender equality, focusing only on the girls, links her to Sciamma and *Water Lilies*. See Claire Vassé, "Entretien Lucile Hadzihalilovic: 'Qu'est-ce que va arriver?' est une question importante quand on est enfant," *Positif* (January 2005): 33.

51 Sheila Johnston, "Film-makers on film: Lucile Hadzihalilovic on Peter Weir's *Picnic at Hanging Rock*," *The Daily Telegraph* (September 24, 2005). www.telegraph.co.uk/ arts/main.jhtml?view=DETAILS&grid=P8&xml=/arts/2005/09/24/bffof24.xml. Accessed January 23, 2008.

52 Wilson, "Miniature Lives": 181.

53 David Macdougall, *The Corporeal Image: Film, Ethnography and the Senses* (Princeton: Princeton University Press, 2006), 67.

54 For a productive contextual discussion about the contemporary French literary trope of corporeal change as a motif to explore immigration and social exclusions, see Susan Ireland, "Deviant Bodies: Corporeal Otherness in Contemporary Women's Writing," *Nottingham French Studies* 45:3 (Autumn 2006): 39–51.

55 Tarr with Rollet, *Cinema and the Second Sex*, 13.

56 Quoted in David Ng, "Blanc Generation: Ghosts of the Modern Workplace," *The Village Voice* (January 11, 2005). www.villagevoice.com/2005-01-11/film/blanc-generation-ghosts-of-the-modern-workplace. Accessed January 21, 2009.

57 Céline Curiol, trans. Sam Richard, *Voice Over* (New York: Seven Stories Press, 2008), 150.

58 Ibid., 224.

59 Ibid., 204.

60 Paul Auster, "Preface," 6.

61 Sellier, "French Women Making Films in the 1990s," 217.

62 Kavaïté perhaps refers here to Polanski's *Repulsion* (1965), albeit with much less psychological sensationalism.

63 Harry Caul (Gene Hackman), the fanatical yet ultimately ineffectual protagonist of Francis Ford Coppola's *The Conversation* (1974) is another role model, of course.

64 Sellier, "French Women Making Films in the 1990s," 217.

Conclusion: Instructive Cinephilia

1 David Bordwell, Kristin Thompson, and Janet Staiger, *The Classical Hollywood Cinema: Film Style and Mode of Production to 1960* (Columbia: Columbia University Press, 1985), 1.

2 Quoted in Christian Keathley, *Cinephilia and History, or The Wind in the Trees* (Bloomington: Indiana University Press, 2006), 7.

3 Antoine de Baecque, *La Cinéphilie: Invention d'un regard, histoire d'une culture 1944-1968* (Paris: Hachette, 2003), 12.

4 David Bordwell, "Games Cinephiles Play," www.davidbordwell.net/blog/?p=2662. Accessed August 4, 2008. The reference to filmgoing as a religious ritual recalls a personal encounter with cinephilia: a visit to the Cinémathèque Française, surely any cine-pilgrim's Mecca, at its old location in the Palais Chaillot in 2004. In the main screening room, as lights went down before a late-night screening of Henri Decoin's *Entre onze heures et minuit* (1949), one English visitor was overheard whispering loudly to her companion, "This place is like a *church*."

5 Keathley, *Cinephilia and History*: 7-8.

6 George Toles, "Rescuing Fragments: A New Task for Cinephilia," *Cinema Journal* 49:2 (Winter 2010): 161.

7 De Baecque, *La Cinéphilie*, 24.

8 Liz Czach, "Cinephila, Stars, and Film Festivals," *Cinema Journal* 49:2 (Winter 2010): 141. See also Marijke de Valck and Malte Hagener (eds.), *Cinephilia: Movies, Love and Memory* (Amsterdam: Amsterdam University Press, 2005).

9 See la Fémis promotional materials, such as http://www.lafemis.fr/index.php?rub =1. Accessed September 27, 2008.

10 A corollary to this conclusion is the future of the Louis-Lumière school, planned by Luc Besson as the pedagogical component of his massive new Cité du Cinéma site, to be built in the 8th arrondissement of Paris. Due to open in 2012, Besson's 6.5-hectare venture will include nine sound stages, offices and space for all aspects of production, and, perhaps most crucially, the relocated Louis-Lumière facilities, whose student-trainees will supplement the 2,000 film workers employed on site.

11 Personal interview with Marina de Van, August 26, 2004.

12 Sylvain Monier, "Ecoles de cinéma: Mode d'emploi," *Première* (April 2009): 96.

13 Personal interview with Matthieu-David Cournot, July 11, 2008.

14 Réné Prédal, *Le Cinéma français depuis 2000: Un renouvellement incessant* (Paris: Armand Colin, 2008), 117. Prédal uses la Fémis mainly as a point of departure, rather than as a concrete source of practice resulting in a particular aesthetic.

15 Personal interview with Noémie Gillot, August 21, 2008.

16 Jean-Claude Carrière, *Raconter une histoire: Quelques indications* (Paris: La Fémis, 1992), 25.

17 Serguëi Mikhaïlovitch Eisenstein and Vladimir Nijny, trans. Jacques Aumont, *Leçons de mise en scène* (Paris: La Fémis, 1989).

18 Alain Bergala, "Les 156 Films Qu'Il Faut Avoir Vus: La Liste," Unpublished la Fémis document: 6.

19 Ibid.

20 Ibid., 7.

21 Personal interview with Noémie Gillot.

22 Thierry Lounas, "'Nous ne disons pas aux élèves quel cinéma faire': Entretien avec Marc Nicolas," *Cahiers du cinéma* 615 (September 2006): 43. Nicolas, throughout, is coy on the subject of la Fémis as an elite institution, noting that genre filmmaking is increasingly taught as part of its curriculum.

23 François Bégaudeau, "*A travers le forêt*," *Cahiers du cinéma* (October 2005): 35.

24 Benjamin Esdraffo and Jean-Marc Lalanne, "'Je suis tenté par la légèreté, le superficiel': Rencontre, Jean-Paul Civeyrac," *Cahiers du cinéma* (February 2002): 79. The format of Civeyrac's first name is given variously as Jean-Paul and Jean Paul; I prefer the latter as it is how he signs his own works. The issue is incidental yet also provides another textual motif for a filmmaker obsessed with confluences and syntagmatic connections.

25 Ibid.

26 Marie-Noëlle Tranchant, "Pur enchantement," *Figaroscope* (October 12, 2005).

27 Quoted in Philippe Azoury, "Civeyrac, lueur d'automne," *Libération* (October 12, 2005).

28 Robin Wood, "The Ghost Princess and the Seaweed Gatherer," in *Personal Views* (London: Gordon Fraser, 1976), 235.

29 A close textual relative to *Through the Forest* is the extraordinary *Frontier of Dawn* (*La Frontière de l'aube*, 2008) of Philippe Garrel (another la Fémis teacher). Garrel's film, exquisitely shot in his customary black-and-white, focuses on a photographer, François, played by the director's son and muse, Louis Garrel, who gets involved with a sensuous but unstable actress, Carole (Laura Smet). After being committed to an institution, Carole kills herself; one year later, François becomes the lover of Eve (Clémentine Poidnatz). Apparently on the path to domesticity, François remains obsessed with Carole's memory: he either imagines, or is genuinely visited by, her spirit, who urges him to join her in oblivion. Poised like Civeyrac's work—in blissful ambiguity between real life and afterlife—Garrel, however, includes one very brief climactic shot, almost imperceptible, that gives a more straightforward prompt about the demonic nature of François's guilty fixation.

30 See Tim Palmer, "Exotic Aesthetics: Long Take Style and Staging in the Films of Mizoguchi and von Sternberg," *Filmhäftet* 122: 4 (July 2002): 1-6; and David Bordwell, *Figures Traced in Light: On Cinematic Staging* (Berkeley: University of California Press, 2005), 83-139.

31 Quoted in Azoury, "Civeyrac, lueur d'automne."

SELECT FILMOGRAPHY

5 x 2 (2004)

Directed by François Ozon; writers François Ozon & Emmanuèle Bernheim; produced by Olivier Delbosc, Philippe Dugay & Marc Missonnier; cinematography by Yorick Le Saux; film editing by Monica Coleman.

With Valeria Bruni Tedeschi (Marion), Stéphane Freiss (Gilles), Françoise Fabian (Monique), Michael Lonsdale (Bernard).

DVD availability: Velocity / Thinkfilm (Region 1).

35 Shots of Rum (35 Rhums, 2008)

Directed by Claire Denis; writers Claire Denis & Jean-Pol Fargeau; produced by Bruno Pésery; cinematography by Agnès Godard; film editing by Guy Lecorne.

With Alex Descas (Lionel), Mati Diop (Joséphine), Nicole Dogue (Gabrielle), Grégoire Colin (Noé), Jean-Christophe Folly (Ruben), Djédjé Apali (Martial).

DVD availability: Cinema Guild (Region 1).

400 Blows, The (Quatre cents coups, Les, 1959)

Directed by François Truffaut; writers Marcel Moussy & François Truffaut; produced by François Truffaut; cinematography by Henri Decaë; film editing by Marie-Josèphe Yoyotte.

With Jean-Pierre Léaud (Antoine Doinel), Claire Maurier (Gilberte Doinel, la mère d'Antoine), Albert Rémy (Julien Doinel), Guy Decomble ("Petite Feuille," the French teacher).

DVD availability: Criterion Collection (Region 1).

Actresses (Actrices, 2007)

Directed by Valeria Bruni Tedeschi; writers Valeria Bruni Tedeschi, Noémie Lvovsky & Agnès de Sacy; produced by Olivier Delbosc & Marc Missonnier; cinematography by Jeanne Lapoirie; film editing by Valeria Bruni Tedeschi & Anne Weil.

With Valeria Bruni Tedeschi (Marcelline), Noémie Lvovsky (Nathalie), Louis Garrel (Éric), Mathieu Amalric (Denis).

DVD availability: Wild Side Video (Region 2, Amazon.fr) with English subtitles.

All Is Forgiven (Tout est pardonné, 2007)

Directed by Mia Hansen-Løve; writer Mia Hansen-Løve; produced by Lola Gans, Philippe Martin, Géraldine Michelot & David Thion; cinematography by Pascal Auffray; film editing by Marion Monnier.

With Paul Blain (Victor), Marie-Christine Friedrich (Annette), Victoire Rousseau
   (Pamela enfant), Constance Rousseau (Pamela adolescente).
DVD availability: Les Editions Pelléas (Region 2, Amazon.fr) with English subtitles.

L'Après-midi de Monsieur Andesmas (2004)

Directed by Michelle Porte; writers Marguerite Duras & Michelle Porte; produced
   by Marin Karmitz; cinematography by Dominique le Rigoleur; film editing by
   Colette Culbert.
With Michel Bouquet (Monsieur Andesmas), Miou-Miou (La Femme de Michel
   Arc), Paloma Veinstein (La Petite fille), Anne Isserman (Valérie), Patrick Roques
   (Michel Arc).
Not available on DVD.

Baise-moi (2000)

Directed by Virginie Despentes & Coralie; writers Coralie & Virginie Despentes;
   produced by Dominique Chiron & Philippe Godeau; cinematography by
   Benoît Chamaillard; film editing by Aïlo Auguste-Judith, Francine Lemaitre
   & Véronique Rosa.
With Karen Lancaume (Nadine), Raffaëla Anderson (Manu), Céline Beugnot
   (Blonde at Billiards), Adama Niane (Boy at Billiards).
DVD availability: Vision Video Ltd. (Region 2, Amazon.co.uk) with English subtitles.

Betty Blue (37°2 le matin, 1986)

Directed by Jean-Jacques Beineix; writers Philippe Djian & Jean-Jacques Beineix;
   produced by Jean-Jacques Beineix & Claudie Ossard; cinematography by
   Jean-François Robin; film editing by Marie-Aimée Debril (extended version),
   Monique Prim & Pablo Ferro.
With Jean-Hugues Anglade (Zorg), Béatrice Dalle (Betty), Gérard Darmon (Eddy),
   Consuelo De Haviland (Lisa).
DVD availability: M6 Vidéo (Region 2, Amazon.fr) with English subtitles.

Breathless (A bout de souffle, 1960)

Directed by Jean-Luc Godard; writers Jean-Luc Godard & François Truffaut;
   produced by Georges de Beauregard; cinematography by Raoul Coutard;
   film editing by Cécile Decugis & Lila Herman.
With Jean-Paul Belmondo (Michel Poiccard), Jean Seberg (Patricia Franchini),
   Daniel Boulanger (Police Inspector Vital), Jean-Pierre Melville (Parvulesco).
DVD availability: Criterion Collection (Region 1).

Ça brûle (2006)

Directed by Claire Simon; writers Jérôme Beaujour, Claire Simon & Nadège Trébal;
   produced by Samuel Chauvin, Gilles Sandoz & Ruth Waldburger; cinematography
   by Pascale Granel; film editing by Daniel Gibel & Julien Lacheray.

With Camille Varenne (Livia), Gilbert Melki (Jean Susini), Kader Mohamed (Moisi), Marion Maintenay (Amanda).
Not available on DVD.

Car Keys (Clefs de bagnole, Les, 2003)
Directed by Laurent Baffie; writer Laurent Baffie; produced by Laurent Baffie; cinematography by Philippe Vene; film editing by Anne Lafarge.
With Laurent Baffie (Laurent), Daniel Russo (Daniel), Pascal Sellem (Pascal, le barman), Karine Lyachenko (La barmaid).
DVD availability: Tartan Video (Region 2, Amazon.co.uk) with English subtitles.

A Christmas Tale (Conte de Noël, Un, 2008)
Directed by Arnaud Desplechin; writers Emmanuel Bourdieu & Arnaud Desplechin; produced by Pascal Caucheteux; cinematography by Eric Gautier; film editing by Laurence Briaud.
With Catherine Deneuve (Junon), Jean-Paul Roussillon (Abel), Anne Cosigny (Elizabeth), Mathieu Amalric (Henri), Melvil Poupaud (Ivan), Emmanuelle Devos (Faunia).
DVD availability: Criterion Collection (Region 1).

Class, The (Entre les murs, 2008)
Directed by Laurent Cantet; writers François Bégaudeau, Robin Campillo & Laurent Cantet; produced by Caroline Benjo & Carole Scotta; cinematography by Pierre Milon; film editing by Robin Campillo.
With Nassim Amrabt, Laura Baquela, Cherif Bounaïdja Rachedi, Juliette Demaille.
DVD availability: France Télévisions Distribution (Region 1; Region 2, Amazon.fr).

Dancing (2003)
Directed by Patrick-Mario Bernard, Xavier Brillat & Pierre Trividic; writers Pierre Trividic & Patrick-Mario Bernard; produced by Patrick Sobelman; cinematography by Xavier Brillat & Emmanuel Caula; film editing by Stephane Huter & Christine Maffre.
With Patrick-Mario Bernard (René Bernard / Son double), Pierre Trividic (Patrick Kérisit), Jean-Yves Jouannais (Maurice / Ses doubles), Peter Bonke (Arne Nygren).
DVD availability: Seven7 (Region 2, Amazon.fr) with English subtitles.

Darling (2007)
Directed by Christine Carrière; writers Pascal Arnold, Christine Carrière & Jean Teulé; produced by Edouard Weil; cinematography by Gordon Spooner; film editing by Mathilde Grosjean.
With Marina Foïs (Catherine / Sophie / Cécile Nicolle / dite "Darling"), Guillaume Canet (Joël Epine / dit "Roméo"), Océane Decaudain (Catherine / Darling petite), Anne Benoît (Suzanne Nicolle / la mère de Darling).

DVD availability: Paramount Home Entertainment (Region 2, Amazon.fr) with English subtitles.

Demonlover (2002)

Directed by Olivier Assayas; writer Olivier Assayas; produced by Sylvie Barthet, Jean Coulon, Claude Davy, Xavier Giannoli, Andres Martin & Edouard Weil; cinematography by Denis Lenoir; film editing by Luc Barnier.

With Connie Nielsen (Diane de Monx), Charles Berling (Hervé Le Millinec), Chloë Scvigny (Elise Lipsky), Dominique Reymond (Karen).

DVD availability: Palm Pictures / Umvd (Region 1).

District B13 (Banlieue 13, 2004)

Directed by Pierre Morel; writers Luc Besson & Bibi Naceri; produced by Luc Besson, Bernard Grenet & Mehdi Sayah; cinematography by Manuel Teran; film editing by Stéphanie Gaurier & Frédéric Thoraval.

With Cyril Raffaelli (Capt. Damien Tomaso), David Belle (Leïto), Tony D'Amario (K2), Bibi Naceri (Taha Bemamud).

DVD availability: Magnolia (Region 1).

Diva (1981)

Directed by Jean-Jacques Beineix; writers Daniel Odier, Jean-Jacques Beineix & Jean Van Hamme; produced by Claudie Ossard, Irène Silberman & Serge Silberman; cinematography by Philippe Rousselot; film editing by Monique Prim & Marie-Josèphe Yoyotte.

With Wilhelmenia Fernandez (Cynthia Hawkins), Frédéric Andréi (Jules), Richard Bohringer (Gorodish), Thuy An Luu (Alba).

DVD availability: Lions Gate (Region 1).

Dobermann (1997)

Directed by Jan Kounen; writer Joël Houssin; produced by Frédérique Dumas-Zajdela & Eric Névé; cinematography by Michel Amathieu; film editing by Bénédicte Brunet & Eric Carlier.

With Vincent Cassel (Yann Le Pentrec / aka Dobermann), Tchéky Karyo (Inspecteur Sauveur Cristini), Monica Bellucci (Nathalie / Nat the gipsy), Antoine Basler (Jean-Claude Ayache / dit "Moustique").

DVD availability: Universal Pictures Video (Region 2, Amazon.fr) with English subtitles.

Ecoute le temps (2007)

Directed by Alanté Kavaïté; writer Alanté Kavaïté; produced by Antoine Simkine; cinematography by Dominique Colin; film editing by Agnès Mouchel.

With Emilie Dequenne (Charlotte), Mathieu Demy (Julien), Ludmila Mikaël
(Charlotte's Mother), Etienne Chicot (Bourmel), Bruno Fleder (Jérôme Blanc).
DVD availability: Lifesize Ent. (Region 1).

L'Ennemi public no. 1 (2008)

Directed by Jean-François Richet; writers Abdel Raouf Dafri & Jean-François Richet;
produced by Thomas Langmann; cinematography by Robert Gantz; film editing
by Bill Pankow & Hervé Schneid.

With Vincent Cassel (Jacques Mesrine), Ludivine Sagnier (Sylvie Jeanjacquot),
Mathieu Amalric (François Besse), Gérard Lanvin (Charly Bauer), Samuel le Bihan
(Michel Ardouin), Olivier Gourmet (Le Commissaire Broussard).

DVD availability: Momentum Pictures (Region 2, Amazon.co.uk) with English
subtitles.

Esquive, L' (2003)

Directed by Abdel Kechiche; writer Ghalya Laroix; produced by Franck Cabot-David,
Jacques Ouaniche & Charles Taris; cinematography by Lubomir Bakchev; film
editing by Ghalya Laroix.

With Osman Elkharraz (Krimo), Sara Forestier (Lydia), Sabrina Ouazani (Frida),
Nanou Benhamou (Nanou).

DVD availability: TVA Films (Region 2, Amazon.fr).

Et toi, t'es sur qui? (2007)

Directed by Lola Doillon; writer Lola Doillon; produced by Saga Blanchard;
cinematography by Romain Lacourbas; film editing by Enrica Gattolini.

With Lucie Desclozeaux (Elodie), Christa Theret (Julie / dite Batman), Gaël Tavares
(Vincent), Nicolas Schweri (Nicolas).

DVD availability: Universal Studio Canal Video (Region 2, Amazon.fr) with English
subtitles.

France, La (2007)

Directed by Serge Bozon; writers Serge Bozon & Axelle Ropert; produced by Lola Gans,
Philippe Martin, Géraldine Michelot & David Thion; cinematography by Céline
Bozon; film editing by François Quiqueré.

With Sylvie Testud (Camille), Pascal Greggory (Le Lieutenant), Guillaume Verdier
(Le cadet).

DVD availability: Kino (Region 1).

French Gigolo, A (Cliente, 2008)

Directed by Josiane Balasko; writer Josiane Balasko; produced by Patrick Batteux;
cinematography by Robert Alazraki; film editing by Marie De La Selle &
Claudine Merlin.

With Nathalie Baye (Judith), Eric Caravaca (Patrick / Marco), Isabelle Carré (Fanny),
  Josiane Balasko (Irène).
DVD availability: Paramount Home Entertainment (Region 2, Amazon.fr).

Friday Night (Vendredi soir, 2002)
Directed by Claire Denis; writers Emmanuèle Bernheim & Claire Denis; produced
  by Bruno Pésery; cinematography by Agnès Godard; film editing by Nelly Quettier.
With Valérie Lemercier (Laure), Vincent Lindon (Jean), Hélène de Saint-Père (Marie).
DVD availability: G.C.T.H.V. (Region 2, Amazon.fr).

Gabrielle (2005)
Directed by Patrice Chéreau; writers Patrice Chéreau, Anne-Louise Trividic & Joseph
  Conrad; produced by Patrice Chéreau, Ferdinanda Frangipane & Joseph Strub;
  cinematography by Eric Gautier; film editing by François Gédigier.
With Isabelle Huppert (Gabrielle Hervey), Pascal Greggory (Jean Hervey), Claudia Coli
  (Yvonne), Thierry Hancisse (The Editor-in-Chief).
DVD availability: IFC (Region 1).

Hate (Haine, La, 1995)
Directed by Mathieu Kassovitz; writer Mathieu Kassovitz; produced by Adeline
  Lecallier, Alain Rocca, Christophe Rossignon & Gilles Sacuto; cinematography
  by Pierre Aïm; film editing by Mathieu Kassovitz & Scott Stevenson.
With Vincent Cassel (Vinz), Hubert Koundé (Hubert), Saïd Taghmaoui (Saïd),
  Abdel Ahmed Ghili (Abdel).
DVD availability: Criterion Collection (Region 1).

Histoire de Richard O, L' (2007)
Directed by Damien Odoul; writer Damien Odoul; produced by Damien Odoul;
  cinematography by Patrick Ghiringhelli; film editing by Sophie Delecourt.
With Mathieu Amalric (Richard O.), Rhizlaine El Cohen (Celle qui tue Richard),
  Stéphane Terpereau (Le Grand), Alexandra Sollogoub (La jeune fille du
  restaurant).
DVD availability: Bac (Region 2, Amazon.fr).

In My Skin (Dans ma peau, 2002)
Directed by Marina de Van; writer Marina de Van; produced by Stéphanie Carreras,
  Laurence Farenc, Alain Rocca & Laurent Soregaroli; cinematography by Pierre
  Barougier; film editing by Mike Fromentin.
With Marina de Van (Esther), Laurent Lucas (Vincent), Léa Drucker (Sandrine),
  Thibault de Montalembert (Daniel).
DVD availability: Fox Lorber (Region 1).

Innocence (2004)

Directed by Lucile Hadzihalilovic; writers Lucile Hadzihalilovic & Frank Wedekind; produced by Geoffrey Cox, Alain de la Mata, Patrick Sobelman & Paul Trijbits; cinematography by Benoît Debie; film editing by Adam Finch.

With Zoé Auclair (Iris), Bérangère Haubruge (Bianca), Lea Bridarolli (Alice), Marion Cotillard (Mademoiselle Eva), Hélène de Fougerolles (Mademoiselle Edith).

DVD availability: Homevision (Region 1).

Instinct de mort, L' (2008)

Directed by Jean-François Richet; writers Abdel Raouf Dafri, Jacques Mesrine & Jean-François Richet; produced by Thomas Langmann; cinematography by Robert Gantz; film editing by Hervé Schneid.

With Vincent Cassel (Jacques Mesrine), Cécile de France (Jeanne Schneider), Gérard Depardieu (Guido), Gilles Lellouche (Paul), Roy Dupuis (Jean-Paul Mercier), Elena Anaya (Sofia), Michel Duchaussoy (Pierre André Mesrine), Florence Thomassin (Sarah).

DVD availability: Momentum Pictures (Region 2, Amazon.co.uk) with English subtitles.

Intimacy (Intimité, 2001)

Directed by Patrice Chéreau; writers Hanif Kureishi, Anne-Louise Trividic & Patrice Chéreau; produced by Patrick Cassavetti, Jacques Hinstin, Peter McAleese, Lesley Stewart & Charles Gassot; cinematography by Eric Gautier; film editing by François Gédigier.

With Mark Rylance (Jay), Kerry Fox (Claire), Susannah Harker (Susan / Jay's wife), Alastair Galbraith (Victor).

DVD availability: Koch Lorber Films (Region 1).

Irreversible (Irréversible, 2002)

Directed by Gaspar Noé; writer Gaspar Noé; produced by Vincent Cassel, Brahim Chioua, Emmanuel Gateau, Richard Grandpierre, Gaspar Noé & Christophe Rossignon; cinematography by Benoît Debie & Gaspar Noé; film editing by Gaspar Noé.

With Monica Bellucci (Alex), Vincent Cassel (Marcus), Albert Dupontel (Pierre), Jo Prestia (Le Tenia).

DVD availability: Lions Gate (Region 1).

It's Easier for a Camel . . . (Il est plus facile pour un chameau . . ., 2003)

Directed by Valeria Bruni Tedeschi; writers Valeria Bruni Tedeschi, Noémie Lvovsky & Agnès de Sacy; produced by Maurizio Antonini, Paulo Branco & Mimmo Calopresti; cinematography by Jeanne Lapoirie; film editing by Anne Weil.

With Valeria Bruni Tedeschi (Federica), Chiara Mastroianni (Bianca), Jean-Hugues
    Anglade (Pierre), Denis Podalydès (Philippe).
DVD availability: New Yorker Video (Region 1).

Mes stars et moi (2008)
Directed by Laetitia Colombani; writer Laetitia Colombani; produced by Christophe
    Rossignon; film editing by Véronique Parnet.
With Kad Merad (Robert), Catherine Deneuve (Solange Duvivier), Emmanuelle Béart
    (Isabelle Séréna), Mélanie Bernier (Violette Duval).
DVD availability: Universal Studio Canal (Region 2, Amazon.fr), with English subtitles.

Musée haut, musée bas (2008)
Directed by Jean-François Ribes; writer Jean-Michel Ribes; produced by Frédéric
    Brillion & Gilles Legrand; cinematography by Pascal Ridao; film editing by
    Yann Malcor.
With Josiane Balasko (La Mère en Chanel), Michel Blanc (Mosk), Isabelle Carré
    (Carole Province), Gérard Jugnot (Roland Province), Valérie Lemercier (Valérie),
    Tonie Marshall (Laurence), Yolande Moreau (Madame Stenthels), Dominique
    Pinon (Simon).
DVD availability: Warner Home Video (Region 2, Amazon.fr).

On the Ropes (Dans les cordes, 2007)
Directed by Magaly Richard-Serrano; writers Pierre Chosson, Gaëlle Macé & Magaly
    Richard-Serrano; produced by Nathalie Mesuret; cinematography by Isabelle
    Razavet; film editing by Yann Dedet.
With Richard Anconina (Joseph), Maria de Medeiros (Térésa), Louise Szpindel (Angie),
    Stéphanie Sokolinski (Sandra).
DVD availability: TF1 Vidéo (Region 2, Amazon.fr).

OSS 117: Cairo, Nest of Spies (OSS 117: Le Caire, nid d'espions, 2006)
Directed by Michel Haznavicius; writers Jean Bruce, Jean-François Halin & Michel
    Haznavicius; produced by Eric Altmayer & Nicolas Altmayer; cinematography
    by Guillaume Schiffman; film editing by Reynald Bertrand.
With Jean Dujardin (Hubert Bonisseur de la Bath/OSS 117), Bérénice Bejo (Larmina),
    Aure Atika (La Princesse At Tarouk), Philippe Lefebvre (Jack Jefferson), Constantin
    Alexandrov (Setine).
DVD availability: Music Box Films (Region 1).

OSS 117: Lost in Rio (OSS 117: Rio ne répond plus, 2009)
Directed by Michel Haznavicius; writers Jean Bruce, Jean-François Halin & Michel
    Haznavicius; produced by Eric Altmayer & Nicolas Altmayer; cinematography by
    Guillaume Schiffman; film editing by Reynald Bertrand.

With Jean Dujardin (Hubert Bonisseur de la Bath/OSS 117), Louise Monot (Dolorès Koulechov), Rüdiger Vogler (Von Zimmel), Alex Lutz (Heinrich), Reem Kherci (Carlotta), Ken Samuels (Bill Trumendous).
DVD availability: Gaumont (Region 2, Amazon.fr) with English subtitles.

Persepolis (Persépolis, 2007)
Directed by Vincent Paronnaud & Marjane Satrapi; writers Vincent Paronnaud & Marjane Satrapi; produced by Tara Grace, Marc Jousset, Kathleen Kennedy, Xavier Rigault & Marc-Antoine Robert; film editing by Stéphane Roche.
With Chiara Mastroianni (Marjane "Marji" Satrapi), Catherine Deneuve (Mrs. Satrapi / Marjane's mother), Danielle Darrieux (Marjane's grandmother), Simon Abkarian (Mr. Satrapi / Marjane's father).
DVD availability: Sony Pictures (Region 1).

Plaisir (et ses petits tracas), Le (1998)
Directed by Nicolas Boukhrief, writers Nicolas Boukhrief & Dan Sasson; produced by Marc Baschet, Frédérique Dumas-Zajdela & Cédomir Kolar; cinematography by Jean-Max Bernard; film editing by Jacqueline Mariani.
With Vincent Cassel (Michael), Mathieu Kassovitz (Roland), Julie Gayet (Véra), Foued Nassah (Marcel), Florence Thomassin (Lise), Caroline Cellier (Hélène), Michele Placido (Carlo).
DVD availability: Universal (Region 2, Amazon.fr) with English subtitles.

Porn Theatre (Chatte à deux têtes, La, 2002)
Directed by Jacques Nolot; writer Jacques Nolot; produced by Pauline Duhault & Eric Zaouali; cinematography by Germain Desmoulins; film editing by Sophie Reine.
With Vittoria Scognamiglio (Cashier), Jacques Nolot (50-Year-Old Man), Sébastien Viala (Projectionist).
DVD availability: Strand Releasing (Region 1).

Regarde-moi (2007)
Directed by Audrey Estrougo; writer Audrey Estrougo; produced by Xavier Durringer and Bruno Petit; cinematography by Guillaume Schiffman; film editing by Marie-Pierre Renaud.
With Emilie de Preissac (Julie), Eye Haidara (Fatima), Lili Canobbio (Eloise), Terry Nimajimbe (Jo).
DVD availability: Paramount Home Entertainment (Region 2), with English subtitles.

Ring Finger, The (L'Annulaire, 2005)
Directed by Diane Bertrand; writers Diane Bertrand & Yoko Ogawa; produced by Bruno Berthémy, Bertrand Faivre, Soledad Gatti-Pascual, Alfred Hürmer & Kate Ogborn; cinematography by Alain Duplantier; film editing by Nathalie Langlade.

With Olga Kurylenko (Iris), Marc Barbé (L'homme du laboratoire), Stipe Erceg (Costa, le marin), Edith Scob (La dame du 223).
DVD availability: Second Sight (Region 1; Region 2, Amazon.co.uk).

Romance (1999)
Directed by Catherine Breillat; writer Catherine Breillat; produced by Catherine Jacques & Jean-François Lepetit; cinematography by Giorgos Arvanitis; film editing by Agnès Guillemot.
With Caroline Ducey (Marie), Sagamore Stévenin (Paul), François Berléand (Robert), Rocco Siffredi (Paolo).
DVD availability: Lions Gate (Region 1).

See the Sea (Regarde la mer, 1997)
Directed by François Ozon; writers Marina de Van, Sasha Hails & François Ozon; produced by Nicolas Brevière, Olivier Delbosc & Marc Missonnier; cinematography by Yorick Le Saux; film editing by Jeanne Moutard.
With Sasha Hails (Sasha), Marina de Van (Tatiana), Samantha (Sioffra / The Baby), Paul Raoux (Sasha's Husband).
DVD availability: Zeitgeist Films (Region 1).

Sequins (Brodeuses, 2004)
Directed by Eléonore Faucher; writers Eléonore Faucher & Gaëlle Macé; produced by Alain Benguigui, Audrey Tondre, Bertrand Van Effenterre & Thomas Verhaeghe; cinematography by Pierre Cottereau; film editing by Joële Van Effenterre.
With Lola Naymark (Claire Moutiers), Ariane Ascaride (Mme. Mélikian), Jackie Berroyer (M. Lescuyer), Thomas Laroppe (Guillaume).
DVD availability: New Yorker Video (Region 1).

She's One of Us (Elle est des nôtres, 2003)
Directed by Siegrid Alnoy; writers Siegrid Alnoy, Jérôme Beaujour & François Favrat; produced by Béatrice Caufman; cinematography by Christophe Pollock; film editing by Plantin Alice & Benoît Quinon.
With Sasha Andres (Christine Blanc), Carlo Brandt (Degas), Pierre-Félix Gravière (Sébastien), Catherine Mouchet (Patricia).
DVD availability: Homevision (Region 1).

Sitcom (1998)
Directed by François Ozon; writer François Ozon; produced by Olivier Delbosc & Marc Missonnier; cinematography by Yorick Le Saux; film editing by Dominique Petrot.
With Évelyne Dandry (La mere), François Marthouret (Le père), Marina de Van (Sophie), Adrien de Van (Nicolas).
DVD availability: New Yorker Video (Region 1).

Sombre (1998)

Directed by Philippe Grandrieux; writers Sophie Fillières, Philippe Grandrieux & Pierre Hodgson; produced by Catherine Jacques; cinematography by Sabine Lancelin; film editing by Françoise Tourmen.

With Marc Barbé (Jean), Elina Löwensohn (Claire), Géraldine Voillat (Christine).

DVD availability: Koch Lorber Films (Region 1).

They Came Back (Revenants, Les, 2004)

Directed by Robin Campillo; writers Robin Campillo & Brigitte Tijou; produced by Simon Arnal, Caroline Benjo & Carole Scotta; cinematography by Jeanne Lapoirie; film editing by Robin Campillo & Stephanie Leger.

With Géraldine Pailhas (Rachel), Jonathan Zaccaï (Mathieu), Frédéric Pierrot (Gardet).

DVD availability: Haut et Court (Region 1).

Those Who Remain (Ceux qui restent, 2007)

Directed by Anne Le Ny; writer Anne Le Ny; produced by Jean-Philippe Andraca & Christian Bérard; cinematography by Patrick Blossier; film editing by Idit Bloch.

With Vincent Lindon (Bertrand Liévain), Emmanuelle Devos (Lorraine Grégeois), Yeelem Jappain (Valentine), Anne Le Ny (Nathalie).

DVD availability: Universal Studio Canal Video (Region 2, Amazon.fr) with English subtitles.

Through the Forest (A travers le forêt, 2005)

Directed by Jean Paul Civeyrac; writer Jean Paul Civeyrac; produced by Philippe Martin & David Thion; cinematography by Céline Bozon; film editing by Florence Bresson.

With Camille Berthomier (Armelle), Aurélien Wiik (Renaud / Hippolyte), Morgane Hainaux (Roxane), Alice Dubuisson (Bérénice).

DVD availability: Seven7 (Region 2, Amazon.fr), part of *8 Films de Jean Paul Civeyrac*, with English subtitles.

Time Out (Emploi du temps, L,' 2001)

Directed by Laurent Cantet; writers Robin Campillo & Laurent Cantet; produced by Simon Arnal, Caroline Benjo, Barbara Letellier & Carole Scotta; cinematography by Pierre Milon; film editing by Robin Campillo & Stephanie Leger.

With Aurélien Recoing (Vincent), Karin Viard (Muriel), Serge Livrozet (Jean-Michel).

DVD availability: Miramax Home Entertainment (Region 1).

Toi et Moi (2006)

Directed by Julie Lopes-Curval; writers Sophie Hiet & Julie Lopes-Curval; produced by Alain Benguigui; cinematography by Philippe Guilbert; film editing by Anne Weil.

With Marion Cotillard (Léna), Julie Depardieu (Ariane), Jonathan Zaccaï (Mark), Eric Berger (François), Sergio Peris Mencheta (Pablo), Chantal Lauby (Eléonore).

DVD availability: Koch Lorber (Region 1).

Trouble Every Day (2001)

Directed by Claire Denis; writers Claire Denis & Jean-Pol Fargeau; produced by Georges Benayoun, Françoise Guglielmi, Philippe Liégeois, Kazuko Mio, Jean-Michel Rey & Seiichi Tsukada; cinematography by Agnès Godard; film editing by Nelly Quettier.

With Vincent Gallo (Shane), Tricia Vessey (June), Béatrice Dalle (Coré), Alex Descas (Léo).

DVD availability: AVENTI (Region 2, Amazon.fr).

Twentynine Palms (2003)

Directed by Bruno Dumont; writer Bruno Dumont; produced by Allen Bain, Rachid Bouchareb, Jean Bréhat, Christel Brunn, Darren Goldberg, Muriel Merlin, Axel Möbius, Jesse Scolaro & Christoph Thoke; cinematography by Georges Lechaptois; film editing by Dominique Petrot.

With Yekaterina Golubeva (Katia), David Wissak (David).

DVD availability: Wellspring (Region 1).

Very Long Engagement, A (Un Long dimanche de fiançailles, 2004)

Directed by Jean-Pierre Jeunet; writers Sébastien Japrisot, Jean-Pierre Jeunet & Guillaume Laurant; produced by Francis Boespflug, Bill Gerber, Jean-Louis Monthieux & Fabienne Tsaï; cinematography by Bruno Delbonnel; film editing by Hervé Schneid.

With Audrey Tautou (Mathilde), Gaspard Ulliel (Manech), Dominique Pinon (Sylvain), Chantal Neuwirth (Bénédicte).

DVD availability: Warner Home Video (Region 1).

Water Lilies (La Naissance des pieuvres, 2007)

Directed by Céline Sciamma; writer Céline Sciamma; produced by Bénédicte Couvreur & Jérôme Dopffer; cinematography by Crystel Fournier; film editing by Julien Lacheray.

With Pauline Acquart (Marie), Louise Blachère (Anne), Adele Haenel (Floriane), Warren Jacquin (François).

DVD availability: Koch Lorber Films (Region 1).

Work Hard, Play Hard (Violence des échanges en milieu tempérés, 2003)

Directed by Jean-Marc Moutout; writers Olivier Gorce, Ghislaine Jégou & Jean-Marc Moutout; produced by Milena Poylo, Gilles Sacuto & Anne-Dominique Toussaint; cinematography by Claude Garnier; film editing by Marie-Hélène Mora.

With Jérémie Renier (Philippe Seigner), Laurent Lucas (Hugo Paradis), Cylia Malki (Eva), Olivier Perrier (Roland Manin).

Not available on DVD.

Recommended resources for Region-2 DVD technical information,
including whether French releases feature English subtitles:
www.dvdfr.com
www.dvdaf.com
www.excessif.com

SELECT BIBLIOGRAPHY

D'Arvor, Olivier Poivre. "Great Time for French Culture." *Culturesfrance* newsletter
     (January 2008): 2–8.
Audé, Françoise. "Actrices cinéastes, leur amour du jeu." *Positif* (May 2002): 21–24.
———. *Cinéma d'elles, 1981–2001.* Lausanne: Editions L'Age d'Homme, 2002.
Austin, Guy. *Contemporary French Cinema: An Introduction.* Manchester: Manchester
     University Press, 1996.
Baeque, Antoine de. *La Cinéphilie: Invention d'un regard, histoire d'une culture
     1944–1968.* Paris: Hachette, 2003.
Bainbridge, Caroline. *A Feminine Cinematics: Luce Irigaray, Women and Film.*
     New York: Palgrave Macmillan, 2008.
Beugnet, Martine. *Cinema and Sensation: French Film and the Art of Transgression.*
     Edinburgh: Edinburgh University Press, 2007.
Bordwell, David. *Planet Hong Kong: Popular Cinema and the Art of Entertainment.*
     Cambridge, MA: Harvard University Press, 2000.
———. *Figures Traced in Light: On Cinematic Staging.* Berkeley: University of California
     Press, 2005.
Bordwell, David, Janet Staiger, and Kristin Thompson. *The Classical Hollywood Cinema:
     Film Style and Mode of Production to 1960.* London: Routledge, 1985.
Brakhage, Stan. *Essential Brakhage: Selected Writings on Filmmaking by Stan Brakhage.*
     New York : Documentext, 2001.
Bresson, Robert. *Notes sur le cinématographe.* Paris: Gallimard, 1975.
Buchsbaum, Jonathan. " 'The *Exception Culturelle* Is Dead.' Long Live Cultural
     Diversity: French Cinema and the New Resistance." *Framework* 47:1 (2006): 5–21.
Butler, Alison. *Women's Cinema: The Contested Screen.* New York: Wallflower, 2002.
Carrière, Jean-Claude. *Raconter une histoire, quelques indications.* Paris: La Fémis, 1992.
Céléstin, Roger, Eliane DalMolin, and Isabelle de Courtivron (eds.). *Beyond French
     Feminisms: Debates on Women, Politics and Culture in France, 1981–2001.* New York:
     Palgrave Macmillan, 2003.
Céléstin, Roger, and Eliane DalMolin. *France from 1851 to the Present: Universalism in
     Crisis.* New York: Palgrave Macmillan, 2007.
Ciment, Michel. "Éditorial: Premières oeuvres." *Positif* 514 (December 2003): 3.
Club des 13, Le. *Le Milieu n'est plus un pont mais une faille.* Paris: Editions Stock, 2008.
Conway, Kelley. "The New Wave in the Museum: Varda, Godard, and the Multi-Media
     Installation." *Contemporary French Civilization* 32:2 (Summer 2008): 195–217.

Creton, Laurent, ed. *Le Cinéma à l'épreuve du système télévisuel*. Paris: CNRS Editions, 2002.

———. *Économie du cinéma: Perspectives stratégiques*. Paris: Armand Colin, 2005.

Curiol, Céline. *Voice Over*, trans. Sam Richard. New York: Seven Stories Press, 2008.

Darrieussecq, Marie. *Pig Tales: A Novel of Lust and Transformation*, trans. Linda Coverdale. New York: The New Press, 1998.

Downing, Lisa. "French Cinema's New 'Sexual Revolution': Postmodern Porn and Troubled Genre." *French Cultural Studies* 15:3 (2004): 265–280.

Drouhaud, Sarah. "Production cinéma: toujours plus d'argent." *Le Film français* 2873 (March 16, 2001): 9–11.

———. "Production cinéma: plus d'argent pour plus de films." *Le Film français* 2927 (March 15, 2002): 12–13.

———. "Production cinéma: tassement des investissements pour autant de films." *Le Film français* 2981 (March 14, 2003): 12–14.

———. "La Production cinéma en sortie de crise." *Le Film français* 3089 (March 11, 2005): 14–16.

———. "La Production française au taquet." *Le Film français* 3145 (March 24, 2006): 13.

———. "La Production française se stabilise à haut niveau." *Le Film français* 3200 (March 30, 2007): 16–17.

———. "Beau fixe sur la production française." *Le Film française* 3254 (March 26, 2008): 6–7.

Drouhaud, Sarah, and Fabrice Leclerc. "2003: la hausse contrastée de la production française." *Le Film français* 3036 (March 19, 2004): 14–16.

Eisenstein, Sergueï Mikhaïlovitch, and Vladimir Nijny. trans. Jacques Aumont. *Leçons de mise en scène*. Paris: La Fémis, 1989.

Ezra, Elizabeth, and Sue Harris. *France in Focus: Film and National Identity*. New York: Berg, 2000.

Farchy, Joëlle. *L'Industrie du cinéma*. Paris: Presses Universitaires de France, 2004.

Gentile, Mary. *Film Feminisms: Theory and Practice*. London: Greenwood Press, 1985.

Gimello-Mesplomb, Frédéric. "Le Prix de la qualité: L'État et le cinéma français (1960–1965)." *Politix* 16:61 (May–June 2003): 97–115.

———. "The Economy of 1950s Popular French Cinema." *Studies in French Cinema* 6:2 (2006): 141–150.

Gregory, Abigail, and Ursula Todd, eds. *Women in Contemporary France*. New York: Berg, 2000.

Hayward, Susan. *Luc Besson*. Manchester: Manchester University Press, 1998.

———. *French National Cinema*, 2nd. ed. New York: Routledge, 2005.

Hayward, Susan, and Phil Powrie, eds. *The Films of Luc Besson: Master of Spectacle*. New York: Manchester University Press, 2006.

Hayward, Susan, and Ginette Vincendeau, eds. *French Film: Texts and Contexts*. 2nd. ed. London: Routledge, 2000.

Herpe, Noël, trans. Thierry Jutel. "Will There Ever Be a New French Cinema?" *Film Criticism* 27:1 (Fall 2002): 5–19.

Higbee, Will. "'Elle est où, ta place?' The Social-Realist Melodramas of Laurent Cantet: *Ressources humaines* (2000) and *Emploi du temps* (2001)," *French Cultural Studies* 15:3 (2004): 235–250.

Ince, Kate. "From Minor to 'Major' Cinema? Women's and Feminist Cinema in France in the 2000s," *Australian Journal of French Studies* XLV:3 (September-December 2008): 277–288.

Ireland, Susan. "Deviant Bodies: Corporeal Otherness in Contemporary Women's Writing," *Nottingham French Studies* 45:3 (Autumn 2006): 39–51.

Jäckel, Anne. "The Inter/Nationalism of French Film Policy," *Modern & Contemporary France* 15:1 (February 2000): 21–36.

Jordan, Shirley. "Close-up and Impersonal: Sexual/Textual Bodies in Contemporary French Women's Writing," *Nottingham French Studies* 45:3 (Autumn 2006): 8–28.

Jouve, Valérie, Sébastien Ors, and Philippe Tancelin. *Bruno Dumont*. Paris: Dis voir, 2001.

Keathley, Christian. *Cinephilia and History, or The Wind in the Trees*. Bloomington: Indiana University Press, 2006.

Kraidy, Marwan M. *Hybridity, or the Cultural Logic of Globalization*. Philadelphia: Temple University Press, 2005.

Krzywinska, Tanya. *Sex and the Cinema*. London: Wallflower Press, 2006.

Lamome, Stéphanie. "Girl Power," *Première* 366 (August 2007): 78–84.

Lanzoni, Rémi Fournier. *French Cinema From Its Beginnings to the Present*. New York: Continuum, 2004.

Levaco, Ronald, ed. and trans. *Kuleshov on Film: Writings of Lev Kuleshov*. Berkeley: University of California Press, 1974.

Lounas, Thierry. "Nous ne disons pas aux élèves quel cinéma faire: Entretien avec Marc Nicolas." *Cahiers du Cinéma* 615 (September 2006): 42–43.

MacDougall, David. *The Corporeal Image: Film, Ethnography and the Senses*. Princeton: Princeton University Press, 2006.

Maule, Rosanna. *Beyond Auteurism: New Directions in Authorial Film Practices in France, Italy and Spain since the 1980s*. Chicago: Intellect Press, 2008.

Mazdon, Lucy. *Encore Hollywood: Remaking French Cinema*. London: BFI, 2000.

———, ed., *France on Film: Reflections on Popular French Cinema*. London: Wallflower, 2001.

Michael, Charlie. "French National Cinema and the Martial Arts Blockbuster," *French Politics, Culture & Society* 23:3 (2005): 55–74.

Miller, Ann. *Reading* bande dessinée: *Critical Approaches to French-Language Comic Strip*. London: Intellect Books, 2007.

Murray Levine, Alison J. "Mapping *Beur* Cinema in the New Millennium." *Journal of Film and Video* 60.3–4 (Fall/Winter 2008): 42–59.

Neupert, Richard. *A History of the French New Wave Cinema*, 2nd.ed. Madison: University of Wisconsin Press, 2007.

———. "Kirikou and the Animated Figure/Body." *Studies in French Cinema* 8:1 (Spring 2008): 41–56.

O'Shaughnessy, Martin. *The New Face of Political Cinema: Commitment in French Film Since 1995*. London: Berghahn, 2007.

Palmer, Tim. "Exotic Aesthetics: Long Take Style and Staging in the Films of Mizoguchi and von Sternberg." Filmhäftet 122: 4 (July 2002): 1–6.

———. *"Le Samouraï,"* in Phil Powrie, ed., *The Cinema of France*. London: Wallflower, 2006.

———. "Style and Sensation in the Contemporary French Cinema of the Body." *Journal of Film and Video* 58:3 (Fall 2006): 22–32.

———. "Under Your Skin: Marina de Van and the Contemporary French *cinéma du corps,*" *Studies in French Cinema* 6:3 (Fall 2006): 171–181.

———. "Threading the Eye of the Needle: Contemporary French Pop-Art Cinema and Valeria Bruni Tedeschi's *Il est plus facile pour un chameau . . .*" In *France at the Flicks: Trends in Contemporary French Popular Cinema*. Waldron, Darren, and Isabelle Vanderschelden, eds. Newcastle: Cambridge Scholars Publishing, 2007.

———. "An Amateur of Quality: Postwar French Cinema and Jean-Pierre Melville's *Le Silence de la mer,*" *Journal of Film and Video* 59:4 (Winter 2007): 3–19.

———. "Paris, City of Shadows: French Crime Cinema Before the New Wave." *New Review of Film and Television Studies* 6:2 (August 2008): 113–131.

Palmer, Tim, and Liza Palmer. *"Les Enfants terribles*: An Interview with Françoise Marie." *Film International* 34 (Fall 2008): 94–98.

Pardo, Carlos. "Crime, pornographie et mépris du peuple: Des films français fascinés par le sordide." *Le Monde Diplomatique* 2.00 (February 2000): 28.

Powrie, Phil, ed. *French Cinema in the 1990s: Continuity and Difference*. Oxford: Oxford University Press, 1999.

———. "Unfamiliar Places: 'Heterospection' and Recent French Film on Children." *Screen* 46:3 (Autumn 2005): 341–352.

Prédal, Réné. *Le Jeune cinéma français*. Paris: Nathan, 2002.

———. *Le Cinéma français depuis 2000: Une renouvellement incessant*. Paris: Nathan, 2008.

Quandt, James. "Flesh and Blood: Sex and Violence in Recent French Cinema." *Artforum* 42:6 (2000): 24–27.

Ramanathan, Geetha. *Feminist Auteurs: Reading Women's Films*. London: Wallflower, 2006.

Rivi, Luisa. *European Cinema after 1989: Cultural Identity and Transnational Production*. New York: Palgrave Macmillan, 2007.

Rouyer, Philippe, and Claire Vassé. "Entretien: François Ozon, La vérité des corps," *Positif* 522/23 (July/August 2004): 41–45.

Satrapi, Marjane. *Persepolis: The Story of a Childhood*. New York: Pantheon, 2004. Originally published as *Persepolis 1* and *Persepolis 2*. Paris: L'Association, 2000; 2001.

———. *Persepolis: The Story of a Return*. New York: Pantheon, 2005. Originally published as *Persepolis 3* and *Persepolis 4*. Paris: L'Association, 2002; 2003.

Sellier, Geneviève. "French Women Making Films in the 1990s," in Céléstin, Roger, Eliane DalMolin, and Isabelle de Courtivron. eds. *Beyond French Feminisms: Debates on Women, Politics and Culture in France, 1981–2001*. New York: Palgrave Macmillan, 2003.

Serceau, Daniel. *Symptômes du jeune cinéma français*. Paris: Editions du cerf, 2008.

Sitney, P. Adams, ed. *The Avant-Garde Film: A Reader of Theory and Criticism*. New York: New York University Press, 1978.

———. *Modernist Montage: The Obscurity of Vision in Cinema and Literature*. New York: Columbia University Press, 1990.

Sowerwine, Charles. *France Since 1870: Culture, Society and the Making of the Republic*, 2nd. ed. New York: Palgrave Macmillan, 2009.

Sterritt, David. "Time Destroys All Things: An Interview with Gaspar Noé." *Quarterly Review of Film and Video* 24 (2007): 307–316.

Tarr, Carrie, with Brigitte Rollet. *Cinema and the Second Sex: Women's Filmmaking in France in the 1980s and 1990s*. New York: Continuum, 2001.

Tarr, Carrie. *Reframing Difference: Beur and Banlieue Filmmaking in France*. Manchester: Manchester University Press, 2005.

———. "Director's Cuts: The Aesthetics of Self-Harming in Marina de Van's *Dans ma peau*." *Nottingham French Studies* 45:3 (Fall 2006): 78–91.

Temple, Michael, and Michael Witt, eds. *The French Cinema Book*. London: BFI, 2004.

Vanderschelden, Isabelle. "Strategies for a 'Transnational'/French Popular Cinema." *Modern & Contemporary France* 15:1 (2007): 37–50.

———. "The '*Cinéma du Milieu*' Is Falling Down: New Challenges for Auteur and Independent French Cinema in the 2000s." *Studies in French Cinema* 9:3 (Fall 2009): 243–257.

Vincendeau, Ginette. "Women's Cinema, Film Theory, and Feminism in France." *Screen* 28:4 (1987): 4–18.

Waldron, Darren, and Isabelle Vanderschelden, eds. *France at the Flicks: Trends in Contemporary French Popular Cinema*. Newcastle: Cambridge Scholars Publishing, 2007.

West, Dennis, and Joan M. West, "Women, Beauty Parlors, and Love: An Interview with Tonie Marshall." *Cinéaste* 26:2 (March 2001): 29–31.

Williams, Linda. "Cinema and the Sex Act," *Cinéaste* 27:1 (Winter 2001): 20–25.

———. *Screening Sex*. Durham: Duke University Press, 2008.

Wilson, Emma. "*État présent*: Contemporary French Women Filmmakers," *French Studies* LIX:2 (2005): 217–223.

———. "Women Filming Children." *Nottingham French Studies* 45:3 (2006): 105–118.

———. "Miniature Lives, Intrusion and *Innocence*." *French Cultural Studies* 18:2 (2007): 169–183.

Wood, Robin. *Personal Views: Explorations in Film*. London: Gordon Fraser, 1976.

Film Reviews and Critical Commentaries from French-language Periodicals

Cahiers du cinema
Charlie-Hebdo
La Croix
Les Echos
L'Express
Le Figaro
Le Film français
France-soir
L'Humanité
Les Inrockuptibles
Le Journal de Dimanche
Libération
Le Monde
Le Nouvel Observateur
Le Point
Positif
Première
Studio
Télérama
La Tribune

Personal Interviews

Matthieu-David Cournot, July 11, 2008.
Marina de Van, August 26, 2004; April 3, 2005; July 14, 2008.
Lola Doillon, October 23, 2008.
Thomas Favel, July 10, 2008.
Noémie Gillot, August 21, 2008.
Julie Lopes-Curval, September 5, 2010.
Françoise Marie, March 30, 2008.
Arielle Pannetier, July 10, 2008.

INDEX

5x2, 6, 147; and art cinema, 121; and cinéma du corps, 62, 68
8 Femmes. See 8 Women
8 Women, 81, 141
9 Songs, 65
23 Quai du Commerce, 1080 Bruxelles. See Jeanne Dielman
35 Rhums. See 35 Shots of Rum
35 Shots of Rum, 121
36 Quai des Orfèvres, 117
37°2 le matin. See Betty Blue
99 Francs, 63, 108
The 400 Blows, 16, 24, 27, 35–36
Les 400 coups. See The 400 Blows

A Bout de souffle. See Breathless
L'Académie des Arts et Techniques du Cinéma. See French Film Academy
Academy Awards: and The Hurt Locker, 155; and Persepolis, 49
À ce soir, 42
action (genre), 115, 185
actor-filmmakers, 163, 226–27n52; Anne le Ny, 41–42, 227n60; Jean-Marc Barr, 64; Marina de Van, 43–44, 82–83, 201–2; Mia Hansen-Løve, 41–42; Valeria Bruni Tedeschi, 123–24, 125–32. See also critic-filmmakers
actorly (aesthetics), 43–45
Actresses, 6, 158, 236n46; analysis of, 128–31; and pop-art cinema, 98, 122
Actrices. See Actresses
actrices cinéastes. See actor-filmmakers
Adjadj, Marc, 84
Adler, Laure, 166

admissions (French), 49, 99, 100, 108–9, 118, 124, 154–56, 234n22, 235n38, 238–39n5
adolescence, 10, 23; in Ça brûle, 190; in Et toi, t'es sur qui?, 24–32, 225n30; and feminine cinema, 162, 165; in LOL (Laughing Out Loud), 156; in Persepolis, 48–50; in Water Lilies, 33–40. See also cinéma d'ado
adultery, 65, 72, 122, 123
aesthetics (cinematic): actorly, 43–45; aquarium, 140, 145; corporeal, 11, 39, 61, 77, 88–92, 158, 160, 213, 231n50; and female filmmakers, 167; gender inversion, 178–79, 182, 184, 190–91; hallucinatory, 180; home movie, 26; naturalism, 65, 66, 134, 137, 191, 199, 200; obsolescence, 53. See also digital video; expressionism; lyrical; neorealism; style
Agent 117 of the Office of Strategic Services, 108
Agents secrets, 101, 117
Aïe, 41
Aja, Alexandre, 133
Akerman, Chantal, 73, 160, 205
A l'intérieur. See Inside
All Is Forgiven, 11, 21, 41, 227n65; analysis of, 42–47
Almendros, Néstor, 191
Alnoy, Siegrid, 12, 120, 189, 192; and Our Children, 177–78; and She's One of Us, 178–84
Altmayer brothers (Nicolas and Eric), 109, 116

Amalric, Mathieu, 120, 129
Les Amants criminels. See Criminal Lovers
A ma soeur! See Fat Girl
Amélie, 174
L'Ami de mon ami. See Boyfriends and Girlfriends
L'Amoureuse, 123
Les Amours d'Astrée et Céladon. See The Romance of Astree and Celadon
Anatomy of Hell, 62, 63
animation (French), 51–52, 227–28n66. See also *bande dessinée*
Annaud, Jean-Jacques, 166
L'Année dernière à Marienbad. See Last Year at Marienbad
L'Annulaire. See The Ring Finger
Antichrist, 65
Antonioni, Michelangelo, 72, 120, 138
L'Appartement, 101
L'Après-midi de Monsieur Andesmas, 122
aquarium (aesthetics), 140, 145
Arbid, Danielle, 164
Argento, Dario, 171
Arnold, Martin, 210
art cinema, 11, 42, 68, 70– 72, 78, 229n5, 235n38; and *Actresses*, 130; and *cinéma du corps*, 153; and Claire Denis, 122; and *Demonlover*, 148; and *La France*, 139–40; and *Les Invisibles*, 186; and *It's Easier for a Camel . . .*, 124, 126; and Lucile Hadzihalilovic, 174; and popular cinema, 95, 98, 119–21, 124, 132, 137, 143, 146, 149, 162, 215; and *They Came Back*, 138; and women, 161. See also avant-garde cinema; lyrical
art et essai. See art cinema
Arthur (franchise), 115
L'Ascension du haut mal. See Epileptic
As If Nothing Happened, 85, 227n58
Assault on Precinct 13, 99
Assayas, Olivier, 4, 12, 41, 186, 239n18; and *cinéma du corps*, 58, 65, 81; as

critic-filmmaker, 195; and *Demonlover*, 143–49; and pop-art cinema, 98
L'Association, 49–50
L'Association des Directeurs de la Photographie Cinématographique (AFC), 204
Astérix (franchise), 118
Asterix at the Olympic Games, 100
Astérix aux Jeux Olympiques. See Asterix at the Olympic Games
Astérix et Obélix: Mission Clèopâtre, 118
A travers la forêt. See Through the Forest
Attal, Yvan, 123–24, 132
L'Auberge Espagnole, 23
Au Coeur du mensonge, 123
Audé, Françoise, 161, 162–63
Audiard, Jacques, 9, 132
audiences. *See* admissions; spectatorship
Audry, Jacqueline, 170
Auster, Paul, 184
Austin, Guy, 163
auteurism, 4, 19–22, 44, 51, 52, 54, 95, 98, 119–20, 122, 197; and avant-garde cinema, 163; and *cinéma du corps*, 69; and debutants, 164, 226n52; and feminine cinema, 164; and feminism, 163; and la Fémis, 79; and horror genre, 134–35; and Luc Besson, 114; and Olivier Assayas, 146, 147–48; and Valeria Bruni Tedeschi, 123, 127, 128, 132; and women, 155, 160–62, 163
autobiography: in *The 400 Blows*, 24; in *Actresses*, 128, 236n46; in *Innocence*, 241n45; in *It's Easier for a Camel . . .*, 123; and Laetitia Masson, 154; in *On the Ropes*, 178; in *Persepolis*, 49–50, 56; and popular cinema, 235n40; in *Water Lilies*, 35–36
avances sur recettes, 5, 16–17, 19, 21, 23, 148
avant-garde cinema, 184, 214, 231n50; and art cinema, 122; and auteurism,

163; and *cinéma du corps*, 59, 60, 64-65, 70, 76, 78, 84, 86-88, 93, 153; and cinephilia, 196; and *Demonlover*, 146; and found footage, 210; and *Innocence*, 173-74, 186; and Jean-Luc Godard, 182; and pop-art cinema, 124, 126; and women, 153, 154, 161. *See also* art cinema; lyrical
Azuelos, Lisa, 155-56, 239n5

Baby Blues, 154
Back and Forth, 76
Baffie, Laurent, 96, 97, 98, 107, 113, 114, 125, 127, 235n31; and cinephilia, 196
Bainbridge, Caroline, 168
Baise-moi, 57, 230n16; and *cinéma du corps*, 64, 67, 68
Le Baiser mortel du dragon. See *Kiss of the Dragon*
Balasko, Josiane, 154, 179, 238n5
Le Bal des actrices, 141, 237n67
bande dessinée, 49-50, 51, 53
Bangalter, Thomas, 39, 73
banlieue: cinema, 30, 99, 118, 179; riots in, 31, 237n57
Banlieue 13. See *District B13*
Banlieue 13: Ultimatum, 118, 235n31
Barbe bleue. See *Bluebeard*
Barney, Matthew, 67
Barougier, Pierre, 87
Barratier, Christophe, 105
Barr, Jean-Marc, 64
Battles Without Honor or Humanity (pentalogy), 105
La Baule-les-Pins, 123
Baye, Nathalie, 179
Bazin, André, 196-97
The Beaches of Agnes, 122
Béart, Emmanuelle, 155
Beauchard, David, 50
Le Beau Serge, 18
Beau Travail, 71

Beauty and the Beast, 70
Beauvois, Xavier, 32
Becker, Jacques, 9
Bégaudeau, François, 134
Beigbeder, Frédéric, 63
Beineix, Jean-Jacques, 18, 97, 235n31
Being Light: and *cinéma du corps*, 64
La Belle et la bête. See *Beauty and the Beast*
Bellour, Raymond, 166
Bellucci, Monica, 70; and *Irreversible*, 72, 88, 230n28; and Vincent Cassel, 101
Belmondo, Jean-Paul, 103
Bemelmans, Ludwig, 174
Bercot, Emmanuelle, 166, 205
Bergala, Alain, 206-7, 218
Bergman, Ingmar, 148, 209
Bernard, Patrick-Mario, 64
Bernard, Raymond, 139
Bernheim, Emmanuèle, 147
Berri, Claude, 96, 100
Bertolucci, Bernardo, 65
Bertrand, Diane, 4, 11; and *cinéma du corps*, 61, 120, 153-54; and *The Ring Finger*, 88-92
Besson, Luc, 7, 19, 114-16, 118, 119, 234n22, 239n18, 243n10
Betty Blue, 72, 97
Bibliothèque du Film (BiFi), 4, 205, 210, 224n15
The Big Blue, 114
Bigelow, Kathryn, 155
Bien sous tous rapports, 80
Bienvenue chez les Ch'tis. See *Welcome to the Land of the Chtis*
biopic (genre), 99, 107, 146
Birthday Girl, 101
Blame it on Fidel!, 47
Blaq Out, 198, 209
blockbusters: and genre films, 117; and Luc Besson, 116; and *Persepolis*, 49; and pop-art cinema, 98, 119

Bloody Mallory, 133

Bluebeard, 62

Blueberry. See *Renegade*

Blyton, Enid, 174

Boarding Gate, 143, 146

Boisson, Noëlle, 21

Bond, James (franchise), 108, 109, 111, 113

Bonello, Bertrand, 93

Boon, Dany, 118

Bord de mer. See *Seaside*

Bordwell, David, 4, 124, 196, 197, 226n51

La Bouche de Jean-Pierre, 169

Bouhnik, Laurent, 93

Bourdieu, Emmanuel, 205

boxing (genre), 178–79, 199

box office. See admissions

Boyfriends and Girlfriends, 36

Boys Don't Cry, 203

Bozon, Céline, 140, 237n64; and la Fémis, 202

Bozon, Serge, 4, 12, 237n65; as critic-filmmaker, 195; and *La France*, 138–43, 212; and pop-art cinema, 98, 146, 147, 149

Brakhage, Stan, 59, 64–65, 76, 87, 173–74, 186, 231n50

Breathless (1960), 15, 16, 18, 39, 103, 232n4

Brechtian effects, 121, 141–42

Bréhat, Jean, 78

Breillat, Catherine, 31, 64, 229n13; as author, 63; and *Baise-moi*, 230n16; and *cinéma du corps*, 58, 61–62, 66, 68; and feminine cinema, 163, 165; on women in the film industry, 153

Breitman, Zabou, 41

Bresson, Robert, 203, 206, 208; and *La France*, 139–40; influence on Céline Sciamma, 34, 36, 37, 226n44

Brève traversée. See *Brief Crossing*

Brice de Nice, 2, 107–9, 118, 233n15

Brief Crossing, 62

Brillat, Xavier, 64

Brisseau, Jean-Claude, 93

Brodeuses. See *Sequins*

Les Bronzés 3: Amis pour la vie, 118

Brotherhood of the Wolf, 101, 116–19

The Brown Bunny, 65

Bruce, Jean, 108

Bruni Tedeschi, Valeria, 12, 192; and *Actresses*, 128–31, 158, 168; and feminine cinema, 166, 168; and *It's Easier for a Camel . . .*, 123–28, 168, 241n45; and pop-art cinema, 98, 122, 132, 134, 142, 146, 147, 149, 153, 164, 189, 236n46; and the *Tournées*, 177

Buchsbaum, Jonathan, 7

Buet, Jackie, 164–65, 172, 175

Buñuel, Luis, 205, 206, 218

Burgeau, Jean-Pol, 71

Butler, Alison, 168

Cabrera, Dominique, 163

Ça brûle, 190–92

Cahiers du cinéma, 41, 47, 60, 119, 122, 147, 148, 197, 206

cameos, 41; directorial, 39–40

Caméra d'or, 18

camera movement. See long takes; techniques

Campillo, Robin, 12; and pop-art cinema, 98, 142, 146, 147, 149; and *They Came Back*, 132–38; and *Time Out*, 179

Camping, 118

Campion, Jane, 71, 160

Camus, Isabelle, 107

Canal+, 5–6, 8, 10, 148, 169, 236n55

Canet, Guillaume, 185

Cannes Film Festival, 18; Actors-Turned-Directors series, 42; and *Actresses*, 132; and *La Bouche de Jean-Pierre*, 169; and *cinéma du corps*, 59, 61, 65, 69; and *The Class*, 134;

and *Demonlover*, 144, 148; and la
Fémis, 205; and François Ozon, 62;
International Critics Week series, 18;
and *Irreversible*, 69; and *Persepolis*, 49,
56. See also *Caméra d'or*; *Un Certain
Regard*
Cantet, Laurent, 18, 134, 179
captions. *See* dialogue
La Captive, 205
Caramel, 164
Caravaca, Eric, 42
Carion, Christian, 132, 185
Car Keys, 96, 104, 107, 113, 123, 125, 127,
196
Carlos, 146
Carne, 169
Carné, Marcel, 203
Carpenter, John, 147
Carrière, Christine, 157-60, 202
Carrière, Jean-Claude, 206
Carron, Cheyenne, 164, 165
Cassatt, Mary, 171
Cassel, Jean-Pierre, 101
Cassel, Vincent, 11, 108, 233n10; in
Irreversible, 72, 88, 230n28; and the
Mesrine franchise, 98, 99-107, 109,
111, 233n9, 233nn11-12
Cat People, 70
Catwoman, 118
Cavayé, Fred, 186
celluloid, 64, 76, 87, 140, 145, 164, 174,
200, 203, 205, 208, 212
censorship, 68, 228n69, 230n16; and
cinéma du corps, 67
Centre National de la Cinématographie
(CNC), 5, 6, 7, 10, 16, 19, 20, 95, 116,
117, 119, 132, 161, 177, 232n2, 235n38
Centre Pompidou, 166
Un Certain Regard, 18, 169
César Awards, 8, 11, 18, 43; Best First
Film, 18, 21, 42, 154, 164, 166,
240n20; and Isabelle Mergault, 154;

and Marina Foïs, 157; and the Mesrine
franchise, 99; and Mia Hansen-Løve,
41; and *Persepolis*, 48, 56; and *Pour
elle*, 186; and *Séraphine*, 107; and
Ursula Meier, 236n51, 240n20; and
Valeria Bruni Tedeschi, 123
Cette femme-là, 117
Ceux qui restent. See *Those Who Remain*
CGI, 52-54, 93, 97, 118
Chabrol, Claude, 18, 123
La Chambre des officiers. See *The Officer's
Ward*
Les Chansons d'amour. See *Love Songs*
Chatonsky, Grégory, 210
La Chatte à deux têtes. See *Porn Theatre*
Chéreau, Patrice, 2; and *cinéma du corps*,
65, 68; and *Gabrielle*, 121; and Valeria
Bruni Tedeschi, 123, 128
children: in *La Bouche de Jean-Pierre*,
169; in contemporary French cinema,
46-47, 240-41n38; and feminine
cinema, 167; in *Our Children*, 177-78;
point of view, 26, 47-48, 167, 169, 176
Children of Paradise, 203
Chirac, Jacques, 167
The Choir, 175
Chomet, Sylvain, 52
Les Choristes. See *The Choir*
A Christmas Tale, 201, 227n58
Chrysalis, 117
Chytilová, Vera, 84
Ciboire de Criss!, 50
Ciment, Michel, 20
cineliteracy, 3, 13, 21, 41, 195, 196; and
cinéma du corps, 69-70; and la Fémis,
79, 206; and the French film industry,
196; and Lola Doillon, 23; and Lucile
Hadzihalilovic, 176; and Marina de
Van, 78; and Olivier Assayas, 147; and
Persepolis, 52; and pop-art cinema, 96,
98. *See also* cinephilia
Cinema and the Second Sex, 161-62

cinéma d'ado (genre), 24, 33–34
Cinéma d'elles, 162–63
cinéma du corps, 11, 31, 57–93, 120–22,
    153, 182; and Bruno Dumont, 185;
    critical reception of, 60, 66–70,
    230n15; definition of, 57; and
    Demonlover, 145, 146; and Diane
    Bertrand, 153–54; and Flanders, 139;
    and Innocence, 175; and Les Invisibles,
    186; and Lucile Hadzihalilovic, 174;
    and Vincent Cassel, 100
cinéma du look, 2, 18, 97, 114, 144
le cinéma gore (genre), 133
cinéma rural (genre), 185, 187
Les Cinémas de la Zone, 169
Cinémathèque Française, 4, 166, 205,
    242n4
cinephilia, 3, 12, 23, 34, 106, 109, 156,
    242n4; and Anne le Ny, 41–42;
    and cinéma du corps, 58–59; and la
    Fémis, 217; and Marjane Satrapi, 54;
    and Olivier Assayas, 146, 147; and
    practice, 195–215. See also cineliteracy
City of Lights, City of Angels (COLCOA),
    106–7
Civeyrac, Jean Paul, 12, 243n24; and
    Céline Bozon, 140; and cinephilia, 195,
    208–10; and Through the Forest, 208,
    210–14, 244n29
Clark, Larry, 67
The Class, 134
Classe tous risques, 103
Clean, 143
La clef. See The Key
Les Clefs de bagnole. See Car Keys
Cléo de 5 à 7. See Cleo from 5 to 7
Cleo from 5 to 7, 172
Cliente. See A French Gigolo
The Closet, 118
Clouzot, Henri-Georges, 133
Club des 13, 9–10, 240n20
Cocteau, Jean, 70, 204, 209

Cold Water, 146
Colin, Dominique, 187
Collectif Jeune Cinéma, 17
Colombani, Laetitia, 154, 155, 238n5
comedy (genre), 11, 47, 95, 107–9, 116,
    118, 154, 155, 162, 185, 196, 232n5
Comment je me suis disputé . . . [ma vie
    sexuelle]. See My Sex Life . . . or How I
    Got into an Argument
commercial cinema. See popular cinema
Comme si de rien n'était. See As If Nothing
    Happened
communication: in Et toi, t'es sur qui?,
    27–28, 225n30; in Water Lilies, 34–35;
    in Twentynine Palms, 74
compte de soutien, 5
Conner, Bruce, 210
conspiracy thriller (genre). See suspense
    thriller
Constantine, Eddie, 113
Un Conte de Noël. See A Christmas Tale
Conway, Kelley, 166–67
corporeal (aesthetics), 11, 39, 61, 77, 88–
    92, 158, 160, 213, 231n50
The Corporeal Image, 176
Corps à corps, 117
Cotillard, Marion, 100, 170, 192
Cournot, Matthieu-David, 204
Crash, 86
Craven, Wes, 133
crédit d'impôt, 6, 8
Créteil International Women's Film
    Festival, 164
Creton, Laurent, 7
Crime on a Summer Morning, 103
crime thriller (genre), 11, 95, 100, 107.
    See also policier
Criminal Lovers, 62, 81
Crimson Rivers, 116
Criterion, 198
critic-filmmakers, 148, 195
La Croix, 135

Les Croix de bois. See Wooden Crosses
Cronenberg, David, 86
Cultural Exception, 1–2, 114
Cultural Services of French Embassy, 132,
    177
culture (French): and Agnès Varda, 167;
    continuation of, 93; death of, 1–2;
    as export, 177; and feminine cinema,
    166; as industry, 184; and It's Easier
    for a Camel . . ., 126–27; and Musée
    haut, musée bas, 97; and popular
    cinema, 232n1. See also film
Culturesfrance, 1
Curiol, Céline, 64, 183–84, 189

Dagoit, Marie-Laure, 63
Dahan, Olivier, 93
Daisies, 84
Dalle, Béatrice, 72, 74
Les Dames du Bois du Boulogne, 203
Dancing, 57, 64
Dans les cordes. See On the Ropes
Dans ma peau. See In My Skin
Dante 01, 39, 117
Darling, 157, 167, 168, 173, 188, 191;
    analysis of, 158–60
Darrieussecq, Marie, 64, 179
D'Arvor, Olivier Poivre, 1
Days of Heaven, 191
De Baecque, Antoine, 196–98, 214
De Beauvoir, Simone, 151
Debie, Benoît, 75–76, 174–76
debutants, 10–11, 15–21, 31, 42–43,
    46–48, 51–52, 54, 69, 106, 153, 214,
    225–26n38, 227n65; and Anne le Ny,
    44; and auteurism, 164, 226n52; and
    autobiography, 24, 35–36; and Céline
    Sciamma, 34–36, 39–40; and Eléonore
    Faucher, 200; and experimentation,
    120; and feminine cinema, 164,
    165, 167; and la Fémis, 205; and
    Lola Doillon, 21–24, 26; and Lucile

Hadzihalilovic, 170, 171, 176; and
    Marina de Van, 78; and Mia Hansen-
    Løve, 44, 45; and sexism, 154. See
    also jeune cinéma
Deep in the Woods, 133
Déjà fait, 23
De l'amour, 99
De Laubier, Jean-Baptiste. See ParaOne
Delbosc, Olivier, 6
Demi-tarif. See Half Price
Demonlover, 57, 181; analysis of, 143–46;
    and cinéma du corps, 65, 81; critical
    reception of, 146–47; and pop-art
    cinema, 147–49
Demy, Mathieu, 185
Deneuve, Catherine, 155, 201,
    228n66
Denis, Claire, 4, 11, 239n18; and
    aesthetics, 229n4; and Agnès
    Godard, 174; and art cinema, 122;
    and cineliteracy, 69–70, 229n5; and
    cinéma du corps, 58–61, 73, 78, 81, 89,
    120, 121, 153; and dialogue, 235n37;
    and feminine cinema, 162–65; and
    Friday Night, 127; and Olivier Assayas,
    147; and Trouble Every Day, 71, 77,
    81; and use of dialogue, 74; and use
    of lighting, 74–75; and Valeria Bruni
    Tedeschi, 123
Depardieu, Julie, 192
Deren, Maya, 38, 160
Despentes, Virginie, 64
Desplechin, Arnaud, 79, 186; and
    cinephilia, 201
Les Destinées, 41, 146
Les Destinées sentimentales. See Les
    Destinées
Destricted, 67
Deux filles, 23
Deux ou trois choses que je sais d'elle.
    See Two or Three Things I Know
    About Her

De Van, Marina, 11, 43–44, 192; on being a female filmmaker, 160, 161; and *cinéma du corps*, 58, 61, 79–80, 89, 120, 153; and cinephilia, 201–2; and la Fémis, 78–79, 203; and François Ozon, 80–81; and *In My Skin*, 81–88, 231n50

Devers, Claire, 163

Les Diables, 47, 241n38

Les Diaboliques, 133

dialogue (cinematic), 235n37; in *Actresses*, 129–31; in *All Is Forgiven*, 44–46; in *Car Keys*, 96; and Claire Denis, 71; in *Darling*, 157, 159; in *Déjà fait*, 23; in *Demonlover*, 143; in *Ecoute le temps*, 189; in *Et toi, t'es sur qui?*, 26–31, 34; in *La France*, 138, 141; in *Gabrielle*, 121; in *In My Skin*, 82; in *Innocence*, 173, 175; *L'Instinct de mort*, 105, 106, 233n11; in *It's Easier for a Camel . . .*, 125–28; in *LOL (Laughing Out Loud)*, 156; in *OSS 117: Cairo, Nest of Spies*, 110; in *OSS 117: Lost in Rio*, 112, 113; in *Our Children*, 177–78; in *Persepolis*, 50, 53, 55, 228–29n66; in *Le Plaisir . . . (et ses petits tracas)*, 101; in *Un Pur esprit*, 47; in *The Ring Finger*, 91, 92; and the roles of Marina de Van, 81; in *She's One of Us*, 182; in *They Came Back*, 133, 136; in *Those Who Remain*, 44; in *Through the Forest*, 212; in *Toi et Moi*, 193; in *Trouble Every Day*, 74; in *Twentynine Palms*, 74; in *Water Lilies*, 34, 36, 37–38, 40. *See also* communication; slang

Digital Factory, 115

digital video (DV), 26, 47; and *Car Keys*, 96; and *cinéma du corps*, 64; and *Demonlover*, 145; and la Fémis, 205; and Jean Paul Civeyrac, 208, 211–14; and Laetitia Masson, 154; and Marina de Van, 86–87

District B13, 118

Diva, 18, 97

divorce: in *5x2*, 121; in *All Is Forgiven*, 45–47; in France, 43, 151; in *A French Gigolo*, 179; in *Intimacy*, 65; in *Persepolis*, 50. *See also* marriage

Dobermann, 97, 117

Dogma, 142

Dog Star Man, 87

Doillon, Jacques, 21–22, 123

Doillon, Lola, 11, 21–32, 36, 41, 44, 50, 71, 156, 192, 225nn26–27, 225n38

domestic drama (genre), 64, 146, 162, 165, 178–79

domesticity, 34, 41– 43, 45, 46, 131, 137, 155, 162, 165, 178, 181, 185, 186, 190, 199, 244n29

domestic thriller (genre). *See* suspense thriller

Doucet, Julie, 50

Le Doulos, 103

Le Doux amour des hommes, 209

The Dreamers, 65

Ducastel, Olivier, 141

Dugowson, Martine, 163

Dujardin, Jean, 2, 11, 233nn15–16; and the OSS 117 franchise, 98, 106–14, 126

Dumont, Bruno, 11, 18, 31, 57, 179; and cineliteracy, 70, 229n5; and *cinéma du corps*, 58–61, 65–67, 73, 78, 81, 120, 185; and cinematography, 75; and *Flanders*, 139; and *Twentynine Palms*, 71, 77; and use of dialogue, 74

Duras, Marguerite, 122, 163, 164

Duthillel, Laure, 42

Du Weltz, Fabrice, 174

Eastern Promises, 101

L'Eau froide. *See Cold Water*

ecocriticism, 187, 190, 191–92

L'Ecole Louis-Lumière, 195, 203, 204, 243n10

L'Ecole Nationale Supérieure des Métiers de l'Image et du Son. *See* La Fémis

Ecorchés, 164

Ecoute le temps, 184–92

Eden Log, 117

editing: in *Irreversible*, 76; in *She's One of Us*, 181, 182; in *Trouble Every Day*, 72; in *Ugetsu*, 211. *See also* long takes; techniques

Eisenstein, Sergei, 206

The Elementary Particles, 63

Elig, Raphael, 39

Elizabeth Films, 148

Elle est des nôtres. See *She's One of Us*

Elsaesser, Thomas, 198

empirical cinema, 60

L'Emploi du temps. See *Time Out*

Enemy of the State, 147

Les Enfants du paradis. See *Children of Paradise*

Les Enfants terribles, 209

Enfin veuve, 154

L'Ennemi public no. 1, 98, 99, 107; analysis of, 102–3. *See also* Mesrine

Entre les murs. See *The Class*

Ephron, Nora, 155

Epileptic, 50

Erice, Victor, 171

erotic thriller (genre). *See* suspense thriller

Espion/s, 117

L'Esquive, 30

Estrougo, Audrey, 30, 164–66, 179

Etre et avoir, 47, 241n38

Et toi, t'es sur qui?, 11, 21–22, 36, 46–47, 52, 156, 225n30; analysis of, 24–32; and long takes, 225nn26–27

EuropaCorp, 115, 116, 118, 185

experimentation. *See* avant-garde cinema

L'Express, 152

expressionism: and *Mine-Haha, or The Corporeal Education of Young Girls*, 170; and *Persepolis*, 54–55

The Eye, 133

Eyes Without a Face, 133

Fantômes, 208

Farrugia, Dominique, 96

Fassio, Anne, 47, 164

Fat Girl, 62, 68

Faubourg 36, 105

Faucher, Eléonore, 177; and cinephilia, 200

Faucon, Bernard, 171

La Faute à Fidel. See *Blame it on Fidel!*

Fear(s) of the Dark, 52

feminine cinema, 12, 21, 153–93; and la Fémis, 204; and *Water Lilies*, 35. *See also* feminism; women

feminine cinematics, 168. *See also* aesthetics; style

feminism, 192; and auteurism, 163; and *Daisies*, 84; in *Darling*, 157–58; and film, 156, 162; in France, 151–52; and icons, 165, 167; and *In My Skin*, 83; in *Julie and Julia*, 155; in *LOL (Laughing Out Loud)*, 156; in *Persepolis*, 50–51; and *Romance*, 62; and scholars, 161, 163, 167. *See also* feminine cinema; women

La Fémis, 12, 21, 34, 41, 86, 93, 169, 218, 243n14, 243n22; and Céline Bozon, 140; and Céline Sciamma, 32, 39; and cinephilia, 195, 202–8; and Claire Simon, 190; and debutants, 153; and Emmanuèlle Bernheim, 147; and Jacques Fieschi, 147; and Jean Paul Civeyrac, 208, 209; and Laetitia Masson, 154; and Marina de Van, 79, 80; and Philippe Garrel, 244n29

Ferran, Pascale, 8–9, 166, 241n49

Ferreira Barbosa, Laurence, 123

Festival des Cinémas Différents, 17

Fidélité Films, 6

Fieschi, Jacques, 147

The Fifth Element, 116

Fight Club, 147

Fillières, Sophie, 41, 127, 132, 192; and
    la Fémis, 205

film (French): and culture, 93, 98, 115,
    122, 161, 186, 204, 217; and identity,
    116, 119; and misogyny, 156. *See also*
    culture; film industry

Le Film français, 4, 7 8, 10, 21, 49; and
    feminine cinema, 165–66

film industry (French): and cineliteracy,
    196; contemporary, 5–10, 61,
    115–19, 234n25, 234n27; and la
    Fémis, 205-6, 209; and the North
    American industry, 133–34, 155,
    161, 239n10; and sexism, 165; and
    state intervention, 169; and women,
    153–54, 156, 161–62, 164, 176, 192,
    239n11

films du milieu, 9–10

Film socialisme, 122

Film Society of Lincoln Center, 42

Fin août, début septembre. See *Late
    August, Early September*

Fincher, David, 147

first-time filmmakers. *See* debutants

Fissures. See *Ecoute le temps*

Flanders, 139

Flandres. See *Flanders*

Foïs, Marina, 157, 160

Fontaine, Anne, 154, 238n5

formalism: and *cinéma du corps*, 59, 65,
    66, 78, 86, 87; in *Innocence*, 174

Forman, Milos, 206

Les Fragments d'Antonin, 139

Fraisse, Geneviève, 152

La France, 2, 145, 180, 212, 237n64;
    analysis of, 138–42

Franju, Georges, 133

Frédéric, Léon, 171

French American Cultural Exchange
    (FACE), 132, 177

French culture. *See* culture (French)

French film. *See* film (French)

French Film Academy, 10, 18, 48

A French Gigolo, 179

French literature. *See* literature

French New Wave. *See* New Wave

Friday Night, 127, 147

friendship: in *Et toi, t'es sur qui?*, 24–27;
    in *Water Lilies*, 33, 37

From Here to Eternity, 112

From Paris with Love, 116

Frontière/s, 133, 185, 236–37n57

Fukasaku, Kinji, 105

Fuller, Samuel, 70, 139

Furia à Bahia pour OSS 117, 113

Gabrielle, 2, 121, 142

Gallo, Vincent: as director, 65; in *Trouble
    Every Day*, 72

Gance, Abel, 133, 139

Gangsters, 117

Gans, Christophe, 79, 133

Garcia, Nicole, 154, 238n5

Gardiens de l'ordre, 117

Garrel, Louis, 129, 244n29

Un Gars, une fille, 107

Gaumont, 109, 115

Gavras, Julie, 47

gay: characters, 208; nightclubs, 72;
    relationships, 64

gaze: and cinephilia, 199; female, 168;
    male, 167, 190–91

gender: and *cinéma du corps*, 67, 83; and
    clichés, 154; and filmmaking, 161, 163,
    165; in France, 152, 192; in *Innocence*,
    172; and *It's Easier for a Camel . . .*, 128

gender inversion (aesthetics), 178–79,
    182, 184, 190–91

General Agreement on Tariffs and Trade
    (GATT), 7, 114

genre (cinematic): action, 115, 185; biopic,
    99, 107, 146; boxing, 178–79, 199;

cinéma d'ado, 24, 33–34; cinéma gore, 133; cinéma rural, 185, 187; comedy, 11, 47, 95, 107–9, 116, 118, 154, 155, 162, 185, 196, 232n5; crime thriller, 11, 95, 100, 107; domestic drama, 64, 146, 162, 165, 178–79; filmmaking, 179, 184, 243n22; heritage, 62, 118, 146, 162; horror, 133–36, 138, 175, 236n55; musical, 140–41; policier, 11, 95, 100, 103, 107, 116, 117, 133, 162, 187, 232nn4–5; road movie, 64, 141, 162, 236n51; romantic comedy, 192–93; spy thriller, 110, 117; suspense thriller, 57, 62, 65, 97, 107, 117, 133–35, 143–47, 174, 184–89, 236n55, 238n73; war, 138–42, 237–38n68

genre d'ados. See cinéma d'ado

Les Gens normaux n'ont rien d'exceptionnel, 123

Gentile, Mary, 168

Gentille, 127

German expressionism. See expressionism

Gershon, Gina, 144

Giannoli, Xavier, 93, 148

Gimel, Augustin, 17

Girerd, Jacques-Rémy, 52

The Girl from Paris, 185

globalization, 27, 117; and animation, 227–28n66; in Demonlover, 143, 146; and film festivals, 65; French resistance to, 1–2

Godard, Agnès, 74–75, 174

Godard, Jean-Luc, 15, 18, 39, 122, 142, 182, 206, 218, 232n4

Go Fast, 117

Good Men, Good Women, 204–5

gothic, 171, 172

Gothika, 133, 236n55

Graine de star, 107

Le Grand bleu. See The Big Blue

Grand détournement, 109

La Grande illusion, 139

Grandrieux, Philippe, 235n37; and cinéma du corps, 58, 64–67, 120

La Grande vadrouille, 118

Grangier, Gilles, 114

Green, Eugène, 140

Guy, Alice, 160

Hadzihalilovic, Lucile, 12, 35, 120, 182, 192; and Innocence, 168–77, 241nn45–46, 241n50

La Haine. See Hate

Half Price, 26, 47

Halin, Jean-François, 109, 110

hallucinatory (aesthetics), 180

Haneke, Michael, 96

Hansen-Løve, Mia, 11, 21, 41–48, 227n65

Happy Memories, 41

Harry Potter (franchise), 174

Harry un ami qui vous veut du bien. See With a Friend Like Harry

Hate, 30, 237n57; and Vincent Cassel, 101, 232–33n8, 233n12

Haute tension. See High Tension

Hawks, Howard, 178, 206; influence on Anne le Ny, 42, 44

Hayward, Susan, 95

Hazanavicius, Michel, 109–11, 126

Heading South, 134

Les Herbes folles. See Wild Grass

heritage (genre), 62, 118, 146, 162

L'Heure d'été. See Summer Hours

Higbee, Will, 67, 134

High Tension, 133

The Hills Have Eyes, 133

Une Hirondelle a fait le printemps. See The Girl from Paris

His Girl Friday, 178

L'Histoire de Richard O., 57, 120

Hitchcock, Alfred, 109, 113, 210

home movie (aesthetics), 26

Homer, 206

Un Homme perdu, 164

homosexuality. *See* gay; lesbianism

Honoré, Christophe: and *cinéma du corps*, 93; and *Love Songs*, 141; and pop-art cinema, 132, 146

La Horde, 133

horror (genre), 133–36, 138, 175, 236n55

Hôtel de France, 123

Hou. *See* Hsiao Hsien, Hou

Houellebecq, Michel, 63

Hsiao-Hsien, Hou, 148, 204–5

Humains, 133

Humanité. See Humanity

Humanity, 61

Human Resources, 18, 134

Huppert, Isabelle, 121

The Hurt Locker, 155

Huth, James, 108, 233n15

hybrid (cinematic): and *cinéma du corps*, 78; and *La France*, 139–40; and genre filmmaking, 133; and pop-art cinema, 98, 117; and Valeria Bruni Tedeschi, 98, 124

identity vertigo. See *vertige identitaire*

The Idiots, 65

L'Ile et elle, 166

Il est plus facile pour un chameau. See *It's Easier for a Camel . . .*

Ils, 133, 185

Immortel (ad vitam), 117

Ince, Kate, 167

In My Skin, 2, 44, 181; analysis of, 81–82, 84–88; audience response to, 83–84; and *cinéma du corps*, 57, 78, 89, 91; and cinephilia, 201–2

Innocence, 35, 120, 168, 169, 186–88, 191, 241n45; analysis of, 171–77; critical reception of, 170–71

Les Inrockuptibles, 124, 156

Inside, 133

The Insider, 147

L'Instinct de mort, 98, 99, 107, 110, 111,

114, 233n11; analysis of, 102–6; and cinephilia, 199. *See also* Mesrine

Institut des hautes études cinématographiques (IDHEC), 79, 169, 195, 203, 205

Institut Lumière, 75

International Federation of Film Critics, 176

In the Realm of the Senses, 68

Intimacy, 57; and *cinéma du corps*, 65, 68, 120

Intimité. See Intimacy

Les Invisibles, 147, 186

Irigaray, Luce, 168

Irma Vep, 146

Irreversible, 39, 57, 179; analysis of, 72–77; audience response to, 59, 229n7; and *cinéma du corps*, 61, 67, 68, 70, 81, 87, 88, 91, 92; cinematography in, 75–76; and *Demonlover*, 146; narrative design, 71, 121; premiere at Cannes, 69; and production method, 64; sound in, 73–74; and Vincent Cassel, 100

Irréversible. See Irreversible

I Stand Alone, 67, 169

Italian neorealism. *See* neorealism

It's Easier for a Camel . . ., 241n45; analysis of, 123–28; and pop-art cinema, 98, 122, 130, 132

J'Accuse, 139

Jäckel, Anne, 119

Jaoui, Agnès, 154, 166, 238–39n5

Jeanne and the Perfect Guy, 141

Jeanne Dielman, 73

Jeanne et le garcon formidable. See Jeanne and the Perfect Guy

Jean-Philippe, 203

Je déteste les enfants des autres, 47, 164, 185

jeune cinéma, 3–4, 10–11, 15–21, 24, 32; and *All Is Forgiven*, 41; and *Et toi, t'es sur qui?*, 28–29; and *Those Who Remain*, 41; and *Water Lilies*, 34. *See also* debutants

Jeunet, Jean-Pierre, 19, 117, 139, 140, 174

Je vais bien, ne t'en fais pas, 42–43

Je vous trouve très beau, 154, 240n20

Jousse, Thierry, 186

Joyeux Noël. See *Merry Christmas*

Les Justes, 167

Kafka, Franz, 179, 227n60

Karina, Anna, 182

Karouby, Annabel, 107

Kassovitz, Mathieu, 19, 30; and *cinéma du corps*, 66; and *Gothika*, 133, 236n55; and *Hate*, 237n57

Kavaïté, Alanté, 184–90, 192, 242n62

Keathley, Christian, 196–99

Kechiche, Abdellatif, 30

Kessler, David, 119

The Key, 117, 186

Kirokou and the Sorceress, 52, 53

Kirokou et la sorcière. See *Kirokou and the Sorceress*

Kiss of the Dragon, 117

Klapisch, Cédric, 23, 132

Kounen, Jan, 63, 97

Kristeva, Julia, 83

Kubrick, Stanley, 70

Kuleshov, Lev, 38, 226n49

Kuroneko, 134

Kurosawa, Akira, 175

Kurys, Diane, 123, 163, 164

Labaki, Nadine, 164

Labrune, Jeanne, 163

Un Lac. See *A Lake*

Lady Chatterley, 8, 241n49

A Lake, 64–65

Lang, Fritz, 218

Lang, Jack, 6

Langmann, Thomas, 100, 102, 105, 116

language. *See* communication; dialogue; slang

The Last Mistress, 62

Last Year at Marienbad, 121

Late August, Early September, 41

Late Spring, 121

Leaving, 42

Le Besco, Isild, 26, 47

Le Besco, Maïwenn, 132, 141, 166, 192, 237n67, 241n45

Leçons de mise en scène, 206

Leconte, Patrice, 41, 132

Ledoyen, Virginie, 174–75

Lemming, 42

Lenoir, Denis, 145

Le Ny, Anne, 11, 21, 41–47, 165, 227n58

Leone, Sergio, 105

Le Pêcheur, Didier, 93

Le Pogam, Pierre-Ange, 115

lesbianism, 33, 37–38

Leterrier, Louis, 115

La Lettre du cinéma, 138

Lewis, C. S., 174

Lewton, Val, 133

Libération, 66, 119, 143; and chauvinism, 156

Lioret, Philippe, 42–43

literature (French), 63

Livret de phamille, 50

LOL (Laughing Out Loud), 155–56, 239n5

Un Long dimanche de fiançailles. See *A Very Long Engagement*

long takes: in *5x2*, 121; in *Actresses*, 131; in *Ça brûle*, 191; and Catherine Breillat, 62; in *Et toi, t'es sur qui?*, 26, 32, 225nn26–27; in *Innocence*, 172–73, 174; in *Irreversible*, 77, 88; in *Porn Theatre*, 65; in *She's One of Us*, 182; in *Through the Forest*, 210–14; in *Twentynine Palms*, 72–73; in *Water Lilies*, 36–37

Lopes-Curval, Julie, 18, 156, 177, 192–93

Lovers, 64
Love Songs, 141
Lubitsch, Ernst, 209
Lucas, George, 148
Lucky Luke, 108
Lvovsky, Noémie, 79, 123, 128, 129, 154, 166, 239n5; and la Fémis, 202, 205
Lynch, David, 96, 144
lyrical (style). and 35 Shots of Rum, 121–22; and Ça brûle, 191; and cinéma du corps, 88–89, 120; and cinephilia, 196, 198, 209; and Darling, 158–60; and Ecoute le temps, 188, 190; and feminine cinema, 168; and In My Skin, 86; and Innocence, 171; and popular cinema, 215; and The Ring Finger, 90–91; and Through the Forest, 211–13. See also art cinema; avant-garde cinema

Ma 6-T va crack-er, 30, 99
MacDougall, David, 176
Mackenzie, David, 65
Madeline (children's series), 174
La Main du diable, 133
mainstream cinema. See popular cinema
Maïwenn. See Le Besco, Maïwenn
Majorettes, 23
Maléfique, 133
Malick, Terrence, 191
Ma mère, 57
Mann, Michael, 147
Mann, Sally, 171
Marceau, Sophie, 156
Marchand, Corinne, 172
Mariages!, 107, 239n5
Marie, Françoise, 195
marriage: in All Is Forgiven, 45–46; in Darling, 157; in France, 43; in Gabrielle, 121; in It's Easier for a Camel . . ., 127; in Persepolis, 50; in Those Who Remain, 45–46. See also divorce

Marshall, Tonie, 151, 164
Martineau, Jacques, 141
Martyrs, 133
masculinity, 35, 63, 108, 110, 111, 134, 163, 178, 185–86, 188, 192; in Ecoute le temps, 189–90. See also men
The Mask of Horror, 133
Le Masque d'horreur. See The Mask of Horror
Masson, Laetitia, 154, 163, 205
Masters of Cinema, 198
Matisse, Henri, 214
Maule, Rosanna, 115, 148, 163, 239n18
Megaton, Olivier, 115
Melville, Jean-Pierre, 16, 23, 40, 206, 237n64
memory, 61, 89, 90, 109, 244n29
men: and banlieue cinema, 179; in Ecoute le temps, 189–90; in Et toi, t'es sur qui?, 25; in the films of Catherine Breillat, 62; in Innocence, 175; in Mes stars et moi, 155; in Persepolis, 50, 56; and popular cinema, 12, 155, 156, 167, 179, 184–86, 190, 192; in Tell No One, 188; in Water Lilies, 35. See also masculinity
Menu, Jean-Christophe, 50
Mères et filles, 156
Mergault, Isabelle, 154, 240n20
Merrill's Marauders, 139
Merry Christmas, 139
Mesrine (franchise), 11, 233n9, 233n11; and popular cinema, 98, 99–107, 109, 110, 114, 115
The Messenger: The Story of Joan of Arc, 101
Mes stars et moi, 155, 156, 168
The Metamorphosis, 179
"Metaphors on Vision," 173–74
La Meute. See The Pack
Michael, Charlie, 17, 116
Miller, Claude, 9, 41

Millet, Catherine, 63

Mimi, 190

Mine-Haha, or The Corporeal Education of Young Girls, 170, 241n50

minimalism: in *Innocence*, 174; and *It's Easier for a Camel . . .*, 124; and *Persepolis*, 56; and sound, 39; in *Water Lilies*, 34, 37

minimum garanti (MG), 6

Ministère de la Culture. *See* Ministry of Culture & Communications

Ministry of Culture & Communications, 1, 16, 17, 169

Ministry of Foreign and European Affairs, 1, 51, 132, 177

Ministry of Industry and Commerce, 16

Mirrors, 133

mise-en-scène: in *Car Keys*, 96; and Catherine Breillat, 62; and *cinéma du corps*, 71; in *Demonlover*, 143; in *Ecoute le temps*, 187; in *Et toi, t'es sur qui?*, 27; in *Gabrielle*, 121; in *In My Skin*, 85; in *Innocence*, 170; in *Persepolis*, 52–53, 55; in *The Ring Finger*, 91–92; in *She's One of Us*, 181; in *Through the Forest*, 213; in *Trouble Every Day*, 77; in *Water Lilies*, 38–39; and Yoko Ogawa, 89–90. *See also* settings

Mitchell, John Cameron, 65

Miyagawa, Kazuo, 175

Mizoguchi, Kenji, 206, 211, 212, 226n52

Moll, Dominik, 185; and la Fémis, 205

Le Monde, 41, 128

Le Monde diplomatique, 66

Mon meilleur ami. See *My Best Friend*

Monsieur Hulot (character), 182

Moreau, David, 133

Moreau, Yolande, 42, 240n20

Morel, Pierre, 115, 116, 118, 234n22

Mornas, Pierre-Olivier, 85

Les Morsures de l'aube, 133

Mothlight, 173

Motion Picture Association of America, 68

Moutout, Jean-Marc, 85, 181

MR 73, 117

Mulholland Drive, 96, 144–45

Mulvey, Laura, 163

Musée d'Orsay, 146

Musée haut, musée bas, 97–98, 107

Museum of Fine Arts, Boston, 42, 132, 176

musical (genre), 140–41

My Best Friend, 41

My Life to Live, 182

My Sex Life . . . or How I Got into an Argument, 42

La Naissance des pieuvres. See *Water Lilies*

Narnia (children's series), 174

Nathalie . . ., 147

naturalism (aesthetics), 65, 66, 134, 137, 191, 199, 200

Ne le dis à personne. See *Tell No One*

Nénette et Boni, 123

neorealism, 54, 55

The Nest, 117, 236n55

Neupert, Richard, 24, 53

New Directors New Films, 17

A New Life, 64–65

New Wave (French), 2, 11, 16–17, 24, 39, 41, 58, 79, 95, 114, 122, 147–49, 197; and *Love Songs*, 141; and narrative, 186

New Wave (Japanese), 134

Nicloux, Guillaume, 186

Nicolas, Marc, 207–8, 243n22

Nid de guêpes. See *The Nest*

Ni d'Eve ni d'Adam, 208

Night and Fog in Japan, 142

Nikita, 114

Ni pour, ni contre (bien au contraire), 23

Noé, Gaspar, 11; and cineliteracy, 70, 229n5; and *cinéma du corps*, 58–61, 66, 67, 69, 78, 81, 120;

as cinematographer, 75–76; and
  Innocence, 176; and *Irreversible*,
  71, 81, 121, 230n28; and Lucile
  Hadzihalilovic, 169, 174; and use of
  digital formats, 64; use of sound,
  73–74, 241n46; and *Vinyan*, 174
Nolot, Jacques, 65
North by Northwest, 109, 113
Nos enfants. See *Our Children*
Nos enfants chéris. See *Our Precious
  Children*
Notorious, 113
Nous C Nous, 107
Nouvelles fictions, 17
Novo, 57

Objective Burma!, 139
obsolescence (aesthetics), 53
Ocean's Thirteen, 101
Ocean's Twelve, 101
Ocelot, Michel, 52, 53
Odoul, Damien, 58, 166
The Officer's Ward, 139
Ogawa, Yoko, 61, 89–90
Olivia, 170
Once Upon a Time in America, 105
On dirait que . . ., 195
One Missed Call, 133
Onibaba, 134
On the Ropes, 178–79, 199–200
Orphée. See *Orpheus*
Orpheus, 204, 209
Oscar Awards. *See* Academy Awards
O'Shaughnessy, Martin, 134
Oshima, Nagisa, 142
OSS 117 (franchise), 11, 196; and pop-art
  cinema, 126; and popular cinema, 98,
  106–15
OSS 117: Cairo, Nest of Spies, 98, 233n13;
  analysis of, 106–13. *See also* OSS 117
OSS 117: Le Caire, nid d'espions. See *OSS
  117: Cairo, Nest of Spies*

OSS 117: Lost in Rio, 98; analysis of,
  106–14. *See also* OSS 117
OSS 117 n'est pas mort, 108
OSS 117: Rio ne répond plus. See *OSS 117:
  Lost in Rio*
Oublie-moi, 123
Our Children, 177–78, 180
Our Precious Children, 185
Ozon, François: and *5x2*, 121; and *8
  Women*, 141; and *Angel*, 241n49; and
  cinéma du corps, 62–63, 66–68; and
  la Fémis, 202; and Marina de Van,
  80–81, 84
Ozu, Yasujirô, 121, 126, 206

The Pack, 133
Le Pacte des loups. See *Brotherhood of
  the Wolf*
Païni, Dominique, 166
Palm Pictures, 148
Palud, Xavier, 133
Pandora's Box, 170
ParaOne, 39
Pardo, Carlos, 66–68
Paronnaud, Vincent, 11, 21, 48, 52–54
Les Particules élémentaires. See *The
  Elementary Particles*
Partir. See *Leaving*
Par un beau matin d'été. See *Crime on a
  Summer Morning*
Pasolini, Pier Paolo, 70
Le Passager, 42
pedophilia, 171
Persepolis, 11, 21, 48, 227–28n66; analysis
  of, 51–56
Persépolis. See *Persepolis*
Persona, 62, 82, 209
La petite Lili, 41
Le Petit lieutenant, 117
Petits frères, 22, 23
Peur[s] du noir. See *Fear(s) of the Dark*
Peut-être, 117

photo-novella, 193

The Piano Teacher, 96

Picasso, Pablo, 218

Picnic at Hanging Rock, 170–71

Pig Tales, 179

Piranha 3-D, 133

Pitof, 118

Le Placard. See The Closet

Les Plages d'Agnès. See The Beaches of
   Agnes

Le Plaisir . . . (et ses petits tracas), 101,
   103, 117

Play Time, 182

Le Point, 124, 128

La Pointe-Courte, 16

point of view: in 99 Francs, 63; in All Is
   Forgiven, 43; of children, 26, 47–48,
   167, 169, 176; in Et toi, t'es sur qui?,
   31; and feminine cinema, 168, 182;
   feminist, 179; in La France, 142; in
   Water Lilies, 35; of infants, 173–74; in
   In My Skin, 87; in Innocence, 171; in On
   the Ropes, 199; in OSS 117: Lost in Rio,
   112; in Regarde-moi, 179; in She's One
   of Us, 182, 183; in Through the Forest,
   212, 213; in Toi et Moi, 193; of women
   on rape-revenge format, 64

Polanski, Roman, 169, 242n62

policier (genre), 11, 95, 100, 103, 107, 116,
   117, 133, 162, 187, 232n4–5

Pollock, Christophe, 181

polyphonic approach, 184

Ponette, 22, 23

pop-art cinema, 5, 11, 95–98, 122–49,
   176, 180, 214, 236n51, 237nn67–68;
   and cinephilia, 196; and Ecoute le
   temps, 184, 189; and feminine cinema,
   164

popular cinema, 95–119, 184, 214, 232n1,
   234–35n31, 237n68; and art cinema,
   124–25, 132, 137, 143, 146, 149, 162,
   215; and autobiography, 235n40;

and Demonlover, 148; and Ecoute le
   temps, 185, 186; and feminine cinema,
   153–56, 161, 167, 192; and the horror
   genre, 133; and Laetitia Colombani,
   155; and Luc Besson, 234n22; and
   Lucile Hadzihalilovic, 174; and lyrical
   style, 215; and men, 12, 155, 156,
   167, 179, 184–86, 190, 192; and They
   Came Back, 138; and A Very Long
   Engagement, 139

pornography: and cinéma du corps, 66–68;
   in Demonlover, 144–46; internet, 65,
   81, 144, 145; in Porn Theatre, 65; use
   of porn actors in Baise-moi, 64

Porn Theatre, 65

Porte, Michelle, 122

Positif, 20, 60, 62, 69, 124, 163

La Possibilité d'un île. See The Possibility
   of an Island

The Possibility of an Island, 63

Pour elle, 186, 188

Pourqoui (pas) le Brésil. See Why (Not)
   Brazil?

Powrie, Phil, 47, 118, 240–41n38

Prédal, Réné, 15, 67, 79, 133, 164, 204,
   236n53, 243n14

Premenons-nous dans les bois. See Deep in
   the Woods

Première, 4; and cinéma du corps, 67;
   and feminine cinema, 164–65; and
   Luc Besson, 114–15, 119; and Vincent
   Cassel, 100–101

La Première mort de Nono, 169

Pretty Woman, 179

Princes and Princesses, 52

Les Princes et les princesses. See Princes
   and Princesses

Prix Jean Vigo, 18

Prix Louis-Delluc, 18

La Prophétie des grenouilles. See Raining
   Cats and Frogs

Provost, Martin, 107

psychological thriller (genre). *See* suspense thriller
Un Pur esprit, 47–48

Quand la mer monte. See *When the Sea Rises*
Quandt, James, 67
Qui a tué Bambi?, 117

Raconter une histoire, 206
Raging Bull, 178
Raining Cats and Frogs, 52
Ramanathan, Geetha, 167
rape, 58; in *5x2*, 63; in *Baise-moi*, 64; in *Demonlover*, 145; in *Irreversible*, 72, 77, 81, 121, 229n7; in *Twentynine Palms*, 72, 77
Rashomon, 175
Read My Lips, 101
realism: in *All Is Forgiven*, 44; in *Innocence*, 171; and Jean Paul Civeyrac, 208; and Laurent Cantet, 134; in *Those Who Remain*, 44
Rebel Without a Cause, 104–5
Regarde la mer. See *See the Sea*
Regarde-moi, 30, 164, 179
Renaissance, 52, 117
Rendez-vous du cinéma français, 163
Rendez-Vous with French Cinema, 42
Renegade, 116, 117; and Vincent Cassel, 101
Renoir, Jean, 9, 139, 218, 226n52
Repulsion, 169, 242n62
Resnais, Alain, 9, 120, 122, 126
Les Ressources humaines. See *Human Resources*
Rétention, 80
Les Revenants. See *They Came Back*
Ribes, Jean-Michel, 97, 98
Richard-Serrano, Magaly, 178–79; and cinephilia, 199–200
Richet, Jean-François, 30, 236n55; and

the Mesrine franchise, 99, 102, 233n9, 233n11
Richie, Donald, 42
The Ring Finger, 57; and *cinéma du corps*, 61, 88–93, 154; and cinephilia, 199
Les Rivières pourpres. See *Crimson Rivers*
RKO, 133
road movie (genre), 64, 141, 162, 236n51
Rochefort, Jean, 96
Roche, Stéphane, 52, 53
Roehler, Oskar, 63
Rohmer, Eric, 36, 122
Rollet, Brigitte, 161–62, 165, 167, 179
Rollin, Jean, 133
Romance, 57; and *cinéma du corps*, 61–62, 67, 68
The Romance of Astree and Celadon, 122
romantic comedy (genre), 192–93
romantic thriller (genre). *See* suspense thriller
Romero, George, 135
Rope, 210–11
Rozen, Anna, 63
Russian Ark, 211

Sacha, Jean, 108
Sade, 147
Safari, 117
Sagnier, Ludivine, 102, 164
Saint Ange, 174–75
Salis, Robert: and *cinéma du corps*, 93
Salo, 70
Sans toit ni loi. See *Vagabond*
Sarrouy, Emmanuelle, 17
Sartre, Jean-Paul, 104
satire: in *Daisies*, 84; in *Persepolis*, 53
Satrapi, Marjane, 11, 21, 48–56, 228n69, 240n20
Savage Nights, 147, 227n58
Schlöndorff, Volker, 206
Sciamma, Céline, 11, 21, 32–40, 44, 50,

85, 140, 192, 225–26n38, 241n50; and
    la Fémis, 202
Scorsese, Martin, 178, 233n12
Scott, Tony, 147
Screen, 163
screenplays: and *cinéma du corps*, 71–72;
    and Robin Campillo, 134; and Valeria
    Bruni Tedeschi, 128
Seaside, 18
The Second Sex, 151
Secret défense, 117
See the Sea, 57, 64; as homage to *Persona*,
    62; and Marina de Van, 81
self-mutilation, 2, 11; in *In My Skin*,
    82–84, 86, 202; and Marina de Van, 81
self-reflexivity, 142, 232–33n8; and art
    cinema, 120; in *Le Bal des actrices*,
    141; and *jeune cinéma*, 44; and Laetitia
    Masson, 154; in *Toi et Moi*, 193
Sellier, Geneviève, 168, 184, 186
La Séparation, 42
Sequins, 200–201
Séraphine, 107
Serreau, Coline, 154, 162–64, 239n5
Se souvenir de belles choses. See *Happy
    Memories*
settings: brutalist architecture in *In My
    Skin*, 85; modernist in *Water Lilies*,
    32–33, 35–37; sexualized in *The Ring
    Finger*, 92. See also *mise-en-scène*
Seul contre tous. See *I Stand Alone*
Sevigny, Chloë, 144
sex, 11; in *La Bouche de Jean-Pierre*, 169;
    and capitalism, 63; and *cinéma du
    corps*, 57–58, 65–69, 72, 73, 76–77;
    in *Demonlover*, 148; in *Et toi, t'es
    sur qui?*, 24–25, 26, 29, 31–32; and
    female desire, 61, 190; in the films of
    Catherine Breillat, 62; and homosexual
    desire, 62, 112; in *Les Invisibles*,
    186; oral, 80; in *The Ring Finger*, 91;
    sadomasochism, 81; sexuality, 10, 27,

68, 78, 120, 163; in *She's One of Us*,
    182; unsimulated, 57, 65, 120, 230n16;
    and violence, 67, 120; in *Water Lilies*,
    33. *See also* adultery; gay; lesbianism;
    pornography; rape; violence; virginity
Sex Is Comedy, 62
sexism, 154, 165
Shakespeare, William, 206
Sheitan, 133, 185; and Vincent Cassel, 101
She's One of Us, 120, 187, 188, 191;
    analysis of, 178–84
Shindo, Kaneto, 134–35
Shortbus, 65
Sight and Sound, 60, 69
Le Silence de la mer. See *The Silence of
    the Sea*
The Silence of the Sea, 16, 36
Silent Hill, 133
Simon, Claire, 190–92
Sitcom, 42, 62, 81
slang, 28–30, 34
Snow, Michael, 76
Société pour le Financement du Cinéma
    et de l'Audiovisuel (SOFICA), 6, 8
society (French): in *35 Shots of Rum*,
    121–22; and *cinéma du corps*, 58,
    86, 91; and the economy, 134; and
    feminine cinema, 168; and French
    cinema, 5; and solitude, 85–86, 157
Soderbergh, Steven, 100
Sokurov, Alexander, 211
Les Solitaires, 208, 209
Sombre, 57; and *cinéma du corps*, 64–65,
    87, 120
Sony Classics, 49
sound: and *cinéma du corps*, 73–74,
    77; in *In My Skin*, 87; and Lucile
    Hadzihalilovic, 241n46
Sous le sable. See *Under the Sand*
spectatorship: and art cinema, 119–20;
    and auteurism, 148; and *cinéma
    du corps*, 11, 58–60, 64, 69, 70, 74,

76-78, 83, 88, 92, 120, 229n7; and cinephilia, 195, 197, 198, 206-7; and *Demonlover*, 145, 146, 148; and *Ecoute le temps*, 188; and feminine cinema, 168; and *La France*, 141-42; and *In My Skin*, 202; and *Innocence*, 172, 175; and *Irreversible*, 229n7, 230n28; and the Mesrine franchise, 105; and the millionaires, 154, 238-39n5; and the OSS 117 franchise, 110; and pop-art cinema, 98, 138; and popular cinema, 96, 155; and *Through the Forest*, 213, 214; and Vincent Cassel, 102; and women, 153, 155, 156. *See also* admissions

Spirit of the Beehive, 171

spy thriller (genre), 110, 117

star system, France, 95

steadicam, 26, 145, 205

Studio, 4; and feminine cinema, 166; and Jean Dujardin, 108; and Luc Besson, 119; and Valeria Bruni Tedeschi, 236n46

Studio Canal, 6, 23, 148

style (cinematic), 229n4; abstraction, 38-39, 64-65, 79, 120, 158-60, 171-73, 186-87, 212, 213, 229n5; in *All Is Forgiven*, 44; and art cinema, 120-21; in *Ça brûle*, 192; in *Car Keys*, 96; and *cinéma du corps*, 59, 60, 64-65, 71, 73-75, 77, 78, 81, 230n15; and cinephilia, 195-96, 198; and feminine cinema, 157, 160, 162, 165-68; in *Innocence*, 168-69, 171, 172, 174; and Luc Besson, 115; and the OSS 117 franchise, 113-14; in *Sequins*, 200; in *She's One of Us*, 182-83; in *Those Who Remain*, 44; in *Through the Forest*, 210-12, 214; in *Water Lilies*, 34, 37. *See also* aesthetics; digital video; long takes; minimalism; naturalism; neorealism; realism; techniques

Subway, 114, 115

suicide, 169, 244n29

Summer Hours, 42, 146

supernatural thriller (genre). *See* suspense thriller

Sur mes lèvres. See *Read My Lips*

suspense thriller (genre), 57, 62, 65, 97, 107, 117, 133-35, 143-47, 174, 184-89, 236n55, 238n73

Suspiria, 171

Swimming Pool, 62

Tachou, Frédéric, 17

Taken, 115-16, 185

Tardieu, Carine, 47

Tarkovsky, Andrei, 148

Tarr, Carrie, 83, 118, 161-62, 165, 167, 179

Tati, Jacques, 131, 181, 206, 236n51

Tautou, Audrey, 139

Taxi (franchise), 115, 116, 119

Taxi 2, 119, 235n34

techniques (cinematic): in *35 Shots of Rum*, 121-22; in *Actresses*, 129-31; in *Ça brûle*, 191-92; and Catherine Breillat, 62; in *A Christmas Tale*, 201; and *cinéma du corps*, 70-71, 77, in *Darling*, 158-60; in *Demonlover*, 145-46, 148; in *Ecoute le temps*, 186-90; in *Et toi, t'es sur qui?*, 28, 31; in *La France*, 139-41; in *Gabrielle*, 121; in *In My Skin*, 83-88, 202; in *Innocence*, 171-76; in *Irreversible*, 76, 77; in *It's Easier for a Camel . . .*, 125-27; and the Mesrine franchise, 99, 102-3, 105, 233n9; in *On the Ropes*, 199-200; and the OSS 117 franchise, 111, 113-14; in *Our Children*, 177-78; in *Persepolis*, 52, 54; and Philippe Grandrieux, 64-65; in *Un Pur esprit*, 47-48; in *The Ring Finger*, 90-92; in *Sequins*, 200-201; in *She's One of Us*, 181-83; in *They Came Back*, 136, 138;

in *Through the Forest*, 211–14; in *Toi et Moi*, 193; in *Trouble Every Day*, 77; and *Vidocq*, 118; in *Water Lilies*, 36, 39. *See also* editing; long takes

technology: in *Ecoute le temps*, 187; in *Et toi, t'es sur qui?*, 27, 28, 225n30

teenagers. *See* adolescence

Télérama, 60

Tell No One, 117, 185–86, 188

The Tenant, 169

terminal illness, 227n58; in *Those Who Remain*, 43, 45–46

Terzian, Alain, 96

Testud, Sylvie, 138, 140

La Tête de maman, 47

Teulé, Jean, 157

They Came Back, 132–33, 180, 236–37n57; analysis of, 135–38

They Live, 147

Thompson, Danièle, 154, 235n37, 239n5

Thompson, David, 144

Those Who Remain, 11, 21, 41, 227n60; analysis of, 42–47

Three Men and a Cradle, 162

thriller (genre). *See* suspense thriller

Through the Forest, 208, 244n29; analysis of, 210–14

Time Out, 134, 179, 180

Toi et Moi, 192–93

Toles, George, 197, 199

Too Much Flesh, 64

Toronto International Film Festival, 169

Tournées, 132, 177

Tourneur, Jacques, 70, 133

Tourneur, Maurice, 133

Tout est pardonné. See *All Is Forgiven*

transnationalism, 117, 119, 139, 144, 234n28

The Transporter (franchise), 115, 116

Tribeca Film Festival, 132

Trinh Thi, Coralie, 64

The Triplets of Belleville, 52

Les Triplettes de Belleville. See *The Triplets of Belleville*

Tristesse beau visage, 208

Trois hommes et un couffin. See *Three Men and a Cradle*

Trouble Every Day, 57; analysis of, 72–77; and *cinéma du corps*, 58, 59, 61, 68, 70, 81, 86, 87, 91, 121; lighting in, 74–75; narrative design, 71; premiere at Cannes, 69; sound in, 74

Truffart, François, 106–7

Truffaut, François, 9, 20, 24, 33, 66, 114, 206

Truismes. See *Pig Tales*

Tuel, Laurent, 203

Twentynine Palms, 57; analysis of, 72–78; and *cinéma du corps*, 61, 65, 68, 91; cinematography in, 75; narrative design, 71; premiere at Cannes, 69; sound in, 74

Two or Three Things I Know About Her, 142

Ugetsu, 211

Under the Sand, 81

unemployment (French), 30–31, 115

UniFrance, 17, 42, 151, 163

Vagabond, 162

Valette, Eric, 133

Vanderschelden, Isabelle, 10, 116–17, 232n1

Vanity Fair (magazine), 101

Van Sant, Gus: influence on Céline Sciamma, 34

Varda, Agnès, 16, 22, 122, 162, 206; and feminine cinema, 163–67

Variety, 116

Vendredi soir. See *Friday Night*

Venice Biennale, 166

Vénus beauté (institut). See *Venus Beauty Institute*

Venus Beauty Institute, 151

La Vérité si je mens!, 118

Vers le sud. See Heading South

Vertige, 133

vertige identitaire, 152

Vertigo, 113

A Very Long Engagement, 117, 139, 234n27

Veysset, Sandrine, 163

Vidocq, 118

La Vie de Jésus, 18

Une Vieille maîtresse. See The Last Mistress

La Vie nouvelle. See A New Life

La Vie selon Luc, 208

viewers. *See* admissions; spectatorship

The Village, 175

Villiers, Aruna, 115

Vincendeau, Ginette, 95, 162, 169, 171

Vinyan, 174

violence, 230n16; child abuse, 137, 169;
    and *cinéma du corps*, 69, 73, 81, 83, 88;
    and *Demonlover*, 145; domestic abuse,
    157, 184; and pop-art cinema, 103.
    See also self-mutilation

*Violence des échanges en milieu tempéré.
    See Work Hard, Play Hard*

virginity: in *Et toi, t'es sur qui?*, 25, 26,
    28, 31–32; in *LOL (Laughing Out Loud)*,
    156; in *Water Lilies*, 33, 37–38

Viridiana, 205

Vivre sa vie. See My Life to Live

Voice Over, 183–84

Voix sans issue. See Voice Over

Volckman, Christian, 52

Von Trier, Lars, 65

Wajda, Andrej, 206

Walsh, Raoul, 139

war (genre), 138–42, 237–38n68

Warner Bros., 118

Warner France, 117

Water Lilies, 11, 21, 44, 46–47, 52, 85,
    225–26n38, 241n50; analysis of,
    32–40

Wedekind, Frank, 170

Weil, Edouard, 148

Weir, Peter, 170–71

Welcome to the Land of the Chtis, 118, 185

Welles, Orson, 206, 218

Wenger, Eric, 39

When the Sea Rises, 42, 240n20

White Material, 121

Why (Not) Brazil?, 154

Wild Grass, 122

Williams, Linda, 68

Wilson, Emma, 161, 163–65, 171, 176

Winterbottom, Michael, 65

With a Friend Like Harry, 185

women: civil rights in France, 51, 151–53,
    164–65, 192; and la Fémis, 169, 204;
    as film critics, 161; as filmmakers, 12,
    21, 107, 126, 151, 153–93, 239nn10–11;
    the films of Catherine Breillat, 62; and
    the millionaires, 154, 238–39n5; as
    subjects, 12, 22, 23, 50, 107, 154–93;
    as victims, 160. *See also* feminine
    cinema; feminism

Wooden Crosses, 139

Wood, Robin, 73, 211, 237n59

Work Hard, Play Hard, 85, 181

Yamakasi, 119

*Les Yeux sans visage. See Eyes Without
    a Face*

Young Adam, 65

young cinema. *See jeune cinéma*

Yves Saint Laurent: and Vincent Cassel,
    101–2

Zonca, Erick, 66

Wesleyan Film

A series from WESLEYAN UNIVERSITY PRESS
Edited by LISA DOMBROWSKI & SCOTT HIGGINS
Originating editor: JEANINE BASINGER

Anthony Mann
New and Expanded Edition
by Jeanine Basinger

It's the Pictures That Got Small
Hollywood Film Stars on 1950s Television
by Christine Becker

The South Korean Film Renaissance
Local Hitmakers, Global Provocateurs
by Jinhee Choi

The Films of Samuel Fuller
If You Die, I'll Kill You!
by Lisa Dombrowski

Kazan Revisited
edited by Lisa Dombrowski

Physical Evidence
Selected Film Criticism
by Kent Jones

The New Entrepreneurs
An Institutional History of Television
Anthology Writers
by Jon Kraszewksi

Action Speaks Louder
Violence, Spectacle, and the American
Action Movie
Revised and Expanded Edition
by Eric Lichtenfeld

Hollywood Ambitions
Celebrity in the Movie Age
by Marsha Orgeron

Brutal Intimacy
Analyzing Contemporary French Cinema
by Tim Palmer

Soul Searching
Black-Themed Cinema from the March
on Washington to the Rise of Blaxploitation
by Christopher Sieving

A Splurch in the Kisser
The Movies of Blake Edwards
by Sam Wasson

About the Author

TIM PALMER is associate professor of film studies at the University of North Carolina Wilmington. His articles have appeared in journals such as *Cinema Journal, Journal of Film & Video, Studies in French Cinema*, and the *French Review*. He is co-founder and co-editor-in-chief of the journal *Film Matters*.

Library of Congress Cataloging-in-Publication Data

Palmer, Tim, 1975–

Brutal intimacy: analyzing contemporary French cinema /
Tim Palmer.

   p. cm. — (Wesleyan film)

Includes bibliographical references and index.

ISBN 978-0-8195-6826-7 (cloth: alk. paper) —

ISBN 978-0-8195-6827-4 (pbk.: alk. paper) —

ISBN 978-0-8195-7000-0 (e-book)

1. Motion pictures — France — History. I. Title.

PN1993.5.F7P23   2011

791.43'0944'09 — dc22   2010043477